The Future of the Black Colleges

Journal of the American Academy of Arts and Sciences

CONTENTS

	v	*Preface*
ANDREW F. BRIMMER	539	*The Economic Outlook and the Future of the Negro College*
HENRY ALLEN BULLOCK	573	*The Black College and the New Black Awareness*
C. ERIC LINCOLN	603	*The Negro Colleges and Cultural Change*
VIVIAN W. HENDERSON	630	*Negro Colleges Face the Future*
WILLIAM J. TRENT, JR.	647	*The Future Role of the Negro College and Its Financing*
S. M. NABRIT	660	*Reflections on the Future of Black Colleges*
MICHAEL R. WINSTON	678	*Through the Back Door: Academic Racism and the Negro Scholar in Historical Perspective*
PATRICIA ROBERTS HARRIS	720	*The Negro College and Its Community*
MACK H. JONES	732	*The Responsibility of the Black College to the Black Community: Then and Now*
ELIAS BLAKE, JR.	745	*Future Leadership Roles for Predominantly Black Colleges and Universities in American Higher Education*

CONRAD K. HARPER 772 *The Legal Status of the Black College*

WINFRED L. GODWIN 783 *Southern State Governments and Higher Education for Negroes*

TOBE JOHNSON 798 *The Black College as System*

THOMAS F. PETTIGREW 813 *The Role of Whites in the Black Colleges of the Future*

ST. CLAIR DRAKE 833 *The Black University in the American Social Order*

898 *Notes on Contributors*

900 *Recent Issues of Dædalus*

SUMMER 1971: THE FUTURE OF THE BLACK COLLEGES

Issued as Vol. 100, No. 3, of the Proceedings of the American Academy of Arts and Sciences

Preface to the Issue "The Future of the Black Colleges"

THE YEARS that saw the founding of Cornell University and Johns Hopkins, of Stanford and the University of Chicago, were also the years when many small colleges were established in the South to serve the educational needs of the newly-freed slaves. While great nineteenth-century industrial entrepreneurs like Ezra Cornell, Johns Hopkins, Leland Stanford, and John D. Rockefeller —to name only some of the more conspicuous—gave amounts ranging from half a million to tens of millions of dollars to found great teaching and research universities where none had previously existed, and while many others, less famous, gave impressive sums to expand and refurbish modest college establishments that had already taken root, there were no comparable benefactions for private Negro higher educational institutions. Only in the twentieth century, and then mostly through the generosity of a handful of individuals and bodies like the General Education Board of the Rockefeller Foundation and the Julius Rosenwald Fund, did the struggling black colleges begin to receive support in single-gift amounts larger than that of a few thousand dollars.

The Morrill Act of 1862 is justly celebrated as the most important single piece of federal legislation affecting higher education in the nineteenth century; it established the basis for the land-grant institutions that developed throughout the country, most successfully perhaps in the states of the Middle West. Less is written about the Morrill Act of 1890, the so-called Second Morrill Act, which made possible the establishment of separate Negro land-grant colleges in the southern and border states. No one would seriously contend that the Second Morrill Act had consequences for the education of black men and women in any way comparable to what the Civil War legislation accomplished for those who took advantage of its educational opportunities.

The "separate but equal" principle, even if faithfully adhered to, could never have created in Alabama, Georgia, or Mississippi state institutions like those that developed in Wisconsin, Michigan, or California. The states where blacks were to be found in overwhelming number before the First World War were not those that had reputations for being generous in their appropriations for public education. They were, for both blacks and whites, the major "underdeveloped educational areas" of America.

So long as college and university education was uncommon—and it was that until well into the twentieth century—and so long as even high school education was not an occupational requirement—it is important to recall that only about 15 per cent of the age group fourteen to seventeen were enrolled in high schools even as late as 1910—it was possible to ignore the very substantial differences that existed between the educational opportunities available to whites and blacks. When, however, both those situations changed, the full extent of the discrimination against blacks was apparent. This is not to say, however, that the discrimination was recognized, or that significant steps were taken to reduce its adverse effects. Even after World War II, when something like mass higher education was becoming a reality for the white youth of the nation, the overwhelming majority of blacks were excluded from a college option.

The Negro colleges—still small and impoverished—enrolled the greatest number of those few blacks who were able to pursue their studies beyond high school. These colleges were largely "invisible," as their inhabitants were, to all white citizens except the handful who had philanthropic or other reasons for being concerned with them. These colleges did not figure among the institutions celebrated by those who thought to extol American higher educational achievement. They were isolated in all the ways that racism and segregation required. The choices their presidents, trustees, alumni, students, and faculties were in a position to make were in all instances severely restricted. The stigma of race attached to everything they sought to do; they were educating black men and women to live and work in a segregated society.

In this environment, superficially so inimical to growth, numbers of black men and women sought to create educational opportunities suited to the society they lived in. They disagreed, over curriculum, of course, but also over more fundamental issues. Ought they to aspire to imitate "white institutions," serving black citizens as other colleges and universities served the white majority, or ought they to admit their distinctiveness, and seek to educate with other purposes in mind? Their graduates were desperately needed, to teach and minister to the segregated black communities of the South, but also to care for their health and welfare. What priorities ought to be given to what purposes? The struggle was perpetual, carried on constantly with insufficient resources of every kind.

These colleges inspired loyalties, sometimes not altogether different from those common in other American higher educational institutions. To read the articles in this issue of *Dædalus,* however, is to be aware of how deep are the passions that many of these institutions evoke. There is gratitude for what they were able to do, despite adverse circumstances, but with it goes an only slightly concealed anger. Both need to be reckoned with. The passion is not only for a system of higher education that operated—whether well or badly—under adverse circumstances, but also for a system that suffered the most severe rebuke of all—that of not being taken seriously. The anger—and it can only be read as such—relates to a society that did so little for men and women who suffered for no other reason than being born black.

These institutions, particularly after the Supreme Court decision of 1954, had to contend with all their old problems but with many new ones as well. They had been founded to serve a segregated society. But if, as the Supreme Court decreed, segregation was no longer permissible—if the whole structure built on the myth of "separate but equal" was to be dismantled—what place did these institutions have in the new order of things? Belatedly, great numbers of colleges and universities in the North vied for black students (and, also, for black professors and trustees). If the doors were no longer closed to the black man or woman, what compelling reason was there for supporting financially-embarrassed institutions that had been established in the first instance only because no other facilities were open to the black citizen?

The availability of new opportunity has opened an entirely new dialogue within the black community. Many are not at all persuaded that the new doors are in fact as open as some pretend; they are skeptical of the private colleges that send their recruiters out in such number to search for black students. They ask whether these practices, together with "faculty raiding," do not deprive the black colleges of their most precious human resources, reducing their effectiveness at a time when they might otherwise be growing in strength. Many are not at all persuaded that the advantages offered by these institutions are as advertised; they ask what they will lose if they choose to go through these new doors rather than through those that have been open to them for a century.

There is a considerable division about what the black colleges have accomplished in the past, and what they are in fact capable of doing in the future. Some—almost certainly the minority—accept that many of the black colleges are antiquated; only the strongest, they say, ought to be maintained. Others find a mixture of arrogance and ignorance in such a proposal. For them, the problem of the education of blacks is a national obligation; the federal government is duty-bound to provide financial and other assistance. If a black youth wishes to enroll in a college or university that is overwhelmingly white, that is his choice to make. If he prefers to stay with other blacks in an institution where blacks are in control, that ought also to be permitted. Some who argue in this way insist that a "black" institution, with all the same library and laboratory equipment, will never be like a "white" institution, and ought not to aspire to become so.

This issue on "The Future of the Black Colleges" seeks to address itself to some of the more compelling questions that presently preoccupy those concerned with the higher education of black men and women. Inevitably, the problem of financing such education figures prominently. So, also, do questions relating to curriculum, organization, and purposes more generally. There has been a continuing interest in exploring what has happened to a people whose whole life-experience has been in such great measure determined by racial injustice. The black colleges are still too "invisible"; this issue of *Dædalus* seeks to contribute something to making them less so, and it attempts to do this in the only way that makes sense—to draw attention to the opinions and reflections of those for whom race is a daily concern, not subject to the vagaries of public opinion or the mass media. The issue is intended to draw attention to a group of institutions still too little reflected on. Finally, it is intended to raise questions that have nothing to do with the institutions themselves but relate to the fabric of American society.

A great debt is owed the Ford Foundation for making this issue possible. Without the meetings and conferences that its support permitted, this volume would not now exist.

S.R.G.

ANDREW F. BRIMMER

The Economic Outlook and the Future of the Negro College

I. *The Economic Outlook*

THE ECONOMIC future of the predominantly Negro college as a segment of American higher education seems reasonably assured when viewed over the next decade. However, the outlook for particular groups of these colleges is far from promising. This is the general conclusion which emerges from an assessment of prospective changes in the American economy, their probable impact on the Negro population, and the resulting implications for the Negro colleges.

Before presenting the results of this analysis, I must stress the perspective from which it was undertaken. In the first place, I have no specialized knowledge of the problems and opportunities faced by the Negro colleges.[1] This fact was recognized when I was invited to prepare this essay. Instead, it was felt that an overview of the economic environment in which these colleges will have to operate in the years ahead might serve as a background against which experts in higher education can appraise the future of these institutions. On the other hand, it does appear appropriate to sketch some of the implications for Negro colleges of the principal economic changes that are now visible on the horizon.

In looking ahead, one must be careful to avoid allowing his vision to outrun the evidence. In the case of the national economy, it is difficult to visualize the contours of economic activity more than a decade ahead. So for this essay, the analysis is based primarily on the projections of the American economy in 1980 prepared by the Bureau of Labor Statistics (BLS) in the U. S. Department of Labor.[2] In employing these data, the objective is not to present the projections as such; rather, the aim is to extract from them enough information to enable us to judge the probable effects of a changing economy on the Negro population and their subsequent demand for the services of Negro colleges. With this objective in mind, the rest of this essay is devoted to (1) a discussion of the main contours of the national economy in 1980; (2) the economic position of the Negro in 1980; (3) the economic characteristics of the Negro college; and (4) the economic outlook for these institutions over the present decade.

The American Economy in 1980

In 1980, according to the BLS projections, the American economy may be producing goods and services at a $1.4 trillion annual rate. That would be the value of gross national product (GNP), measured in 1968 prices—the base year for the projections. This would represent an increase of 65 per cent, compared with total output of $865.7 billion achieved in 1968. To achieve this target would require an annual growth rate of about 4.3 per cent, and productivity (output per man-hour) would have to rise by 3.0 per cent a year. Unemployment may average about 3 per cent per year.[3] On the assumption that the economy will be operating under peacetime conditions (that is, assuming that the Vietnam war will be over and no new military conflicts will have ensued), there should be no serious obstacles to achieving this level of output. The outcome also assumes that the appropriate mix of monetary and fiscal policies will be adopted to assure that an economy operating at full employment will not generate unacceptable inflationary pressures.

The over-all structure of demand for output probably will not change appreciably during the current decade. The largest share of the GNP (just over three-fifths) traditionally has been taken by consumers, and roughly the same proportion will prevail in 1980. In that year, personal consumption expenditures may amount to approximately $900 billion, an increase of about $363 billion (or by two-thirds) from the 1968 level. A much larger share of consumer outlays will be made for durable goods and services, and a smaller share will go for nondurable goods. Purchases of durables may absorb about 10 per cent of consumer expenditures in 1980, compared with roughly 9½ per cent in 1968. This relative rise will be stimulated by the increasing number of new families making expanded purchases of furniture and household equipment. Spending for services may account for just under 30 per cent of consumer outlays in 1980, versus about one-quarter in 1968. In this case, the sharp rise will reflect the rapid advance in consumer expenditures for medical care, private education, and recreation.

The other major sector of the private economy—gross private domestic investment—may rise to $222 billion in 1980 from just over $126 billion in 1968. It may account for only a moderately larger share (15½ per cent) of GNP in 1980 than it did in 1968 (when it took 14½ per cent). Expenditures for residential construction, reflecting the high priority assigned to housing as a goal of national policy, will probably increase by at least 75 per cent (to $53 billion) by 1980, compared with the $30.2 billion level attained in 1968. Investment in plant and equipment may rise from $89 billion in 1968 to $152 billion in 1980. Spending for equipment during this decade is expected to grow more rapidly than spending for plants and other structures. In particular, the rate of construction growth for certain kinds of institutional buildings (including those to serve higher education) is expected to be slow.

The role of government in the economy may decline relatively over the current decade, but purchases of goods and services by governmental units will still be a major factor in 1980. In that year, total government purchases may amount to $290 billion, compared with $200 billion in 1968.[4] Within this total, purchases by the federal government are expected to be about $107.3 billion in 1980; they were $99.5 billion in 1968. Thus, the federal government would absorb about 7½ per cent of GNP in 1980, down from 11½ per cent in 1968. However, the composition of federal purchases would have changed appreciably—with a sizable decline in the share going for military purposes (reflecting the passing of the Vietnam war) and a substantial rise in the share devoted to domestic needs, including housing and community development, educational improvements, and the expansion of social welfare programs. In the case of state and local governments, purchases are expected to advance from $100.7 billion in 1968 to $182.4 billion in 1980. Their share of GNP would rise from 11.6 per cent to 12.8 per cent. To cover these sharply higher outlays, state and local units will rely much more heavily on grants from the federal government (including revenue sharing) and higher tax collections in their own jurisdictions. Education will continue to absorb the major share of funds at the state and local level. In particular, since states usually pay for public higher education, they will continue to face heavy pressure for enlarged expenditures. Despite a slowdown in the rate of population growth, there is unlikely to be any letup in enrollment in public institutions of higher education, and by 1980 a larger percentage of college-age young people are expected to attend both community junior colleges and state universities. Increased demand for improvements in health facilities will also add to spending by state and local governments. Programs for conservation, urban renewal, redevelopment, and rehabilitation of central cities (as well as traditional road-building activities) will generate further increases in outlays.

The final major sector (net foreign purchases of goods and services) is expected to expand to roughly $13 billion by 1980, a gain of $10½ billion over the 1968 level. This enormous expansion in foreign trade and other international activity by American businesses will generate a variety of new opportunities for college graduates. It will also pose a number of challenges for institutions of higher education, including demands for training in foreign languages and greater specialization in programs devoted to foreign areas.

Labor Force and the Growth of Employment

The above assessment of the outlook for GNP in 1980 points to a conclusion of major importance: By the end of the decade, the national economy will be concentrating even more heavily on the production of services—thus continuing a trend evident for a number of years. This further growth in the demand for services is hard to quantify, but the BLS projections suggest that the pace is more likely to accelerate than to slow down. By 1980, there may be about 100 million workers in the total labor force, compared with 82 million in 1968—a gain of just over one-fifth. However, by the end of the decade, close to seven in every ten workers (or 68 million) may be employed in service-producing sectors. In 1968, the proportion was six in ten, and it was five in ten in 1950.

By 1980, the service industries will employ almost as many people (21 million) as manufacturing (22 million); in 1968, the latter held the lead by some 5 million workers (20 million to 15 million). The rise in employment in service industries (which include such diverse categories as private household workers and personal, business, health, and educational services) will be stimulated by a significant increase in population, expanding economic activity, a rapid climb in disposable personal income, and a growing demand for medical, educational, and other services. At the same time, output per man-hour in these labor-intensive service industries is not likely to be boosted very much by technological advances, so the expansion of employment opportunities also will be rapid. Consequently, service industries are expected to absorb about 28 per cent of the expansion in the total labor force during the current decade, although they accounted for only 18 per cent of the total jobs in 1968.

Wholesale and retail trade (traditionally the largest of the service industries) is expected to expand about in line with the total economy, and this sector may employ about 20½ million people in 1980, compared with 16½ million in 1968. The growth of employment in retail trade (reflecting the impact of technological developments such as vending machines and electronic computers for inventory control and billing) will be rather modest. The expansion of jobs in wholesale trade will be more rapid, especially in establishments selling motor vehicles and equipment and industrial machinery.

Employment in other major service-providing industries may expand parallel to the economy as a whole. This will probably be true for transportation, communications, and public utilities, as well as for finance, insurance, and real estate.

The expansion of employment in government service is expected to slacken noticeably in the current decade. During the 1960's, employment in government rose more rapidly than in any other sector —increasing by 4½ per cent a year, almost two and one-half times the rate for total employment. However, in the last half of the decade, much of the faster growth centered in the federal government and was associated with the Vietnam war. This stimulus has already weakened, and the assumption is that it will disappear entirely in the next year or so. On the other hand, population growth and the demand for both new and improved government services also generated jobs in the public sector; these will continue during the current decade. Nevertheless, the annual rate of growth in government employment in the 1970's may be about 2.9 per cent a year—considerably below that of the 1960's. By 1980, total government employment is projected at 16.8 million, compared with 11.8 million in 1968. The bulk of the gain will be at the state and local level, while federal government employment will rise only moderately. Even among state and local units, however, the pace of expansion is expected to be slower than it was in the 1960's. This can be traced primarily to an anticipated slackening in the rate of growth of educational services, which represent about half of total employment in state and local governments.

While the service-producing industries are expected to provide most of the new employment opportunities in the current decade, the goods-producing sectors will probably offer only a moderately greater number of jobs. As mentioned above, the total output of goods will increase to unprecedented levels during the 1970's, but technological improvements and the rise in productivity will keep the growth of jobs to a minimum. In two industries (mining and agriculture) employment is projected to decline. In manufacturing, employment growth will be slower than during the 1960's. Only in construction—where few technological advances are anticipated in the face of rising demand for housing and other structures—is the pace of employment expected to quicken during the 1970's.

Reflecting these trends, the goods-producing industries may provide about 31½ million jobs by 1980, up only slightly from the 29 million provided in 1968. Consequently, their share of total employment will decline from roughly 36 per cent in 1968 to less than a third by 1980.

Underlying this pattern of potential expansion of employment in major sectors is the continuation of a trend that may be of considerable importance to young people contemplating college who may have to earn all or part of their expenses. This is the anticipated further shift to part-time employment. For example, in 1956, part-time employees represented 6.8 per cent of the total employed labor force; by 1968, they represented 11.1 per cent; by 1980, the proportion is expected to be even larger. To a considerable extent, the increased reliance on part-time employees can be traced to the growth of retail trade and service industries (especially to their increased location in suburban areas) which attempt to set their hours to accommodate the needs of working customers.

Occupational Upgrading

During the decade of the 1970's, a sharp advance is anticipated in the level of skills required by both industry and government. White-collar occupations will continue their fifty-year record as the fastest growing occupational group. Jobs in this category will expand from 35.6 million in 1968 to 48.3 million in 1980, and the white-collar share of total employment is expected to rise from approximately 46 per cent in 1968 to about one-half (50.8 per cent) in 1980. Employment in blue-collar occupations will probably grow much more slowly. By 1980, jobholders in this group may number 31.1 million, compared with 27.5 million in 1968. Thus, its share of total employment may drop from 36.3 per cent in 1968 to 32.7 per cent by the end of the decade. While many blue-collar occupations (especially those in the skilled craft and foreman group) require years of specialized training, the vast majority of blue-collar jobs demand few skills.

Despite a substantial increase in farm production during the current decade, the number of farm workers will continue to shrink, declining from 3.5 million in 1968 to 2.6 million in 1980. Their share of the labor force will drop from 4.6 per cent in 1968 to about 2.7 per cent in 1980. Service occupations will expand rapidly during the 1970's, rising by more than one and one-half times as fast as all occupations combined. Employment is projected to climb to 13.1 million in 1980, up from 9.4 million in 1968.

As we focus more closely on the principal occupations, the enormous expansion expected in job opportunities at the top of the occupational ladder stands out clearly. Professional and technical workers, which numbered 10.3 million in 1968, are expected to increase to 15.5 million by 1980. This growth would lift their share of total employment from 13.6 per cent in 1968 to 16.3 per cent in 1980. Thus, this group will expand about twice as fast as all occupations combined. Increasing population, expanding economic activity, and rising personal incomes will account for much of the greater demand for professional and technical personnel. In addition, the increasing concentration of population in metropolitan areas and the growing need to cope with urban problems (such as urban renewal, mass transportation, and environmental protection) will also stimulate new demands for these highly trained workers. The business and academic sectors will also have a greatly enlarged need for professional and technical personnel to help carry on industrial expansion and to press the quest for scientific and technical knowledge.

The number of managers, officials, and proprietors will increase more slowly than total employment in the 1970's. By 1980, employment in this group will reach 9.5 million, compared with 7.8 million in 1968. Its relative share of employment will remain unchanged at about 10 per cent of the total. Within the group, however, considerable divergence in growth rates is anticipated. Reflecting the steady decline of self-employment, the number of manager-proprietors will continue to shrink. In contrast, the demand for salaried managers and officials is expected to grow rapidly, as both industry and government become increasingly dependent on trained management specialists. For instance, in both sectors there will be a growing need for technical managers to plan research and development programs and to make decisions on the installation and use of automated machinery and computer-based information systems.

In the case of clerical and sales workers, technological innovations and new merchandising techniques will have a mixed impact on employment. Rapid technological developments associated with computers, office equipment, and communication devices will limit the growth of clerical employment in some fields. On balance, however, the number of clerical workers is expected to rise from 12.8 million in 1968 to 17.3 million in 1980, lifting their share of total employment from 16.9 per cent to 18.2 per cent. Employment of sales workers is projected to expand from 4.6 million in 1968 to 6 million in 1980. This rate of growth would be slightly faster than that for total employment, and the proportion of all jobs held by sales workers would remain at just over 6 per cent.

Although total economic activity is projected to expand considerably during the 1970's, the number of craftsmen, foremen, and workers with similar skills is expected to expand more slowly than the labor force as a whole. By 1980, there may be about 12.2 million of these highly skilled workers, compared with 10 million in 1968. Their share of total employment will ease downward moderately to 12.8 per cent in 1980. While opportunities to enter these skilled occupations may become somewhat more open (especially in manufacturing which employs the greatest number), barriers to entry (such as long apprenticeships and racial discrimination) may continue to limit the expansion of the work force in this category. This may be especially true of construction where craftsmen and other skilled workers make up a much higher proportion of the labor force—one-half of the total, compared with one-fifth in manufacturing and transportation and less than one-tenth in other industries.

Employment of semiskilled workers has risen sharply over the years as American industry shifted increasingly to mass production based on technological innovations. In recent years, however, these techniques have become firmly rooted, and the outlook is for a more moderate rate of growth in semiskilled occupations. In fact, during the decade of the 1970's, such jobs may expand only half as rapidly as total employment. By 1980, they may number 15.4 million, compared with 14 million in 1968. So by 1980, their share of total employment will have shrunk to 16.2 per cent—from 18.4 per cent in 1968. Whereas about three-fifths of semiskilled workers were employed as factory operatives in 1968, this ratio is expected to decline over the current decade, and by 1980 a greater proportion of the total will be found in transportation, especially as drivers of motor trucks handling local and long-distance freight shipments.

The number of laborers employed outside agriculture may remain constant at about 3½ million during the current decade. If so, their share of total employment will decline from 4.7 per cent in 1968 to 3.7 per cent in 1980. This outcome is expected as the net result of a rising demand for labor approximately offset by rising productivity as industry continues to substitute mechanical equipment for manual labor.

As already indicated, the demand for service workers will expand rapidly over the decade. The diverse occupations in this group cover a variety of jobs and require a wide range of skills—including household workers, beauty shop operators, policemen, as well as janitors and sanitation workers. Between 1968 and 1980, the number of service workers may rise from 9.4 million to 13.1 million. This would be a rate of growth about one and one-half times as rapid as that for total employment. Private household employment will register the slowest expansion, from 1.7 million in 1968 to 2.0 million in 1980. The fastest growing service area will be health services, where a gain of 90 per cent is expected, raising the total from 800 thousand to 1.5 million between 1968 and 1980.

These changing demands for labor—and especially the growing emphasis on skills—should be kept in mind when we turn to a consideration of the future of the Negro college. These unfolding occupations will be the primary determinants of where the graduates of these (and other) colleges will find employment.

Educational Attainment and the Emergence of a Youthful Labor Force

The occupational upgrading discussed in the preceding section will be sustained by substantial improvements in educational qualifications during the 1970's. By the end of the decade, it will be rare indeed to find among workers out of school anyone who has not received some high school education. In 1980, there may be about 77 million adult workers (twenty-five years of age and over), compared with roughly 64 million in 1968. Of these, only 5 million (or 6½ per cent) will have less than eight years of schooling; in 1968, 7 million (or 11 per cent) were in this category. Approximately two-thirds of the adult labor force (52 million) will have completed at least four years of high school in 1980, compared with less than three-fifths (37 million) in 1968. Those with at least four years of college may number 13 million and represent about one-sixth of all adult workers in 1980; there were 8½ million in this group in 1968, accounting for one-eighth of the total. Furthermore, just over 9 million adult workers (or 12 per cent of the total) will have gone to college but without completing a four-year course.

At the same time, the American labor force will become a younger body of workers. The influx of teenagers and young adults (twenty to twenty-four years of age) will slacken during the current decade—in contrast to the experience in the 1960's when they accounted for a significant share of labor force expansion. On the other hand, the number of workers in the early stages of their careers (in the twenty-five to thirty-four age group) will increase sharply. By 1980, there should be about 26 million jobholders in this group, up from 16½ million in 1968, an increase of nearly 60 per cent. By the end of the decade, about one-quarter of all workers will be in this age group, compared with one-fifth in 1968. This dramatic rise reflects the further progression of the sharp climb in the birth rate in the late 1940's and early 1950's. As these young, highly trained people move through industry and government service and up the occupational ladder, they will exert considerable pressure on older employees and on traditional ways of conducting business.

Immediately above them in terms of age, they will find a group whose numbers will remain relatively thin. This latter group (aged thirty-five to forty-four) will have expanded only moderately by 1980—to 19 million from 17 million in 1968. Workers in this age range were born in the era of low birth rates that prevailed in 1936-1945, years still dominated by the Great Depression and World War II. But workers in this age group (despite the thinness of their ranks) by the end of this decade will be holding positions of maximum responsibility and normally will be performing at or close to the peak of their capacities. Because of their relative fewness, a sizable number of workers in the younger age group may be able to move into positions of greater responsibility somewhat earlier than their formal education and work experience would have indicated.

The next age group (those forty-five to sixty-four years old) by 1980 will be showing an even greater effect of the depression years on birth rates. Their number is projected to rise only moderately—from 27½ million in 1968 to 29 million in 1980—and their share of the total labor force will shrink from 33 per cent to about 29 per cent. These workers are normally at the top of their career ladders, and most of the authority to direct the nation's resources and chart its future course will rest with them. However, because their ranks, too, will be relatively thin by 1980, many members of younger age groups behind them will have a greater opportunity to participate in the conduct of affairs at the top level of decision-making. Finally, the number of workers still employed beyond the normal retirement age of sixty-five will remain about unchanged (at roughly 3 million) during the decade.

In concluding this assessment of the outlook for the American economy during the decade of the 1970's, the main contours visible on the horizon can be summarized briefly: We should expect a sizable growth in total output and employment, with a further marginal shift toward the provision of services relative to the production of goods. There should be a significant upgrading in occupations and a sharp increase in the demand for skills. The average age of the labor force will decline appreciably, and its level of educational attainment will rise noticeably. The net outcome will be greatly enhanced opportunities for college graduates—and a serious deterioration in the employment outlook for persons with little education and few marketable skills.

II. The Negro in the American Economy in 1980

What are the implications of these prospective economic changes for the American Negro? How are black people expected to share in the gains from economic growth during the decade of the 1970's?

While these questions cannot be answered with certainty, through the use of economic projections similar to those employed in the assessment of the outlook for the national economy we can set rough boundaries to our expectations. Again, the time horizon is the period 1968-1980.[5]

According to the U.S. Bureau of the Census, the Negro population should be about 32.5 million in 1980, compared with 22 million in 1968. The Bureau has projected the total population of the United States at approximately 243 million in 1980, versus 198 million in 1968. Thus, the Negro population is expected to grow by 10.5 million, or 48 per cent, while the total population expands by 45 million, or 23 per cent. Consequently, while Negroes represented 11 per cent of the total in 1968, they may account for almost one-quarter of the net increase, and by 1980 their share of the total may have climbed to 13.4 per cent.[6]

During the present decade, the proportion of the Negro population participating in the labor force is expected to remain essentially unchanged (at roughly 60 per cent of the total).[7] However, participation rates will probably change in opposite directions among Negro men and women, and they may converge when compared to those for white workers. Historically, the proportion of Negro women in the labor force has been considerably higher than for white women—a reflection of the greater need of the former to contribute to family incomes. Yet, the labor force participation rates of the two groups have been converging in recent years, and the trend is expected to continue through the 1970's. For instance, in 1968, 49 per cent of Negro women were in the labor force, compared with 40 per cent of white women. By 1980, it is anticipated that the difference will have shrunk further, as the rate for Negro women eases off to 47 per cent while that for white women rises to 42 per cent. These results will arise from a somewhat lessened pressure on Negro women to work (reflecting relative improvement in the economic position of Negro men) and a greater tendency for white women to seek paid employment outside the household. Among Negro men, the labor force participation rate may increase moderately from 75.9 per cent in 1968 to 77.5 per cent in 1980. The participation rate for white men (which was 80.4 per cent in 1968) is expected to edge downward. For Negro men, the years ahead will probably bring more steady employment and a reduced tendency for them to withdraw from the labor force because of discouragement over job prospects. The net result should be noticeable improvement in their basic economic position.

Reflecting these trends, there should be about 12 million Negroes in the labor force in 1980, an increase of 3 million from the 1968 level. This would represent an annual rate of growth of 2.4 per cent, about one and one-half times as rapid as that for whites (1.6 per cent). So Negroes would account for 16.5 per cent of the growth in the total labor force between 1968 and 1980, and their share of the total would be 12 per cent by the end of the decade.

For Negroes, the pattern of change in the work force between 1968 and 1980 will be essentially the same as that for whites. Here also a large proportion of labor force growth will be concentrated among workers in the twenty-five to thirty-four age group, but a relatively larger percentage of the increase for Negroes will be found here. Moreover, while a greater percentage of Negro teenagers will remain in school—along with their white counterparts—a relatively larger proportion of the former will also enter the labor force during the current decade. This behavior will entail considerable risk, in view of the ever-rising demand for skills discussed earlier.

Occupational Upgrading Among Negroes

In general, Negroes are expected to share significantly in the over-all upgrading in occupations which seems to be on the horizon. Assuming that they improve their position in the 1970's at the same rate registered during the 1960's, their occupational distribution will change appreciably by 1980. By the latter year, they may hold over 10 per cent of the professional and technical jobs, compared with about 6 per cent in 1968. Their share of managerial, official, and proprietory occupations may rise from under 3 per cent in 1968 to almost 4 per cent in 1980. Significant gains are also anticipated in the proportion of clerical, sales, and craftsmen jobs held by Negroes. On the other hand, they might continue to account for about the same percentage of farm workers and laborers, while a noticeable decline is expected in their share of service jobs.

These occupational changes are expected to have a major impact within the black community as well. In this instance, however, we can make detailed projections only through 1975.[8] In the latter year, professional and technical workers might represent 12 per cent of the Negro labor force, compared with 7.8 per cent in 1968. Since this is one of the most rapidly expanding occupational groups, the ratio will undoubtedly be much higher in 1980. In contrast, in 1968, about 14.3 per cent of the white labor force consisted of professional and technical workers, so the Negro-white differential was 6.5 percentage points in favor of whites. By 1975, the proportion of whites in this occupational category may rise only slightly to 15 per cent, and the differential may shrink to only 3 percentage points. The managerial group is expected to account for about 3 per cent of the Negro labor force in 1975, compared with 2.8 per cent in

1968. Here also the percentage can be expected to rise further by 1980, but a sizable gap would remain compared with the proportion for whites (which was about 15 per cent in 1968). By 1975, a considerably higher proportion of the Negro labor force will be engaged in clerical and sales occupations. As mentioned, most of the relative shift will be away from the blue-collar and unskilled jobs.

Further Improvement in Educational Attainment Among Negroes

Underlying this anticipated upgrading in jobs held by Negroes is a further improvement in their educational attainment—continuing a trend evident during the last decade. For, example, the proportion of Negro men in the age group twenty-five to twenty-nine with four years of high school or more rose from 36 per cent in 1960 to 60 per cent in 1969; the corresponding gain for white men was from 63 per cent to 78 per cent. Negro women made similar but less striking advances. Moreover, in the 1960's, there was a major increase in the number of Negroes attending college.

If these trends in schooling for both whites and Negroes continue during the decade of the 1970's, the gap between the two will narrow considerably. On this assumption, by 1980, Negro women on the average may have completed about 12.1 years of schooling compared with 12.6 years for white women. This would mean that the educational differential would shrink from 0.9 years in 1967 to only 0.5 years in favor of white women. Among Negro men, the median years of schooling may rise to 11.4 years by 1980, compared with 12.8 years for white men, further narrowing the gap to about 1.4 years compared with a differential of 1.9 years in 1967. Moreover, substantial improvement can also be expected in the quality of education received by Negroes over the next decade.

Future Trends in the Income of the Negro Community

While Negroes will obviously share significantly in the output of the American economy that is expected to reach $1.4 trillion by 1980, we have no direct way to identify their share of GNP. On the other hand, we do have a reliable estimate of aggregate money income earned by Negroes as defined by the Bureau of the Census. This series does distinguish between income recipients according to color. In 1968, aggregate money income as measured by this series amounted to $488.4 billion. Of this amount, $454.5 billion was earned by the white population, and $33.9 billion was received by nonwhites, representing 6.9 per cent of the total. In 1956 the income of the nonwhite population amounted to $14 billion or 5.7 per cent of the total. During recent years the share of aggregate money income received by nonwhites has been increasing. If we assume that the same annual increase in the proportion received by nonwhites during the period 1956-1968 continues during the next decade, nonwhites would receive about 8.8 per cent of aggregate money income in 1980. If present over-all trends continue, aggregate money income might amount to $843 billion in 1980, expressed in 1968 prices. The division might be $769 billion accruing to the white population and $74 billion accruing to nonwhites.

Thus, during the 1970's, sizable gains will undoubtedly be registered in the aggregate money income of nonwhites as well as for whites. But the relative improvement for nonwhites would probably be substantially greater. This can be seen most clearly when the income figures are expressed in per capita terms. In 1968 aggregate money income per head was $2,465; it was $2,590 for whites and $1,590 for nonwhites. By 1980 the total may rise to $3,465 per capita. The corresponding figures for whites and nonwhites may be about $3,648 and $2,277, respectively. Consequently, for whites aggregate money income might increase by 40 per cent; but for nonwhites the gain in per capita terms might be 50 per cent.

In conclusion, the Negro community is expected to share somewhat more fully in economic growth in the current decade than they did in the last. However, this projected result is based on the assumption (which may prove to be optimistic) that they will be able to acquire skills at an accelerated rate and that racial discrimination and other barriers to participation in an open economy will be appreciably lessened. But even if the most favorable outcome materializes, it will still be necessary to press on with the campaign for equal opportunity in 1980.

III. The Economics of the Negro College

Given this improved economic outlook for the Negro community, how will it affect the prospects for the predominantly Negro colleges? To establish a benchmark for answering this question, it might be helpful to examine the general economic situation confronted by these institutions as a group.

In this part of the discussion, however, it is necessary to remember that there are really two distinct subgroups: Of the 115 black colleges in operation in 1969, about 34 were publicly controlled (mainly by southern states); the remaining 81 were privately controlled, including around 70 closely related to religious bodies.

The Pattern of Enrollment

In 1969, these predominantly Negro colleges enrolled about 155,000 students. This was just over one-third of the 434,000 black students in schools of higher education in 1968, the latest year for which we have a fairly good estimate.[9] The remaining two-thirds were in predominantly white institutions. Among the Negro colleges, those under public control accounted for about three-fifths of the students, compared with two-fifths for the private colleges. Roughly the same division prevailed in 1959 when their total enrollment was around 89,000. Thus, in general terms, the black colleges are still playing a significant (although relatively declining) role in the education of black youth; although the latter still represented less than 6 per cent of the 7.3 million student population in higher education in 1969, about one-third of them were studying at institutions serving primarily a Negro student body. The demand for spaces in entering classes of black college freshmen (which expanded at an annual rate of 5 per cent during the last decade) has placed a heavy burden on Negro colleges and apparently will continue to do so for some time. However, the rate of increase in enrollment in these schools appears to be slowing—especially in the privately controlled institutions.

Looking ahead, we can extend our view of future enrollment only through 1978, and this must rest primarily on official U.S. government estimates.[10] According to these data, by 1978, about 10.3 million students are expected to be enrolled in degree-granting institutions, of which 8.1 million will be in four-year colleges and universities and 2.2 million in institutions offering two-year programs. In the ten years 1968-1978, total enrollment might advance by almost 50 per cent.

For Negro students, the rate of increase in enrollment will probably be even greater. This likelihood is strongly suggested by a variety of evidence. For example, although the college attendance rate for nonwhites of college-going age is currently less than half the rate for whites, the situation may change significantly in the years ahead as a greater percentage of Negro youths graduate from high school. Evidence also shows that the college attendance rate among nonwhites who have graduated from high school is roughly 80 per cent of that among whites. In addition, it seems that a higher proportion of nonwhites than white seniors plan to enroll in college—suggesting that Negroes are strongly motivated toward college as a vehicle for social and economic improvement.[11] Given these trends, college enrollment of Negro students may increase one and one-quarter to one and one-half times as fast as that for all college students through 1978. At this rate of growth, there would be between 700,000 and 750,000 Negro college students in 1978, representing about 7 per cent of the total, compared with less than 6 per cent in 1969.

The vast majority of the increased enrollment, however, is expected to occur at predominantly white institutions. Even if enrollment at Negro colleges increases through 1978 at the 5.1 per cent annual rate recorded between 1959 and 1969 (which seems unlikely), the growth in their student bodies would amount to only 88,000, raising their total enrollment to just over 240,000. Thus, their share of all black college students would remain in the neighborhood of one-third. Among these institutions, however, those under private control may attract somewhat less than two-fifths of the projected increase through 1978—which was their share of total enrollments at Negro colleges in 1968.

On the other hand, one should have serious doubts about the continuation of some of the essentially separate, publicly-controlled Negro colleges. With increased emphasis on desegregation as a goal of public policy at the national level, many of the states currently maintaining such schools may find it best to merge them or otherwise combine them with predominantly white institutions. But pointing in the opposite direction is growing pressure from the black community to maintain as separate institutions (mainly because of local pride) some of the Negro colleges with which they have been identified over the years. Which of these competing tendencies will prevail cannot be foreseen with certainty, but the move toward consolidation appears to be the more likely outcome.

Financial Resources of the Negro Colleges

The financial outlook for the black colleges is mixed. Among the strongest are the thirty-odd publicly controlled schools. In the last decade or so, as the segregated system came increasingly under attack as being both separate and unequal, a number of southern states rushed to provide essentially "catch-up" appropriations for previously neglected Negro colleges. These funds went for current operations as well as for building programs. Yet, complaints are still heard about lagging funds for salaries and new programs.

As a general rule, for both private and publicly controlled black colleges, in-depth financing and capitalization have fallen short of the levels required, and most of them suffer from low endowments, declining values of physical plants, and difficulties in gaining access to long-term financing. In fact, much of the recently announced increase of $29 million in funds from the U.S. Office of Education expressly for black schools apparently was made in recognition of this financing problem. Of the total, $20 million was earmarked for direct loans for construction. In the past, many of these schools could not take full advantage of some federal government assistance programs because they could not raise their share of the required matching funds.

It is difficult to obtain consistent data relating to trends in finances of the Negro colleges. However, for the private colleges, the experience of the ten predominantly Negro schools supported at least in part by the United Methodist Church probably provides a fairly good picture of the situation.[12] These ten schools represent about one-fifth of the privately controlled black colleges, and they had about one-eighth of the enrollment in such schools in 1969.

In the academic year 1968-1969, the United Methodist Church (UMC) was associated with eighty-three senior colleges, of which eleven[13] enrolled mainly Negro students. In 1959-1960, the total number was seventy-four, of which eleven were Negro colleges. In 1968-1969, these eighty-three schools enrolled 97,186 students; enrollment at the ten (see note 13) black institutions in that year was 7,965, or 8.2 per cent of the total. These data reflect an increase of 45 per cent in regular enrollment at the eighty-three colleges between 1959-1960 and 1968-1969; at the black colleges, enrollment rose by 32 per cent. In all of the UMC related colleges, there were 6,451 faculty members in 1968-1969, compared with 4,448 in 1959-1960. The faculty at the ten Negro schools numbered 407 (or 9.2 per cent) in the earlier year and 558 (or 8.7 per cent) in the most recent year. The typical black UMC related college had about two-thirds the enrollment of its average white counterpart.

An analysis of the financial statistics for the UMC colleges suggests that the black schools among them lagged significantly in two critical areas over the last decade. The relative deterioration centered in the value of their endowments and physical plant. For all of the schools, the value of their endowments (the bedrock on which their financial position must rest) rose from $190.6 million in 1959-1960 to $296.7 million in 1968-1969. For the black colleges, the increase was from $9.7 million to $11.8 million over the same period. Thus, the latter's share of the total declined from 5.1 per cent to 4.0 per cent. Even more striking, the endowment per student at the black colleges dropped by 10 per cent (from $1,620 to $1,470), while at all UMC colleges it rose by 7 per cent (from $2,860 to $3,060). Thus, measured in terms of the amount available per student, the black colleges' average endowment was only three-fifths that of their white counterparts in 1959-1960, and it had fallen to less than one-half by 1968-1969.

The Negro colleges made substantial improvements in their physical facilities during the last decade, but the relative gain was less than that achieved by all UMC colleges combined. In 1959-1960, the value of physical plant was put at $298 million for the group as a whole, and this had risen to $741 million by 1968-1969. For the ten Negro colleges, the corresponding figures were $21 million in 1959-1960 and $45 million in 1968-1969. This meant that all UMC colleges multiplied the value of their physical plant two and one-half times while the Negro colleges little more than doubled the value of their facilities. But in terms of investment per student, the latter expanded their holdings by 61 per cent (from $3,500 in 1959-1960 to $5,650 in 1968-1969). For all UMC colleges, the gain was 72 per cent (from $4,450 to $7,650). Nevertheless, the black college-UMC ratio of per student investment eased off slightly over the decade (from 75 per cent to 74 per cent).

In the case of total current income and educational and general expenditures, the Negro colleges made slight improvements in their relative position. In 1959-1960, they had total current income of $6.5 million, and this rose to $20.4 million by 1968-1969. The parallel figures for all UMC colleges were $92 million and $251 million, respectively. Current income from educational and general sources rose in tandem (from $4.6 million to $14.1 million for Negro colleges and from $61.0 million to $174.6 million for all UMC schools). Thus, the black colleges' share of both total income and educational receipts advanced moderately—from 7.5 per cent to 8.1 per cent.

On the expenditure side, the Negro colleges also expanded somewhat more rapidly than all UMC schools during the last decade. In 1959-1960, the black colleges' total outlays were $6.2 million, of which $4.3 million were for educational and other purposes (excluding additions to physical plant). By 1968-1969, their total outlays had risen to $21.3 million, and those for education had climbed to $14.6 million. For all UMC colleges, the figures were: 1959-1960, total expenditures, $90 million; educational outlays, $57.6 million. 1968-1969, total expenditures, $249.6 million; educational outlays, $166.7 million. Thus, the black colleges raised their proportion of total expenditures by UMC colleges from 6.9 per cent to 8.5 per cent, and their share of educational outlays rose from 7.5 per cent to 8.7 per cent.

On the other hand, their ability to borrow long-term funds remained relatively unchanged—although their total indebtedness rose along with that of all UMC schools. In 1959-1960, the latter had outstanding borrowings of $50.1 million, and the level rose to $207.3 million by 1968-1969. For the Negro colleges, the corresponding figures were $2.4 million and $11.3 million. So the latter's share of total indebtedness was essentially the same in both years (5.0 per cent and 5.5 per cent, respectively).

Financial Position of Publicly Controlled Negro Colleges

In the case of publicly controlled black colleges, we do not have financial data comparable to the UMC statistics for private colleges. But several fragments of information we were able to collect do provide a rough indication of the general situation among the public institutions.

One body of data, comparing educational and general expenditures per student by four-year public colleges, was obtained from the Council for Financial Aid to Education. In 1968-1969, all four-year institutions spent for these purposes about $2,538 per student. At all four-year black schools, the average was $2,467, or roughly 97 per cent of that for all schools combined. Among public institutions, the average outlay was $2,483 for the total and $2,554 at Negro colleges—some 3 per cent more. During much of the 1960's, apparently average outlays by the public Negro colleges rose more rapidly than any other group. For example, between 1962-1963 and 1968-1969, for all four-year colleges the rise amounted to 20 per cent, compared with 83 per cent for all black schools combined. For all publicly controlled institutions, the increase amounted to 16 per cent but it was 137 per cent at Negro colleges. (For comparison, the increases in per student expenditures by the UMC private schools were 95 per cent for the total—from $915 to $1,790—and 134 per cent—from $750 to $1,760—for the black schools, between 1959-1960 and 1968-1969.) So, judged by expenditures per student, all black colleges—including the public institutions—made significant strides in strengthening their financial positions.

Another bit of information on finances of the publicly controlled Negro colleges was provided by the Office for Advancement of Public Negro Colleges (OAPNC), a group recently formed to promote their interest, and the U. S. Office of Education.[14] By combining these data, one can get a fairly good view of trends in the sources of current fund income of the public Negro colleges. In both 1959-1960 and 1967-1968, state support of black public institutions accounted for a somewhat larger proportion of total fund income than for all public colleges and universities.[15] However, over time, the proportion for the black schools has risen slightly. In 1959-1960, the states provided about 45 per cent of the Negro colleges' current revenue, but the ratio had moved up to 50 per cent by 1967-1968. For all public colleges, the corresponding figures were 41 per cent and 39 per cent, respectively, virtually unchanged over the decade. Federal government support of the public Negro colleges fluctuated widely over the decade, but the trend was generally downward. In contrast, all public institutions combined became somewhat more heavily dependent on federal support. In 1959-1960, about 14 per cent of the black schools' receipts came from the federal government, and in 1967-1968 the ratio was 10 per cent. For all of the publicly controlled group, the federal share climbed from 17 per cent to 20 per cent. Here also the experience of the black schools reflected their relative inability to raise matching funds required under federal assistance programs.

Public Negro colleges have relied on tuition to about the same extent as all schools in this class. In both 1959-1960 and 1967-1968, both groups received between 10 per cent and 12 per cent of their current funds from this source. On the other hand, the black institutions have consistently relied more heavily on income from auxiliary enterprises (such as dormitories, cafeterias, and bookstores). In both 1959-1960 and 1967-1968, about one-quarter of their current receipts originated in these enterprises. Among all public schools, the proportion was about one-sixth in both years.

One of the most striking developments associated with the publicly controlled Negro colleges in recent years is their strong effort to raise funds from private sources. While private support for all public institutions of higher education was trending downward, the predominantly black schools have been able to attract private funds much more readily. In 1959-1960, they received only 0.3 per cent of their current receipts from private contributions; the corresponding figure for all public institutions was 2.6 per cent. By 1967-1968, the black schools had been able to lift the proportion to 1.0 per cent, while for public colleges as a whole it declined to 1.2 per cent. Foundations have been the main source of increased private support for the publicly controlled Negro colleges. In 1959-1960, many of them had received no income from foundations. These institutions were unable to share in the fund-raising efforts of the United Negro College Fund, so other general welfare foundations had to be tapped. Moreover, as indicated above, these schools recently formed their own association with the primary aim of appealing for private support.

In concluding this assessment of the financial position of the Negro colleges, several points should be kept in mind. During the last decade, the black colleges continued to compete fairly strongly for students, but the rate of increase in their enrollments appears to be slowing, especially in the privately controlled institutions. The over-all financial position of these predominantly black colleges is quite mixed. Some of these schools (especially those under public control) have made noticeable strides in terms of income for current operations and for construction of facilities. However, endowment resources (held mainly by the private institutions) have advanced only moderately, and all of the black colleges are plagued by lagging funds for salaries and new programs. So, in general, these black colleges and universities entered the decade of the 1970's beset by an agenda of financial difficulties somewhat more challenging than that faced by their predominantly white counterparts.

IV. The Future of the Negro College

Against this background of economic change and the evolving financial circumstances of the predominantly black institutions, we can now turn to the most difficult part of this assignment: the assessment of their prospects in the decade ahead. In my judgment, their future will be shaped to a considerable extent by a new structure of demand for college graduates, a significant change in college attendance patterns, and continued limitations on the availability of financial resources.

Future Demand for Negro College Graduates

As stressed several times in this essay, the current decade will be characterized by a sharp increase in the demand for highly trained people of all types. This will include Negro college graduates along with everyone else. Here, however, the black colleges—and their student bodies—will be confronted by a dramatically shifting demand for skills by industry and government, compared with the traditional composition of their graduating classes. As is generally known, Negro college students historically have concentrated in those fields where employment was virtually assured by patterns of racial segregation and discrimination.

This legacy is still traceable in the distribution of degrees granted by the publicly controlled black colleges. For example, in 1967-1968, degrees in education represented close to half of all bachelor's degrees, and the graduates were distributed almost equally between elementary school teaching and other education fields. The concentration in education was much less than it was in 1955-1956 (when it accounted for two-thirds of the graduating classes), but it was ahead of all other fields by a considerable margin. Moreover, about four-fifths of all those receiving master's degrees from these publicly controlled Negro institutions in 1967-1968 did their work in education. Over this twelve-year period, degrees in the social sciences rose from 11 per cent to 17 per cent of all bachelor's degrees awarded by these schools. Degrees in business fields increased from 3.5 per cent to 8.5 per cent. The share of English and literature rose from 3.6 per cent to 6.2 per cent in the same period. However, in the scientific fields, the shift was less marked. Here the proportion rose from 7.4 per cent to 9.2 per cent of the total, but the share of biology remained unchanged at 4.4 per cent. Degrees in mathematics expanded from 2.3 per cent to 4.5 per cent.

Over the current decade, the demand for college graduates is expected to run substantially counter to the typical supply of degree holders leaving the Negro colleges. Elementary and secondary education will probably experience the most striking change in supply-demand conditions. Long plagued by a shortage of classroom personnel, teaching is on the verge of a dramatic change in circumstances: even before the decade is very far advanced, the total supply of teachers is expected to exceed demand by a significant margin—if recent entry patterns in this occupation continue. In scientific fields, there may also be a surplus of mathematicians and life scientists (especially of biologists), if students continue to concentrate in these areas in the same proportion as in the recent past.

In contrast, several other scientific and technical fields will continue to face shortages during the 1970's. These include chemistry, geology, geophysics, and engineering. Although transfers among these fields can be expected to occur frequently, over-all shortages may still prevail. Professional health occupations can also anticipate continued shortages. The shortfall in the supply of physicians and dentists may be especially serious owing to the limited capacity of existing medical and dental schools, which may be relieved only slightly by institutions scheduled to be launched during the 1970's.

Outside the scientific and medical fields, other areas of potential shortages include counseling, social work, urban planning, and a number of occupations involved in the planning and administration of state and local governments.

In view of these shifting supply and demand conditions, the Negro colleges will have to make major adaptations in their curricula and programs—if they are to remain viable. In general, the areas of new opportunity will call for a heavy investment in highly qualified faculty and instructional equipment. On the basis of recent trends, many of the Negro colleges (particularly among those privately supported) would find it difficult to generate the resources needed to upgrade their educational efforts along the required lines.

Changing Preferences for College Attendance

Another obstacle the Negro colleges will have to face during the current decade is the growing competition for students stemming from the rapid multiplication of community colleges. As indicated earlier, they have already come under competitive pressure from predominantly white universities and liberal arts colleges.

During the decade 1968-1978, it is anticipated that most of the increase in the number of community colleges will center in those offering two-year programs. The total enrollment in these institutions may expand by more than two-thirds, from 1.3 million to 2.2 million over this period. This would represent an annual rate of growth of 5.4 per cent, about one-third faster than that for enrollment at all institutions of higher education and two-fifths faster than the rate for four-year colleges and universities. In 1968, the two-year colleges already had 18 per cent of the total enrollment, and by 1978 this may rise further to 21 per cent.

Of considerable importance to Negro colleges—and the potential students which they must attempt to attract—these new community colleges will be located primarily in urban areas. Thus, they will be in close proximity to the Negro population which will become even more urbanized over the current decade. Since these new institutions will almost certainly be commuter schools charging little tuition—and most probably eligible for an increasing amount of federal aid—they will obviously be attractive places for black students from poor families seeking some college education as a vehicle for economic and social advancement.

These new two-year colleges should not be confused with the twenty-six predominantly black junior colleges already in existence. Most of these were begun during the 1960's, and about one-third of them are publicly supported. However, of the twenty-six, nearly three-fifths are church-related, and all but a few of these are not accredited. The future of this latter group appears particularly unpromising.

Family Income and Educational Expenditures

One of the strongest factors favoring the Negro colleges is the strong incentive black families have to send their children to college. To support their judgment, they are apparently spending a substantially larger share of their smaller incomes for this purpose than are white families. To a large extent, this is not a wholly new situation. For example, between 1950 and 1960, spending for education by Negro families showed a gain of 4.2 per cent for every 1 per cent increase in their disposable personal income, compared with a 3.1 per cent rise in expenditures for the same purpose by white families for a 1 per cent increase in their disposable income.[16]

More recent studies show that both the incentive for black students to attend college and the willingness of their families to pay a sizable share of the cost remain strong. For instance, a study of 1966 high school seniors' future plans, based on their view of the best way to get ahead in life, showed that 82 per cent of nonwhite youths planned to enter college, compared to 77 per cent of the white students.[17] The burden of college attendance on the incomes of Negro families is clearly considerable. Thus, in 1969, for example, the average family income of students in the thirty-four predominantly black publicly supported colleges was below $4,000. At the same time, the average tuition and room and board charges were $914 for in-state students. These costs represented nearly one-quarter of the average family income. Most students obviously needed some financial assistance from nonfamily sources.

This situation is not unique to Negro families, of course. A recent study by the College Scholarship Service (CSS), based on the information submitted by all families seeking assistance in underwriting at least some of the cost of their children's education, found that the average family had a median income in 1969 of $9,740. A substantial fraction of the applicants had a justifiable need for aid, and the mean financial need was for 47 per cent of the total college budget.

If we use this last ratio (47 per cent) as a benchmark and apply it to the average student at the black public colleges, he would have needed at least $430 in assistance had his family income equaled the median of the CSS family. Adjusting for the fact that median income for Negroes in 1969 was $6,971 (or 72 per cent of the CSS family), this student might have expected $658 in scholarship or other assistance.

In fact, a substantial number of black students have found assistance through federal loan and work-study programs. The National Defense Student Act of 1958 provided student loans, and the Economic Opportunity Act of 1964 provided aid for those engaged in work-study arrangements. A study of student assistance conducted in the late 1960's found that over half of all students in Negro colleges received scholarship aid of some kind.[18] For all black colleges in this survey, the average dollar amount of aid per student assisted varied between $305 and $348. For those students in the public school example mentioned above, had they received that amount of assistance, they (or their families) would have been required to provide the difference—which would have amounted to roughly between $566 and $609, or nearly two-thirds of the cost of college. This still would have represented about one-sixth of their average family income.

Clearly black families are paying a considerable part of the cost of college education for their children. Consequently, it is not surprising that Negro students have enrolled in substantial numbers in the less expensive, predominantly black colleges. And while the incomes of Negro families are expected to register sizable gains during the current decade, the prospects are that—as long as there is a noticeable differential in tuition and other costs—many black students will continue to enroll in these Negro colleges in the future.

Availability of Resources

Finally, the future of the Negro colleges will turn critically on their ability to attract resources, both human and financial. We are in a much better position to pinpoint the nature of the problems they will face than we are to foresee solutions.

Undoubtedly, one of the most difficult tasks will be to attract and hold a good faculty. In the typical black college there has always been a need to rely heavily on faculty members whose qualifications were somewhat less than desirable. Moreover, a sizable proportion of their faculties (particularly in those institutions under private sponsorship) has consisted of white Americans or foreign nationals, especially Chinese and Indians.

On the whole, however, the Negro colleges have been able to fill their classrooms to roughly the same extent as their white counterparts. This is clearly implied by trends in faculty-student ratios. For example, the ten UMC Negro Colleges discussed earlier had a faculty-student ratio of 1:14.8 in 1959-1960, compared with 1:15.2 for all members of the UMC group. By 1968-1969, the ratios at both types of institutions were essentially unchanged—1:14.3 for the black schools and 1:14.9 for all schools combined.

At the publicly controlled Negro schools, however, the average faculty member apparently was responsible for a significantly larger number of students—larger even than one would expect for schools in the public sector where faculty-student ratios are normally higher than at private schools. Thus, in 1968-1969, the ratio for the thirty-four publicly supported Negro colleges was 1:18.7. In the same year, the ratio for all public four-year colleges was 1:14.7. In all four-year private colleges it was 1:9.9. As we move through the decade of the 1970's, all schools can be expected to see an increase in student enrollment per faculty member. It has been estimated that by 1977-1978 the ratio in all four-year public colleges will have climbed to 1:16.8, and in their private counterparts it may have reached 1:10.5. On balance, black schools (both public and private) may fare less well in this regard than colleges in general.

In the matter of faculty qualifications, it is impossible to obtain a summary measure that would provide a true index of quality. However, the proportion of a college's faculty with Ph.D.'s is probably a reasonable proxy. In 1968-1969, about 27 per cent of the faculty at publicly supported Negro schools held Ph.D.'s. While no similar figure is readily available for all public institutions, it is undoubtedly higher. For the country as a whole, the percentage of faculty holding Ph.D.'s rose appreciably from 1956 to 1966. But as undergraduate enrollments climbed sharply from 1963 to 1966, the ratio declined moderately. All of this decline was borne by public institutions.[19] As black public colleges also had a sizable increase in enrollment, they probably shared in the general experience.

Increased resources to meet rising faculty salaries will also be an obstacle for the black colleges. Over the last decade, faculty salaries at all colleges and universities rose somewhat more rapidly than wages and salaries in general. For instance, between 1959 and 1966, they advanced at a 5.5 per cent average annual rate. The gain was roughly the same at both private and public institutions. Nevertheless, salaries at Negro colleges generally remain well below those in their white counterparts. Among publicly controlled institutions in 1968-1969, salaries paid by the Negro schools were 75 per cent to 93 per cent of those received by educators in the various academic ranks in all public schools of higher education. The lowest ratio was for full professors, and the highest was for instructors. For both assistant and associate professors, the ratio was about 84 per cent. Roughly the same pattern prevailed when salaries paid by the public Negro colleges were compared with those paid by all private independent universities—except that the ratios for the Negro schools were even lower.[20]

During the last few years, salaries at the publicly controlled Negro colleges have risen somewhat more rapidly than salaries at other institutions generally, but the gap is still considerable. The same is probably true in the case of the private black schools. This condition will create increasingly serious problems for the Negro institutions in the years ahead. For some time now many of the predominantly white schools have made a vigorous effort to attract able black faculty members, and these have come mainly from the Negro colleges. This form of competition will undoubtedly continue, and the shortfall in salaries will make it even harder for the black schools to compete. Thus, it is to be expected that the average quality of the faculty remaining on predominantly black campuses (especially those that are nonaccredited) will decline over the current decade.

Future Sources of Funds

Looking ahead, it seems obvious that many of the Negro colleges will face even greater financial stringency than in the past. The publicly controlled schools will probably suffer with all other public institutions from the growing reluctance of state legislatures and local authorities to provide resources on the scale that is increasingly required. The black private schools—along with their white counterparts—will run the risk of placing themselves beyond the reach of their potential student bodies if they raise tuition and other charges to the full extent necessary to cover their rising costs of operation.

Under these circumstances, it is obvious that alternative means of adjustment must be found. For some, the solution—perhaps unhappily—will probably be to cease operation. This may be especially true for some of the dozen or so private four-year Negro colleges that are not accredited, all of which are church-related. A similar fate may await most of the seventeen existing privately controlled black junior colleges, fifteen of which are not accredited. In fact, some of the marginal four-year colleges are already reducing their scale of operation as enrollments fall and budget deficits become deeper. In the future, such marginal existence will become even more uncertain in a rapidly changing educational environment—characterized by increasing demands of students and more liberal opportunities for enrollment of black students outside the formerly protective barriers of segregation.

Among those institutions which do survive, many of them—particularly among those in the public sector—may cease to be predominantly black schools. The pressure to eliminate all deliberately maintained patterns of segregation in public education will undoubtedly claim some of the existing Negro schools. Already several of them have gone this route. For example, in 1968-1969, over three-fourths of the students at West Virginia State College were white. About half of the students at Lincoln University in Missouri, and one-third of those at Delaware State College and Kentucky State College were white. In fact, all of the historically Negro publicly supported colleges now enroll some white students and have a number of white faculty members. This will become the pattern increasingly over time, especially where the schools are located close to urban areas. For these schools thus transformed into general public institutions, state financial resources would seem to be assured.

Private Negro colleges in the future will probably have to continue to rely heavily on tuition and student fees to support their operations. With family incomes in the Negro community rising more rapidly than for the economy as a whole, the ability of Negro parents to pay higher education costs should also improve. Their situation will be strengthened further by the expanding opportunities for part-time employment for students who wish to work and study at the same time.

Nevertheless, these private Negro schools will find it necessary to seek voluntary support on an increasing scale. Since many of them are church-related, the relative decline in the share of support they received through religious contributions is of major importance. For example, in 1968-1969, black private coeducational colleges obtained about 16 per cent of all their voluntary financial support from religious denominations. In 1962-1963, the proportion had been 42 per cent. The corresponding figures for their white counterparts were 15 per cent and 20 per cent, respectively, at the beginning and end of the decade. Support by the alumni of the private black colleges is one of the weakest areas of voluntary support. For all four-year black colleges in 1968-1969, alumni contributed less than 2 per cent of total current fund income compared with 24 per cent for all four-year institutions combined. Among the predominantly black schools in this sample, the public institutions were the most successful in obtaining funds from their graduates; they increased the share of total current funds from this source to 12.6 per cent in 1968-1969 from 3.1 per cent in 1962-1963. In the same period, the black private colleges lost ground as far as alumni contributions are concerned—with the proportion dropping from 2.0 per cent to 0.9 per cent. In contrast, the predominantly white private colleges experienced an increase in alumni support from 17 per cent of total current funds in 1962-1963 to 27 per cent in 1968-1969.[21] To a considerable extent, of course, the relatively low level of alumni support for the black schools reflects the lower incomes in the Negro community as well as the nature of the occupations typically entered by black college graduates (mainly school teaching and public service). As Negroes' incomes rise to higher levels in the future—and as they broaden the scope of their career paths—the trend of alumni support for the black schools should rise accordingly.

In the end, however, it seems quite evident that the Negro colleges, especially those under private control, will have to look increasingly to the federal government for financial support. Thus, they will have to follow essentially the same course that their white counterparts will have to pursue. How heavy their reliance on federal sources of funds will have to be cannot be estimated with precision. However, it probably will be relatively greater than for the average college. Since these black colleges will have to draw a larger proportion of their students from families with below-average incomes, the amount of assistance per student they will require will also be somewhat larger than for their white counterparts. For example, one study has suggested that by 1976 a typical undergraduate student from the lowest family income quartile may have a need for financial aid totaling $1,274. Of this amount, perhaps $1,109 (or 87 per cent) might have to come from the federal government, consisting roughly of three-quarters grants and one-quarter loans. If public policy had as its goal bringing about equality of educational opportunity for children of equal scholastic ability, the total aid required would have to rise to $2,361 in 1976, and the federal share might have to be $2,196 (or 93 per cent), with grants accounting for almost four-fifths and loans for just over one-fifth. In contrast, for a typical undergraduate from a family in the very next income quartile, the need for aid would be substantially less. Here the amount needed to meet the minimum demand might be only $391, and the federal contribution would have to be $303. Loans would account for virtually all of this amount (95 per cent), and only 5 per cent would have to be in the form of grants. Even a policy in pursuit of educational equality would entail little additional direct burden on the federal government to aid this average student from a slightly better-off family. In this case, the total need for aid might climb to $1,008, and the federal share might have to be $920, or 92 per cent. But of this sum, just under half could be in the form of loans, and the rest would have to be grants.[22]

The extent to which the required aid will be forthcoming from the federal government obviously cannot be predicted. Nor can the division between direct aid to students and aid to institutions be foreseen. Yet, given the high priority the federal government can be expected to continue to assign to education, along with the elimination of poverty and the broadening of economic opportunity, it appears reasonable to assume that a sizable expansion in federal aid to higher education is likely as the decade progresses. And the black colleges which can demonstrate their capacity to serve (particularly those under private control) will undoubtedly share in, and benefit from, the increased availability of financial resources.

V. *Concluding Observations*

On the basis of the foregoing survey, I am left with a few overriding convictions. Despite being caught in the crosscurrents of economic, social, and cultural changes, most of the predominantly Negro colleges will probably survive—and expand—during the decade of the 1970's. Some of the weaker institutions (primarily the unaccredited church-related private schools) may well fall by the wayside. Many of the publicly supported Negro colleges will undoubtedly be transformed into mainly white institutions, but fully open to black students as well. On the other hand, most of the reasonably sound, traditionally Negro private colleges will probably continue roughly along the path they have traveled historically, except that they will have to modernize their programs and cater to a new generation of students seeking an education which will enable them to compete in an economy undergoing dramatic changes in the demand for skills.

The expanding economy will bring increased advantages to the Negro community in terms of improvements in income and employment opportunities. These will mean an enhanced ability on the part of Negro parents to finance a greater share of the educational costs of their children. Nevertheless, access to schools with relatively low tuition and other charges will continue to be of major importance to them. And it is here that the Negro colleges will be able to continue to make a significant contribution. This will be especially true if the federal government finally decides to provide a substantial share of the financial resources which higher education will require—and which only the federal government can supply over the years ahead.

So, I come away from this assessment of the prospective impact of economic change on the future of the Negro colleges with a feeling of greater optimism than I brought to the task. The passage of time will determine whether this hopeful view is justified.

I am grateful to Miss Harriett Harper for assistance in the preparation of this paper.

References

1. Although I have served as a trustee of Tuskegee Institute since 1966, my familiarity with the day-to-day issues faced by the institution is still limited. My service on one or two other college boards (including the Board

of Overseers at Harvard) provides for additional observations, but my lack of specialized knowledge remains substantial.

2. "The U. S. Economy in 1980: A Preview of BLS Projections," *Monthly Labor Review* (April 1970), pp. 4-34.

3. If the slower rate of growth recorded in 1969 is taken into account, the growth rate required to generate the 1980 GNP would be 4.4 per cent, and the annual gain in productivity would have to be 3.2 per cent. If the unemployment rate were to average 4 per cent, GNP might be about $12 billion lower, but the structure would be about the same.

4. It should be remembered that these figures refer to government *purchases* recorded in the GNP accounts; they do not refer to the *budgets* of the federal, state, and local governments.

5. I have examined the economic outlook for the Negro in considerable detail in another essay. See "The Black Revolution and the Economic Future of Negroes in the United States," *The American Scholar* (Autumn 1969), pp. 629-643.

6. Both of these projections assume a decrease in fertility over the current decade. However, the decline is expected to center primarily in the white population.

7. In most cases, data used in this section refer to all races except white. For the country as a whole, Negroes make up about 92 per cent of all non-whites.

8. The Bureau of Labor Statistics' detailed projections of the Negro labor force through 1980 will appear too late to be used in this essay. In the absence of these, the 1975 BLS projections were used.

9. U. S. Department of Labor, *Manpower Report of the President* (March 1970), p. 184.

10. See Kenneth A. Simon and others, *Projections of Educational Statistics to 1977-78,* Office of Education, U. S. Department of Health, Education, and Welfare (1969).

11. See Alice M. Rivlin and others, *Toward a Long-Range Plan for Federal Financial Support for Higher Education,* U. S. Department of Health, Education, and Welfare (January 1969), pp. 6-7.

12. "Education Statistics for Senior Colleges Related to the United Methodist Church, 1959-60 and 1968-69," Nashville, Tennessee. The ten schools in this group were Bennett College, Bethune-Cookman College, Claflin College, Clark College, Dillard University, Huston-Tillotson College, Paine College, Philander-Smith College, Rust College, and Wiley College.

13. One of these was Meharry Medical College, the data for which are not included in this summary.

14. OAPNC, *Public Negro Colleges: A Fact Book* (Atlanta, July 1969); and

"Financial Statistics of Institutions of Higher Education, 1959-60," U. S. Department of Health, Education, and Welfare.

15. In the case of all public institutions, the most recent data refer to 1966-1967.

16. See Andrew F. Brimmer, "The Negro in the National Economy," in John P. Davis, ed., *The American Negro Reference Book* (Englewood Cliffs, N. J.: Prentice-Hall, 1966), p. 281, table 14.

17. Joseph Froomkin, *Aspirations, Enrollments and Resources: The Challenge to Higher Education in the Seventies,* Office of Education, U. S. Department of Health, Education, and Welfare (1970), p. 22, table 2-10.

18. A. J. Jaffe, Walter Adams, and Sandra G. Meyers, *Negro Higher Education in the 1960's* (New York: Praeger, 1968), p. 37.

19. Rivlin and others, *Toward a Long-Range Plan,* p. 12.

20. OAPNC, *Public Negro Colleges,* p. 13.

21. Basic data are from the Council for Financial Aid to Education.

22. Froomkin, *Aspirations,* p. 97.

HENRY ALLEN BULLOCK

The Black College and the New Black Awareness

THIS ESSAY has as its main purpose an assessment of colleges for black people in light of the new black awareness. Growing out of a general ecological frame of reference, it makes the assessment based upon the degree to which this kind of college assists black students in their adjustment to the demands of their social-cultural environment. It exposes the college organization to historically polarizing social climates consisting of assimilation and separatism, observes the adequacy with which it provides adjustment to this climate, and suggests methods of reorganization by which the functions of the institution can be brought more in harmony with student needs.

We assume this to be a logical approach, for every educational institution has an ecological existence which is dependent upon a sustained relationship between itself and a larger societal segment. There is a force that places all vital activity under the influence of the universal life triad we know as organism, function, and environment.[1] It compels the view that the environment is eternally making demands upon living things that respond through organized functions. Wherever life abounds, organization becomes its basic characteristic quality. We see it in the plant and animal communities that shape the vital qualities of our organic world, and particularly in the human communities so strongly governed by a complex of organizations that defines the basic mode of human adjustment.

Colleges for black people, when observed within the context of a modified definition of environment, adequately meet the basic requirements of this ecological view. The kind of environment against which the black American has struggled most intensely has been mainly social-cultural rather than physical in nature. Characterized by racism, it has compelled him to struggle to gain and maintain social survival within the intentions of our democratic professions rather than to achieve a mere biological survival of black people. Since these colleges have been, by tradition, instrumentalities in the struggle of black people against the demands of a social-cultural environment that denies black survival at the equalitarian level, it is legitimate and logical that we assess their efficiency within this framework.

Basic here is a point of view that may very well be unpopular with many who head and support our institutions of higher learning. It is the idea that colleges for black people, first established under the American assimilation ideal, are now experiencing institutional discontinuity under the force of a new black awareness that rejects this ideal. Many educators would disagree with this position. They have perceived the functions of these colleges within the framework of the general purposes of American education: to teach the social order from the White Anglo-Saxon Protestant (WASP) point of view, and to prepare black students to plug neatly into the occupational fields provided by advancing American technology. They would assume an inadequacy of the black labor supply to meet the new opportunities opening to qualified black workers, and they would increase the output of these colleges to meet these demands.

Our position rejects the basic structure of their argument. First, it denies that a truly black college has ever existed; it claims that the illusion which formed a basis for this misconception resulted from the fallacious tendency to define an institution in terms of the racial composition of its clientele rather than the nature of its output. It contends, therefore, that what has been mistakenly called a black college is a "white" college for black people—a college that trains black students for participation, like white students, in a society dominated by a WASP culture. Second, it posits the idea that the degree of racism inherent in American society creates a barrier between the aspirations that these colleges hold for their black students and the actualization of such aspirations in the student's after-college life. The racism places white and black students in two separate social-cultural environments and demands two different kinds of adjustment, and imposes upon colleges for black people an additional function that requires them to be different. We logically derive the assumption, in the third instance, that these colleges now exist in "institutional discontinuity"—aiming their functions in one direction while they are more realistically required in another. This is exactly what the black students have been trying to say through their campaign for black studies in their colleges, and we utilize the innovative ideas carried by this thrust as an important part of our suggestion for a modification.

A model illustrating the current discontinuity of colleges for black people is presented in figure 1. It describes the dynamics of the historical process that made the discontinuity possible. It says that these colleges, designed to actualize the assimilation ideal, have been blocked from the realization of their chief goal by the barrier of American racism, that the disappointment of black people resulting from this blockage has created a new set of aspirations and, therefore, requires a new kind of institutional arrangement.

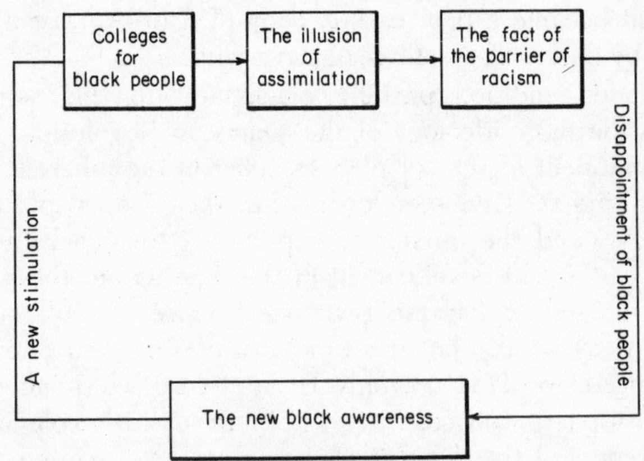

FIGURE 1. An illustrative model of the central position.

Colleges for Black People and the American Assimilation Ideal

The American assimilation ideal may be defined as a form of ethnic and cultural suicide. In its most traditional sense, it has required that all Americans, though of different cultural origins, surrender their prior heritage and accept that of an Anglo-Saxon nature which has become so dominant in our society. More specifically, it has required that the bloods as well as the cultures of our diverse peoples be mixed through a "melting pot" apparatus so that in the end there would actually be formed one people with one culture that is distinctly American.[2]

The black American embraced this ideal under the influence of certain conditions that made him think that he, too, could become an essential ingredient in the melting pot. The first of these conditions appeared within the institution of American slavery. Indeed the very nature of this institution fostered a natural and unintended trend toward black assimilation. A significant transference of African culture through the Africans involved in the slave trade became inadvisable from the point of view of the slave owner. The plantation economy was not organized to absorb a mixture of African and Western cultures; very few of the African culture traits were useful to it, and there was the overpowering fear that such a mixture would foster insurrections.[3] Having been so robbed of their African heritage, these blacks really had no other alternative than to seek to acquire Western ways as a means of survival. Therefore, "The Negro" culture that resulted from this adjustment became a poor carbon copy of Euro-American culture, distorted by the restrictive force of slavery itself.[4]

A second condition pushing blacks toward this assimilation ideal was the basic ideology of the American Revolution. Inspired by a commitment of the colonists to belief in the inherent equality of all men and the divine endowment of their inalienable rights to "life, liberty, and the pursuit of happiness," the blacks' drive for a chance at the full development of the race within the American assimilation context became revitalized. Once, again, they were encouraged by whites, but this time in a positive and direct sense. The Sugar Act of 1764 not only brought forth eloquent defenses of the position of the colonists within the British colonial orbit, but also rendered them aware of their dual role as *oppressed* and *oppressor*.[5] In the protest that he made in his *Rights of the British Colonists* James Otis contended for the Negro's inalienable right to be free. Abigail Adams, in letters to her husband, very pointedly reminded the colonists of the inconsistency of their fight for their own rights while daily denying these rights to the blacks. Thomas Jefferson, in his *Summary View of the Rights of British America*, claimed the abolition of slavery as the great object of desire of the colonists, and charged the British with blocking this liberal move.[6] Although the southern colonists rejected these views and caused them to be stricken from the document that eventually became the Constitution of the United States, black Americans heartily imbibed them and used them as a basis for their many petitions for freedom before the New England courts.

Third, there was the black assimilation thrust that formed the basis for the abolitionary movement. One cannot deny that there was a separatist movement paralleling this strong interest in assimilation. It was, as Harold Cruse expressed it, a strain of "nationalism" whose beginning can be traced to Martin R. Delaney, Edward Blyden, Alexander Crummel, Henry M. Turner, and George Washington Williams.[7] However, in the face of a strong integrationist impulse, so aggressively launched by Frederick Douglass and his associates, this nationalist group was not given much recognition.[8]

Blacks persisted in their pursuit of the assimilation ideal. Just before the close of the nineteenth century, a fourth condition began to prevail. It was a debate concerning the assimilation of blacks which black intellectuals seem to have completely misread. The debate alternated in tones that stretched between the extremes of modified equalitarianism and permanent inequality under paternal supervision.[9] At the equalitarian extreme stood Lewis H. Blair of Richmond, Virginia, who staunchly advocated the elevation of the Negro as an essential to the prosperity of the South.[10] Other voices, however, drowned out the sound of this equalitarian view. Bishop Charles B. Galloway of the Methodist Episcopal Church, South, raised his voice not in support of assimilation but in defense of a kind of benevolent paternalism that would keep the black American forever unassimilated but useful to the southern economy.[11] Edmund Ruffin, in his speech before the Virginia State Agricultural Society in 1852, went even further in his denial of the assimilation concept. Discussing the question of domestic economy and the influence of slavery upon private enterprise and the manners of the society, he had developed a "mudsill" idea, and had pictured domestic slavery as essential for providing leisure for the development of high morals and cultural refinement among the "superior classes."[12]

Despite this meandering pathway to an eventual rejection of black assimilation on the part of southern opinion-makers, black intellectuals who would eventually shape the goals for their colleges persisted in following the assimilation ideal. This ideal became the "carrot on the stick" that black people chased for more than three hundred years.

Each college that was established for black Americans aspired for the actualization of this assimilation ideal. One gleans this first from the objectives which were set up as a part of their founding charters and have persisted as professed goals ever since.[13] Public colleges, by the very nature of their source of support, were stimulated to be most verbal about their assimilation goals. Having grown largely out of normal schools aimed at training teachers, their goals were basically expressed in terms of service to the state. One such college, quite representative of this general group of public institutions, presents the following as an expression of the law that brought it into being:

> The Agricultural and Industrial Normal School has been established by the State Board of Education for the purpose of training colored teachers to meet fuller demands for more efficient and practical instruction in the public school. In carrying out the purpose, it should be the aim of the institution to impart knowledge, discipline the mind, train the hand, and influence the heart of its students that they shall go out of the school fully qualified to discharge every duty faithfully and well.

As the school advanced its curriculum to the college level, to these goals were added this statement:

> The school also recognizes the fact that scientific farming and other industrious pursuits, pursued on a scientific basis is the hope of the South, and it is endeavoring to fulfill its place in furnishing better Negro farmers and mechanics, as well as teachers, to instruct youth in literary and industrial training.

Greater maturity of this college brought higher aspirations, and its aims in the general area of assimilation became more expansive. It aspired to "make maximum contribution to the advancement of the total civilization of the state, nation, and world by so training man that he can gain a reasonable mastery of the human and natural resources." The statement ends with the aspiration that the school would direct the student in "gaining a complete knowledge and understanding of the natural and human resources and of the value of developing and utilizing them to the end that (the state) may take its rightful place in the vanguard of the states and Nation."

Another public college, though put more succinctly, expresses the same pattern of aspirations through an appeal to "local patriotism." It would "serve the citizens of the state at the point of their greatest needs, and endeavors to bring the student's training into closer relationships with life's occupations."

However, some of the public colleges have been much more direct and pointed in the expression of their assimilation aims. One such institution states its basic purposes in this manner:

> The purpose of the school is to secure to all pupils not only the opportunity of high culture and liberal learning, but also a good English education and especially the practical study of branches pertaining to the sciences and art, artistic, commercial, mechanical and agricultural industry, by which pupils may be qualified to become homemakers and breadwinners, and as instructors to teach the same to pupils in the public schools.

Although all of the colleges were apparently conscious of the problems that existed beyond the pale of assimilation, the private ones were a bit more bold in alluding to these problems in the statement of their objectives. References to the job of training black leadership punctuate their list of purposes, and some even more boldly admit of the aspiration of training students for the promotion of desirable change. An example of this may be seen in the following statement of purpose presented by one college of this group:

> The college aims to provide, under guidance, an opportunity for vital contacts with inspiring men and women, with the important areas of human knowledge, and with varied experiences in living by means of which the student, in his fundamental task of building personality, may grow so that the continuing process of his personal development will be purposefully directed; so that he will be able to live successfully in a changing and imperfect social order; and so that he will be willing to, and able to lend intelligent and active assistance in promoting desirable social change.

Another such college very concisely blurs its more "rebellious" intentions in this very terse statement of its aims and purposes: "This college intends that its students shall become self-directed learners and self-reliant persons capable of dealing effectively with challenges and issues both now and in the future."

No attempt is made here to survey the aims and objectives of colleges for black people. Space is too limited, and everybody knows already, whether he admits it or not, that these colleges for black people aim to do for black students what those for whites do for their students—to teach them to live in a WASP dominated society. Neither do I accept these objectives as evidence of what the colleges actually did, but what they aspired to do, or felt that they should be doing. I do wish, however, to call attention to the fact that not all of the colleges are absolutely naïve about what they are doing, that some are rather subtly committed to developing students to challenge the social order.

It is safe to conclude, however, that each college for black people had as its chief goal the assimilation of its students into the general stream of American culture. Not even the controversy that developed between Booker T. Washington and W. E. B. Du Bois deviated from this common objective. Both of these contestants planned to educate blacks from the assimilation point of view. The only difference was the place at which each would begin. Washington would start at the lower end of the class structure, Du Bois at the upper end with the Talented Tenth. Whites supported both efforts not because they really wanted to make blacks equal to themselves, but because they felt that the Washington approach would create a mass of well-trained cheap labor for the southern economy and the Du Bois way would train a professional and proprietary class to guide the black communities that would remain separate and forever apart from the general society. Thus black and white educational leaders became strange bedfellows who could sleep together without stirring too much, not because they agreed on the question of assimilation but because their disagreement would serve the same end—the development and preservation of a biracial society. The carrot had been shaped upon the stick.

There was some historical evidence of great rumblings from black Americans as they responded to their developing educational opportunities, but even here there was no evidence of a strong thrust against the assimilation course on which colleges for black people had been set. James McPherson suggested the idea that there was a black power force operating within plans for the education of black people during the period 1865-1915.[14] This was certainly true according to the manner in which he defined black power. McPherson perceived it to be a movement of black people to gain control over their schools, and he does an excellent job of portraying this struggle and assessing its degree of success. He shows that by 1915, 60 per cent of the teachers of all secondary schools and colleges founded or supported by northern missionary sources were black.[15] Although only 28 per cent of the teachers of the twenty-nine colleges included in this study were black in 1894, they had increased to 50 per cent by 1915.

Nevertheless, there were two limiting forces in operation here. One pertained to the degree of control which blacks gained, the other to a more precise definition of the black power concept. Although blacks gained significant control over the operation of their schools, they had relatively no control over the purse strings that determined their support. Also, but in a more basic sense, blacks were seeking to operate the schools but not to restructure the methods, content, or purposes of the education of their children. Because of this limitation, which McPherson seems to recognize, he was dealing only with the struggle of white liberals against the currents of a strong self-help movement that blacks had launched. It was a struggle that was not disturbing to the strange bedfellows. Therefore, as early as 1915, colleges for black people had been firmly anchored within the context of the assimilation ideal. Founded by whites, supported by whites, and, in many instances, taught by whites, they had become poor carbon copies of those created for white students. The ideals for which they stood would not be questioned for almost half a century.

Colleges for Black People and Their Social-Cultural Environment

One cannot find serious fault with the ecological position of these colleges when they are interpreted within the framework of assimilation. They were appropriately timed, strategically located, and rationally organized.

They came upon the American educational scene when black people hungered for a leadership that would guide them through the darkness that the institution of segregation had imposed upon them. Over 100 of the 123 predominantly black colleges that are

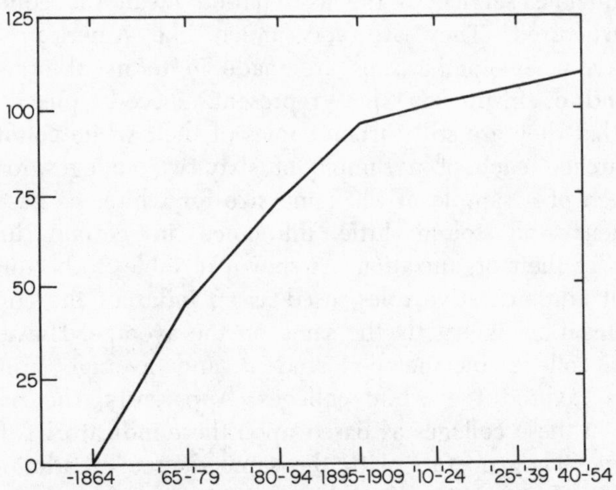

FIGURE 2. Cumulative frequency showing the founding of colleges for black people, 1837-1954.

now in operation came into existence before the first decade of the current century. Although there was bitter southern opposition to the status of freedmen at the close of the Civil War, no special position for black people had been established. Slavery had been overthrown, and Union forces were in control of southern society. These forces had shown decided favor toward establishing a social order in which the freedmen would be allowed to participate freely. In fact, the South had accused the "yankees" of even more: the aim to humiliate southerners by placing them beneath their former slaves. Therefore, it was a logical response for the teachers and those who supported the schools to aspire to make their black charges like themselves.

It was not long before a complete complex of these colleges became distributed, mainly throughout the South and where the black population had begun to settle. Approximately 60 per cent of them were found in Alabama, Georgia, Mississippi, North Carolina, South Carolina, and Texas. These states accounted for more than 60 per cent of the southern black population in 1960. Some were clustered, with as many as three in the same town. They were arranged this way because of the abounding enthusiasm of church officials and benevolent societies to act in behalf of black education wherever the spirit struck them. But as table 1 suggests, they were generally established in the midst of black people, where black problems tended to abound.

In obvious service to the assimilation ideal, the colleges are well structured. They are very much like American colleges generally, when comparisons are made in terms of organization and kind of institution they represent. Piece-by-piece analysis shows that they are still carbon copies of their white counterparts. We matched each of a sample of sixty-two colleges for blacks with each of a sample of the same size for whites as based upon enrollment and found little difference in certain important features of their organization. As shown in table 2, the number of different administrative roles, used as an index of the complexity of organization, is exactly the same on the average. However, the average college income per student and average number of teachers favored the white colleges. Apparently, the basic difference in these colleges as based upon these indicators is financial in nature. They operate with the same degree of administrative complexity, but on a significantly smaller budget than those serving white students.

TABLE 1. Number of Colleges for Black People Distributed by State and the Per Cent Black Population in Each State, 1960

State	Number of black colleges	Proportion of blacks to total population
Alabama	10	30
Arkansas	6	22
Delaware	1	14
D.C.	2	54
Florida	5	18
Georgia	10	28
Kansas	1	4
Kentucky	2	7
Louisiana	5	32
Maryland	5	17
Mississippi	12	42
Missouri	4	9
North Carolina	11	25
Oklahoma	1	7
South Carolina	10	35
Tennessee	6	16
Texas	13	18
Virginia	6	21
West Virginia	3	5
Total	113	19

SOURCE: Compiled from U.S. Bureau of Census, various volumes of characteristics of the population, 1960.

TABLE 2. Comparison of Samples of Sixty-Two Colleges for Black People with a Similar Number for White People as Based Upon Selected Characteristics of Organization

Selected characteristic	Black (averages)	White (averages)
Enrollment	2,060	2,031
Income per student	$1,818	$2,338
No. administrative roles	14	14
No. teachers	129	170

SOURCE: All data for matched colleges were compiled from Otis A. Singletary, ed., *American Universities and Colleges* (Washington, D.C.: American Council on Education, 1968).

However, differences between them do tend to show up in the area of degrees (see table 3). The Ph.D. was the highest degree offered by two colleges of each sample, and approximately 3 per cent of each offered the master's as its highest. All, of course, offered a baccalaureate degree. Where faculty members are distributed

TABLE 3. Per Cent Distribution of Black and White Samples of Matched Colleges According to Highest Degree Held by Faculty Members

Degree	Black (per cent)	White (per cent)
Bachelor's only	9	7
Master's	60	45
Doctorate	31	48
Total	100	100

according to the highest degree earned, differences appear to be significantly favorable to the white colleges. These institutions have 15 per cent fewer master's in proportion to their total teaching force and 17 per cent more doctorates. Obviously, the professional staffs are greater in white colleges because the professional curricula tend to be greater. Nevertheless, the degree of complexity of organization fails to separate colleges for black people and those for whites into radically different kinds when enrollment is held constant.

Despite the apparent similarities we have derived from our comparisons, one must be conscious of the vast differences that exist between colleges for blacks and those for whites. First, those for blacks remained small while those for whites grew and became rather complex institutions whose academic climates are sufficiently varied to touch the different boundaries of human knowledge. In all our comparisons, we placed the best colleges for black people in company with only the smallest, and, in some instances, the poorest of the white colleges, whose academic programs are severely limited if not inadequate. We have compared Howard University, one of our best, with Georgetown University—not with Harvard, Yale, Princeton, or Rice University (which is actually smaller in enrollment). Tuskegee has been compared with Florence State College, and Morehouse College with Saint Leo College. No matter how we matched them, we could not escape the brutal fact that *all* colleges for black people had remained the smaller and simpler institutions when compared with *all* colleges for whites.

Second, the actual professional functions of the facilities have been basically different. The difference has not been so much in terms of academic degrees, though some difference is there, as in the scholarly productivity of professors employed by the two sets of institutions. It would be superfluous to document this difference. With some very notable exceptions that one may find within the faculties of such colleges for blacks as Howard, Atlanta University complex, and Fisk, the writing pens of members of the faculties of these institutions have been virtually silent. Only in the instance when one or two or at most a few black professors have broken through and forged ahead in the production of scholarly literature, and have developed some kind of bibliography of their own writings, does one find exceptions. In general, however, the Ph.D. in colleges for black people is stillborn. He gets his degree and proceeds to teach his classes. The entire atmosphere of this kind of college makes it possible for less mature professors to survive. The administration is usually not interested in scholarly performance, though this kind of activity is tolerated, and the spoon-feeding method of teaching certainly does not call for it. Again, we rush to say that there are exceptions, but these exceptions do not destroy this fact: colleges for black people are not producers of scholarly or publishable literature. The self-study reports received by the Southern Association of Colleges and Schools silently attest to this conclusion.

Third, there is the matter of student quality—the quality of in-put. When measured in terms of how assimilated they have become—how much of the middle-class American culture they have acquired by the time they finish high school—evidence of the retardation of black students is overwhelming. As indicated in table 4, they enter college "behind" as based upon these standards of assimilation, and they never "catch up." All through their college careers, teachers are reminding them of this fact, and the information itself becomes a self-fulfilling prophesy. Admittedly, a continuation of this kind of retardation is due to the method of

TABLE 4. Averages for Colleges for Black and White People as Based Upon Selected Characteristics of Entering Students

Selected characteristic	Black	White
Per cent composing top half of graduating class[a]	72	75
Average SAT verbal[b]	349	524
Average SAT mathematics[a]	365	541
Average ACT verbal[c]	11	19
Average ACT English[a]	11	19
Average ACT mathematics[b]	13	18

[a] All sixty-two colleges in each sample.
[b] Based upon seventeen colleges in each sample.
[c] Based upon twenty-three colleges in each sample.

teaching in these colleges. It is a spoon-feeding operation in which the teacher, in the classroom, tells the student all he is supposed to have read during his study hours. This often robs the student of his own study motivation and the responsibility of doing his own thinking. In all too many instances, original thinking on the part of the student is discouraged, leaving his learning activity confined to a regurgitation of the facts the teacher has spit out. On the whole, neither teacher nor student has extended very much individual effort in adding to his store of knowledge the abundance of existing information on the topic before the class. At least one can surmise this from the library records reported to the Southern Association.

Facing this profile of organization which the colleges have developed is a barrier of racism that blocks the actualization of their aspirations to foster the assimilation of their students. This barrier inescapably shapes the social-cultural environment to which these colleges must respond. This environment is very strongly expressed in the places where blacks live; the opportunities they experience for gaining a respectable position in the national economy; how they socialize their children; and the power they have for change either by collective action within the social order or outside of it. Let us review the power of colleges for black people to create adjustment to this kind of social-cultural environment.

A test, though admittedly modest, as to how adequately our colleges have facilitated the assimilation of black people may be made through a comparison of the black status of 1940 with that of 1960. This represents twenty years of college functioning in an effort to actualize this aspiration.

First, there is the place, the spatial position within the communal complex, where blacks live and express their cultural existence. It constitutes the social-cultural matrix where black children grow up. Despite the assimilation aim of our colleges, the South had developed a completely biracial society by 1900, which had firmly matured by 1940. Consisting of black and white castes, black and white communities had become separated from each other in small towns by such boundaries as tracks that placed black people on the fringe of the incorporated limits of these places. The black habitat had become, at best, unsanitary and unsightly homes that were formerly occupied by whites who had managed to abandon them. Black settlement in the larger southern cities had become more scattered but equally as segregated. This is observed for cities where one or more colleges for black people still operate, and where the black population is distributed according to the proportion they represent in each census tract. Although Atlanta, Birmingham, and Memphis give the illusion that they possess several black areas, blacks are actually more segregated in each than they are in New Orleans. Almost all of the census tracts having 50 per cent or more black population are territorially contiguous. Despite the better black residential areas found nearer colleges, the majority of blacks tended to concentrate in the blighted area of the city and form ghettos where the hard core of poverty prevailed.

Twenty years later, by 1960, no improvement in the area of residential segregation had been made. Despite the sustained efforts of colleges for blacks to affect the assimilation of black people, residential segregation was just as pronounced as if these colleges had not existed. This is shown by the segregation index of 1960 for twenty-three cities where one or more such colleges have long existed. This index measures the minimum percentage of nonwhites required to change the block in which they live to produce an unsegregated distribution—one in which the percentage of nonwhites living in each block is the same throughout the city. In 207 cities, the index value ranged no lower than 60.4 in San Jose, California, and as high as 98.1 in Fort Lauderdale, Florida.[16] American racism had begun separating the races in all seriousness by 1900, and no assimilation effort on the part of all our colleges has yet been able to stop it.

The black position in the national economy has failed to register the slightest impact from these colleges that have prepared black people for assimilation into the American economy. The profile of the race as related to the national family of occupations was virtually the same in 1960 as it was in 1940, or 1920, or even in 1890. Over half of the black workers of Atlanta, Memphis, and New Orleans, where one or more colleges for blacks are located, were employed as service workers, laborers, or operatives in 1960. When we apply our analysis to a broader scope and incorporate the nation as a whole, evidence of a persisting occupational gap between black and white workers becomes even more glaring. Leonard Broom and Norval Glenn, using an index based upon the "expected" proportion of blacks in each occupational group according to their proportion in the total labor force, show a persistence of underemployment in face of an increasing number of qualified blacks turned out by the colleges. For example, the ratio of actual to the expected proportion of blacks in professional fields was barely one-third, and fell between 1940 and 1960. Only in the clerical fields and among kindred workers were there signs of improvement during these decades. Even here, the index never reached 1.00 to indicate a representation in the field equal to that in the working force. Overrepresentation continued in the traditional fields where blacks were able to find work in 1890. So slow was the process of upward mobility for black people that Broom and Glenn concluded that assuming the present rate of representation of black workers as professional, technical, and kindred workers, proportional representation could not be achieved for 530 years after 1960.[17]

A turn to the graduates themselves shows no evidence that colleges for black people are making a dent in the hard crust of racism that surrounds the black opportunity in the general economy. In 1938, Charles S. Johnson's report on a sample of 7,663 graduates of these colleges showed that they were mainly used as teachers in schools for blacks or in some occupational field that served a black clientele. From 53 to 88 per cent of the graduates of all types of colleges for blacks, if they were doing professional work at all, were doing it in the black community.[18]

In the larger economy, where colleges for blacks are most diligently seeking assimilation, the relationship between the salary of black workers and white workers who have approximately the same education shows a decided deficiency for blacks when occupation is held constant. In the professional and technical category, nonwhites had approximately the same as, or more, median years of schooling in nearly every detailed occupation as did the total working population in these fields. However, their income for work in these fields was only 68.5 per cent of the total in 1960. Only in the lower occupational classes is the salary scale between the two races equal or favorable to blacks.[19]

The purpose here is not to make an analysis of the current position of the black American in the American economy, nor even to prove that black workers suffer from a concentration at the lower end of the occupational scale. The point we seek to make is that colleges for black people, when measured in terms of their impact in furthering the assimilation of black people into the general economy, are spinning their wheels. Despite the soaring aspirations of black middle-class youths for careers in the higher region of our occupational family,[20] only a few will make it. The others will fare just as if they had not gone to college at all. At a conference called during March of 1968 by W. C. Ferguson and Associates, four hundred national firms were invited to interview ninety-nine top black college graduates in business and technical fields. Only eight of the invited companies had representatives at the conference, and not one graduate was hired. Colleges for black people train for assimilation but they make no progress along this line because their best efforts are blocked by the barrier of racism.

There are two other aspects of the social-cultural environment to which colleges for black people will eventually have to respond. One is the self-fulfilling prophesy of American racism, the other is the potential of black political power.

American racism perpetuates American racism. If the colleges do not address themselves to this fact, they can be of little use to their black clientele. This American way separates people into racial colonies, forces them to become a subculture, and compels them to teach this subculture to their children in such a manner that the racism is perpetuated. This kind of spatial separation of blacks, accompanied by highly institutionalized policies of deprivation, creates a condition in which a struggle for survival at that level is all for which they can hope. Black children, therefore, are socialized into accepting a culture of deprivation, and little room is left for effort or even hope to rise above this level. Oscar Lewis has called this state a "culture of poverty."[21] This condition not only poses a different set of problems for black people, but also compels a different procedure for teaching black children. We are just beginning to realize this, although colleges for black people should have known it all along. Because these colleges have been in hot pursuit of assimilation, they have failed to develop students familiar with this kind of social-cultural matrix within which black children grow up. Consequently, we are now having to hold special institutes for teachers, mainly in colleges for whites, in order to familiarize them with conditions that as black students they should have been taught in the first place.

Colleges for black people have given their students enough confidence in the assimilation ideal to expect a substantial share in the reward structure of our society. Meeting a denial of that share through American racism, the students threaten to institute change outside the social order. These colleges, probably as much as American racism, must take the blame for the more reactionary orientation now developing among blacks. The colleges have ignored the barrier that has ever stood between them and the actualization of their aspirations, and have made little effort to teach their students how to deal with this barrier through organized and established political processes. As Chuck Stone has pointed out, those who became acceptable leaders, though most had gone through these colleges, were not trained political leaders.[22] They were individuals of varied walks of life, who, despite their college training, had managed to forge ahead and gain some prestige among blacks for having done so. One can easily conclude that though the need for social change in American race relations developed along with these colleges, no significant training for black people to effect this change in an orderly fashion was ever *purposely* developed by these colleges.

The Need for Transition to the Black College

Since the 1960's a certain kind of black awareness has been shaping the social-cultural environment out of which colleges for black people have tended to function. It has now become necessary for these institutions to change direction and take on a greater character of "blackness"—to give more serious attention to the barrier of racism that has always stood between them and their assimilation aims.

Probably the beginning of this new awareness can be lodged with the voter registration project that was launched by the Student Non-Violent Coordinating Committee (SNCC) operating at McComb, Mississippi, in 1961. Dropping their demonstrations to desegregate public facilities, members of this group moved to "arouse people and develop momentum to push for political power." By April of 1964, the movement had developed into a new political entity called the Mississippi Freedom Democratic Party (MFDP). It was designed to be recognized by the national party as the official Democratic party of the state. This would have assured black political participation in Mississippi, given black people control over their lives, placed them in control of political patronage in that state, and generally broadened the base of their political action. The struggle of this party for recognition at the Democratic Convention in August 1964 is well known.

Most important is the fact that this movement led to the development of black power and its accompanying ideology. It was a general aspiration to lead black people to gain control over their lives, under conditions that they rather than whites specify. It proceeded from the analogy that black people are a colonized people —made so by American racism as it operates at the individual and institutional levels—and proposed the generation of a black power through political control and economic operations of a socialistic nature within the various black communities.[23]

Almost simultaneous with the black power movement was a revival of the nationalist aspirations of black people which Marcus Garvey had triggered some forty years before. The revival can be mainly attributed to the leadership of Malcolm X. As John Bracey, Jr., has very well said, "Malcolm kept the doctrine of nationalism—self-determination, self-defense, and separatism—before the American public as alternatives to racial integration and nonviolence."[24] On June 28, 1964, he laid down the aims and objectives of the Organization of Afro-American Unity which he formulated after his break with the Black Muslims. These aims included the right of self-defense, the right to the management of ghetto education of blacks, control over the decisions affecting the destiny of black people, the political, economic, and cultural control of black communities, and the preservation and perpetuation of black culture.[25] It was, therefore, a direct attempt to nationalize black culture in this country.

It was not long before these two movements—one led by Stokely Carmichael and the other by Malcolm X—met and set in motion black efforts that encouraged the further development of cultural nationalism among blacks. Eldridge Cleaver came upon the intellectual scene crying "crinkly as yours," and set the content of black culture more clearly than any before him. He questioned the use of white models as black ideals, and advised blacks to depolarize their minds in the interest of blackness. Roland Snellings, the poet and cultural critic, certainly helped to shape cultural nationalism even more. Using black music as an indicator of the main philosophical and cultural attitudes of black people, he too asserted the existence of a black culture and boldly indicated the uses that should be made of it. Other black writers joined the movement by resurrecting old heroes and giving them a new place in the black collective mind. Although they were mostly pouring old wines into new bottles, they did manage to spark an interest in blackness never before experienced by the American society.

There stands before us now not only the fact of black culture, but also an exacting awareness of it. The language of the ghetto, once looked upon with disdain, now stands as an adaptive communication process without which survival in the ghetto would be extremely difficult if not impossible. It is being legitimized as a dialect worthy of being taught in our schools;[26] the Afro hair style has become commonplace; the dasheki is in fashion; the African motif has invaded the realm of high fashion; and soul food is something to flaunt rather than to hide. In short, the trend is away from whiteness as the criteria for ideals and toward blackness as a standard of beauty.

This black awareness is a new type of psychology that haunts the minds of many black people. It is reflecting a growing dissatisfaction with the methods of older organizations whose programs aimed at assimilation, and indicates a turn toward the methods that spark cultural nationalism. This, therefore, constitutes a kind of social-cultural environment that has never before surrounded colleges for black people.[27]

Black students are asking their colleges to be more responsive to this new thrust toward cultural nationalism. They are asking in tones that range from quiet demands to acts of near violence. The first request came from black students in white colleges—from students who felt a need to receive an education more relevant to their needs. They sought to have black studies programs installed as a means of adjustment. These institutions did respond favorably to this request, although in many instances probably to get rid of the "nuisance." Faculty committees were formed, black professors were aggregated, and curricula oriented toward "blackness" were instituted.[28] There is scarcely a single white college with a sizeable black student population that does not carry some kind of black studies program among its varied curricula. Although many of these programs got into trouble, mainly because of the "overbearing" demands of black students, we must admit that black studies now constitute a legitimate branch of learning in many colleges.

By 1968, some black intellectuals had caught the idea and began to present black university models that extended in pattern from courses in black culture to institutions that would, through revolutionary means, develop ideas for the liberation of "third world" people. Marking the two extremes stand the postulations of Darwin Turner and those of Gerald McWorter. Turner would not alter the basic structure of the university, but would give it greater pigmentation by introducing courses oriented toward blackness. There would be a greater emphasis upon Negro history, and added to this course would be those in black literature, sociology, and art.

He would shore up this scheme with a research emphasis for purposes of generating authority for the subject matter of blackness.[29] The black university for McWorter would focus upon the particular needs of the Afro-American community. It would be based upon an educational ideology that is "grounded in an uncompromising goal of psychological independence as is necessary not only to survive in the world, but to prosper."[30] Vincent Harding, falling between the two extremes, would turn the "blackness" of these colleges toward internationalism. He would make the black university "seek to explain, celebrate, and record the experiences of the non-Western World."[31] None of this is absolutely new, for Christopher Jencks and David Riesman, in their controversial article on the Negro college, had already expressed the possibility of the development of a black curriculum by these colleges.[32]

Another set of black leaders questioned and somewhat opposed the entire black studies idea. Bayard Rustin, for example, apparently had serious anxieties about the movement. He questioned whether the whole black studies thrust did not represent a forum for ideological indoctrination, a plan for the development of political cadres for reorganization of the ghetto, rather than a program to train qualified scholars in a significant field of intellectual inquiry. He wondered whether it was a means to achieve psychological identity and strength or a false and sheltered sense of security, the fragility of which would be revealed by even the slightest exposure to reality. He questioned whether it offered the possibility for better racial understanding or was a regression to racial separatism. Roy Wilkins viewed black studies as a possible "cop out." Kenneth B. Clark resigned from the board of directors of Antioch College because its Afro-American Institute was, in his perception, a "racially organized and exclusionary facility on the campus." C. Vann Woodward feared that the new emphasis would warp as much as correct. These and many other articles presented in a well-written report represent great anxieties about black studies.[33]

This complex of views, however, accents rather than weakens the need for the black college as contrasted with the existing institutions that have developed for black people. It recognizes the new black awareness and never hints, in any way, that it is not to be dealt with by our educational institutions. It hints at, though in a subdued manner, the revolutionary potential inherent in this new ethnic aspiration, and suggests the need for bringing the aspiration into the sphere of control as exercised by our institutions.

In its most genuine sense this is exactly what we mean when we suggest that colleges for black people accept an innovative function in the area of social reconstruction by becoming black colleges. American education has never been reconstructionist. It has always maintained a reflective relationship between itself and the existing social, economic, and political framework upon which our society is based. The American public school system began under Puritan influence and was constructed for the purpose of providing religious training and habits of thrift for American children. When, by the opening of the twentieth century, we had received millions of immigrants to our shores, public schools turned toward the job of Americanizing or training the newcomers in American ways. As our industrial order developed and there was an increased need for skilled and more learned people, American schools responded by adjusting their curriculum to meet this need. Always American education was reflecting old ways and never consciously plotting new ones.[34] We are suggesting that the black college should abandon this reflective role by adding the innovative feature of black studies as part of its reconstructive organization. Indeed, many of our colleges for black people have already begun making this shift toward blackness.[35]

What must a black college do to accomplish this end? It must be two schools in one. First, it must prepare its students for full and efficient participation in a WASP dominated society from whose overpowering influence they cannot escape; second, it must train them for a world of blackness in which they must live. It must provide them with the latter preparation because of the problem of racism that most certainly appears in the first situation. The big question, therefore, is how can the college do both. One could very logically ask, if black students have trouble getting *one* college education, how can they manage to get *two*? There is evidence that this dual approach is not so ridiculous after all. It seems that the black student can get the two more easily than he can get the one that has assimilation orientations. Rather convincing evidence in favor of this proposition has come to the forefront almost accidentally. After observing that college students with apparent reading deficiency showed greater comprehension of reading materials concerned with blackness than that involving the general American experience, I decided to make further and more objective tests. Quietly executing an experimental design, in which control and experimental groups were equated for reading comprehension, I treated the respective groups by exposing the controls to form *B* of the standard reading test and the experimentals to a test of equal difficulty but based upon content about black culture. The results were rather astounding. The experimentals were reading on an average of two grade levels above the controls, though both groups were equal in reading ability when compared on a frequency distribution basis. I taught two classes in introductory sociology with differential methods—one conventionally, as usually taught, the other basically around a black focus. Although the same basic principles were emphasized in each instance, students of the black focus class scored significantly higher than those of the conventional class when both classes were exposed to a common test based upon a published teachers manual.[36] These are not the "swallows that make a summer," but they do provide sufficient evidence to foster the belief that people learn quicker and better that in which they are interested and which relates to the lives they live. It is highly probable that much of the apparent retardation of black college students is a function of the degree to which they have consciously or unconsciously "turned-off" the learning process for lack of interest rather than of their ability to absorb that which is being taught. Their retardation might be a message that says, as they have often put it, "the stuff is irrelevant."

If colleges for black people are to gain greater relevance to the black condition, they must make the transition to black colleges as some have already begun to do. They must accept American racism as a barrier to assimilation, and they must prepare students to deal intelligently with this barrier. This means that these colleges must accept the responsibility of transmitting two cultures rather than one: the WASP culture that anchors the racism which black students must learn to manipulate, and the black culture within whose framework these students must gain leadership. I feel strongly that this responsibility can be properly executed through the medium of a general education program built around black culture as a basic curricular theme.

The use of black culture as a curricular theme appears pedagogically sound. In the first place, recent findings by social scientists show conclusively that black culture is a legitimate subject matter within itself, meriting scientific study. We have finally recognized that there is a complex of life-styles that is uniquely black and adequately defines the black existence. Anchored by the historic roots of slavery and nourished by an involuntary separatism institutionalized as segregation, life-styles indigenous to the black communities of this country have been allowed to develop and constitute the core of the black existence. These styles run the gamut of soul, lower-class, and even middle-class black culture patterns.[37] Practically every American college or university has already made black culture an indispensible part of its curriculum, especially in the areas of sociology and anthropology. The black college should be a center that specializes in black culture, and its students should know as much about its nature as students from any other type of college. Black culture concerns them, their people, and their lives.

Also, any meaningful aspiration that black people hold, whether individual or collective, will be shaped by the black experience and can only be actualized in conflict with the larger WASP culture.[38] This is so because black and white interests are juxtaposed at important levels, and a harmonious accommodation to this conflict—by members of each race—must be worked out within the framework of a knowledge and understanding of each culture. The black college must be an active agent in the development of an accommodation of this conflict. Otherwise it will remain a silent bystander, torn with turmoil in the midst of racial strife.

Finally, when these colleges train students for effective leadership within the black community, as has been their traditional purpose, that leadership should derive from an understanding of black culture. The mere fact that one is black does not provide an expertise in blackness. Especially does this apply to black college students who have been reared by parents who hold middle-class orientations and are alienated from their own culture. We are finding that many of these college graduates, when employed by agencies that are oriented toward special services to lower-class blacks, fail to make adequate adjustment because they do not understand the life-styles of such people. Often we find a discontinuity in social service agencies because of this lack of understanding. I do not see the goal of the black college as solely that of training its students for mainstream living. Only a few of their students ever make the mainstream, and most become marginal persons, neither accepted by whites nor desirous of accepting blacks. Therefore, the formal socialization which they receive is basically dysfunctional, not because it does not always provide mainstream status, but because it alienates them from their own heritage.

There is an instructional strategy that, when executed through the theme of black culture, seems to safeguard the student against this dysfunctional influence. It is a method that we call "cultural context teaching." This is a basic pedagogical mechanism that introduces students to conventional disciplines through a black focus that is in fact black culture. Any of the formalized courses constituting the social sciences, humanities, or behavioral sciences can be taught this way. The method is more than a watering down of these disciplines in an ethnocentric effort to turn them black. It is the presentation of basic principles through the medium of black culture. It supplies the student with familiar "perceptual windows" through which he can view the various disciplines from the vantage point of his own life situation. The student's own skills and knowledge are utilized in the learning process rather than negated, and there is elicited from him a greater degree of personal involvement. Our experiments with this method tend to show that black students learn more rapidly this way and withdraw from the classroom climate less often. Most important, however, is the tendency for this method to produce bicultural students—students who are sophisticated in handling the barrier of American racism. Figure 3 presents a generalized model of the cultural context teaching method. It may suffice to draw a few illustrations of this method from introductory sociology, a field in which I have done some experiments.

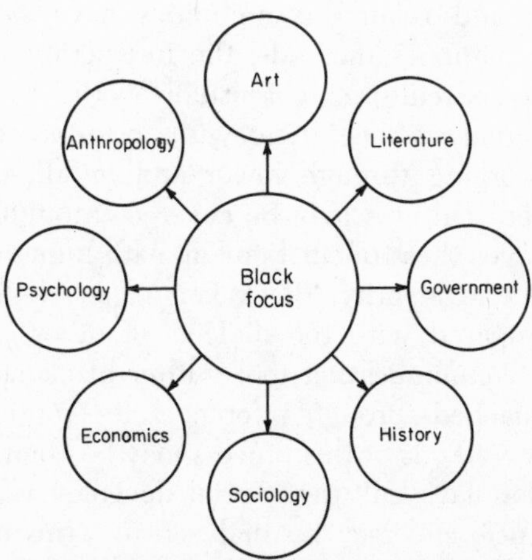

FIGURE 3. Design illustrating cultural context teaching in the general education program.

A conventional course in introductory sociology may be neatly built around (1) sociology as a science—the usual introduction; (2) culture and personality; (3) population and community; (4) social organization—including informal and formal groups—associations, social differentiation in roles and statuses, and social class; (5) social institutions; and (6) social change. There may be variations here and there, but students are usually introduced to the study of human society through some such topical arrangement as this, which is generally presented in this order.

Cultural context teaching would ordinarily start with the community and population because these supply the locus and human resources for all that is blackness. Using a "where do you live?" kind of question, the teacher first introduces the student to the ecology of the human community by way of his own black community. It is here that the student first encounters the tendency for ecological and social-psychological forces to create lower-class communities within the inner city and middle-class communities in the suburbs. He will also notice the operation of traditional policies of racial segregation toward the creation of ethnic colonies, where social isolation inhibits upward mobility and encourages ethnic groups to build cultures that are indigenous to their respective life experiences. The method would explore the black population as a resource for the actualization of black aspirations,[39] and move into demography as it relates to the general population structure.

Once black and related communities have been delineated, particularly by mapping methods, the instruction would move to an analysis of black culture. It is usually better to use a case approach in this analysis, beginning with the more dramatic "soul-pattern" and working through lower and middle-class life-styles. Elements of other cultures may be covered through a comparative method that leaves the student familiar with human culture in the sense of its generic identity. Black language—Negro nonstandard English—is compared with the dialects of other cultures, and is evaluated as a communication tool within black culture.[40] Socialization is approached through references to "coming up black,"[41] and the various methods of this process may be compared as related to black and nonblack cultures. Social deviancy is studied in this frame of reference, and may be analyzed in terms of the norms of the culture in which it occurs. Different phases of social organization are analyzed as they relate to black culture and the larger cultural style; the same is done for social institutions; and the study of social change is initiated through the various patterns of collective movements that tend to rise out of black culture. These movements may be compared with those of the larger community structure and evaluated in relation to black aspirations.

My main position here has been a simple though possibly an unpopular one. It has postulated that the institutions commonly called black colleges are actually white colleges for black people—that they have persistently pursued the American assimilation ideal but have been blocked in this aspiration by a barrier of racism which they have ignored. In this respect, these colleges have experienced cultural discontinuity in a society that is now threatened with a new black awareness. Transition to a black college type would bring racism into focus, where black students can be taught to deal with it constructively, and, at the same time, learn to participate in two cultures. I take this position because I believe that a dignified survival of black people calls for a training for living in two cultural worlds.

References

1. This view of J. W. Bews (*History of Creation,* 1868) may be found also in Amos H. Hawley, *Human Ecology* (New York: The Ronald Press Company, 1950), p. 3.

2. See Milton M. Gordon, *Assimilation in American Life* (New York: Oxford University Press, 1964), esp. p. 85.

3. Saunders Redding, *They Came in Chains* (New York: J. B. Lippincott Company, 1950), p. 30.

4. Melville Herskovitz published his *Myth of the Negro Past* in 1941 and opened a controversy on this question. He maintained that substantial survivals of African cultures existed in the culture of the black population in the United States.

5. John Hope Franklin, *From Slavery to Freedom* (New York: Alfred A. Knopf, 1967), p. 127.

6. *Ibid.,* p. 129.

7. Harold Cruse, *The Crisis of the Negro Intellectual* (New York: William Marrow and Company, 1967), p. 5.

8. Benjamin Quarles, *The Black Abolitionist* (New York: Oxford University Press, 1969), pp. 3-7.

9. See Guion G. Johnson, "A History of Racial Ideologies in the United

States with Reference to the Negro," manuscript in Schomburg Collection, New York Public Library.

10. See Lewis H. Blair, "The Prosperity of the South" (Richmond, Va.: Everett Waddy, 1889), in his *Southern Prophesy* (Boston: Little, Brown and Company, 1964).

11. See Reverend Bishop Charles B. Galloway, "The South and the Negro," an address delivered at the Seventh Annual Conference for Education in the South, Birmingham, Alabama, April 26, 1904.

12. Edmund Ruffin, "The Influence of Slavery, or Its Absence, on Manners, Morals, and Intellect," an address to the Virginia State Agricultural Society, First Annual Meeting, December 16, 1852.

13. Data dealing with aims and objectives of colleges have been gathered from their catalogs and from their self-study reports to the Southern Association of Colleges and Schools. The anonymity of colleges has been maintained by prior agreement with the heads of the respective institutions.

14. James M. McPherson, "White Liberals and Black Power in Negro Education, 1865-1915," *American Historical Review,* 75 (June 1970), 1357-1386.

15. *Ibid.,* pp. 1380-1385.

16. Karle E. Taeuber and Alma F. Taeuber, *Negroes in Cities* (Chicago: Aldine Publishing Company, 1965), pp. 30-35.

17. Leonard Broom and Norval Glenn, *Transformation of the Negro American* (New York: Harper and Row, 1965), p. 111.

18. Charles S. Johnson, *The Negro College Graduate* (Chapel Hill, N. C.: University of North Carolina Press, 1938), p. 95.

19. Daniel O. Price, *Changing Characteristics of the Negro Population* (Washington, D. C.: U. S. Bureau of Census, 1969), pp. 134-135.

20. See Eli Ginsberg, *The Middle Class Negro in the White Man's World* (New York: Columbia University Press, 1967).

21. Oscar Lewis, *La Vida: A Puerto Rican Family in the Culture of Poverty* (New York: Random House, 1966). See also his *The Children of Sanchez: Autobiography of a Mexican Family* (New York: Random House, 1961) and his *Five Families: Mexican Case Studies in the Culture of Poverty* (New York: Basic Books, 1959).

22. Chuck Stone, *Black Political Power in America* (New York: Dell Publishing Company, 1968), p. 8.

23. See Stokely Carmichael and Charles V. Hamilton, *Black Power* (New York: Vintage Books, 1967).

24. John Bracey, Jr., August Meier, and Elliott Rudwick, *Black Nationalism in America* (New York: Bobbs Merrill Company, 1970), p. 412.

25. *Ibid.,* pp. 421-427.

26. See Frederick Williams, ed., *Language and Poverty: Perspectives on a Theme* (Chicago: Markham, forthcoming).

27. For revolutionary ideology spawned by this movement see Lee Lockwood, *Conversation with Eldridge Cleaver, Algiers* (New York: Dell Publishing Company, 1970); George Breitman, ed., *By Any Means Necessary* (New York: Pathfinder Press, Inc., 1970); E. U. Essein-Udom, *Black Nationalism* (New York: Dell Publishing Company, 1967).

28. See Anne-Marie Henschel and Richard L. Henschel, "Black Studies Programs: Promise and Pitfalls," *Journal of Negro Education* (Fall 1969), 423-429. The authors review these programs and their possible implications.

29. Darwin T. Turner, "The Black University: A Practical Approach," *Negro Digest,* 17 (March 1968), 14-20.

30. Gerald McWorter, "The Nature and Needs of the Black University," *ibid.,* pp. 4-13.

31. Vincent Harding, "Some International Implications of the Black University, *ibid.,* pp. 33-38.

32. Christopher Jencks and David Riesman, "The American Negro College," *Harvard Educational Review,* 37 (November 1, 1967), 53.

33. See *Black Studies: Myths and Realities* (New York: A. Philip Randolph Fund, 1969), p. 5.

34. Nathaniel Hickerson, *Education for Alienation* (Englewood Cliffs, N. J.: Prentice-Hall, 1966), pp. 1-18.

35. Illustrations of various degrees of curricular commitment to study black culture on the part of colleges for black people may be found in: Tennessee State University, *Bulletin* (March 1970), pp. 130, 135, 158; Robert D. Reid to Henry A. Bullock, letter of August 10, 1970, naming black literature, Afro-American history, geography of Africa, minority group problems, and Afro-American musicology as courses in black studies offered at Alabama State University; Benedict College Catalog, 1969-1970, shows eleven courses composing its program of Afro-American studies, pp. 41-42; George Rigsby, *Report to the Steering Committee of the Department of Afro-American Studies,* October 6, 1969, showing organization, curriculum, academic program, and staff of the department as operating at Howard University, and Howard University, *The Department of Afro-American Studies,* supplied through courtesy of James E. Cheek, president of the university; Walter L. Jones to Henry A. Bullock, July 24, 1970, verifying an interdisciplinary black studies program at Langston University that includes emphasis on behavioral sciences, humanities, and the creative arts; *Proposal for a Major in African-Afro-American Studies,* at North Carolina A. and T. College, supplied through courtesy of Darwin T. Turner; Tuskegee Institute, *African Studies Program,* through the courtesy of Glenn Howze; and an academic minor

offered at South Carolina State College, Algernon S. Belcher to Henry A. Bullock, July 31, 1970.

36. Henry A. Bullock, "Some Reflections on Cultural Context Teaching," unpublished manuscript.

37. See Ulf Hannerz, *Soulside* (New York: Columbia University Press, 1969) and Charles Kiel, *Urban Blues* (Chicago: University of Chicago Press, 1966).

38. For vivid evidence of this view, one should see, for example, R. A. Schermerhorn, *Comparative Ethnic Relations* (New York: Random House, 1970).

39. This is the kind of analysis which Phillip Hauser makes. See his "Demographic Factors in the Integration of the Negro," in Talcott Parsons and Kenneth B. Clark, eds., *The Negro American* (Boston: Houghton Mifflin, 1966), pp. 71-101.

40. See Williams, ed., *Language and Poverty*.

41. See David Schulz, *Coming Up Black* (New York: Prentice-Hall, 1969).

C. ERIC LINCOLN

The Negro Colleges and Cultural Change

And so they did begin; they founded colleges, and up from the colleges shot normal schools, and out from the normal schools went teachers, and around the normal teachers clustered other teachers to teach the public schools; the college trained in Greek and Latin and mathematics, 2,000 men; and these men trained full 50,000 others in morals and manners, and they in turn taught thrift and the alphabet to nine millions of men, who today hold $300,000,000 of property. It was a miracle—the most wonderful peace-battle of the 19th Century, and yet today men smile at it, and in fine superiority tell us that it was all a strange mistake.

—W. E. B. Du Bois[1]

THE BATTLE of the twentieth century will be to keep the Negro colleges alive and viable. If that can be accomplished, that too will be a "miracle"—for some men are still "smiling in fine superiority," convinced more than ever before that Negro education was indeed "a strange mistake," and continues to be so. *Was it? Is it? Can it survive? Shall it survive? And in what form, if any?* These are the questions before this generation of Americans—a generation already burdened with a pandorian agenda of war and peace, the misassignment of roles, the pollution of the environment, the increase in crime, the decline of religion, the new morality, the old Establishment, sexual inversion, academic diversion, and the virulence of racism—the last mentioned having a critical, uncryptic relationship to the survival of the Negro college and any of the values associated with it.

Among the Seven Sages of Antiquity was Bias, the Greek philosopher whose estimate of the human condition was summed up in one cheerless statement: "Most men are bad." In these days of anxiety about the capacity of man to do what he ought to do, and to be what he ought to be, we live increasingly under the shadow of the suspicion that Bias was right—and this despite the fact that for 2,000 years our civilization has been informed by a religious philosophy which insists that man is essentially good, and that even at his worst, he is redeemable. We wonder, without asking, whether this is so. At every level of social intercourse the evidence to the contrary seems to grow more insistent. We are tempted—and at times we yield to the temptation—to abandon the hope we now hold so tenuously that man is capable of redemption and regeneration, and that the society we have constructed on that conviction is any longer worthy of our confidence and support. But when our despair over human intransigence and perversity impels us to option our own conformance with the best expectations of this society, then we ourselves contribute to the irreversibility of the human predicament.

If most men are bad, some bad men have their better moments. Seneca declares that "God divided man into men that they might help each other." Whether men accept this dictum as a functional principle of social facilitation, or whether there is inherent in human nature some irrepressible inclination to altruism, that men *do* help each other is self-evident. In helping each other they help themselves. Together, all can have a better life than any can have alone. This, I take it, is what society is all about. Imperfect men create imperfect societies. Certainly that is true. And some men are impelled to destroy what others labor to create. Yet, in the midst of destruction new creations are always in process, and amidst the rubble of what was, what is to be is always taking shape.

One hundred years ago this country was torn asunder over the question of whether this was to be a society of free men, or whether some only would be free. In the troublesome complexity of issues which impelled men to fight each other, there were, to be sure, other interests which were less manifest and possibly less respectable. However, the focus of the contending commitments was whether those who were not free might any longer be utilized as the instruments for the freedom, comfort, and prosperity of those who held them enthralled.

It was true then, and it is true now, that no society which predicates its well-being upon the dehumanization of some for the exaltation of others can endure with tranquillity, or can long enjoy, the prosperity it distills from the agony of the oppressed. No man is born a slave. Slavery is a social contrivance. It is always invented by men who feel inadequate and exploitative; and it can only be accepted by men who feel inadequate and accommodative.

Slavery is not always signified by chains. A sophisticated society presupposes sophistication in the methodology through which it structures its systems of preference and prerogative. In such a society the chains are invisible, but no less restraining; and their presence is made manifest in an incorrigible consensus which delimits participation in the social process. The autonomous spirit of the self-confident individual resists every sign and symbol of enthrallment, and refuses to be accommodated to any system which impeaches his humanity. This is the wonderful story of our new generation of black youth—the heart-warming saga of their refusal to capitulate to indignity, or to accommodate themselves to shame. It is the story of their search for origins, for rootages external to and beyond the confinements of a culture organized and structured for their perpetual debasement. It is clear now that Blackamerica will participate in the shaping of its own destiny, and of the destiny of the larger sociopolitical entity of which it is a part. That is why the issue of the black colleges is a critical one. They are the cultural and academic matrices which shape and refine the black response to the perpetual challenges of a hostile and critical white world. But more, they are the intellectual and spiritual prisms through which the spectra of the black experience itself are diffused into the understanding black people need to have about themselves—an understanding which has not been available from any other source in white-oriented America.

Every human experience rests upon some previous experience, and every possibility for tomorrow is contingent to some other possibility which was realized yesterday. Human possibility is created at the intersection of time, place, and circumstance. Manipulate any one of these variables and the life chances of any given individual will be changed. If all the world is a stage, as Shakespeare alleged it to be, then history is the backdrop for the play, and the parts we play and the possibilities inherent in them are at least in part conditioned by other actors, who at other times have stood before the same footlights. Like us, they played their roles in terms of their possibilities.

The great benefactors of society are so often the visionaries who have the peculiar perceptivity to see beyond the exigencies of the present that is here, and to address the future that is to be. Human society is dynamic; it is never a static accomplishment capable of complete realization in a lifetime or a generation. Rather it is always in process—always becoming what it is, always different from what it was; yet never what it will be. To integrate the social flux, men who care about the refinement of human experience create *institutions*, monuments to themselves, sometimes, but history has a way of dealing with what is culturally fraudulent. The true objective of an institution should be to strengthen the fabric of society, to enhance the quality of the life-experience of the individual, and to project the values of the culture out of which it arises. Now the function of culture is to make possible an ordered social life in which individuals may more nearly realize their fullest potentials as persons. The function of an institution is to relate discrete social experiences in such a way as to infuse life with a quality of meaning which accentuates its social value. Hence, an institution is a social instrument directed toward the enhancement of the individual human experience to the ultimate benefit of the whole society. It is created as a response to a need that is felt to be fundamental, and its singularity is that it transcends time and circumstance, addressing itself to successive generations of men and women.

The Negro college is such an institution. Born of the turmoil of a war which made black men free with an imperfect freedom, established in a social environment hostile to its presence and committed to its destruction, the Negro college has survived to become one of the singular assets of the black community and a unique, valuable, contributing component in the educational complex of America. More than that, it is an instrument of freedom. Black freedom. The vision of the men and women who founded this institution which is now a vital aspect of the black heritage, the wise and often sacrificial leadership which nurtured its infancy and guided its development, was informed by their faith in the righteousness of God and by their confidence in the social potential of the Blackamerican. It was their fervent hope, and their reasoned expectation, that an education of high quality in a Christian environment could effect for the Blackamerican a more perfect freedom than he had received; and that in the process of his search for his own dignity and personal autonomy, he would make a contribution to the moral integrity of the society and to the political respectability of the nation.

The twenty-five years or so following the end of the slavocracy represented an extraordinary seedtime for the establishment of Negro colleges. Through the combined efforts of the Freedman's Bureau, various church denominations, and private philanthropy, dozens of these institutions suddenly came into being. There were already two Negro colleges in the North. All of the postwar colleges were in the South; and despite the magnanimous language of the charters of a few of them, they were all established for, and directed toward, the education of *Negroes*. Thereon hangs an interesting tale, and it is necessary to seek no further to lock into the concatenation of events which made predictable the present crisis of the Negro colleges.

When Lincoln University was founded in Pennsylvania (as Ashmun Institute) in 1854, and when Wilberforce was established in Ohio in 1856, they were founded as *Negro* colleges. Despite the fact that the best colleges and universities in the country were located in the North, and that blacks had been matriculating at some of them since the 1820's, the churches founding these colleges[2] consciously designed and intended them for Negroes. There were other colleges already in existence in Pennsylvania and Ohio, of course, but they were white, and while the University of Pennsylvaina did not graduate a black student before 1880, Oberlin had at least eight black graduates by 1856 when Wilberforce was founded, and possibly as many as fifteen. By 1875 when the founding of Negro colleges neared its zenith, Dartmouth, Yale, Harvard, Bates, Geneva, Westminister, Bowdoin, Ohio, Wesleyan, Lafayette, Franklin, and Adrian all had black alumni; and ten years later so did Columbia, Amherst, Bucknell, Mt. Holyoke, Bellvue, Olivet, Denison, Hiram, and the University of Minnesota.[3] Some of the denominations most active in the founding of Negro colleges were already prominent in their sponsorship of institutions of higher education for whites, and in some cases, black students had already been admitted to, and graduated from, their white colleges. It was an anomaly of the times, or possibly of the spirit, which led them to now establish separate colleges for Negroes.

While no one would contend realistically that the admission of black students to the white colleges in the North was routine, the record does seem to suggest that in the two decades following the Civil War when the founding of Negro colleges became a passionate enterprise for a considerable variety of interests, black and white, religious and secular, blacks *were* being admitted in increasing numbers to a steadily increasing number of white institutions. A logical question is why the need for *Negro* colleges seemed so compelling. A convincing argument could be made for the establishment of Negro secondary schools, especially in the South. In the first place, for example, the South did not have a developed system of public school education. Even had there been one, it could hardly have survived under the weight of the avalanche of blacks—children and adults—who looked to education to make them truly free. Education was the white man's magic. It alone could eradicate the pitiful, the grotesque scars of black slavery and make whole men out of tortured bodies and wasted minds. Again, black secondary schools were inevitable because southern whites were no more ready for school integration in 1865 than they were in 1954. Only five southern states made mixed schools legal,[4] and of the few attempts to operate integrated schools under legal consent, none lasted.[5] In Horace Mann Bond's opinion, "Those who argued against mixed schools were right in believing that such a system was impossible in the South."[6] Gunnar Myrdal exclaims that "The great wonder is that the Negroes' right to public education was not renounced altogether."[7]

It seems unnecessary to belabor the obvious, then, that the establishment of Negro secondary schools *in the South* was predicated upon a clear and present necessity. The reasons for the establishment of Negro colleges in the North are less apparent. As the black migration from South to North got under way, segregated public schools followed, of course, and became permanent fixtures in the American plan of public education. The possibilities are more than fair that they may even outlast the segregated institutions of the South. But this phenomenon, bizarre and tragic as it is, sheds no light upon the prior question of the Negro college in the North.

Once the principle of separate, higher education for Negroes was established illogically, it was inevitable that it would be extended logically. If "Negro colleges" were good for blacks in the North where blacks were relatively few in number and where they were admitted to the very best white colleges, then "Negro colleges" must represent a veritable *summum bonum* in the South where the black population was concentrated and where white colleges were less prestigious and generally closed to the admission of black students. If the logic is faulty, it is because we may not have a clear understanding of the "good" being sought in the first place. What were the goals of "Negro" higher education, and were those goals sufficiently different from the goals of "white" education to warrant their institutionalization in "Negro colleges"? The second part of the question is, of course, academic. The institutionalization of *some* spectrum of values in the "Negro college" is already a matter of history. What these values were, is another question; and whether they are still visible and still viable is a matter of grave contention between people who want to see the "Negro college" survive, and those who consider it an anachronistic indulgence at best, an impeditive absurdity at worst.

Dwight Oliver Wendell Holmes in *The Evolution of the Negro College* discloses an interesting spectrum of motivations which express the social consensus for the establishment of Negro colleges in the first place:

First, the Negro having been rescued from the hell of slavery and two and a half centuries of unrequited toil, was worthy of everything the nation could bestow upon him by way of recompense . . . Second, it was the plain duty of a Christian nation to discharge this obligation to the freedmen promptly by providing them with the same means of mental and moral development that has proved effective in the advance of white people. Third, the Negro possessed the same mental capacity as the white man, his apparent mental inferiority being due to the debasing effect of slavery. Fourth, without education, the Negro would rapidly degenerate and become a national menace . . . to the entire nation.[8]

Such was the rationale of the northern philanthropists, the Freedman's Bureau, and the church and missionary societies. White southern opinion varied, but coalesced around the firm opposition to any educational program in which the notion of racial equality might be remotely implicit. The poor whites, who were themselves uneducated, opposed any education at all for Negroes. Their opposition was seconded by the cruder politicians and by the diehards of the old plantation regime who bed-wet themselves with dreams of having their faithful old field hands and mammies back in service in trustful ignorance. The Alabama Constitutional Convention of 1901 provides a revealing portrait of southern opinion about Negroes a full thirty-five years after the southern fantasy had forever lost its reference to any reality that might once have been. One has only to listen to Delegate J. T. Heflin of Chambers County to see how deeply entrenched, and how persistent were southern attitudes about the Negro's place in American society:

I believe as truly as I am standing here that God Almighty intended the negro to be the servant of the white man . . . I am not an enemy of the negro; I am a friend to him in his place . . . I love to think of the old black mammy . . . I think the time will come when the South will erect a monument to the old black mammy for the lullabies she has sung. We like to think of all these things . . . I like to think of the negro from the old-fashioned Southern standpoint. I like to tell him you do this, or you do that, John, and here is a quarter; you black my shoes, or catch my horse, and you do this and that, and all is well; . . . A man goes out and buys a section of land . . . and builds a magnificent home, and there he rears a family, and a negro comes along and builds himself a little house out in the woods and becomes the servant of the white man and looks after his horses, and stands at the door with his hat off and asks, "Boss, you want your shoes shined?" And all is well. He stays in the kitchen where he belongs.[9]

If the Negro belonged in the kitchen shining shoes, or out in the back lot catching horses for the white man, a rush to educate him could hardly be consistent with the southern understanding of his need to know. There were some southerners, of course, who were more realistic in their reading of the future. While they would probably have preferred to keep Negroes uneducated, in the face of the new legal barriers to his exclusion from all schooling, and considering the meddlesome determination of the Yankee do-gooders, it seemed a matter of enlightened self-interest to have the Negro educated *somewhat*, and to have the educating done by southern whites. They could be succeeded in due course by Negro teachers properly indoctrinated to project the southern point of view. The South never did share the northern missionary's optimism over the Negro's intellectual potential. To almost all southerners, the notion of higher education for Negroes was bound to be economically and academically futile because of the Negro's limited capacity to learn, and because whether or not there was any mistake about his ability, there could be none about his opportunity to utilize any educational attainment in the white man's world as they perceived it.

While northern philanthropy was not entirely oblivious of southern objections to Negro education, other factors including white and Negro religious interests combined to overcome the deflective intent of those objections. For example, a review of the statements of the founders and of the literature, the public addresses, and the sermons of the time shows quite clearly that however wide-ranging were the doctrinal, political, theological, or racial differences of the various groups participating in the founding of the Negro colleges, they were all agreed in at least one interest: whatever else the Negro college was to be, it was to be an agency of *moral uplift* for "the Negro race." The American culture was in tacit agreement with itself that Negroes were the subjects of a certain depravity "inherent to the race." Two and a half centuries of the white man's moral example had imperfectly accomplished reliable patterns of moral behavior or understanding in these children of Africa. It was probably not a conviction that education could instill what example had failed to accomplish, but education *could* create a consciousness of deficiency, which once recognized would be constantly attended. In short, the Negro was morally deficient and unlettered; he had no proper awareness of his shortcomings. So long as he was a chattel, his moral behavior was ultimately the responsibility of the white master, and while every Christian master would agree that the morality of his Negroes should be encouraged when convenient, few considered it to be a critical factor in the ongoing life of the plantation. The prevailing view was that it was in the *nature* of the Negro to lie, to steal, to cheat, to fornicate, to avoid work whenever possible, and to be indifferent about it all. He was popularly thought of as a being of sudden passions, short memory, and a forgiving nature—being especially prone to forgive himself. Hence, the white man's burden was in large part a surrogate responsibility for the Negro's incapacity to measure up to the moral requirements of a civilized society. In slavery, the master was ultimately responsible for his slave in the same way that he was responsible for his dog or his mule, and the moral behavior of slaves was viewed with the same tolerance as that of animals or small children. The sudden emancipation of four million black "children" who now expected to function as equals in the body politic—that is, who now by their very freedom were implicitly responsible for their own moral sufficiency—created a perceived threat to organized society and to established social expectations and obligations. The Negro college was thrust into the role of creating moral awareness and exercising moral control over all those within its jurisdiction—a role which has been continually identified with its reason for existence. The presidents, both white and black, of the early Negro colleges were usually ministers and were invariably men with a strong sense of the Negro's moral precariousness. In those colleges controlled by white churches, the sense of black moral vulnerability was the chief reason for the retention of white administrators long after black scholars with equal or better credentials were available. The white president remained because he was an important symbol, a visible representative of the desired standards of morality. So it was that white heads of Negro colleges lingered on through the 1960's, a hundred years after Negro colleges were first established, and long after any serious question of the readiness and the availability of black administrators with the requisite professional qualifications could be raised.

Thousands of white teachers from New England and elsewhere in the North went South to staff the colleges and secondary schools and academies which sprang into existence after the war. Most of them were missionary-minded. The South was the new frontier—a *home* frontier on which the fight against paganism, heathenism, moral indigence, and consummate ignorance could be resumed. A few paid with their lives for their zeal, and many suffered unimaginable indignities and hardships, for the white South was hard set against the "academic" education of Negroes, and it never relinquished the notion that the Negro's moral instruction was a matter of southern white responsibility. The white South contended that it had the understanding, the know-how, and the means to make the Negro behave; that education—higher, lower, or of whatever kind—would not improve the Negro's morals, but would only increase his native cunning thereby extending the limits of his natural perfidy.

Despite the attitudes of the white South, it should not be inferred that the Negro's moral uplift was exclusively the concern of northern liberals. Negroes themselves, perhaps that element Washington had in mind when he referred to "the wisest among my race,"[10] perhaps those included in Du Bois' Talented Tenth, had decided misgivings about their moral adequacy or at least that of the black masses. Negroes had little opportunity for a realistic evaluation of themselves against the idealized white overculture which everywhere engulfed and stifled them. Furthermore, they were constantly reminded of their shortcomings, real and imagined, by the white man, whose own perspectives were seriously distorted by his momentary political ascendancy, which was too easy to confuse with an inherent godliness. Then, too, blacks were the subjects of a highly selective religious indoctrination which enlisted God, the Bible, and the white man's assurance of manifest destiny in the insidious clouding of the black man's claims to humanity. The Negro, so lowly even in his own eyes, was determined to "rise," but in the realities of the moral situation in which he found himself, he may have been already well above the heap. Ironically, the truth could be known only through education, because the truth was a body of information external to the experience of slavery and therefore far beyond the freeman's existing tools of measurement and analysis. The Negro would have to be educated before he could have any defensible notion of who he was and whether he was moral or not.

A major role of the Negro college, then, was to insure the moral acceptability of the Negro vanguard, which would in turn leaven the black masses with teachers and clergymen—and at industrial schools like Hampton and Tuskegee, with farmers and artisans who by precept and example would lift the race by its bootstraps.

In a fit of racial arrogance common to his times and his class, John C. Calhoun of South Carolina once offered the gratuitous confession that "if a Negro could be found who could parse Greek or explain Euclid, I should be constrained to think that he had human possibilities."[11] Calhoun's snide benevolence was no more than an exercise in racist rhetoric, of course, for in his day and in his state it was felonious for black people to learn to read and write, and a public whipping was among the penalties provided for anyone who undertook to teach them. There would come a day with the advent of the Negro college, however, when the parsing of Greek and the explanation of Euclid would become—in the common American tradition—the symbols of academic and intellectual achievement and acceptability. Eventually, the relevance of a classical curriculum to the fundamental needs of the black estate would be aired in fervent debate between Booker T. Washington and W. E. B. Du Bois. That famous controversy was historically necessary for the establishment of an educational perspective for black leadership. After all, with black people having so recently emerged from slavery, the black experience in education was, to say the least, not extensive, and what kind of educational system would prove most functional to what ends in the short run, and in the long run, was conjectural and problematical. Both Washington and Du Bois endorsed the importance of moral uplift in Negro education, though not with the same emphasis. A posture of moral concern in education would be inevitable in a strategy of meekness, and such a posture would likely be exaggerated in selling a bootstrap philosophy. Said Washington:

> The very best service that one can render to what is called the higher education is to teach the present generation to provide a material or industrial foundation. On such a foundation as this will grow habits of thrift, a love of work, economy, ownership of property, bank accounts. Out of it in the future will grow practical education, professional education and positions of public responsibility. Out of it will grow moral and religious strength . . . One farm bought, one house built, one home sweetly and intelligently kept . . . one sermon well preached . . . one life cleanly lived—these will tell more in our favor than all the abstract eloquence that can be summoned to plead our cause.[12]

Washington's sentiments do not veer far from the prevailing notions of his day. Rather they constitute a fair restatement of the Protestant ethic which shaped and conditioned most American thinking for most of our history. Hard work, thrift, money, and morals are inevitably linked, and for Washington moral respectability *for the race* was the first order of business. This could be accomplished through work—work with the hands—in the fields, in the shops, in the kitchens. What counted most was the day-to-day level of visible achievement which could be measured by the Negro-watchers, North and South, whose skepticism Dr. Washington felt it necessary to allay. "There is still doubt," he reminded his critics, "as to the ability of the Negro unguided, unsupported to hew his own path and put into visible, tangible, indisputable form products and signs of civilization."[13]

Certainly Professor Washington cared little for civilization in the abstract. His universe for the purposes of his task as he saw it, was a limited one. But it was also *present* and *real,* and the lives and welfare of the people he sought to lead were irrevocably contingent to the realities of that limited, self-regulated universe. "Patiently, quietly, doggedly, persistently," he counseled, "we must reinforce argument with results . . . Our pathway must be up through the soil, up through the swamps." If the Negro could earn respectability by minding his morals and doing his job well, however humble, tangible rewards would follow in due course.

In Du Bois' thinking, classical education *for some* is necessarily prior to even a society of farmers and artisans, for somebody has to teach the teachers, and education is more than the knowledge of a trade. As a matter of fact, classical education reaches full flower only when the *Lumpenproletariat* is sufficiently leavened to be "raised in morals and manners" as a prerequisite to successful vocational activity. Higher education is not for everybody, but it is crucial to racial progress and it must encompass the whole man in the whole universe of mankind:

> Men of America, the problem is plain before you. Here is a race transplanted through the criminal foolishness of your fathers. Whether you like it or not, the millions are here, and here they will remain. If you do not lift them up, they will pull you down . . . Education must not simply teach work—it must teach life. The Talented Tenth of the Negro race must be made leaders of thought and missionaries of culture among their people. No others can do this work and Negro colleges must train men for it. The Negro race, like all other races, is going to be saved by its exceptional men.[14]

There were many who agreed with Du Bois, but the question *was* asked then as it is asked now—why a *Negro* college? To men who had any understanding of the meaning of being black in a world of whiteness, it was a frivolous question, an asininity. Kelly Miller, the very distinguished dean at Howard University, suggested that "One might as well ask, or had better ask, the rationale of Jewish seminaries or Methodist colleges and universities. These racial and denominational schools impart to the membership of their community something which the general educational institution is wholly unable to inculcate."[15]

That "something" is what contemporary supporters of the still existing Negro colleges are variously trying to discover, re-identify, parallel, sell, or promulgate. For Dean Miller, that something was positive, patent, and critical: "But for the Negro college, Negro scholarship would decay, and Negro leadership would be wanting in effectiveness and zeal. The Negro college must furnish stimulus to hesitant Negro scholarship, garner, treasure and nourish group tradition, enlighten both races with a sense of the cultural worth and achievement of the constituency it represents, and supply the cultural guidance of the race."[16]

Looked at in the context of the culture of which it is a part, and with which it has had to contend, we may well ask whether the Negro college reasonably fulfilled the challenge its most ardent afficionados set for it. A hundred years have passed. They have been years of darkness. They were the years of the terrors of the "reconstruction"—when black citizenship was a travesty of civil justice and the efforts of black men to participate responsibly in the political process evoked derision and anger and savage reprisal. They were years of light—when schools like Clark, Talladega, Atlanta University, and Fisk were created of the synthesis of white concern and black determination. They were years of dismay—when the twin maggots of prejudice and discrimination, spawned in the feculence of racial hatred, emerged to infect all America with an obscene disease. At the crucial moment in her history when she could have opted for a supreme place among civilized nations, America faltered, weakened, and succumbed. Our supreme tragedy is that we have no national will to recover. Racism in America, for all its loathsomeness, seems everywhere regarded as an indisposition to be accepted rather than a stinking chancre to be excised.

But they were also years of promise—when Daniel Hale Williams, a black physician, performed the first successful heart operation at Provident Hospital in Chicago; when William A. Hinton, a black physician on the Harvard faculty, developed a standard test for syphilis; when the Black Tenth Calvary rescued Theodore Roosevelt from certain defeat by Spanish forces in Cuba; when the National Negro Business League was organized in Boston; when Jack Johnson became heavyweight champion of the world; when W. C. Handy gave the blues to America; when Carter Woodson founded the Association for the Study of Negro Life and History; when George Washington Carver was hailed as "the greatest industrial chemist in the world"; when Eva B. Dykes at Radcliffe, and Sadie T. Mossell at Pennsylvania, and Georgiana Simpson at the University of Chicago took the first Ph.D. degrees ever awarded to black women; when the Negro renaissance produced Claude McKay, Jean Toomer, Alain Locke, Langston Hughes, Counter Cullen, and James Weldon Johnson; when Paul Robeson, Roland Hayes, and Marian Anderson interpreted for America and the world America's only indigenous music, the songs of the black experience; and when the art of Henry O. Tanner, Aaron Douglas, Richmond Barthe, and Augusta Savage found its way into the distinctive collections of two continents.

The first hundred years were years of uncertainty and groping for the best way to come to terms with America—as when Booker T. Washington offered his "separate fingers compromise" at the Cotton States Exposition in Atlanta; as when W. E. B. Du Bois, in founding the Niagara Movement, demanded civil justice and denounced accommodation; as when Marcus Garvey and his United Negro Improvement Association sought the unity of black men everywhere under the slogan, "One God, One Aim, One Destiny!" As when Malcolm X sought deliverance in a separate nation, "right here in the United States!" For more than half of that hundred years the NAACP, and the Urban League worked with patience and fortitude to accomplish an "integrated" society through litigation and persuasion; and for a brief moment, Dr. Martin Luther King electrified the world with the possibilities of social change in America through nonviolent protest. The problem persists. The fact that doctrines and strategies once considered radical are now dismissed as conventional and prosaic, and that the emphasis of the struggle is no longer on integration is a revealing commentary on the pervasiveness of the problem and the quality of its continuing resistance. The same facts may also suggest that goals which were once considered sacred and which enjoyed very wide consensus may now be under reevaluation and redefinition.

In a hundred years the 4½ million Blackamericans have become 30 million. The centers of the black population have shifted from the rural South to the great cities. In all too many instances it has been a case of migrating from the plantation to the ghetto. Seventy-five per cent of the black population now live in cities. Fifty-six per cent of all Blackamericans now live outside the old slave states. Like the American Jew, the Blackamerican has become an urban dweller. The "folk image" has been dissipated, and in its place is the developing image of the New Blacks.

In the meantime, the Blackamerican has found time to help

fight five wars at the behest of his country. In one war he fought "to make the world safe for democracy." In another, he fought to guarantee Four Freedoms for all freedom loving people. Through all of them he found less freedom and democracy at home for himself than he found for any of the people he fought and died for in the far off corners of the world. In his fight for his own freedom in his own country he has been essentially alone. Neither the British nor the French nor the Italians, the North Koreans nor the South Vietnamese have ever protested the American debasement of the blacks whose blood is mingled with the soil of Europe and Asia for the freedom of Europeans and Asians. Nor, for that matter, have any of the countless other peoples, here or abroad, who have profited by the sacrifice Blackamericans have made for their freedom. Beyond that, it is an interesting footnote to history, and one well remembered, that Blackamericans have never been called upon by their country to defend the freedom of *any black people anywhere!* In Vietnam we are deeply involved in the "liberation" of a people, who, from all the evidence, seem far more concerned about being liberated from us than from their countrymen. In South Africa, where 3 million Europeans hold 17 million Africans in slavery in their own country, the billions we have invested there belie our alleged concern about human freedom. It is a question of *whose* freedom is at stake; it is a question of *who* is benefited thereby. Who shall die to defend *what* freedom is not a question, nor has it ever been.

Has the Negro college kept the perspectives clear? Has it helped black youth to see itself in its special relation to America and to the world? If it has not, if it has not taught its black constituency to read the fine print of history and to address itself to the realities of difference no less than to the possibilities of synonymity, then the failure of the Negro college is critical, and time is of the essence. There must be changes.

The years have flown swiftly. The hundred years behind us belong to history. The time before us is our own. What is past is beyond resurrection, but it is not necessarily beyond rectification. We live forever in the present, but the present is always the future that has arrived. All our dreams, all our plans, whatever we hope to be is projected. The present is merely the medium through which the past gives perspective to the future. The point is that the individual who understands the circumstances of his own history is the individual who is best equipped to influence the circumstances of his history-to-be.

The Negro college is a part of our history. It is a part of the history of America. We may consign it to death, but we cannot consign it to oblivion. It would persist in the minds of the people and in the shaping of the culture long after its colors were pulled down and its historic old halls gave way to supermarkets and parking lots. You cannot kill an institution by converting its real estate or starving it out of existence. The men and women who founded the Negro colleges recognized the exigencies of *their* times and tried to guard against them. But they also had a kind of clairvoyance which impelled them to address themselves and the institutions they founded to future possibilities—*today's* possibilities. They did not expect the aberrations and disparities of their day to be perpetuated. If they had, to have founded the Negro college at all would have been in direct contradiction to what they believed.

Times change. Institutions change, though less perceptibly. The struggle for human rights and the desire for human recognition persists with the tenacity of time itself. A survey of the attitudes of Negro college graduates in 1910 yielded responses scarcely different from what one hears today at a black rap session on any of a hundred campuses:

"In my opinion, the Negro needs nothing so much as to be let alone. He asks for no more than he merits, but he wants all he does merit. Life is a battle, and every man must be a fighter."

"Long since, I came to the conclusion that right living on our part would not solve the problem."

"I firmly believe that the destiny of the American Negro lies largely in his own hands."

"The Negro must continue to contend for all the rights, privileges, and opportunities accorded other American citizens. He ought to ally himself with any political party that will further these ends."

"The ability to think well should outrank the ability to live well."

"The Negro should be urged to contend peaceably and earnestly for everything needed to make him a man."

"The Negro is passing through a critical period of his existence in America, and no one can say with certainty what the result will be."

"The Negro should qualify himself politically as well as otherwise and become interested in all questions affecting humanity in general and himself in particular."

"I believe that the American Negro must live and die in America."

"The Negro must work and fight and fight and work. He must scorn peace earned at the price of self-respect. He must deport himself as a man, and he must insist on being treated as a man in America."

"The Negro is growing more assertive and manly. He is beginning to meet imposition with opposition, even with his life."

"The Negro needs leaders and instructors who will teach that he is a man."[17]

This last quote above all. The times demand such leaders and teachers no less now than then. In 1910, 53 per cent of the graduates from Negro colleges were teachers.[18] There is no need to search far for the reason: the segregated schools had to be staffed with segregated personnel. There was a bull market for black teachers. Today, the market is off. It will never recover completely. In 1910, 20 per cent of all Negro college graduates were preachers.[19] That market is off too, though not for the same reasons. The black churches and the white churches have shown no strong urge to merge at the local level, but black talent that once saw the black ministry as the principal outlet for leadership has found some other markets for what it has to sell. It is obvious that training teachers and preachers may no longer be the essential *raison d'etre* of the Negro college. Those concerned for the survival of these colleges know this, of course, and for almost a decade now efforts to find viable new emphases have grown increasingly frantic as operating costs have gone up, traditional revenues have gone down, and quality of entering students has been affected by increasingly less bigoted admission policies of white institutions, North and South. The first reaction to the 1954 desegregation decisions of the Supreme Court was an attempt to justify the continuing service-related validity of the Negro college by stressing remedial teaching for large numbers of black students who would not likely be admitted to competing white colleges. Such a decision, while understandable in terms of the vulnerability of the competitive positions of almost all of the Negro colleges, was nonetheless retrogressive. Most Negro colleges came into being as high schools—or less—hopefully masquerading under the dubious rubric of "colleges" and "universities." Even after reaching academic maturity, many of them continued to maintain their own feeders in the form of high school departments or their equivalents. Any increase in subcollege activities by institutions already suffering from a severely qualified "college" image could only lead to a progressive erosion of academic credibility. In an "Open Letter to the Presidents of the Colleges in the United Negro College Fund," Margaret C. McCulloch, a former officer of the American Missionary Association,[20] responded to a letter from the UNCF presidents announcing their intention to expand remedial work in an effort to anticipate the consequences of the 1954 decision. Some of what she had to say bears repeating:

> In many cases you have done heroic things in lifting your institutions from colleges accredited only on a standard "for Negroes only," to colleges meeting and overpassing requirements for recognition on the same basis as "white" colleges. To pass from the first part of your letter reporting on these matters to the latter dealing with the decade ahead . . . rarely have I read a document by educators that showed so little evidence of awareness of the changes in our world or of what is needed to meet them . . . [the] first [defect of your proposal] is the positive harm it will do to Negro youth, doing remedial work with them after their admission to college. The second defect is the complete absence of any affirmative proposals to meet the challenge of the second half of the Twentieth Century . . .
>
> Large scale, low-cost education is a state function, even on the college level. For private Negro colleges to assume this responsibility . . . would be a backward step . . . Further, . . . the private Negro college is not required to admit youth merely on graduation from a state-accredited high school. It can set its own admission requirements. Again, Negro youth are potentially the intellectual equal of white youth; but they are not vastly superior. It is therefore not possible for them during the four years of college to do the full equivalent of a four year course taken by their white brethren and simultaneously to do what is really a part of their high school work on a remedial basis. In planning such a program, you are condemning Negro college education to a prolonged inferiority to white.[21]

Professor McCulloch was painfully right; and what was wisdom in 1955, when the unknowns of racial desegregation could only be guessed at, is still wisdom in 1971, when we have lived through fifteen years of desegregative implementation and have a developed prognosis of what its meaning is for the future of Blackamericans.

We cannot afford to take the low road with the education of Blackamericans ever again, and at this juncture of time, place, and circumstance, the Negro college could not survive another trip through the shadows. Nor should it be required to try. The Negro college is already written off by some educational seers. Harvard Professors Christopher Jencks and David Riesman in their projection of the future of Negro higher education offer black people some cold comfort indeed with the gratuitous suggestion that there will always "be a substantial number of Negroes who want a B.A., are willing to do what they are told to get one, but simply cannot meet the modest standards of even the least selective white colleges." A Negro college, in the opinion of Jencks and Riesman, is one which "will allow them to get the coveted diploma, even if it does not make them competent to do the kinds of work they hope a B.A. implies."[22] Having had some experience with Negro colleges, including owning one of the B.A.'s to which the Harvard professors give such slight consideration, I think perhaps the J. and R. definition is somewhat overdrawn. And because I taught at Negro colleges for something more than a decade before being touched by the grace of white academia, the implication that a diploma from a Negro college is no more than an academic sinecure I consider crude and insulting to every black faculty and every black student body. It is 125 years from South Carolina's John C. Calhoun to Harvard's Jencks and Riesman, but the specter that haunts the garden of black aspiration is that the pattern of American conceptualization about Negro intelligence and Negro institutions has changed little, if any, during that time. Merely to be a Negro, no less now than then, implies a rigidly defined capacity for learning anything, or for properly valuing what is learned or not learned. In consequence, in the minds of many white Americans (and some Negroes who still have identity problems), the Negro college exists for the purpose of formalizing that incapacity with so much academic posturing, and the issuance of impressive looking diplomas which have no currency beyond the stepped-down world in which Negroes are popularly supposed to live and have their mediocre being. That is neither a true nor adequate explanation for the past existence of the Negro college; nor is it an honorable or adequate reason for its continued existence. It is a suggestion that says more about the culture than about its Negro institutions.

From the snotty arrogance of Calhoun to the shallow presumptiveness of Jencks and Riesman is only 125 years or so, but that particular 125 years happens to cover the entire life span of the Negro college. One cannot escape the annoying suspicion that American attitudes on basic questions concerning Negroes persist, and *will* persist without reference to any objective reality. It is hard to avoid the feeling that so far as official, decision-making white America is concerned, a hundred years of effort by a hundred-odd Negro colleges has gone for naught; that the "educated Negro" insofar as he was educated in a Negro college has made no significant impact upon this society; that, in fact, the money and effort, the blood, the sweat, the tears, and the prayers expended on Negro higher education may just as well have been thrown to the proverbial wild hog, with all who dared hope for a return on their investments crying "soo-oo-ee-ee!"

We must return to the beginning. We must go back to origins. The Negro college came into being in consequence of a set of assumptions which reveal rather more about the peculiar American culture which occasioned them than about the colleges themselves. A hundred years or so of "Negro education" has not substantially reduced those assumptions, and the qualifications with which most Americans perceive Negro education and its relevance to whatever higher education is supposed to accomplish has scarcely been demolished, despite the reading of whatever statistics, or the citing of whatever cases of accomplishment. The Negro colleges began with a deficit they will never overcome so long as they are "Negro," because being "Negro" is (and has always been) precisely their deficit. It is a sad but revealing commentary on the times—and on the culture—that these colleges now feel constrained to refer to themselves as *predominantly* Negro! This is the awful price of an illusion about the possibility of survival. There aren't any "predominantly" Negro colleges, of course. There never were. And there aren't likely to be any. To cite the handful of white students on scattered black campuses as a reason to call those colleges "predominantly Negro," is itself farcical and misleading, if not altogether irresponsible. Nobody calls Harvard a "predominantly white college" despite the fact that Harvard's ratio of blacks to whites, however minuscule, is several times the ratio of whites to blacks at Morehouse or Fisk or Miles. But that is really beside the point: a mere numerical predominance of blacks over whites in an academic situation is not what makes a "Negro college"; and the notion of a "predominantly" Negro college is an absurdity, a nullity, a contradiction in terms. A college can no more be predominantly Negro than can a person. People who are "predominantly Negro" or even "part Negro" do not occur anywhere in our society. The reason is quite simple: "Negro" is itself a cultural category, which, while it has very definite connotations, can hardly be the subject of quantitative modification. One can be part Irish, or part Chinese, or even part African, and, given a disproportionate distribution of genes from one stock or another, he could conceivably be "predominantly" whatever the disproportion favors. But if one is a "Negro" within the meaning of American cultural understanding, that is the sum of it. He may be also half-white, or half-Indian, but despite that happenstance, he will continue to be *all*-Negro, and throughout the length and breadth of this fair land he will be so regarded. "Negro" is a subjective reference, and like beauty and some other passion-rousing concepts, may well be in the eye of the beholder.[23]

In consequence of the American understanding of what a Negro is, Negro education was born with a cultural nemesis it has never been able to shake; and if society has been slow to accept its Negroes into white systems of education, it has been fabian in its acceptance of Negro education as a legitimate and valuable academic enterprise. Jencks and Riesman observe that an "all-Negro" college "is likely to develop the familiar pathologies of de facto segregation, with separatism coming to mean inferiority,"[24] and "the minority of Negro colleges that will attract white students in large numbers will . . . thus cease to be Negro colleges in any basic sense."[25] In short, our habits of thinking are such that we cannot separate what is "Negro" from what is inferior, and what is "Negro" ceases to be "Negro" when whites move in because the mere presence of significant numbers of white people changes the tone and character of the enterprise, thereby relieving it of the stigma of Negro inferiority.

This is the generation in which the Blackamerican must reach his final maturity, his absolute manhood, his unqualified freedom. A college or a university should be preeminent as an instrument through which the attainment of these values might ordinarily be accelerated. Education is, or ought to be, the principal means through which society sustains itself, renews itself, improves itself. The first function of higher education should be in the higher social interests which lie behind and beyond mere vocational aspirations and a concern for needs that are merely visceral. In this respect, the Negro college has never reached the fullest expression of its normative possibilities, and it is doubtful that it ever will. The fault does not lie in the Negro college. The fault lies in the society which spawned it and then deformed it before it was born. It is true that a college can be no more than its human constituents and the ideas by which their vision is illumined. It is a dynamic microsystem in which roles, status, values, and personalities do not necessarily lose their urgency in the formal planning and pursuit of education. It is true, also, that sometimes the best intentions of the founders have a way of receding further toward oblivion with successive generations of the principals who carry on the administrative process. But this is not necessarily bad. New exigencies in new times require new strategies. Sometimes old goals, revered and valued in their day, need updating and reevaluating. When new goals and new strategies for reaching them can be merged into the legitimate interests of existing institutions, the whole society benefits and the trauma of precipitous change is avoided.

There are those who call for the end of the Negro colleges on the grounds that they are no longer needed. The absurdity of such a suggestion is matched only by the difficulty of finding the financial means to continue them. The argument is that if they do not voluntarily commit an honorable hari-kari, then the alternative is slow dishonorable atrophy and death. Further, it is said that the Negro colleges have never been competitive financially or academically, and that now, since practically all white colleges of any repute are at least nominally open to black students, and increasingly to black professors, the Negro college can only expect a continued debasement of student body and faculty by having to accept new students with progressively poorer entrance credentials and instructors who could hardly be posted elsewhere.

All of this is true. But it need not be true.

This is a good time to take advantage of the need and the desire for change. The Negro college has not outlived its usefulness, but it has outlived its former goals. It has also outlived its cultural imprimatur and it may have outlived its societal acceptability. But whether any of this is true, there are certain assets which the Negro college has which remain beyond debate. Among them are cultural continuity and solid accomplishment. The black college is an important integrative force in the black subculture. It has been the central tramline of the black experience since the Civil War. What is more, it is probable that for a time at least more black people—American, African, and Caribbean—were educated in the Negro colleges in the United States than in all of the institutions in the rest of the world combined, an achievement which ought to temper the impatient criticism of latter day planners and pundits alike. One cannot escape the fact that the Negro college did a job nobody else wanted and no other institution was doing. It assumed and carried the burden of higher education for a mass of people whose handicaps were many, whose abilities were untested and everywhere held in doubt, and whose hopes and aspirations transcended the realities of their own limitations to achieve what in fact the cultural consensus had already decided they could not, and would not, achieve. The newly freed Negro American knew that he was not truly "American" because he did not, even in his own mind, project the image (or experience the security) of being American. His hope and his dream was that education would provide the magic metamorphosis which would see his deficits corrected and his insufficiencies washed away. The Negro college accepted the impossible task of keeping the dream alive but grounded as painlessly as possible in reality, while providing the intellectual and the cultural experiences which over the long haul would give viability to hope and substance to the dream. In large part it succeeded. The task now is not addressed to a new dream but to the final completion of one that is old. It is the dream of every man to experience the affirmation of his own existence and to see it unequivocably confirmed in the value systems of his own culture, his own society.

When the Negro colleges were founded, few blacks had had the time or the opportunity to acquire property or amass the kind of money required by a system of higher education. They were, after all, turned out of servitude with nothing. The private colleges took over where the Freedman's Bureau left off, but the prime responsibility for the education of the exslaves remained, and remains, where it was—on the federal government. The federal investment in Howard University can be seen only as a limited acknowledgment of a far broader obligation. Today it would be unthinkable (I hope) to add 4½ million new citizens to the country without extensive provisions for their education and training.

In the light of present needs and existing circumstances, the Negro colleges could probably benefit themselves, their black constituencies, and the nation at large by making the obvious transition from private Negro colleges to black national universities. All of the assets I have mentioned plus an extraordinary reservoir of good will are transferable. This generation of Blackamericans has goals not fully anticipated under the old rubric which gave birth to the "Negro" college. Neither a "Negro education" nor an "education for Negroes" is capable of meeting the real needs of today's blacks and tomorrow's Blackamericans. The urgencies of the nineteenth century have been replaced by a whole new set of exigencies. The salient goals of the Negro colleges have been met; some of the others are no longer relevant. The Negro colleges did produce, and sustain, an educated class of professionals—teachers, clergymen, lawyers, physicians, businessmen, and the like—to service a society segregated by color. Their graduates did not always find the personal niche they had a right to expect in the professions for which they prepared: B.A.'s by the thousands carried mail, and B.S.'s did the menial work in America's hotels, swept the railroad cars and terminals, served the drinks, and put down a thousand "hustles" at America's favorite resorts and playgrounds. They had to do this, not because they were better trained to hustle than to hold positions open to whites with commensurate training and credentials, but because they were black. The proof of the pudding is seen in the fact that with rare exceptions blacks with credentials from white institutions fared no better. It wasn't so much that Negro colleges were not turning out "representative" graduates as it was that they were not turning out *white* graduates. Negro college graduates fared well south of segregation. Black graduates from white colleges did too; but they did no better than the graduates of Negro colleges in the world beyond the color line, and even the occasional Harvard or Yale degree, insofar as it represented professional practice, hung from a wall in the ghetto as did those of Clark, Howard, Talladega, and Fisk. The wonder is that in the face of the discrimination that limited their range of possibilities, black people did not give up higher education altogether. The happy result is that little by little Blackamerica approached, and then passed, the critical point that distinguishes a people who know from a people who do not know, and who do not know that they do not know. In short, along with the knowledge and training needed to service the black community, the Negro colleges gave to Blackamerica a critical self-awareness and a perspective for freedom from which there must be no regression. It is time now to pursue more fully the logical consequences of that perspective with the self-confidence of a people who have looked at the sun and not been blinded.

We need our Negro colleges. It would be criminally foolish to permit them to close. All over the South, a malevolent species of "integration" is closing the black schools. The objective seems to be to destroy the black psyche by destroying the institutions from which it derives support. In Athens, Alabama, Trinity School, which was founded by the AMA in 1865, and which still sits atop the old Civil War fort which is so intricately intertwined with its history, is shuttered, closed, and abandoned. It was an excellent school, better perhaps by far than some of those in which its former students have become involuntary intruders. Its principal has been "laid off." Its faculty has been scattered. I went to Trinity. And I went to LeMoyne. And to Fisk.

A system of national colleges could be one answer to the Negro college dilemma. It could capitalize rather than destroy the rich cultural heritage of Blackamerica. It could do much to reestablish American ties with black Africa and broaden the opportunities for sharing a vital element of our national subculture. One school, such as Howard, could represent the national focus on Third World studies—economics, politics, foreign service, medical research, and training with an African or Third World orientation. Another, perhaps Atlanta University or Tuskegee, might become the national center for research in every aspect of black slavery and its consequences—for example, the economic and psychological effects of racism. There could be a continuing investigation of regional history with a view toward new understandings of old problems which beset the nation. Wilberforce, or Lincoln, would be concerned with the peculiar circumstances of the free Negro in the North. Fisk could be the national institute concerned with the art and culture of African and Afro-American peoples. Each national center or institute might have any number of satellite campuses utilizing the facilities and faculties of existing Negro colleges. Rather than have the Negro college retreat into oblivion, it seems to me that the times require, and offer them, an expanded role in the American academic enterprise. Change is the order of the day. When the governor of Georgia and the governor of South Carolina are confident enough to address their inaugural audiences with unequivocal commitments to racial equality during their administrations,[26] there is reason to hope and reason to plan for the complete emergence of the black estate as a full complement to the making and the meaning of America. But America is far behind in discovering much that she should know about herself. That is why a national system of black colleges is imperative. We've got a lot to learn—and the best place to learn it is where it is. The Negro college was a product of the culture, a reflection of the times. Within the limitations which structured it and defined its goals and its possibilities, it fulfilled its *raison d'etre* with reasonable success and, on occasion, with distinction. Now there are new goals and new responsibilities, new possibilities. The black national university is the logical successor to the private Negro college in the common interests of all Americans.

REFERENCES

1. Booker T. Washington and W. E. B. Du Bois, *The Negro Problem* (New York: James Pott and Co., 1963), pp. 46-47.
2. Lincoln was founded by the Presbyterians. Wilberforce was founded by the Methodist Episcopal Church, but was purchased by the African Methodist Episcopals in 1862.
3. "The College-Bred Negro," in *The Atlanta University Publications* (New York: Arno Press, 1968), pp. 48-49.
4. Florida, Mississippi, South Carolina, Louisiana, and Alabama. Alabama required the unanimous consent of the parents of students enrolled.
5. There were a few mixed schools in Mississippi, and at least two in South Carolina. An attempt by black children to attend a "white" school in Louisiana was aborted when the white students became violent.
6. Horace Mann Bond, *The Education of the Negro in the American Social Order* (Englewood Cliffs, N. J.: Prentice-Hall, 1934), p. 57.
7. Gunnar Myrdal, *An American Dilemma* (New York: Harper and Brothers, 1944), p. 888.
8. Dwight Oliver Wendell Holmes, *The Evolution of the Negro College* (New York: Bureau of Publications, Teachers College, Columbia University, 1934), pp. 68-69.
9. Quoted in Horace Mann Bond, *Negro Education in Alabama* (New York: Atheneum, 1969), pp. 173-174.
10. Referred to in the famous Atlanta Exposition Address.
11. Bond, *Education of the Negro in the American Social Order,* p. 146.
12. Washington and Du Bois, *The Negro Problem,* pp. 10-29.
13. *Ibid.*
14. *Ibid.*, pp. 56-75.
15. Kelly Miller, "Howard: The National Negro University," in Alain Locke, *The New Negro* (New York: Arno Press, 1968), p. 321.
16. *Ibid.*
17. "The College-Bred Negro," pp. 91-97.
18. *Ibid.*, p. 66.
19. *Ibid.*
20. The American Missionary Association established or played a key part in the establishment of many of the best known Negro colleges, including Fisk, LeMoyne, Hampton, Tougaloo, and Talladega.

21. *Journal of Negro Education* (Fall 1955), pp. 493ff.

22. Christopher Jencks and David Riesman, *The Academic Revolution* (New York: Doubleday, 1968).

23. "Negroes" light enough to pass immediately cease to be "Negroes" when they are mistaken for white, although no biological, physiological, racial, political, or aptitudinal transformation whatever takes place! Conversely, a white man identified as a Negro becomes the subject of an automatic schedule of negative presumptions. Similarly, graduates of say Clark College in Atlanta, or LeMoyne College in Memphis, both "Negro colleges" would doubtless enjoy superior recognition *on the same merits* from people who mistakenly believe them to be graduates of Clark at Worcester, Massachusetts, or LeMoyne of Syracuse, New York. I am a graduate of the "Negro" LeMoyne, and I have had the experience more than once.

24. Jencks and Riesman, *The Academic Revolution,* p. 449.

25. *Ibid.,* p. 450.

26. *New York Times,* January 13, 1971, p. 1.

VIVIAN W. HENDERSON

Negro Colleges Face the Future

A COLLEGE or other institution of higher learning is in large measure an expression of the culture and social structure of which it is a part. One of the dilemmas or paradoxes faced by predominantly Negro colleges is that the social and racial context within which they were founded and nurtured, many well over one hundred years ago, is of a passing order. While the remnants of that order continue today and will continue into the future, the nation is committed to eliminating it from its midst.

For most of their existence, Negro colleges have served higher education within the context of a social structure built upon concepts of racial dualism, racial segregation, white supremacy, and racial inferiority of black people. Some of the Negro colleges, specifically most of the private colleges, were not founded on these principles. Indeed, they were founded on the hope that former slaves were going to become an integral part of American society. Nonetheless, their development through the years was conditioned by the country's racist policies. They suffer the legacy of those policies today as they face the future. State-supported colleges were founded on the principle that the state was obliged to support something for Negroes which it also supported for whites, but with the understanding that whatever it supported for Negroes would be inferior to that which was supported for whites.

The social context within which Negro colleges have operated has been altered. The courts have engendered national policy committed to racial desegregation in education as well as other aspects of society. Consequently, the question is raised as to the need for Negro colleges in the future and, further, if needed, what will or should be their roles in a racially "integrated" society?

It is not my precise purpose to explore here the function and role of Negro colleges under conditions of racial integration in education. On the other hand, one cannot treat basic questions involving administrative decision-making in Negro colleges without having in focus questions involving their role and function. Several questions must be raised in which role and function condition administrative decision and direction. For example, what direction will the Negro college take as racial dualism in state supported systems of higher education is eliminated? What adjustments in aims and purposes will be needed in adopting and adjusting to the new social context within which higher education is placed? What adaptations will be necessary for Negro colleges to compete for better qualified black students in view of their new accessibility to white institutions? Can Negro colleges attract white students? Should they seek to attract white students or should they be black colleges serving the needs of black people *only*? What impact will the new thrust for black identity ultimately have on the historic and traditional Negro college? What are the responses of the colleges to new student expectations regarding relevancy and participatory democracy?

These are serious questions. They cannot be brushed aside with a business-as-usual posture. Administrative leaders must be involved with these questions. Boards of trustees must be involved with these questions. The faculty and students and alumni are likewise involved with these questions as Negro colleges face the future.

Beyond change in the racial and social context, other forces are at work that affect the framework within which Negro colleges must function in the future. In general, these forces affect the whole of American higher education. However, because of the unique position of Negro colleges in higher education they have special meaning for such colleges.

—Demographic change involving movement of Negroes from the South to other regions of the country. There is a simultaneous shift in the Negro population from rural to urban residence. Migration in the former instance has occurred at a decreasing rate since about 1965. There seems to be no let-up, however, in the movement to urban areas. Urbanization has meant greater national attention to neglect of cities. Demand for education to be more responsive to city needs and the urban mentality of youth is greater. Ghetto problems are more sharply focused as are maldistribution in benefits and burdens between the haves and have-nots.

—Increased sensitivity on the part of public and private policy to provision of equal opportunity in education, jobs, and other areas for all citizens. More federal funds have been made available for less affluent students and higher education has been made more accessible. The number of community colleges has increased significantly since 1960. Seventy-six were started in 1968. Consequently, Negro enrollment in white schools is on the rise in all sections of the country and Negro education is increasingly being handled by non-Negro institutions. This would suggest greater strain on Negro colleges for faculty, staff, and students.

—Escalation in occupational opportunity and greater diversity in occupational demands for black college graduates. This has meant increased pressure on black colleges for diversification in curricula and instructional programs. At the same time black students are demanding curricular adaptations to make black colleges more "relevant" to the black community. Thus black colleges face a dual kind of responsibility. In one instance they must meet needs of students for service in the black community; in the other they must prepare students for participation in the larger society. And this is expected to be done despite extraordinarily limited resources with which to do the job.

—The development of black studies in black and white colleges. This development is welcomed. It means a serious void in race relations education may be filled. White and black people alike may become more appreciative of contributions of black people to the development of domestic and world civilization as well as more aware of problems involving race relations at home and abroad. This too will pose a special strain on Negro colleges as previously all white faculties seek blacks for staffing black studies and other programs.

—Developments of new concepts of human rights including student rights and rights of the poor. Students have almost developed into a separate and distinct class with aims and objectives peculiar to that group. Their demands on education, governments, and the general society are most pronounced. A major demand is for an array of educational reforms including open admissions, participation in governance, student voice in hiring, promotion, and dismissal of teachers, and inclusion of community (poor) people in various aspects of campus decision-making and activity.

—Increase in the cost of education. It appears that there is no end in sight to increments in the cost of operating colleges and universities. Public colleges, while beneficiaries of an education-starved society, must soon face up to the massive task of defining the almost open-ended needs of a heavily taxed public which in essence holds a growing mortgage on the destinies of public higher education. Meanwhile, sources of support for private colleges tend to shrink in relation to the needs of these colleges.

Another important development is the rise of emphasis on black awareness and black identity. One result is a call for the "all black" college or university. Some students, teachers, and community leaders have raised questions regarding what they view as "white oriented" structures, posture, and images of black colleges. They call for an all black student body, all black faculty, all black boards of governance, and even all black money or funding for the colleges. Those who advocate the all black college argue that the push for racial integration has not yielded significant results. More important, they argue for institutions which will direct themselves toward fulfillment of the black experience and for institutions which will devote their entire energies to solving problems of black people and nurturing understanding and learning about the black experience at home and abroad.

These forces and trends are not all-encompassing of developments shaping higher education in the society. They suggest sources of special pressure and constraints on the Negro colleges. They provide at least a partial framework within which some analysis of administration problems of Negro colleges may be made. As these developments occur, educational opportunities for Negro youth become distinct from the welfare of Negro colleges as such. It may be, therefore, that projection of a philosophy regarding Negro colleges and education of Negroes should reflect this fact.

Pressures and constraints are nothing new to Negro colleges. The social context within which they operate is. On the one hand, many well-meaning people see black colleges as symbols of segregated education; some blacks, on the other hand, in pursuit of black empowerment and self-identity see the black colleges as symbols of black awareness and as a resource for development of exclusively black education. One is almost forced, therefore, into a defensive posture regarding black colleges and a rationale for their continuance.

Administrators of Negro colleges will be increasingly confronted with the issue of the all black college or university. The question must be faced in terms of aims, purpose, and objectives. A rather clear posture must be assumed as to direction in which the institution is expected to go. Shall the institution be committed to racial integration of the society and "liberation" of black people via that avenue or shall it be committed to racial exclusion, setting blacks off from the rest of society?

In my own view there is considerable difference between being an all black institution and being a black institution. The former connotes racial exclusion, the latter does not. Yet the black college has every opportunity to do its thing as a black institution with its mission of serving black people as well as preparing them for the total economic, social, and political process. There is not much hope for the institution that chooses racial exclusion as a path for the future. At the same time black colleges must become more relevant. They need to take urban problems more seriously. Urban problems in so many ways are problems that weigh heavily upon black people.

It may be well to summarize some of the "values" of Negro colleges and what they do for a clientele that might not be done if left to higher education in general. On the positive side the black college offers professional realization for certain categories of black professionals and administrators as well as for professors and auxiliary people including secretaries, food handlers, and building and grounds people. These are people who would not normally find their professional expression in the larger society. The black college offers social realization for faculty and students in a way that would not normally be available in the kind of situation in which we participate. These colleges may offer political and economic noncontingencies for employees—a sort of built-in invulnerability up to a point. The black college may provide an important ethnic identity in the area in which it is located; it offers an institutional association at a meaningful level. These colleges also offer a unique opportunity for radicalization of the black community, a radicalization of politics and economics and over-all social awareness. In other words, there is a philosophy associated with these colleges that goes beyond education per se. These are positive values, somewhat intangible and often overlooked, which weigh heavily as part of the framework within which Negro colleges should be viewed.

There are also negative values which must be brought into the picture. The unique place of black colleges in higher education heightens competition for certain scarce values such as status and power. They experience a kind of devaluation on the part of philanthropies, professional organizations, and economic institutions such as corporations and news media. These look upon white institutions one way and black another. Black colleges also suffer from weak community support, weak trustee support, and teachers who have too much work to do.[1]

What this adds up to is that Negro colleges are more than a segment of higher education. A whole life style is caught up in their being and that life style must not or should not be sacrificed as the nation moves to eliminate racial dualism. Nevertheless, in discussing Negro colleges as they face the future, one must consider realistically the fact that these colleges have entered a new era in American higher education. What should be their role in this new era? Should they endeavor to become institutions serving fully integrated student bodies, racially speaking, and offering the best in liberal and professional education? Or should they continue as predominantly Negro institutions endeavoring to meet particular needs of a "disadvantaged" minority? Either role demands self-evaluation and change in policies and curricula on the part of the colleges involved. Administrators of these colleges cannot escape facing up to these alternatives.

In my own view it is disconcerting to focus attention primarily on integration. Although no one can discount the validity of this concern, it is more important to focus on the fundamental question of "quality education." It does little good to focus on the attention of white students as an index of educational quality in a society where racial prejudice continues as a major force underlying decisions involving human interaction. The most important reason for attracting white students to black colleges is to project the fullest meaning of pluralism in the society, to reduce the prevalence of racial isolation in education and thought, and to educate whites and blacks on the dynamics and full meaning of a multiracial society.

One of the problems involved with the integration question is that integration is usually construed to mean doing away with anything in the society that is Negro. This is particularly the case in the field of education, where elementary and secondary schools attended by black children are easily eliminated regardless of worth and the assumption is that only white institutions can be desegregated. A proper question to be raised is whether a college has to be white to be good and good enough for everybody. Many Negro colleges have never practiced racial discrimination. They have served overwhelmingly a black clientele, but many have never excluded whites. The point is, what is wrong with Negro colleges continuing to be Negro or black colleges? They are going to be just that for a long time to come and perhaps it would not be a bad idea for them to remain Negro colleges through the time. A vital part of this argument is that there is nothing wrong with whites going to Negro colleges, just as Negroes go to white colleges and Gentiles attend Brandeis or Yeshiva and Protestants attend Notre Dame.

Unfortunately, the image held of Negro colleges is part of society's image of the Negro. The assumption is that because they serve in the main a Negro clientele they are necessarily inferior; this, of course, is part of the image of inferiority society holds of Negroes in general. The more important aspect of these institutions is their posture and potential as vital to America's educational resources and accomplishment of the democratic ideal.

In sum, at this point Negro colleges are part of the problem of American education. We could easily be talking about Catholic colleges or the Jewish institutions. All the same, we must accept this difference. Negro colleges have faced in the past, they face at present, and no doubt will face in the future problems conditioned by a societal process entrenched with racial practices and racial overtones that go beyond education in general.

Institutions of higher learning have three basic missions: discovery of new knowledge—research; transfer of knowledge to others—teaching; and application of knowledge—public service.[2] The latter has been a particular function of the land grant college. It is fair to say that Negro colleges have focused primarily on teaching. The other two missions have received only passing attention in most Negro colleges. Notable exceptions are the Howard University Law School with its attention to the field of civil rights and Fisk University and Atlanta University in the social sciences. At any rate, public service has been thrust upon Negroes as a basic mission to accompany teaching. Public service in this respect is defined to mean service to black urban ghettos and rural communities. It is an area where affirmative response by the institution is expected in terms of new curricula and programs. Students expect to experience learning by doing, thus being actively involved in correcting ghetto problems (poverty, community development, racial discrimination, political participation). Negro colleges, in other words, are expected to be involved in solving day-to-day problems of black people as well as preparing youth for service in black communities and for the community at large.

Issues growing out of trends and pressures center primarily upon the future of Negro colleges (as Negro colleges) and education of

Negro youth. The latter involves the question of where Negro youth are to receive an education and how to close the gap between college-going Negro youth in the college age population and white youth. What is to be done to educate the educationally and economically disadvantaged (so-called) youth? The basic issues obviously overlap. It has been the Negro college to which society has looked in the past for education of Negro youth. It is clear, to me at least, that for the foreseeable future society will have to continue to look to the Negro college for this mission. This is particularly true in the South, where most of the Negro colleges are located.

From the standpoint of administration in the Negro colleges, three fundamental *problems* are paramount regarding ability to adapt to new trends, circumstances, demands, and conditions: *resources, organization and control,* and *leadership*. The process of decision-making regarding program rests upon these three problems. It is fair to point out that these problems are not confined to Negro colleges. All of American higher education, and in particular the smaller colleges, are confronted with problems of resources, governance, and leadership and management. But because of the legacy associated with history these problems have particular meanings for Negro colleges.

Two major developments have occurred regarding resources. First, whereas the sixty or so private Negro colleges once had a virtual monopoly on whatever funds went to Negro education from private philanthropy, this is no longer the case. Financially starved public Negro colleges have in recent years, thanks to the Cooperative College Development Program and the Office for Advancement of Public Negro Colleges, effectively competed for financial aid from private corporations, individual donors, and private foundations. At the same time, private philanthropy has assumed a posture that is less concerned with institutional support and more concerned with the education of Negro people, regardless of whether the students are in public or private or white or black institutions. This posture has meant that the limited support given by private philanthropy has to be spread over more institutions. In all probability private funds available for Negro education will shrink even further as the new tax on private foundations is implemented by the federal government.

Second, increase in federal funds for higher education has brought a new source of support for Negro colleges. Negro colleges have by no means shared in the federal dollar for higher education as they should. Of the $4 billion that went to higher education in 1969, Negro colleges, public and private, received $119 million, or 3 per cent. The most significant support came under Title III of the Higher Education Act of 1965, the "Developing Institutions" provision.

The problem with federal funds is that they are project oriented and can be obtained only on an annual basis. Multiyear commitments are rare. (This is also the case with funds from private sources but the restrictions are fewer.) Nonetheless, Negro colleges will have to look to federal funds for major support in the future and as a resource to underwrite growth. As a result there is a kind of external pressure on the colleges that leads to increasingly complex, if not disorderly, administrative relationships both within the institution itself and between the institution and other agencies. This, I would argue, is one of the basic problems administrators of Negro colleges will have to face in the future. It may mean administrative reorganization to manage special projects; it means business office organization for specialized accounting for government funds in meeting the many requests imposed by government. Certainly it means that more careful consideration will have to be given to patterns of growth and the kinds of priorities and emphases assumed by the college or university. Growth can easily result in uncontrolled expenses. Most Negro colleges are not tooled up to meet these kinds of problems. Absence of an effective division of labor along with second and third levels of staff specialization is a primary factor in this regard.

The situation of resources is not likely to improve in the near future. Costs rise; new demands for expanded curricula increase and outstrip income. Management of resources therefore becomes more acute.

Negro colleges, like most colleges, operate under the control of a board of trustees. In public colleges control is often in the hands of regents or boards of regents. Governance as a factor in administration is a tedious affair, often conducted in an old-fashioned manner. Boards of trustees meet infrequently; they are not structured nor do they operate in such manner as to provide direction for administrative leaders to follow and implement. They operate primarily to select the president, approve budgets and new buildings, and receive reports. Review of such things as purpose, aims, and objectives occur spasmodically; seldom are there real challenges by the board to the status quo or to the president and how he perceives and directs affairs of the institution.

Perhaps the most significant recent inquiry into governance of Negro colleges was conducted by Samuel Nabrit and Julius Scott under a grant given by the Ford Foundation.[3] The study was completed in 1969 and involved fifty private Negro colleges. Several findings are important to the administration of Negro colleges.

—The quality of the governing board paralleled the quality of the college and vice versa.

—Churches in control of colleges are gigantic "holding companies." They hold very little of the colleges' "stock" but they hold a disproportionate amount of power. Bishops serve as chancellors at several schools with veto power over decisions of the president. In some such schools the bishop appoints all trustees and exerts one-man control. Presidents change rather frequently at such schools.

—Generally speaking, members of boards of trustees in Negro colleges contribute very little in terms of financial resources.

—Most board members cannot communicate with students. The average age of members of boards of trustees in the fifty schools was found to be sixty-five years. The range was from over forty to about eighty years. Only a small percentage of board members were under fifty years of age.

—In no case was there a design to suggest the kind of people the college would like to have on its board of trustees—that is, in terms of geography, age, professions. When alumni on the board were not reelected or renominated by the alumni, boards of trustees felt it impolite not to reelect that person. Finally, there was no mechanism for getting people off the board once they were put on.

—In several cases colleges had violated their charters by having an excess number of board members.

—It was found that no logical analysis is made regarding contributions of board members to the welfare of the college.

—In terms of race, trustees in the African Methodist Episcopal and African Methodist Episcopal Zion schools were found to be predominantly (as much as 98 per cent) black. In Episcopalian and Presbyterian schools they are predominantly white. One public college, Texas Southern, was mentioned as having a majority of blacks on the board.

—The study found very little relationship between the colleges and local communities in terms of community financial support for the college.

—Generally speaking, the colleges do not have a normal budget process. Budgets are made at the top and handed down. In some cases department heads did not have budgets, and if they did have budgets they often received them well after the fiscal year had begun.

—There were few cases of multiple board membership—that is, a trustee serving on two or more college boards of trustees. This was especially true of Negro members of the boards. The general secretary of church departments of higher education often serves on several, if not all, of the boards of colleges affiliated with his church.

—By and large the boards were characterized as being relatively conservative.

Nabrit reached three basic conclusions after the study. First, that the future of these colleges will depend on whether or not an effective governance structure can be developed, one in which the president properly and officially consummates the aspirations of the college rather than his own, and where the board, meeting with the president, can anticipate and plan strategies rather than having to react to an emergency. Too often boards are reluctant to dampen the enthusiasm of a president when he unrealistically proposes, for example, a $30 million fund-raising program.

Second, Negro colleges have simply not addressed themselves to the roles and functions of various officers in the administrative structure.

Third, boards of governors must look at whether or not they can, for example, support five colleges, three of them unaccredited, or whether they ought to support only two.[4]

This brief summary of findings by Nabrit and Scott serves the purpose of suggesting the key role of management, control, and governance in determining directions in which Negro colleges are going as they face the future. While boards of trustees cannot be expected to provide day-by-day leadership, it is important that administrative leadership operate within the framework of policy and general programs set by the governing boards. One would conclude from the study by Nabrit and Scott that, as currently structured, governing boards of Negro colleges do not function so as to set policy and general programs. Consequently, administrative leadership is pretty much left on its own in setting the directions in which the college goes. If resources are to be increased, inroads to be made in local communities for greater support, and organization and management of the college to be improved, then boards of governance will have to be improved and will have to assume a greater role in determining the direction in which the college is to go.

It can be said, of course, that these findings would apply to most colleges and universities, white as well as black. Thus one should be concerned but not necessarily alarmed over the findings. This type of thinking is fallacious. In the first place, we are talking about a group of colleges that have occupied a specific place in American higher education. We cannot model our thinking in terms of the general problem for all schools. Next, the findings should be given serious consideration by Negro colleges as Negro colleges. Improvement is always in order, regardless of the universe involved.

No doubt absence of structure and failure to function on the part of governing boards in Negro colleges has a great deal to do with problems associated with organization and management in these colleges. There must be an organic relationship between the governing boards and the rest of the college if good college management and organization are to be achieved. This is important to achieving flexibility in educational programs, in patterns and methods, in the budget process, and in organizational structure. It is important to achieving a positive philosophy and practice in decision-making.

Negro college administration is often characterized as being a one-man show—that man being the president of the college. He is often accused of being a strong-armed, sometimes benevolent, dictator who is inflexible when it comes to delegation of authority and sharing decision-making. To the extent that this is factual, it is understandable. With limited financial and manpower resources and limited involvement of the board of governors, the president of the Negro college has had to assume a firm posture; this procedure will have to be modified if the best response to current trends and pressures is to be achieved.

By and large division of labor in Negro college administration is too limited. The consequences are constraints on growth and creativity and limited efficiency. Presidents of Negro colleges are overloaded and overworked. This is one of the least understood problems of the Negro college. Presidents (and administrative officers), in the absence of resources with which to devise a good division of labor, find it necessary to deal with many problems below the level of critical significance. In addition, the president is called upon to provide leadership and serve on numerous local and national committees and boards. The number of Negroes available for voluntary service in community and national endeavors is quite limited. These Negro college presidents get the call all too often and they feel obligated to serve lest Negro representatives be omitted.

I do not accept the argument that Negro college presidents are by and large dictatorial and more so than whites. However, it is a fact that administration is an area where Negro colleges must become more sophisticated. New resources must be found for investment in management of the colleges in both fiscal and business affairs. This is particularly the case with the private college. Likewise, the college must become more sophisticated in the management of curricula and instruction.

As suggested earlier, arguments are advanced by some that Negro colleges should face the future as institutions for remedial and compensatory education, junior colleges, or vocational institutions, or that they should be eliminated entirely. This is an area of extreme importance to administrators of Negro colleges. Obtaining resources necessary to do the job, from private foundations and corporate aid to education programs, is closely tied to decisions regarding the kind of education Negro colleges project for themselves. Likewise, the constantly improving self-image Negroes hold of themselves has implications for current change in Negro colleges.

In general, the role of Negro colleges should not be that of *solely* providing compensatory education. Few educational institutions can expect to survive, let alone meet demands of a future student population, with compensatory education as an orientation and purpose. Moreover, Negro colleges should not be expected to shoulder the costly burden of compensatory education while white institutions go their merry way. Yet Negro colleges need not and should not apologize for serving a clientele unhappily burdened with poor preparation for college work but nonetheless having abilities and potential for success in higher education. Roles in this regard are shaped by historical commitment and these roles should not be abandoned. By the same token, there is no reason to abandon service to that part of a historical clientele or others who are properly prepared for fullest exploitation of higher education. There is no reason to abandon competition for the bright student, just as there is no reason to apologize for serving a historical clientele with a disproportionate number poorly equipped for college. Thus, rather than reject the need for Negro colleges, it is important that they be strengthened to serve better more black youth while simultaneously made more attractive to other students, so that institutional differences will not appear to reflect racial differences but student variations in ability, intellectual interests, and career goals.

In other words, the extent to which Negro colleges leave the periphery of higher education and achieve a balance that leads itself to educational ventures that will function well in a multiracial society will depend upon the extent that these colleges, and appreciation of their roles and contributions, are unmarred by the predominance of their racial composition.

Implications, Imperatives, and Prospects

What has been attempted here is a broad analysis of factors conditioning Negro colleges as they face the future and of the significance of such factors to administrative decision-making in the colleges. There is a fundamental belief that these colleges have a future, but the context within which that future will exist is and will be vastly different from the context within which they developed in the past.

The major inference to be gleaned from the analysis is that those responsible for policy in these colleges must give careful attention to the question of what these colleges are to be as they face the future. I have tried to answer this question in several places. Negro colleges will by and large continue well into the future as Negro colleges. The historic Negro college will have the responsibility for educating a diminishing but significant proportion of black youth enrolled in higher education. A significant proportion of black youth will enroll in newly developed community colleges and junior colleges which will be substantially black because they are located so as to make higher education more accessible to "disadvantaged" youth. Negro colleges will be slow in attracting white students not because of policy or lack of quality but because institutionalized and entrenched racism is a barrier to freedom of movement to white youth.

Response by administrations, including governing boards, to social, economic, and political trends affecting Negro colleges should focus on new options for modifying constraints on Negro colleges. Governing boards will have to be more responsive to demands for new and more relevant curricula. This means Negro colleges will face the problem of curricular development that will prepare black youth for work and service in the black community and simultaneously prepare youth for participation in the larger society. It will be foolish for administrators to assume that the black college should assume a posture of preparing youth for service to the black community only. The needs of the black community are great but the resources necessary to meet these needs are not confined to the black community. Moreover, the masses of Negroes will have to look to the larger community for jobs and income just as whites do. Consequently, it will be necessary for colleges to prepare youth to compete for jobs and income and new opportunities that are increasingly accessible to the black youth.

The major purpose of education is to maximize development and participation in the economic and social process. In a sense every person, black or white, has a right to all the training and education he can absorb. Negro and white institutions of higher education have a responsibility to contribute to this end. Negro colleges must adjust curricular and institutional programs to accelerate achievement among those students who enter college with imbalances in their preparation. I question "open admissions" for Negro colleges as open admissions is currently defined. Negro colleges have always taken students with imbalances in high school preparation for college. College board scores have only recently played a role in admission of students to these colleges. They have always taken students with potential for success in college, largely by virtue of motivation for college work, but with poor educational backgrounds. The open admissions debate is largely academic insofar as a Negro college is concerned.

At the same time these colleges must do more for students with limited preparation for college work. I have observed two things more broadly during my five years at Clark College than I did as chairman dealing with the narrow confines of my department of economics at Fisk University. One is that Negro colleges are effectively serving that part of their constituency with better preparation, but, second, there is serious need to adjust curricula and instruction to accelerate achievement of those with imbalances in preparation. The problem here is acceleration not remediations per se. And I am not talking about acceleration in terms of getting the undergraduate degree earlier. I refer primarily to learning more things better during the period of undergraduate education; I refer to better counseling and guidance to accelerate the student's adjustment to college life and work. This is badly needed. Attrition rates are disproportionately high in Negro colleges. This is particularly so in the private colleges where, on the average, loss is about 60 per cent between the freshman and senior year. This is partly due to finance; a significant part is due to absence of counseling and guidance to aid students in their adjustment to college life and work.

Negro colleges face problems much different from colleges in general. I have attempted to place these problems in some degree of order. As they face the future several imperatives and prospects emerge which should command the attention of administration in these colleges. High priority should be given to careful review of aims, goals, and posture of each college with particular attention to changing social, economic, and political environments within which the colleges operate. Their posture relative to the "all black" and "black" institution deserves special attention. Finding new ways of more effectively relating to problems of black people and the poor is especially important to Negro colleges. Negro institutions should explore their involvement in the entire range of urban problems: the disadvantaged, race relations, education, housing, employment, transportation, taxation, ecology, and political participation. Governing boards will have to be restructured as to age, sex, race, and support by the local community. Church-related colleges will have to rethink the role of the church as an institutional sponsor. How much power should the church (and bishops) have over the institution? A better division of labor in the administration of the schools is necessary. Overworked and overloaded presidents of Negro colleges will have to find ways and means of spreading work and responsibilities and decentralizing authority and responsibility.

Administrators of Negro colleges are in general fully aware of the times in which we live. They recognize the paradoxical nature of societal forces conditioning the future of Negro colleges, their roles and contributions. They are aware of those who question their role in a desegregated society and indeed their right to exist. They are aware of the fact that survival in and of itself is not enough; quality of survival is the critical issue. They are aware of those forces which question the "special" mission of Negro colleges. Moreover, it is not enough to survive; the question is, will these colleges prevail?

The prospects in many ways are good, perhaps better than many realize. As they face the future, however, they must realistically assess changing roles, increased competition from white schools for student and faculty, and tighter squeeze on resources.

REFERENCES

1. See remarks by C. Eric Lincoln in Proceedings of the Conference on Negro Colleges, March 6-7, 1969, American Academy of Arts and Sciences, Boston, Massachusetts.

2. James A. Perkins, *The University in Transition* (Princeton: Princeton University Press, 1966).

3. Samuel Nabrit and Julius Scott, Jr., *Inventory of Academic Leadership* (Atlanta: The Southern Fellowship Fund, 1970).

4. Proceedings of the Conference on Negro Colleges.

WILLIAM J. TRENT, JR.

The Future Role of the Negro College and Its Financing

THE NEGRO colleges were born in crisis. They have existed on the edge of poverty since their beginning. Periodically, the question is raised as to whether they have any future. It was seriously raised in 1925 by Thomas Jesse Jones, eminent educator, in a pioneering study for the federal government. It was raised again in 1943 by Ambrose Caliver, the then specialist on Negro education in the Office of Education, Department of the Interior. In that year he published a comprehensive study of the private Negro colleges that came to this conclusion:

> The data presented . . . lead to the obvious conclusion that most of the institutions included in the present study are in serious need of increased revenue; and even those institutions which appear statistically to have adequate resources need increased funds in order to effect improvements in their respective programs. The income of some of the institutions in question is so meager that there is serious question whether they should attempt to continue to operate their present programs without a decided increase in revenue.

Just recently, there has been quite a controversy in professional educational circles as a result of an article on the Negro educational institutions by two Harvard professors who have become authorities on Negro education. In this essay I will not be discussing the question of whether Negro colleges have a future. Rather, an attempt will be made to answer the question: What kind of future will these institutions have in the scheme of things?

Before proceeding, it will be useful to define the terms used to designate these institutions. Prior to the 1954 Supreme Court decision, there were legally "Negro colleges" and "white colleges." After 1954, the terms "predominantly Negro colleges" and "predominantly white colleges" were current. Nowadays, the terms "historically Negro" or "traditionally Negro" are used. And, finally, there are those who refer to the variously defined Negro colleges as "black colleges." I propose to use "Negro" or "white" as the short reference to these colleges, well aware of the fact that the terms are not precise; to use the newer terminology is just too cumbersome. One additional point of clarification. People generally discuss Negro colleges as if they were all alike, with a common fate. This is nonsense. Negro colleges are located along a spectrum of quality ranging from excellent to poor, just as are other institutions. Further, what will happen to these Negro colleges will cover a broad spectrum of possibilities.

Although some of the factors that created the present crisis are of long standing, three new developments since 1954 have had great influence. They are: the new options available to Negro students created by the Supreme Court decision, the recent growth of community colleges, and federal aid to education. Although the initial emphasis of the Supreme Court decision was on public education at the elementary and secondary level, nevertheless, as the years passed there were increasing pressures on the white colleges to admit Negro students. This presented new opportunities. In addition, the rapid growth of two-year community colleges made it possible for many students to go to college and live at home. Large numbers of Negro students are availing themselves of this opportunity. Let's add another influence. If James Coleman is correct in his assumption that Negro children tend to progress faster in desegregated schools, and if the movement toward desegregation in primary and secondary education continues, it means that the Negro high school graduate will be better qualified and will have more real options. His grades and scores will rank high enough so that he can be admitted to white colleges in the region. He can no longer be refused entrance because his scores are below the cut-off point.

Finally, there has been a massive increase in federal funds for higher education over the past two decades. Even though their distribution has been skewed heavily in the direction of the white colleges, these funds have had an impact across the board. The new options and federal financing have greatly affected the role of the Negro college in the South. James W. Bryant, program adviser for the Ford Foundation, recently developed some data on enrollment trends based on information from the U.S. Department of Labor Statistics, the Office of Health, Education and Welfare. He says:

Enrollment statistics for the current year (1969-1970) indicate that Negroes attending post high school institutions (colleges, community colleges, junior colleges) have moved from 434,000 in 1968-1969 to 465,000 in 1969-1970—an increase of 7%. Of this number, 162,000 or 32.84% are in the predominantly Negro colleges—107,000 or 23.01% in public colleges—and 55,000 or 11.83% in the private colleges. Over 65% of all Negro college students are enrolled in predominantly white colleges.*

Twenty years ago, probably 90 per cent of Negroes in college were in Negro colleges. They were fairly evenly divided between the public and the private Negro college. Today, according to these figures, only 35 per cent of Negro students are in Negro colleges—and the percentage is going down. Given the task that they presently have, the question naturally arises: How are the Negro colleges faring financially?

Present Financial Status

In common with all educational institutions, the Negro colleges have serious financial problems. This is especially true of the private Negro colleges. Figures available for 1968-1969 indicate that thirty-one of these colleges had deficits totaling seven and a half million dollars.[1] Recently, special efforts have been made to cope with rising costs by developing new sources of funds and new methods of securing traditional monies. Tuition and fees have been raised regularly and precipitously.

The thirty-five public Negro colleges mounted their offensive on three major fronts—the legislature, the private sector, and the alumni. Graphic and persuasive data on needs have been developed annually by the boards of these institutions in their pleas to the legislature. The public Negro colleges had, over the years, looked longingly in the direction of the private colleges and their fund-raising arm, the United Negro College Fund. They felt that they, too, deserved support from the private sector. The public colleges also organized a special effort seeking private support. This is the Office for the Development of Public Colleges, which is located in

* There are, however, some serious differences in statistics on Negro enrollment in colleges. James Bryant uses an enrollment figure of 434,000 for 1968 fall enrollment. The Research Department of the National Urban League, using data from the Department of Health, Education and Welfare, comes up with a figure of 287,000. Bryant claims that 64 per cent of Negro students are enrolled in other than Negro colleges, while Robert Johnson of the Urban League comes up with 53 per cent. Both, however, show the same trend.

Atlanta, Georgia. It seeks ways and means of securing support from foundations, corporations, and individuals.

The private Negro colleges were in worse condition. They had raised tuition as much as they could without losing too many students. Endowment income was relatively unimportant, except in one or two cases. Leaving aside for the moment the question of federal funds, there were two other major sources of funds—income from the private sector and annually recurring grants from supporting church boards. In both of these areas there has been some ferment within the last decade or so.

Let us first look at the support from church boards. With possibly one or two exceptions, support from churches has been, and continues to be, inadequate. Within the past few years, however, some denominations have attempted to develop imaginative ideas in the area of fund raising. The Methodist church is in the midst of a campaign to raise supplementary funds for its institutions. The Episcopal church, a few years ago, gave some thought to the possibility of carrying on a continuous campaign for its three Negro institutions. Some discussions are going on in the Presbyterian church. The African Methodist Episcopal church talked bravely about their new efforts a few years ago. But nothing happened.

Some new developments have been taking place in the private sector, also. In addition to a sizable increase in the national goals of the United Negro College Fund, some of the private colleges have been developing new programs in two areas—seeking more money through new organizations and developing cooperative services, thereby reducing costs. The newest development in the fund-raising field is the annual local sustentation campaign. The outstanding example of this local support is the annual campaign for Bishop College in Dallas, Texas. In addition, a group of Negro colleges in a state have joined together to find money from individuals, corporations, and foundations in the state. Texas, South Carolina, Georgia, and Virginia are some of the states where these associations of colleges are functioning.

Since budgets can be balanced either by increasing revenue or lowering costs, a few of the private colleges are involved in finding out how to do things together at less cost. A new organization in this field is the United Board for College Development, sponsored by the National Council of Churches. It is involved in exploring possible areas of cooperation among colleges. One of its first projects was cooperative purchasing and accessioning of books for several college libraries. The Alfred Sloan Foundation has been financing still another venture—the Cooperative College Development Program. This organization helps colleges select and train development and fund-raising officers. It also provides professional fund-raising counsel. There are other similar organizations in both these areas.

The colleges have also taken some steps to improve their situation in the public sector. Although there have been dramatic increases in federal funds available for higher education, relatively small amounts have gone to Negro institutions. In order to overcome some of the special problems confronting Negro colleges in their efforts to secure federal funds, two offices have been established in Washington. One of these organizations is known as the National Association for Equal Opportunity in Higher Education. It is a loosely knit organization of presidents of approximately eighty-eight Negro colleges. This group makes a strong and concerted presentation to the administration about the inequities in the allocation of federal funds. On one occasion, representatives of the presidents met with President Nixon to discuss their plight. As a result, there is some evidence that a mandate has gone down to the various departments requesting that they channel more funds to these institutions. The other organization is the College Service Bureau, which is jointly sponsored by the United Negro College Fund and the Phelps-Stokes Fund. Its primary function is to provide information and service to a group of public and private Negro colleges on the availability of federal funds for various educational purposes. In some instances, the Bureau actually gets involved in helping an institution prepare a proposal or request for funds. These two organizations complement one another. The spokesmen call vigorous attention, at the appropriate level, to the plight of the colleges, and the Bureau gets involved in the actual implementation. All of these efforts to strengthen old sources of support and discover new sources of revenue have done little more than postpone the day of reckoning. Costs have gone through the ceiling and income has lagged behind.

Financial Trends

What of the future? At this point, since we will be discussing the future of these institutions and how they will be financed, it would be proper to define the limits of the problem. This essay will treat the historical Negro colleges, which, with few exceptions, are located in the South. They are four-year institutions only—both accredited and unaccredited. A qualification needs to be set forth. Anything that anybody says today about financing the future of the Negro colleges will be drastically affected by political decisions that will be made about aid to education by the federal government. We can analyze the other sources of income and make some guesses as to how they will develop with some degree of certainty. Federal funds are subject to wide variations, depending on the strength and power of the education lobby and the political decisions of the legislature and the executive. As if the factors affecting the decisions about public funds were not complex enough, there are a number of legal tests on the way up to the Supreme Court which will in the near future force a decision on the legality of using public funds to support church-related institutions. Given the demand for higher education on the part of more and more Negro students, how will colleges find funds to meet the need?

Professor Seymour Harris makes some general observations on the trend in growth of sources of support for higher education in the paper he prepared for the Joint Committee Report on the "Economics of Financing Higher Education in the United States."[2] He expects that tuition income will continue to go up, that other private funds will grow, but not nearly as fast as tuition income, that state and local funds, while growing, will grow at a lower rate, and that endowment income will be of major importance only to those institutions already heavily endowed. Obviously, he expects significant increase in federal income. What about the Negro colleges? Let us review the traditional sources of funds.

Tuition and fees. An increase here is severely limited by the economic condition of the Negro family. The private Negro college will suffer severely if tuition charges are increased much more. How much they can, in fact, be increased depends entirely upon the availability of federal funds, and how these funds are made available. The state colleges are tied into a statewide system of charges, and decisions to change these charges will be on a general rather than a racial basis.

State tax funds. Legislatures of the southern states where the public Negro colleges are located will wipe out all racial differentials in the availability of operating and support funds. This will come sooner or later in various states, depending on political decisions that will evolve from increased political sophistication and participation on the part of Negro citizens. This may come, also, as a result of legal action. Just recently in North Carolina, a suit was filed against the state for dual standards of admission, curriculum, and support. Once this corrective action is taken, public Negro colleges will be affected by the same factors that affect the financing of higher education generally. There will still be problems. Competing demands for tax revenue, plus recent student and faculty activities on campus, have tended to dampen somewhat the ardor of legislators and taxpayers for greater funds for higher education.

Annually recurring church grants. Historically, because of miniscule endowments and tuition charges deliberately kept at a low level, the private church-related colleges depended on support from denominations. As a generalization, such support ranged from a "fair" level of support to inconsequential support. There has been some improvement. I expect that there will be more in certain institutions, but the increase will be not at all in keeping with increasing costs. To expect the governing bodies of churches to allocate a larger portion of declining income to education of Negroes is unrealistic. There will be no major increase in church support. What increase there is will be concentrated in a very few colleges supported by certain denominations.

Other private funds: Under this heading I lump the following: alumni, other individuals, and foundations. In this area it is important to make another kind of distinction between public Negro colleges and private Negro colleges. While there has been some increase in private support for public institutions, it is still a tenet of faith that private institutions have the higher priority, since public institutions have tax funds as their basic resource. I do not see any major increase in private funds for public colleges.

The United Negro College Fund. The Fund in its latest campaign (1969) raised a total of $6,875,000 for its thirty-six member colleges. The trend in giving to the Fund has moved up sharply within the past several years. Any estimate as to the ability of the Fund to raise increasingly more money from the private sector must take into account three important factors: the public's attitude toward supporting Negro education through private Negro colleges; the Fund itself, its philosophy, structure, and organization; and the member colleges. All of these factors will be working within a framework of a decline in the proportion of Negro students who will be enrolling in private Negro colleges. The public's attitude will be determined by many factors: race relations, the economy, the type of leadership, and—most important of all—the answer to the question why these institutions should be supported. For the present and near future, the public will support the United Negro College Fund. Education is noncontroversial; it helps prepare Negroes for newer and greater opportunities; it is seen as a way out of our conflicts.

The Fund itself is another matter. It may well be that the Fund has come to the place where, if it is to continue successful in raising money, it must accept more and more responsibility for the quality of education at its member colleges. This is a ticklish business. Nevertheless, it may be necessary for the colleges to relinquish some of their autonomy. The Fund must broaden its educational activities if it is to continue to be successful.

And, finally, what the private Negro college proposes to do by way of educating Negro youth is of grave importance. If the institutions are not unique in some special way that sets them apart from public institutions, what is their reason for existing? In many instances, there are certain unique institutional qualities. In other cases, the educational philosophy, curriculum, and so on can hardly be differentiated from that of the public institution. These colleges have a grave responsibility to examine their special reasons for being, and to exploit the things that they do best.

Because of the variables, it is difficult to make a good hard forecast about support of the private colleges through the United Negro College Fund. The Fund will grow, but whether it will maintain or improve its position relative to the increase in costs is a serious question.

Alumni—individual. Until very recently, the colleges did little to cultivate alumni support. It was not really until the advent of the United Negro College Fund that any serious efforts were made to secure this support, even indirectly. As a consequence of this activity, direct alumni support has grown. It is my guess that this support will probably increase, but will continue to provide an infinitesimal part of the support needed.

Corporate support. The Negro colleges have been the stepchildren of corporate support of higher education. According to the Council for Financial Aid to Education, corporate support of education reached $300,000,000. Although a few Negro colleges receive some direct gifts from corporations, most corporate support for these colleges comes through the United Negro College Fund. At the maximum, this support in 1969 was approximately $4,000,-

000. Any increase in direct corporate support will come from corporations located in the cities or states where local sustentation campaigns are carried on. The conclusion: some increased support, but not significant. The Negro colleges will continue to be the stepchildren of corporate support.

Foundations. Philanthropic foundations played a major role over the years in the support of Negro colleges. The giant in the early years was the General Education Board, a Rockefeller financed foundation. By making judicious grants in selected areas, by supporting a particular institution, by financing faculty training, by financing mergers and cooperative enterprises, foundations have done a much needed job. In the recent past, the most significant grants to Negro colleges have come from the Ford Foundation. Across the board, many grants were made to help improve the quality of some parts of the educational programs of a number of institutions. There were other foundations, also. All of this is changing. I fear that, because the trend in enrollment of Negro youth is increasingly in the direction of the white colleges, the major foundations will reduce their aid to Negro colleges. Foundations will probably make their contributions in this area in three ways: (1) a few Negro institutions will probably be given massive support; (2) scholarship funds will be made available to Negro students enrolled in other than Negro colleges; (3) a limited number of ethnic studies centers will be financed. As a result of this emphasis, the average Negro college cannot expect any significant direct foundation support in the foreseeable future. Foundation support of the United Negro College Fund will continue.

Individuals. A feature of the recent past with respect to financing Negro colleges has been the development of annual sustentation campaigns, either on a local or state basis. This venture is too new to evaluate. Further, there is a basic uncertainty that will affect these efforts. During these times, the Negro colleges, as other colleges, are in ferment, and militancy is growing on campus. Given the present polarization between Negro and white, and between campus and town, it is reasonable to conclude that there will be difficulty from time to time in launching campaigns for the local Negro colleges. In a very dramatic way, this has already happened in a college community. A Negro college decided to mount a capital funds campaign in its community. The structure was set, the leadership chosen, and so forth. Then suddenly there was a violent racial conflict. The campaign was one of the casualties. I do not expect these local campaigns among individuals and businesses to produce much money under the circumstances.

Endowment income. This source of support can be dismissed with a few brief remarks. All thirty-six of the private colleges in the United Negro College Fund together have endowment funds totaling $76,250,000. But the situation is even worse. Five of the colleges hold 62 per cent of these funds. The income is of minor importance to most of the colleges, and practically no new endowment funds are being made available. As a result, the share of the colleges' budgets financed by endowment income will continue to decline.

In summary, income from tuition and fees will go up, but the limit of this increase is set by the rigidity of the facts of economic life. Beyond that point, the private colleges will continue to price themselves out of the market. There will be some modest increase in church support, but this will not be across the board. Some denominations will do better than others. For the state colleges, increased tax funds will be hard to come by. This will vary from state to state, depending on the economic wealth of the state. Except through the United Negro College Fund, I do not see any significant increase in corporate support. The Fund will grow at a constant rate of increase over the next decade. Endowment income will be of even less consequence. Support through local annual campaigns is hard to determine. It is fair to say, however, that because of racial and community strains, this type of support will vary substantially over the years.

This adds up to a modest increase in funds available, but far wide of the mark of keeping up with costs. A large number of private institutions will be incurring operating deficits, and will be forced to revise the quality of their programs, or radically modify their purpose and scope. The state schools are usually required to live within their budgets. If this is generally true, there may be some curtailment of these programs. This estimate can, of course, be drastically affected by federal funds and how they are made available. If the federal government will develop an aid program which includes fellowships, loan funds, work-study funds, and cost of education supplements, directed to and managed by the colleges, the situation will improve greatly. If, however, the aid is student oriented rather than institution oriented, the Negro college will be in trouble. Given these best guesses about the sources of support, what meaning does this have for the future role of these institutions?

The Future of the Colleges

When one discusses the future of institutions that have, over the years, made such stupendous contributions to the growth and welfare and development of a people and a nation, there is always a tendency to color the future by the past, and to hold that the role will not be significantly different or less. Against this tendency are three important facts.

(1) The Negro colleges will in the foreseeable future provide post high school education to a smaller and smaller proportion of Negro students. Given the increased number of Negroes seeking a college education, this does not necessarily mean that there will be an absolute decrease in numbers for a while. But in the long run, there will be a decline in numbers. Further, the proportion of Negro students educated in the private Negro college will continue to be smaller than in the public college.

(2) The proportion of Negro students enrolled in post high school municipal two-year colleges will grow at a rapid rate.

(3) Cost will continue to outpace resources available to pay these costs. The nature and shape of federal financing will determine how long certain marginal institutions can continue to exist as viable educational institutions. This is deliberately put because there is a good possibility that some of the institutions—probably church related—will continue to exist after they have ceased to be viable educational institutions. There are some examples of this today.

Let us look at some of the possible developments in the public institutions. An important factor in their future will be determined by certain political decisions. If these institutions are located in states where opposition to desegregation is still powerful, significant amounts of money will be available to improve the quality of the Negro state schools, thus keeping pressure off the white institutions. This attitude coupled with the desire on the part of some Negroes to have "their own institution" will insure the existence of almost completely Negro state institutions for some time to come. In other states there will be other developments. Pressure, both political and legal, may be brought to bear to wipe out the differentials in per student costs. Under these circumstances, there may be a tendency to consolidate certain special schools or divisions. Thus, the Department of Agriculture at a Negro college may be merged with its white counterpart on the white campus. The decision of students as to what public institutions they wish to attend, plus a decision by the legislature, may well limit the size and growth of the Negro institutions in certain states. I do not, however, expect to see any of the public Negro institutions closed. In fact, in certain areas there is a good possibility that these institutions will enroll a significant number of white students. We may have more situations like West Virginia State College, which was totally Negro some years ago and which is now predominantly white.

The prognostications with respect to the private Negro colleges are more difficult because of the variety of the institutions as to program, financial support, affiliation, location, and so forth. But there are some broad general statements that can be made. There are some private unaccredited colleges. These institutions have not, over the years, been able to attract sufficient revenue to meet the minimum standards. They should close their doors, and some of them probably will if the decision to do so is based on education. Again, I worry about ecclesiastical decisions.

Here is how the picture looks with respect to private Negro colleges which are accredited.

(1) Several of the private colleges have a broader base of support than the others. They will remain in existence, but will have to give serious thought to limiting their curricula.

(2) Some of the private colleges are poorly located. Those that are located in small southern rural communities will find it harder and harder to attract the kind of student they want. In the long run, some of these will fall by the wayside.

(3) Some colleges that would otherwise have serious difficulty surviving, will make it by entering into cooperative relationships with nearby institutions. Where two or more institutions are in one general locality, contractual and other arrangements will be made, thus eliminating needless duplication. In certain special cases, the question of merger should be seriously considered. Here, again, I am afraid that the decision will be an ecclesiastical one rather than an educational one.

(4) There are at present several centers of educational groupings among Negro colleges. There is a strong possibility that these institutions will find significant support from major foundations and state governments.

(5) Some colleges should seriously consider becoming junior colleges. They may just have the level of support for two years.

(6) There are a few colleges that should be closed.

(7) Attempts will be made at several institutions to have them

become "black universities" or "black colleges." If by this is meant all Negro faculty, all Negro students, a specialized curriculum concentrating on black studies, or black image, or whatever, the problem of support will be critical. Federal and state support will not be available. In view of pressures to keep the white academies outside the pale (where they should be), the black institutions must of necessity find themselves unable to qualify for tax exemption certification, and will thereby lose foundation and corporate support. Of course, there is always the possibility that enough support could be found from a sufficiently large number of Negro donors who would not be interested in the tax exemption. I am not sanguine about this as a real alternative.

(8) Increasing numbers of students will be seeking a college education. If any facilities are closed for lack of financial support, then, to meet the demand, the states would have to provide the facilities. This can be done either by expanding existing institutions or building new colleges. Obviously, it would be cheaper to take over an existing private facility. This will happen in a few instances.

All prognostications with respect to the future role, particularly of the private Negro college, have been couched in language which employs the terms "ought" and "should." Whether these guesses do, in fact, come true, depends on a complex of factors. If decisions are made on the basis of sound educational philosophy and practice, these changes are likely to take place. If racial pride and reverence for past achievement are the determining factors, a goodly number of institutions that might be radically altered or closed up will probably remain open rendering poor educational service. If the decision to do or not to do is ecclesiastical, it can be safely predicted that some church colleges which should be closed will remain open.

All of these projections are subject to the scope and extent of federal aid for higher education. If the federal government adopts the recommendations of the Special Report of the Carnegie Commission on Higher Education, the historical Negro college will improve the quality of its educational program. One thing, however, that federal funds will not do—they will not significantly modify the trend in enrollment of Negro students in Negro colleges.

References

1. These data are taken from the audits of member colleges of the United Negro College Fund.
2. Hearings of the Joint Committee on Education, 1969.

S. M. NABRIT

Reflections on the Future of Black Colleges

Private Negro Colleges

THE DIFFERENTIAL between white and Negro family incomes is approximately $3,300 a year; the difference between tuition, room, and board costs in the prestigious white colleges and those in most black colleges comes to about $2,000 per year. So long as these differences persist, Negroes will not find an alternative to the black colleges even were they to seek it.

* * *

It is the very real economic differential that makes the black colleges less competitive in quality; they are obliged to match their costs with the ability of black students to pay. Even with very low tuition and other fees, the black colleges are obliged to provide some financial assistance to approximately 50 per cent of their student bodies.

* * *

The majority of American college students are drawn from families with incomes above $7,000; at black colleges, the preponderant number come from families with incomes below that level.

* * *

If the Negro private colleges had received one-eighteenth of the 1.8 billion dollars in gifts and grants to higher education from private sources in 1969-1970, they would have received 100 million dollars. They, in fact, received approximately 15 million dollars. There was no exception to the rule that where the Negro in America is concerned, it is assumed that he deserves less and receives less. No serious funding for these institutions has ever been contemplated by the boards of education of the several religious denominations, the philanthropic foundations, or the federal government. The accumulated wealth of the Negro in America is such that he cannot sustain these institutions with his own contributions alone. This economic condition will continue for at least another generation.

* * *

Most institutions are currently experiencing operating deficits or are siphoning off from their endowments in order to balance their budgets. Few are hard-nosed enough to curtail programs and make budgetary cuts in order to live within their income.

* * *

The Negro colleges received grants to supplement salaries seven to eight years ago. These grants expire in 1973-1974 and endowment increases or new grants have not been made to sustain these better salaries. In an inflationary economy, with white institutions actively recruiting black professors, no Negro college is in a position to cut salaries today.

* * *

The black colleges are in a vise that is being tightened by several pressures: (1) The social change brought on by integration that drains them of some of their better students, both academically and economically. (2) The pressure of federal agencies to accelerate what appears to be a one-way integration, namely, integration of white institutions by blacks. (3) The decrease in gifts and grants by liberals who honestly feel that in order to expedite integration anything currently operated by blacks ought to be abolished. The liberal who perceives everything in terms of white norms and values may be the worst enemy of the Negro institutions. (4) The turmoil created by black separatists, who are disillusioned and frustrated and who would give up all the integrationist gains of the sixties for a less competitive, separate arena, increasing the pressure constantly being exerted by the die-hard segregationists. (5) The strain on operating costs caused by efforts to retain top personnel who are finding new opportunities elsewhere.

* * *

Only one of the black colleges is generously endowed. Some five others have an endowment cushion which supports an enrollment of one thousand students. If black colleges feel it necessary to increase enrollments in order to achieve economy of size and diversity of curriculum, it will be necessary not only to increase tuition but also to increase basic endowment income and/or stable gift support as well.

Many colleges try to eliminate small classes; they do not understand the principles of economy of size and are bewildered by the requirements of larger enrollments. Unless selective admissions are made which concentrate majors in each field in small classes and effectively make use of the faculty already employed, enrollment increases may only increase the requirement for additional faculty in the more generalized areas.

* * *

The colleges have been further misled by the ease with which funds could be borrowed from the government for self-liquidating auxiliary enterprises; only later did they discover the difficulty of obtaining matching funds to expand the academic facilities required. They have not carefully projected their future enrollments and are leaving out of the equation the changing habits of students with respect to dormitory life and parietal regulations.

* * *

The enrollment in black colleges is affected by the amount of integration achieved in white colleges (see table). One statistic released in 1969 suggested that black freshman enrollment in private colleges had risen to 15.2 per cent. This statistic suggested that more Negroes had entered white private colleges in 1969 than had in fact done so. Howard University, with 9,000 students, had been reclassified private, though it is almost wholly publicly supported. When Howard was classified public, the percentage of Negro fresh-

Enrollment by Types of Institutions in Southern Regional Education Board States, Fall 1968

	Total enrollment	Negro enrollment	Negro as a per cent of total
Predominantly white public senior	750,230	16,833	2.2
Traditionally Negro public senior	75,633	74,376	98.3
Predominantly white private	264,657	5,373	2.0
Traditionally Negro private	44,624	44,196	97.7
Public junior colleges	262,571	21,715	8.3
Totals	1,397,715	162,493	11.6

SOURCE: J. S. Anzalone and Barbara Sherry, "Black Student Enrollment in Higher Education," Southern Regional Education Board, p. 3. The states included are: Alabama, Arkansas, Florida, Georgia, Kentucky, Louisiana, Maryland, Mississippi, North Carolina, South Carolina, Tennessee, Texas, Virginia, and West Virginia.

man enrollment in private colleges was reduced to 3.5 to 4 per cent. In *College and University Bulletin* (1971), published by the American Association of Higher Education, it was reported that of the 1970-1971 black freshmen who scored highest on admission tests, 10,000 enrolled in black colleges and 2,000 enrolled in white colleges.

* * *

Within a four-year period, 1964-1968, according to U.S. census figures the enrollment of Negroes in colleges increased 85 per cent. Still, 78 per cent of the baccalaureate degrees awarded Negroes in 1968-1969 came from black colleges.

* * *

If Peter Muirhead's figures* are correct—that 90 per cent of the disadvantaged youth who enroll in junior colleges become dropouts—and since junior colleges have received the great increases in black enrollments in recent times, and have either eliminated most of these students or shunted them into terminal tracks, one wonders about the true significance of these figures in respect to where Negroes will be educated in the future.

* * *

The Negro colleges have not merely provided talent for a limited region of America. Demographers have recently pointed out that among migrant black males in the greater Boston area, there is a higher percentage of college graduates than the total percentage of college-educated persons in the indigenous population. These migrant Negroes were largely educated in Negro colleges.

* * *

When Clark Kerr appeared before the House of Representatives Special Subcommittee on Education, chaired by Representative Edith Green, he was asked by her if it was possible to devise a "need test" for institutions seeking more funds. Kerr replied that such a test would be difficult to develop because some small colleges facing bankruptcy are too small to be effective and too small to be attractive to students who want a large range of courses and other features found only at larger institutions. Was this an inadvertent or a deliberate kiss of death to the small colleges' quest for federal assistance?

* Muirhead made his statement to junior college executives who sought an increase in their allocation of Title III funds.

There are many alternatives that can mitigate the circumstance of size:

1. Small colleges may move into larger population centers, as Bishop did when it left Marshall, Texas, for Dallas.

2. Neighboring small colleges may specialize, emphasizing quality rather than quantity.

3. Neighbors are in a position to exchange students and/or teachers as St. Augustine's, Shaw, and Meredith are presently doing.

4. Small colleges can use the resources of large neighboring public or private universities, as St. Augustine's and Shaw do with North Carolina State and Knoxville College does with the University of Tennessee.

5. Students may exchange with students from distant institutions for a semester or a year, as Texas Southern and the University of Wisconsin have done.

6. Research participation between large and small colleges with computer related libraries is another possibility.

7. Faculties from distant institutions may serve as visiting teachers on campuses of small colleges, as Brown does at Tougaloo.

8. Television network satellite or direct cable connections can be effective for groups of small colleges, such as the University of Texas Center.

9. Electives can be offered in alternate years in order to increase the range of choice.

* * *

If training and experience mean anything, the four-year college is superior to the junior college, with its lower qualifications for teachers, and to the universities, where much of the freshman and sophomore studies are conducted by inexperienced graduate students.

* * *

Private education at the elementary and secondary levels was largely phased out as public education became available and improved in quality. Obviously, some higher education will have the same experience. Albany State, Fort Valley State, Jackson State, Morgan State, Maryland State, and North Carolina Central State were once private, church-related Negro colleges. The University of Houston and the University of Chattanooga are examples of white private institutions that turned public in recent years. Lincoln University of Pennsylvania is endeavoring to become one of the state-supported colleges, after having been a Presbyterian Negro college and thereafter an independent college and a state-assisted college. There is a long precedent for private Negro colleges changing to become state colleges.

* * *

The Negro colleges have been practically the sole source of higher educational opportunities for Negroes for most of a century. They have also been the birthplaces of significant liberation movements: W. E. B. Du Bois, the Niagara Movement, the NAACP; the legal battles leading to the 1954 court decision in school cases; and the student sit-ins of the mid-sixties. These institutions, in addition, have been history-in-the-making for the Negro and remain his cultural reservoirs. They have taught him that he is somebody, which is antithetical to the teachings of his outside social environment. These institutions have provided role models for raising his aspirations. From these institutions communication was established with the controllers of power in our country. Booker T. Washington, R. R. Moton, John Hope, Emmett Scott, Mordecai Johnson, James Shepherd, and William Hale are examples of Negro college leaders who effectively indicated what the Negro thought and what his wants and aspirations were. The loss of these institutions may cut this line of communication, so unlike the political patronage system, which employs people to give only the advice that is desired.

* * *

That "something of value" which we talk about as black experience, relevancy, racial aspiration, and solidarity will be lost to Negroes if these institutions pass without replacement with new kinds of institutions able to conserve the threatened values. If the present black colleges are not able to survive for economic reasons, less competent and more vocal institutions will arise in their stead. Some type of archive for black experience will exist.

* * *

No one denies that the current attainments of the Negro in America are largely due to his institutions of higher education. The real question is whether the genuine satisfaction that they have found in institutions manned by blacks will be experienced by Negroes in the white institutions that now accept them. It is doubtful, too, that any predominantly white institution will address itself to ghetto concerns in the same way that urban Negro colleges could if they were adequately funded for this purpose and oriented toward this goal. Obviously, collective white experience is of a different order, and especially is that true of the white power structure. For many years, the effective teaching of the disadvantaged in the inner city must be done by Negro teachers. This will be true even if immediate integration takes place. Some institutions must also relate to the continuing education of these teachers. It is unrealistic to expect this from white colleges with different priorities.

* * *

There are certain economic factors crucial to the existence and survival of any college. A small college with a special commitment to train leaders for a particular religious denomination either has to be fully funded by the denomination at a breakeven level or it must admit students whose goals and objectives may differ radically from those of the college so that fees plus gifts or grants can balance out the costs and provide a suitable number of curricular options. This is the plight of many small colleges, and most of the private Negro colleges are in this category.

* * *

The African Methodist Episcopal Church is the only Negro group that endeavors to support several colleges. Only two of their six are regionally accredited, and these two receive generous supplemental support from their white communities. But these colleges are assured of survival to a larger degree than the more prestigious colleges for blacks because black Methodists are determined to keep them alive.

* * *

If a church must limit the amount to be given, it can be more effectively used if it is concentrated in a single college or a small number of institutions. The contribution from the churches is not so much related to the affluence of the denomination as to the order of its priorities and the extent of its educational commitment. Some churches feel that they have performed their educational mission for Freedmen; they would like to shift the responsibility for support to others. Recently, under the pressure of black militancy within the church groups, there has been a much greater response for support of education than in periods when support was considered merely a Christian duty rather than a response to a call for reparations.

The Episcopal church and the United Presbyterians announced a phasing out of direct support for their black colleges (each has three) over a three-year period. This is evidence of the fact that the churches are not willing to support indefinitely black higher education. During the one hundred years of direct support, their financial contributions in relation to operating costs have decreased. Neither church has provided endowments sufficient to offset its annual contribution. Neither has operated the colleges under boards of trustees with experience in fund-raising. Each set of colleges would have suffered if the contemplated action had been consummated. The militancy among their respective black clergy was the chief reason for postponement of this action. Like so many other decisions about higher education, the decision was political rather than one based on educational merit.

* * *

The costs of operating church-related colleges have increased far more rapidly than have the contributions of the churches. This makes the churches' control of these colleges like that of a holding company with a small investment in their operations.

* * *

Viewed in economic terms, it will be difficult to maintain all of the existing private Negro colleges in the future. Their problems will be more exaggerated than those of the white small college because black small colleges are dependent upon white organizations for funding. Integration was the escape mechanism sought by these white organizations for elimination of this responsibility. The church and foundations alike have supported Negro causes after providing for their own. Militant calls for reparations will not change the order of priorities permanently.

* * *

Some of these institutions will and should close. Some should merge to form more viable units. Churches will be forced to examine closely their ability to support multiple institutions. Most of these institutions have been integrated even though student resentment is causing some of them to reassess their commitments to integration. Some will gain state assistance and survive. A few will lower their aspirations and become junior colleges and preparatory schools. Many of them are capable of competing in the market for paying students and available philanthropy, and they will continue to flourish.

Public Negro Colleges

It is far more difficult to predict the fate of the public Negro colleges. A unitary system of completely integrated colleges with freedom of movement in administration, faculty, and student body is the Negro's goal as much as it is the ideal for the country. Most Negroes would have cheerfully abandoned their advantaged positions in the segregated college to obtain equal opportunities in a new kind of America. Unfortunately, the Negro has become disillusioned with the pace at which America will transform itself. He does not believe that the national commitment exists to expedite this behavioral change. He is now trying to salvage some of his gains while preventing the elimination of those institutions which have given him managerial training and experience. The Negro has heard people talk about phasing out the black public colleges but has never heard plans for merging them with white public colleges. The difference, of course, means that in phasing out there is a loss of tenure, employment, and leadership. He wonders if it is worth that to attend an integrated college as an outsider to the making of all decisions.

* * *

Nine of the southern states have been directed to eliminate their dual systems in higher education. It is up to the several states to present acceptable plans for accomplishing this. North Carolina has, on the surface, put all its colleges in a common system with each college responsible for higher education in its geographic area. The difficulty arises in that some areas will have only colleges, while others will have graduate schools. Another complication arises when a Negro school and a branch of the university exist in the same geographic area.

* * *

Suits were filed in Alabama and Tennessee to prevent the states from developing branches of the white universities in the cities where there is already a black public college. Both suits were lost, but at the same time the states were directed to desegregate. The decision by Tennessee to permit a branch of the University of Tennessee to be located in Nashville was fought by Tennessee A. and I., the black state college. The state argued that whites would not enroll in Tennessee A. and I. because of the lower base of financial support, the smaller number of Ph.D.'s, and the quality of the curriculum. Since it has damned the black college, the state is finding it difficult to develop a program designed to integrate Tennessee A. and I. as ordered by the court. The court also ruled that the new branch of the University of Tennessee could operate only as an evening school.

* * *

Demographic conditions have favored the West Virginia black colleges in becoming predominantly white. There were no competing public white colleges in their vicinity. Lincoln in Missouri was assisted in becoming 40 per cent white by the forced closing of the white junior college in Jefferson City. Central State and Kentucky State have made progress in desegregation, but new senior college locations may jeopardize such action in Ohio. Morgan State and Texas Southern have clearly indicated serious intent to integrate. The University of Houston changed from private to state and is located only a few blocks from Texas Southern. Integration slowed at Texas Southern and started at the University of Houston when it became public. The big problem is what to do in Houston, Greensboro, Baton Rouge, Shreveport, Tallahassee, Huntsville, Montgomery, Nashville, and other places where two public institutions exist and operate on a dual basis.

* * *

The advocates of "megaversities" would say: merge them completely or phase out the black college. When you have 7,000 students on one black campus, how can you assimilate them into a campus of 18,000? What are the limits in size to efficiency and opportunities for individual expression? No one has yet developed a concept of ideal size that is generally accepted. As far as state expenditures are concerned, there is little economy in size in enrollments above five thousand. Broader curriculums can be offered in larger institutions and Ph.D. programs can be better supported if undergraduates carry much of the burden of higher per capita costs at the graduate level. Small colleges are being developed within universities to conserve some of the values of small institutions. Specialization in the colleges according to disciplines is one technique for reducing size and not increasing costs. Each college may contribute to the other if each has specialties and expertise not found in the other. Collaboration of this sort enriches the offerings for all students without requiring managerial mergers.

* * *

One novel idea that has been suggested is that the achievement of instant integration of all students might be accomplished by assigning all incoming white freshmen to one quarter of a year on the Negro campus and black students to one quarter on a white campus. To the white college, it is quite easy to plan use of the facilities of the black public college for special programs, but infinitely more difficult to plan creatively for the use of the faculties without discrimination.

* * *

The specialized programs of the public black college are the first casualties of the integration. Such programs as, for example, engineering, agriculture, law, and pharmacy will be dropped in the black public colleges. An argument can be made for this on economic grounds. But a program on a Negro college campus that has sufficient enrollment to justify it will be endangered if the state desires to lower the status and alter the role and scope of the black college. In some cases, this is a punitive action because the black college urged desegregation of the white colleges. In many instances, the loss of these highly specialized programs will militate against developing leadership in these areas among blacks because, by use of the national screening devices, fewer Negroes will qualify for these competitive places on the white campuses.

* * *

The public black colleges on the average are better funded than many of the private black colleges, but compare less favorably with their white counterparts. Even where current per capita funding is equal, the lag persists in facilities, quality, and programs because of the many years that these colleges shared unequally in state financing and in state aspirations.

* * *

If one of the options for survival of the black college is state or federal assistance, that alternative disappears if the black public colleges disappear. For the same rules of law that force integration or phasing out of black public colleges will not permit support of black private colleges that violate the same principle of open enrollment and unitary system support. The enforcers of the rules have not attempted to determine whether the current generation of blacks wants separation or merely freedom of movement from one kind of institution to the other until it is no longer necessary to have a racial strategy for full acceptance.

Earl McGrath, in *The Predominantly Negro Colleges and Universities in Transition* (New York, 1965), gave the Negro colleges a generally positive visibility and left an overly optimistic view about their needs. On the other hand, Christopher Jencks and David Riesman, in their satirical article, "The American Negro College," *Harvard Educational Review,* 37 (1967), and later in *The Academic Revolution* (New York, 1968), put most of the Negro colleges on the defensive, making them the disaster area of American education.

* * *

Like most American colleges, Negro colleges are not all the same. They cannot be grouped in a presentation that either condemns or praises them. Not one is a Harvard or a Berkeley, but when compared with other institutions of their size and with their resources, they are like other American institutions. In fact, their greatest fault has been that they have been forced to imitate in order to be accredited and have not been encouraged to be innovative and independent. They are still assessed by a few foundations and agencies which pass on to the larger giving public their impressions of the colleges' worthiness according to standards set by others rather than those set by the colleges and the communities they are intended to serve. During the sit-ins, which accelerated the pace of integration and the attainment of the great American ideal, there were subtle pressures and veiled suggestions that such non-academic activities by students in the colleges could lead to censure. The tumult was supposed to have destroyed the learning climate. Today, tumult and tension pervade all college campuses and colleges are being forced to reassess their position of non-involvement with society.

* * *

If we are to achieve black-white comparability in college enrollment, we need to plan for 800,000 Negroes in college immediately and about one million in 1975. Obviously, the leadership, the job opportunities, and the escape of Negroes into middle-class America largely depend upon improving the ratio of educated blacks to educated whites. If Negroes become 12 per cent of those enrolled in colleges, more places must be created where high tuition and living cost levels, poor inner city schooling, traditional screening procedures, and competition for places will not work against the Negro. This more than doubling of the capacity for lower income persons in an inflated and inflating educational economy puts severe pressures on limited spaces in prestigious institutions even when there is a genuine desire on their part to help solve the problem. It means more than doubling existing space in colleges where Negroes are enrolled at present. This would require not only a more meaningful retention by junior colleges but also a reduction by 25 per cent of the high school dropout rate, a virtual academic revolution. While this revolution is hoped for, one can be more sanguine about the commitment of the black colleges to keep the doors of opportunity open and to carry the burden of remediation in much the same way as at present, remaining invisible in their herculean efforts and in foundation support but highly visible in their shortcomings.

Cross Currents

The black colleges are caught between the pressures of their own assessments of their best long-range interests and that applied by the militant black separatists who are willing to destroy the institutions if that is necessary in order to gain control of them. If churches and foundations respond more readily to the demands of separatists, this puts the colleges in the position of being competing Establishment interests. It raises the question whether such agencies support separatism, not because of the militancy of their demands, but because this is more in harmony with the unexpressed wishes of the donors. Will this attitude on the part of donors force the colleges from the center toward a militant black separatist stand at the extreme left?

* * *

These colleges need manpower more than anything else, but they also need libraries, laboratories, buildings, and supplies. Though their plants are relatively new, they do not have adequate plant funds for upkeep. Currently, more Ph.D.'s are being turned out among whites than we had anticipated when Alan Cartter made his predictions for the American Council on Education. By the strange quirk of separatism, these Ph.D.'s will not be available for the needs of the black colleges on any permanent basis. This is because faculty people will not take tenured jobs where the social climate can force them out when they become too old to make changes or when they will lose rank and salary by changing locations. No one knows when the black separatist demands will abate.

The black colleges wish only to remain black in a genuinely traditional sense. They were the first colleges to urge integration. Unfortunately, the foundations have provided funds to encourage integration in white colleges but have negatively damned the black colleges by subscribing to the doctrine that only that which is white is worthy of integration.

* * *

The economics of the black community will require that its educational needs be met at the lowest per capita cost. The black colleges with a traditional commitment to this segment of the population cannot price themselves out of the market by raising their costs to the level of their white competitors. So their salaries and facilities must remain less pending a revolutionary change in philanthropic attitudes toward them.

* * *

The sure way to dry up the Negro colleges is to make it the dead end of professional aspirations for black teachers. The black colleges wish for their faculties and students open mobility for jobs in our society. The black colleges would like to make the choice difficult for prospective and present faculty people by becoming fully competitive in climate, salaries, and creativity.

* * *

The Department of Health, Education, and Welfare has recently directed the black private colleges in Virginia as well as the public ones in that state to desist from dissemination of information which indicates that these colleges are primarily for blacks or that they focus on a type of education that is restricted or specially designed for blacks.

* * *

Someone is planning for the black colleges—government, foundations, and commissions—someone is mapping grand strategies for their demise. Who is mapping the strategy for their survival?

Some Remedial Steps

In 1968-1969, the federal government spent $4 billion on higher education. Of this amount, approximately $85 million was spent on Negro colleges. This amount includes loans to students and colleges as well as grants. The rate of growth of support for academic science has decreased from 15 per cent annually from 1963 to 1967 to 1 per cent in 1968-1969. At the present inflation rate, this represents an actual loss in purchasing power. Research and development funds account for 86 per cent of all academic support for 1968-1969. Research and development support was the opening wedge for federal support to colleges because it was noncontroversial. Now that cutbacks in support for research and development are in the future, the major universities and colleges would like to have the government shift to direct block grants for higher education, but still hope to receive 85 per cent of all grants for higher education.

* * *

Most of the bills presented to the Congress at the instigation of the universities have embodied provisions for inequitably funding higher education to the disadvantage of the colleges. House Bill 35, 1969, the Miller/Daddario bill, which was an Institutional Grants Bill, is an indication. It would have appropriated $400 million annually according to a formula which used number of doctoral degrees awarded, amount of research support currently conducted on federal grants or contracts, and the number of persons awarded bachelor's degrees who subsequently moved into graduate study for the doctorate. Of the $400 million, 110 black colleges would have received less than 1 per cent and 90 per cent would still flow to the universities. About 9 per cent would go to other small colleges. This could be rectified by putting more weight on the number of bachelor's degrees awarded.

* * *

If the federal government recognized the need to subsidize research and would separate the function of research and the education of researchers from other aspects of higher education, it would be unnecessary to obfuscate the issue of support for higher education through research support. Then a $1,000 grant to each college in the country on a per capita basis would provide a federal subsidy for each student wherever he happened to be enrolled. The students would seek admission as they do and the government would pay the amount to the college without any relationship to the college's tuition charges. This would assist and upgrade the educational resources of all colleges. It would also slow down the rate of tuition increase, which was nearly 10 per cent in 1969-1970, when colleges had projected a 29 per cent increase over the next ten years. Payment to the student rather than the institution would be more awkward and would dislocate many students.

* * *

Various states have already taken significant action in aid to higher education. Some southern states give out-of-state study grants to students. Rhode Island and North Carolina have building authorities which permit private colleges to float building bonds that are tax exempt. This lowers the cost of borrowed money to private colleges. Maryland approved a bond issue of $1,250,000 to be given to the University of Baltimore, a private university, for expansion of its plant. Oklahoma supports television instruction which is available to the private colleges and universities. Several southern states have provided funds to four-year private institutions to subsidize the students in the first two years in lieu of operation of public junior colleges. Virginia reversed itself in the action it had taken to phase out the School of Agriculture at Virginia State, the Negro college. The action was intended as an economic measure, but the college viewed it as a first step in its emasculation.

* * *

The present administration in Washington has recently agreed to waive the required matching funds for student loan money for those colleges that enroll 50 per cent or more of their students from families whose incomes are below $7,500. If this could be extended to include loans for academic facilities and dormitories, it would greatly assist the poorer colleges. Almost all of the black colleges would fall into this category.

* * *

The several states could recognize that the state is relieved of the educational cost of each student who is enrolled in a private college. It could compensate for not having the full cost of educating its citizens by making assistance subsidies to private colleges, as Pennsylvania does, or by providing scholarship grants to the colleges, as New York does. States could make offsetting grants to students for attending private colleges.

* * *

The colleges and their supporting boards could take some steps to improve their position:

(1) They could improve their governance structure and broaden the base for appeals. In so doing, they could become independent except where they exist as a mission function rather than as acceptable educational alternatives.

(2) The management in some of the institutions is below any good standard of acceptance. Frequently it is not owing to a lack of business procedures or acumen in the business office, but rather to unrealistic adventures into financing plant without an assessment of fund-raising potential.

(3) Board committees on finance should function and provide expertise and guidance when it is lacking in the chief administrator.

(4) Public college boards should not put their personal concern and gain ahead of that of their institution. An appointment to such a board should not be a political payoff. Public trustees should be appointed according to their ability to serve the college, not the governor.

(5) Church boards should not make colleges independent without a guarantee of continuing income from endowments or grants in perpetuity from the church equal to that given by the church during its period of maximum support. Churches are leaving colleges stranded in a period when endowment income is difficult for experts to develop and almost impossible for those trustees and administrative officials who never have shouldered this responsibility.

(6) Conference politics should not be able to force a church with limited funds to operate a large number of colleges when its resources dictate one or two good ones instead.

* * *

The plant assets of the private Negro colleges amounted to \$248,574,000 at their 1967 book value. The public colleges had a book value of \$364,355,000 at the same time. The endowment of the private Negro colleges had a book value of \$130,318,000 in 1967 while the public ones for Negroes had a book value of \$1,947,000. These data are based on ninety-eight colleges from U.S. Office of Education statistics. We can round off the total assets, physical and endowment, to about \$750,000,000. It seems inconceivable that a continued productive use of these resources cannot be found in higher education. We are opening new junior colleges every year and still cannot remain abreast of the needs.

Obviously, if the federal government has to fund colleges, it will make some of the rules. Accreditation or process of it with a regional agency would be one criterion. Efficient size and per capita cost might well be others.

* * *

Federal support alone, however, will not be sufficient to maximize the usefulness of the "widow's mite" which is currently invested in Negro higher education. The private foundations and industry must step up their giving.

MICHAEL R. WINSTON

Through the Back Door: Academic Racism and the Negro Scholar in Historical Perspective

The Anomalous Social and Intellectual Position of the Negro Scholar

IN 1939 when Rayford W. Logan was president of the Howard University chapter of the American Association of University Professors, he wrote to the national office of the AAUP to inquire about the accommodations for Howard professors at the Association's annual meeting held that year in New Orleans. Ralph Himstead, executive secretary of the AAUP, replied that the Negro members of Howard's chapter would be permitted to attend the meeting, but of course they could not be guests at the hotel and would have to enter through the back door. The incident would scarcely be worth recalling today except that it indicates the anomalous social and intellectual position of the Negro scholar in American life. Like Negro intellectuals in general, the small groups of scholars have been regarded by hostile whites as either freaks or a menace, discomfiting because their very existence challenged the prevailing racial stereotypes and the system of racial accommodation in which whites were presumed superior, blacks inferior.

Until relatively recent years, a virtually impermeable racial barrier excluded Negroes from white universities and their superior facilities for teaching and research. In addition, the Negro scholar has found himself isolated in Negro colleges and universities which were themselves marginal financially and intellectually, existing precariously on what Edward Shils has called in a slightly different connection an "intellectual periphery."[1] John Hope Franklin has written of the dilemma of isolated Negro scholars and their humiliation at the hands of racist archivists and librarians. "The world of the Negro scholar," he said, "is indescribably lonely, and he must, somehow, pursue truth down that lonely path while, at the same time, making certain that his conclusions are sanctioned by universal standards developed and maintained by those who frequently do not even recognize him. Imagine the plight of the Negro historian trying to do research in archives in the South operated by people who cannot conceive that a Negro has the capacity to use the materials there."[2] Separated by social convention from their white peers, Negro intellectuals and scholars have been alienated also by cultural tradition from the majority of Negroes, who, in addition to sharing most of the anti-intellectual biases of most white Americans, have the traditional hostility of other basically peasant peoples to intellectuals of their own group.[3] Negro intellectuals and scholars have therefore been necessarily dependent on white philanthropy or state legislatures, with all of the limitations and difficulties such support implied in a society based on white supremacy. This essay will discuss briefly what I view as the principal forces controlling the fate of Negro scholars in America: racism, the development of Negro colleges, and the nascent mobilization of Negroes for "intellectual self-defense." Within this framework it is possible to make an assessment of what kinds of research contributions Negro scholars have made or not made to the broader world of American scholarship.

Politics and Pedagogy: The Institutional Setting of Negro Scholars

American Negroes have developed two major institutions, the Negro church and the Negro school. Of the two, only the school was a point of contact between Negroes and whites because of the problems of financial support on the one hand, and on the other the broad range of relationships inherent in any educational enterprise, no matter how caste-ridden. Because Negro colleges existed as institutions within a society dominated by whites, they were necessarily a reflection of the power relations between the two racial groups. As a consequence of this, the internal development of Negro schools has been related directly to the shifting political and social relations between whites and Negroes in the society. It has also meant that the Negro school, especially the college, has occupied a strategic intermediary position in race relations and has been therefore more of a focus of political pressures and social tension than is commonly expected to be true of educational institutions. To Negroes, denied political participation by statute, business opportunities by lack of resources and custom, and broad areas of social expression by segregation, colleges have been regarded as vehicles for expressing a variety of interests, many bearing only a slender and tangential relationship to education as a process of intellectual development. It is not surprising, therefore, that to Negroes as well as whites, Negro colleges have very often been conceived of in ways which ultimately distort the primary purposes of education. The demands of political expediency often eclipsed the educational needs of the students or the intellectual interests of the faculty. This is fundamental to an understanding of the history of the higher education of Negroes, and especially to an understanding of the peculiar conditions in which Negro scholars have had to work. A brief survey of the history of Negro higher education makes clear the range of obstacles to the development of a strong tradition of scholarship in Negro institutions. Since whites have had the dominant role in determining both the character and degree of support to Negro schools, it is useful to review shifting white attitudes to Negro education as well.

The White Dilemma: The Black Trojan Horse

The attitudes of whites toward the education of Negroes in the United States have been conditioned by three powerful and very often conflicting motives; guilt, fear, and sentimental philanthropy. Despite the passage of more than a century, the Freedmen's Aid Society's sentiments of 1868 are still relevant: "The Freedmen, though of African origin, have for the most part been born on our soil [and] reared under our institutions . . . Their injuries appeal to our sense of justice, we must not forget that we are implicated in slavery. Our fathers covenanted to protect it . . . By their unpaid toil [the Freedmen] and their fathers contributed largely to the wealth of our country. By their aid during the rebellion they contributed to the preservation of the Union."[4] Fear has also been the companion of guilt. The Freedmen's Aid Society report for 1872 notes, for example, that "Patriotism, philanthropy and religion with united voice, urge us to consider this subject [Negro education] and make provisions that this calamity which threatens us may be averted. Four millions of ignorant citizens in a national crisis may wreck the Republic . . . This people . . . if neglected and left in ignorance will fall an easy prey to wicked and designing men, and become a terrible scourge to the nation."[5] J. L. M. Curry of the Peabody Fund made the point crystal clear when he addressed the general assembly of Alabama in 1889. "If you do not lift them up," he said, "they will drag you down to industrial bankruptcy, social degradation and political corruption."[6] But the fear was complex and, in many instances, inarticulate. On the one hand an ignorant black rabble was a menacing Trojan horse, but on the other a truly educated class of Negroes would upset not only the cherished doctrine of the innate intellectual superiority of whites, but, more important, make impossible any prolonged maintenance of political and economic white supremacy. That has been the chief dilemma in the history of white involvement in Negro education. It explains why so-called "industrial education" appealed to white southerners and northerners alike. While the available evidence will not warrant the flat conclusion that a "conspiracy" existed among powerful whites to establish industrial education as the only type of education available to Negroes, it is clear that most of the philanthropic support for Negro education for fifty years went to the trade schools after the John F. Slater Fund adopted a policy in 1882 that it would "favor" schools with industrial programs.[7] The Peabody Fund, whose trustees had lobbied against the Civil Rights Bill in 1873, was also a powerful force for mobilizing northern support for industrial rather than collegiate education.[8] Opposition to higher education was strenuously advocated by the Peabody Fund's general agent, J. L. M. Curry, who maintained that the education provided for Negroes at Atlanta, Fisk, Howard, and other American Missionary Association—Freedmen's Bureau schools was a tragic mistake based on a fanciful view of the Negro's mental capacities. He said that the educational program of these schools "was unsettling, demoralizing, [and] pandered to a wild frenzy for schooling as a quick method of reversing social and political conditions . . . The curriculum was for a people in the highest degree of civilization; the aptitudes and capabilities and needs of the Negro were wholly disregarded. Especial stress was laid on classics and liberal culture, to bring the race *per saltum* to the same plane with their former masters, and realize the theory of social and political equality."[9]

Caroline and Olivia Stokes, Collis P. Huntington, William H. Baldwin, Andrew Carnegie, John Wanamaker, Robert C. Ogden, George Eastman, John D. Rockefeller, Paul and Felix Warburg, and Julia Rosenwald were the most prominent supporters of industrial education and the accommodationist philosophy of Booker T. Washington.[10] In 1907 the Southern Education Association announced its policy that "in secondary education emphasis should be placed upon agriculture and industrial occupations."[11] Liberal southerners argued that in addition to practical considerations there were biological grounds for rejecting college education and favoring some "special education" for a race whose immutable destiny it was to occupy a servile status in "advanced civilizations" like the United States. "The Negro race," Charles H. McCord wrote, "is not only a child race: it is a spoilt race. It has had too much coddling on the one hand, and on the other hand it has been spanked without discretion."[12] As a southern liberal, he counseled patience to those whites exasperated by the rising tide of Negro protest. Racial peace could be achieved if they would only understand that Negroes could not be held responsible for their unfortunate inferiority, and that with the "right kind" of education the protests would cease. McCord "scientifically" demonstrated that Negro social behavior was characterized by "inordinate vanity, superstition and nonmoral religion, love of orgy and carousal, improvidence and lack of foresight, cunning and deceit, weakness of will and lack of inhibitive power, incapacity for sustained labor, lack of cleanliness and true self-respect, animal sexuality, moral insensitivity and a callousness to the suffering of others."[13] The point of the recital was that it made clear how unsuited Negroes were for higher education. McCord was, however, more candid than most white Americans about his reasons for deriding higher and favoring "industrial" education for Negroes. Characteristically, McCord argued that the colleges founded by New England whites for Negroes were "victims" of the "old Jesuitic curriculum and a discredited psychology. Their professors still worship the fetich of 'classical culture' and 'mental discipline.' " Having condemned the colleges, he praised industrial education. "It is one of the most hopeful signs of the time as regards the Negro that he is here and there in greater numbers accepting the teaching of General Armstrong and Doctor Washington.[14] And schools like Tuskegee Institute and Hampton Institute, together with the State Normal and Industrial Schools for Negroes, are forcing a recognition of the new doctrine in the old line colleges."[15] Industrial education would draw the fangs of "the Negro menace" by reducing the worst illiteracy, social deviance, and naked anger produced by the white supremacist social system; but industrial education would not give Negroes enough education to challenge seriously their legal and political domination by whites.[16]

The grip of the industrial education lobby was strengthened by popular southern writers like Joel Chandler Harris, a purported "friend" of Negroes. Harris, as Sterling Brown has pointed out, made Uncle Remus the mouthpiece of the new white supremacist orthodoxy, which is revealed in his evaluation of Negro education:

> Hit's de ruinashun er dis country . . . Put a spellin' book in a nigger's han's en right den en dar you loozes a plowhand . . . What's a nigger gwineter l'arn outen books? I kin take a bar'l stave an' fling mo' sense inter a nigger in one minnit dan all de schoolhouses betwixt dis en de state er Midgigin . . . Wid one bar'l stave I kin fa'rly lif' de vail er ignunce.[17]

Small wonder, then, that the few institutions like Atlanta, Fisk, and Howard which tried valiantly to provide a genuine collegiate education to Negroes languished in poverty and neglect while the propaganda centers for industrial education, Hampton and Tuskegee, prospered and received the lion's share of philanthropic support until the 1930's when it became clear to virtually all observers that industrial education had been a cynical political strategy, not a sound educational policy.[18]

It is not surprising that perceptive Negro intellectuals like Dean Kelly Miller of Howard University thought of the industrial education movement as a vicious scheme to destroy the higher aspirations of the race and the means of their realization. Negroes were being denied adequate opportunities for higher education, Miller said, "by the flaming sword of prejudice, kept keen and bright by avarice and cupidity."[19] The debate between advocates of industrial education and advocates of college education for Negroes is meaningless when viewed strictly in educational terms. The real conflict was about the status of Negroes in American life. One group, believing that Negroes should have no higher status than laborers, argued for industrial education and social subordination, while the other, believing that Negroes had the same intellectual aptitudes as whites, argued for higher education and social equality. Governor William C. Oates of Alabama made clear to a graduating class of Tuskegee in 1894 the views of "friendly white southerners" when he was invited to deliver the commencement address. Responding to John C. Dancy's praise of higher education earlier in the program, Oates said: "I want to give you niggers a few words of plain talk and advice . . . You might as well understand that this is a white man's country, so far as the South is concerned, and we are going to make you keep your place. Understand that."[20] Some years later, in an address to Negro students at Biddle University (now Johnson C. Smith University) in May 1909, President William Howard Taft concluded that "your race is adapted to be a race of farmers, first, last and for all times."[21] Although industrial education is a dead and now almost completely forgotten issue, it was what Buell Gallagher has called a great "detour" in the education of Negroes. The significance of this was that the colleges were forced to operate at a mere survival level, and in such circumstances faculty development, especially any sustained research program, was out of the question until relatively recent years.

Racist Scholarship and the Emergence of Negro Scholars

The growth of American universities and the spread of graduate work based on German models (beginning at John Hopkins in 1876) coincided with the defeat of Reconstruction and the triumph of social Darwinism as taught by Herbert Spencer, William Graham Sumner, and Lester Ward. Viewed in that context, it is scarcely surprising that the first two generations of Negro scholars worked in an atmosphere dominated by anti-Negro thought. From 1870, when Edward Bouchet, the first Negro to receive a doctorate at an American university, was awarded a Ph.D. in physics at Yale, to the late 1920's, when the number of Negro Ph.D.'s began to increase at a steady rate, American scholarship not only reflected the racial attitudes of the larger society, but actively propagated anti-Negro views which strengthened the "iron ring" of public policy and private prejudice designed to trap Negroes in a position of social and economic inferiority.[22] It is impossible to understand the development of scholarship by American Negroes if this background is ignored. Since these facts are usually overlooked in discussion of the type of research done by Negroes, it will be useful to review them here.

Among the leaders in the academic world who succeeded in imposing an anti-Negro bias in scholarship were the historians William A. Dunning and John W. Burgess, whose books on the Civil War and Reconstruction influenced a generation of American historians and the shapers of national policy toward the Negro. Largely through their efforts it became the dominant view that slavery was a benign institution and Reconstruction a tragic error based on the mistaken idea that Negroes should or could be citizens and enjoy the legal protections of the Constitution. At the time that Dunning was at the height of his influence as a historian he described life in the South during Radical Reconstruction as "a social and political system in which all the forces that made for civilization were dominated by a mass of barbarous freedmen."[23] Thus the oppressive racial policies of the South appeared to be vindicated by the best northern scholarship (Burgess and Dunning were at Columbia University); if it was folly to extend the franchise and education to Negroes, then it was wisdom to enforce white supremacy and segregation, and acceptable to use Ku Klux Klan terrorism and lynching to "keep the Negro in his place."

While the nation's leading historians were busy showing how "disastrous" it had been during Reconstruction for Negroes to be allowed minimal legal freedoms, a formidable body of purportedly "objective scholarship" was being produced in the emerging disciplines of sociology and psychology (at that time strongly under the influence of social Darwinism) to show that Negroes were innately incapable of rising above the status imposed by white terrorism.[24] This work was especially powerful in its influence because it was "scientific" and enjoyed the support of the leading universities of the United States. Among the distinguished social science professors was G. Stanley Hall, who held the first Ph.D. in psychology in the United States, and made an academic reputation as the founder of the psychology laboratory at Johns Hopkins (1883) and the *American Journal of Psychology* (1887). Hall used his academic authority in support of anti-Negro propaganda while he was president of Clark University (1899-1919). In 1905, his article "A Few Results of Recent Scientific Study of the Negro in America" noted that a "new scientific study of the negro has arisen, and is fast developing established results which are slowly placing the problems of the future of this race upon a more solid and intelligent basis, and which seem destined sooner or later to condition philanthropy and legislation, make sentiment more intelligent, and take the problem out of the hands of politicians, sentimentalists, or theorists, and place it where it belongs,—with economists, anthropologists, and sociologists." What were these research findings which were to "condition philanthropy and legislation"? First, that the "color of the skin and the crookedness of the hair are only the outward signs of many far deeper differences, including cranial and thoracic capacity, proportions of body, nervous system, glands and secretions, vita sexualis, food, temperment, disposition, character, longevity, instincts, customs, emotional traits, and diseases." Speaking as the leading authority on psychology of his day, Hall associated the alleged peculiar emotional intensity of Negroes with unbridled sexuality, leading him to discuss the question of rape, lynching, and social control. "During slavery regular hard work, temperance, awe of his white masters, were potent restraints . . . Now idleness, drink and a new sense of equality have destroyed these restraints of imperious lust, which in some cases is reinforced by the thought of generations of abuse of his own women by white men upon whom he would turn the tables. At any rate, the number, boldness, and barbarity of rapists, and the frequency of the murder of their victims have increased till whites in many parts of the South have told me that no woman of their race is safe anywhere alone day or night . . . As a preventative of crime, lynching has something to be said for it, but more to be said against it! This wild justice is brutalizing upon those who inflict it."[25]

The brutality and viciousness and ineducability attributed to Negroes by the psychologists were explained by appeals to anatomy and physiology since these disciplines were even more "scientific." It was argued that Negroes were intellectually inferior to whites and incapable of higher education because of a genetically determined arresting of development of the brain after puberty. The most influential academic statement of this view was by Robert Bennett Bean, a professor of anatomy at the University of Virginia Medical School. The "Negro brain" developed normally as far as perception, memory, and motor responses were concerned, but logical critical thinking or the comprehension of abstract ideas were beyond its grasp because of its arrested physiological development.[26]

The degree to which this point of view prevailed is illustrated by Albert Bushnell Hart, distinguished Harvard historian and influential figure in American scholarship. Hart wrote, for example, that "the theory that the Negro mind ceases to develop after adolescence perhaps has something in it."[27] What makes Hart's statement particularly interesting is that he served for twenty-three years on the board of trustees of Howard University,[28] and had thereby a powerful voice in shaping the opportunities for Negro students and scholars. He was one of the Howard trustees in 1926 who opposed the appointment of a Negro president for the first time in its history.

An example of the sociological research sponsored by white universities was Howard W. Odum's *Social and Mental Traits of the Negro: A Study in Race Traits, Tendencies and Prospects,* published in 1910 as volume 37 of the Studies in History, Economics and Public Law, edited by the faculty of poltical science of Columbia University. Odum, president of the American Sociological Society in 1930, and editor of *Social Forces,* 1922-1954, was one of the most influential southern liberals in academic life, serving as Kenan Professor and head of the Sociology Department at the University of North Carolina, and director of the Institute for Research in Social Science. In recognition of his work Harvard conferred upon him an LL.D. in 1939.[29] In his *Social and Mental Traits of the American Negro,* Odum wrote a summary of his investigations, relating the proper education of the race to its genetic tendencies, which is worth quoting at length because it represents the opinion of probably the majority of American social scientists well into the 1930's and 1940's. "Inherited tendency," he said,

and environment of the race conditions constitute a powerful influence in the education of the negro child . . . Back of the child, and affecting him both directly and indirectly, are the characteristics of the race. The Negro has little home conscience or love of home, no local attachment of the better sort . . . He has no pride of ancestry, and he is not influenced by the lives of great men. The Negro has few ideals and perhaps no lasting adherence to an aspiration toward real worth. He has little conception of the meaning of virtue, truth, honor, manhood, integrity. He is shiftless, untidy and, indolent . . . The Negro is improvident and extravagant, lazy rather than industrious, faithful in the performance of certain duties, without vindictiveness, he yet has a reasonable amount of physical endurance. But he lacks initiative; he is often dishonest and untruthful. He is over-religious and superstitious. The Negro suspects his own race and the white race as well; his mind does not conceive of faith in humanity—he does not comprehend it . . . One of the crying weaknesses of the negro school is the lack of moral strength on the part of the women teachers. It is but natural that children accustomed to gross immoralities at home and sometimes seeing indications of the same tendency on the part of the teachers, should be greatly affected by it at school. Thus with mental stupidity and moral insensibility back of them the children are affected already in practice and thought, in deeds and in speech.[30]

Perhaps even more revealing of the dominant patterns of thought is Odum's view of the work of the Negro colleges:

The young educated negroes are not a force for good in the community but for evil. The Negro quickly outgrows the influence and control of his instructors; especially has this been noted in cases where the [northern] whites have taught them . . . They imitate the whites and believe themselves thereby similar to them.[31]

Finally, his view of the problem of crime is enlightening:

Nurtured with some hatred toward the whites, taught no morals, with a fanatical religion, itself leading to erratic actions, with little regard for common decency, and bred in filth and adultery, the negro is considered peculiarly liable to crime. The reformed negro criminal is rarely seen, and it is well known that the negro offender is not cured by the ordinary punishments.[32]

The Emergence of Negro Scholars

The success of white supremacist propaganda during "the nadir," 1877-1901 and after, was so great that the early efforts of

Negroes to contribute to the advancement of knowledge have been largely forgotten. As early as 1787 Negroes in Philadelphia began organizing societies embracing literary and other learned interests, and as many as forty-six groups were active before the Civil War. In cities like New York, separate Negro organizations were also formed because of the racial policy of white learned societies. In 1834, for example, the New York Zoological Institute announced that "the proprietors wish it to be understood that the people of color are not permitted to enter except when in attendance upon children and families."[33]

The earliest efforts are more important for illustrating the interest of Negroes in learning and the means by which they cultivated a separate social life than for any residue of solid achievement in the advancement of knowledge. By far the most important organization not related to a university was the American Negro Academy, established in Washington, D.C., in 1897 by the Reverend Alexander Crummell.[34] Crummell was regarded by his contemporaries as "among the most scholarly black men of the age,"[35] based no doubt on his education at Queens College, Cambridge (A.B. 1853), his association in England with Bishop William Wilberforce, James A. Froude, and Thomas Babington Macaulay, his essays and addresses published while a missionary in Africa, and the character of his ministry as rector of St. Luke's Episcopal Church in Washington.[36]

The Academy had five stated purposes:

(1) The promotion of literature, science, and art,
(2) The culture of a form of intellectual taste,
(3) The fostering of higher education,
(4) The publication of scholarly work,
(5) The defense of the Negro against vicious assaults.

The Academy published occasional papers in defense of Negroes and held regular meetings in Washington until the mid-1920's. A typical product was the first paper, Kelly Miller's critique of Frederick L. Hoffman's *Race Traits and Tendencies of the American Negro,* a book published under the auspices of the American Economic Association in 1896 that maintained that genetic inferiority of Negroes was responsible for Negro social disorganization and concluded that the Negro population would be overwhelmed by disease and death, eventually disappearing altogether as an element in the American population. The Academy published too many significant papers to discuss them here, but a mere listing of a few titles will illustrate the direction of its program:

"The Conservation of Races," W. E. B. Du Bois

"Civilization the Primal Need of the Race," Alexander Crummell

"A Comparative Study of the Negro Problem," Charles C. Cook

"The Educated Negro and His Mission," William S. Scarborough

"The Ballotless Victim of One-Party Government," Archibald H. Grimke

At the same time that the American Negro Academy was active, there emerged the first generation of Negro Ph.D.'s, some of whom made major contributions to American scholarship. For rather obvious reasons, the number was small. Between 1876 and 1914 only fourteen Negroes earned the Ph.D. Of this small group, two, W. E. B. Du Bois and Carter G. Woodson, stand out as the most productive researchers and organizers of efforts to counter anti-Negro scholarship.

W. E. B. Du Bois was in many respects the most outstanding pioneer Negro scholar in the United States, but a historian like George Washington Williams (*History of the Negro Race in America*, 2 volumes, 1882), although not as thoroughly or broadly trained, would also deserve the title "pioneer." After graduation from Fisk University (A.B. 1888), Du Bois studied at Harvard (A.B. 1890, A.M. 1891, Ph.D. 1895) under Albert Bushnell Hart, Justin Winsor, William James, Josiah Royce, George Santayana, and F. W. Taussig and at the University of Berlin (1892-1894) under Gustav Schmoller, Adolph Wagner, and Heinrich von Treitschke. He achieved a solid reputation in both history and the infant discipline of sociology. In 1896 his doctoral dissertation, *The Suppression of the African Slave Trade to the United States of America, 1638-1870,* was published as volume one of the Harvard Historical Studies. The most important work of Du Bois' early years as far as scholarship is concerned, however, was his study of Negroes in Philadelphia, which he worked on from August 1, 1896, to January 1, 1898. He had become convinced that social reform would result from social science research. "The Negro problem," he said, "was in my mind a matter of systematic investigation and intelligent understanding. The world was thinking wrong about race, because it did not know. The ultimate evil was stupidity. The cure for it was knowledge based on scientific investigation."[37]

Du Bois' Philadelphia research was published as *The Philadelphia Negro: A Social Study* by the University of Pennsylvania in 1899. It was the first systematic sociological study of a racial group in an American city, and, in the opinion of later sociologists, a model of the kind of social research method that many years later became standard in American universities.[38] Beyond its intrinsic value as a classic work of social research, *The Philadelphia Negro* represented a dedication to the concept of disinterested scholarship that was rare in those years, particularly when the subject involved race or class.

While engaged in his Philadelphia research, Du Bois presented an ambitious plan of systematic study of the Negro throughout the United States to the forty-second meeting of the American Academy of Political and Social Sciences in Philadelphia, November 19, 1897. At the heart of his plan was cooperative research. "We hear much of higher Negro education," he said,

> and yet all candid people know there does not exist today in the center of Negro population a single first-class fully equipped institution, devoted to the higher education of Negroes, not more than three Negro institutions in all the South deserve the name of "college" at all, and yet what is a Negro college but a vast college settlement for the study of a particular set of peculiarly baffling problems? What more effective or suitable agency could be found in which to focus the scientific efforts of the great universities of the North and East, than an institution situated in the very heart of these social problems, and made the center of careful historical and statistical research? Without doubt the first effective step toward the solving of the Negro question will be the endowment of the Negro college which is not merely a teaching body, but a center of sociological research, in close connection and co-operation with Harvard, Columbia, Johns Hopkins, and the University of Pennsylvania.[39]

Some may now smile knowingly at the almost pathetic hopefulness of the young Du Bois that white scholars would cooperate with such an enterprise. Despite the resounding silence in response to his proposal, Du Bois began what he later called his "real life's work," at Atlanta University where he was professor of history and sociology from 1896 to 1910. There he attempted to carry out his plan without the benefit or assistance of "the great Northern and Eastern universities." Each year he convened a conference to discuss cooperative research studies of particular problems related to Negroes. The studies were organized in ten-year cycles, so that there would be systematic follow-up of changes in the social and economic status of rural as well as urban Negroes. Du Bois edited the Atlanta University Studies alone from 1897 to 1910, when he was assisted by Augustus Granville Dill. A partial listing of the publications suggests the scope and significance of this path-breaking undertaking in the social sciences:

(1) Social and Physical Condition of Negroes in Cities,
(2) The Negro in Business,
(3) The College-Bred Negro,
(4) A Select Bibliography of the American Negro,
(5) The Negro Common School,
(6) The Negro Artisan,
(7) The Negro Church,
(8) The Negro American Family,
(9) The Health and Physique of the Negro American,
(10) Some Notes on Negro Crime, Particularly in Georgia.

Two things should be especially noted. First, even after the Atlanta University Studies received well-deserved praise from some segments of the American academic community, neither financial assistance adequate to the task, nor cooperation were forthcoming from the foundations or the large universities. Second, despite the low level of support, the Atlanta studies under Du Bois' direction were careful research efforts, the first of their kind in any American university and obviously superior to the work supported at that time by white universities. Apart from the annual *Yearbook* of the *Journal of Negro Education*, beginning in 1932, nothing comparable has been attempted since, an indictment of the black as well as white institutions. Prolonged residence in the South during the reign of terror that accompanied the movement to disfranchise and segregate Negroes destroyed much of Du Bois' faith in the efficacy of social research as a means of achieving social reform. In his own words:

> At Wilberforce I was [my people's] captious critic. In Philadelphia I was their cold and scientific investigator, with microscope and probe. It took but a few years of Atlanta to bring me to hot and indignant defense. I saw the race-hatred of the whites as I had never dreamed of it before—naked and unashamed! The faint discrimination of my hopes and intangible dislikes paled into nothing before this great, red monster of cruel oppression. I held back with more difficulty each day my mounting indignation against injustice and misrepresentation.[40]

In 1910 Du Bois, with some reluctance, abandoned his professorial career at Atlanta to become director of publicity of the NAACP and editor of its journal, *The Crisis: A Record of the Darker Races*, which he made into the most influential publication among Negroes, and the clearest, most uncompromising condemnation of

American racism and Western imperialism for the twenty-two years of his editorship. "My career as a scientist," he said later, "was to be swallowed up in my role as master of propaganda."[41]

Although Du Bois returned to Atlanta University as professor of sociology, 1933-1944, after his break with the NAACP, the turbulent years of bitter political and social struggle prevented a return to the conventions of his earlier "scientific" approach to scholarship.[42] The historical works written during this period, *Black Reconstruction* (1935) and *Black Folk: Then and Now* (1939), for example, were marked by advocacy and an understandable impulse to "set the record straight." Keenly aware of the problem of tendentious writing, Du Bois appended a chapter to his *Black Reconstruction* called "The Propaganda of History," which is not only a brilliant apologia, but also an invaluable source for understanding the preoccupation with race of the generation of Negro scholars that followed in his footsteps. Demonstrating that white scholarship, "when it regarded black men, became deaf, dumb and blind," Du Bois concluded that "in propaganda against the Negro since emancipation in this land, we face one of the most stupendous efforts the world ever saw to discredit human beings, an effort involving universities, history, science, social life and religion."[43]

Du Bois' popularization of the idea of the Talented Tenth and the encouragement he gave in the pages of *The Crisis* to younger Negroes achieving intellectual distinction may have had a greater impact on American scholarship than his own careful research efforts of the period 1896-1910. His early books were probably not read widely by contemporary white scholars, or at least I have found little evidence of it in their writing, but his inspiration of younger Negroes to undertake careers of scholarship despite awesome handicaps bore fruit in the lean years between the two world wars.

A near contemporary of Du Bois, Carter G. Woodson (1875-1950) should be mentioned also as a major force in stimulating research among Negroes, particularly historical studies. Educated at Berea College (before the state of Kentucky made it illegal in 1906 for even a private college to have a biracial student body),[44] the University of Chicago, and Harvard (Ph.D. 1912), Woodson's career was a tortuous and at times eccentric amalgam of scholarship and advocacy. At Howard University for only one year, 1919, as dean of the School of Liberal Arts and head of the graduate faculty, he withdrew from university teaching entirely after a dispute with the white president, J. Stanley Durkee, and spent the remaining thirty years in a lonely crusade to rescue the record of the Negro's past from oblivion. His own writings are rather sharply divided into scholarly efforts and energetic popularizations of Negro history for school children and general readers. Examples of the former are his superb *Education of the Negro Prior to 1861* (1915), *A Century of Negro Migration* (1918), *The History of the Negro Church* (1921), and *Free Negro Heads of Families in the United States,* which he edited in 1925. Quite different in method and quality were the popular *The Negro in Our History* (1922) and *Negro Makers of History* (1928).

As Woodson grew older and more militantly defiant, his popularizations increasingly fell heir to many of the pitfalls of that genre of writing. As far as scholarship is concerned, perhaps his development of the Association for the Study of Negro Life and History, founded in Chicago in 1915, and of the *Journal of Negro History,* founded in 1916, was more significant than his individual contributions as a historian. Woodson announced in the first issue of the *Journal of Negro History* the path it would take:

> Excepting what can be learned from current controversial literature, which either portrays the Negro as a persecuted saint or brands him as a leper of society, the people of this age are getting no information to show what the Negro has thought, and felt, and done . . . The aim of the Association [for the Study of Negro Life and History] is to raise the funds to employ several investigators to collect all historical and sociological material bearing on the Negro, before it is lost to the world . . . Our purpose then is not to drift into the discussion of the Negro problem. We shall aim to publish facts, believing that facts properly set forth will speak for themselves.

Almost single-handedly, Woodson made the *Journal of Negro History* into one of the respected American historical journals, a remarkable achievement by any standard. Unfortunately, within a few years of his death it began a steady and tragic decline.

Between 1920 and 1945, there emerged a more broadly differentiated group of Negro scholars, though the total number was still of course small.[45] Some sense of the numbers involved is suggested by the fact that between 1930 and 1943 a total of 317 Negroes had earned the Ph.D. By 1946, universities awarding the largest number were Chicago (40), Columbia (35), University of Pennsylvania (28), Harvard (25), Cornell (25), Ohio State (22), and Michigan (20). By 1943, 40 per cent of the Ph.D.'s held by

Negroes were in the social sciences, and of those, 53 per cent were in the fields of history and sociology.[46] The increase was generally related to the increasing social differentiation of the Negro population, particularly the steady growth of an urban middle class able to sustain the investments of time and money required by graduate study. There was also the rapidly changing status of the Negro colleges. After the First World War there was increased pressure to upgrade the colleges and make their faculties conform more closely to what were becoming regional and national standards. This created a demand for Ph.D.'s that had scarcely existed before, when college presidents considered the degree a luxury rather than a necessity. Until the 1930's Negro colleges in the South were unaccredited, but few persons today recall that the reason had little relation to their quality as institutions. Prior to 1930 the Southern Association of Colleges and Secondary Schools had refused to consider accreditation of Negro colleges because approval of a school automatically carried with it membership in the association. Membership entitled the institution to representation at association meetings, and the majority of the members objected to attendance by Negroes. After repeated protests to the SACSS by Negro colleges because their graduates encountered difficulties in admission to graduate and professional schools in the North and West (they were, of course, excluded by law at that time from all southern graduate schools), the SACSS "solved" the problem by agreeing to review Negro colleges for rating purposes with the proviso that acceptable ratings would not entail admission to the Southern Association.[47] Only one school received an "A" rating in 1930, and as a result a strong impetus was created for the other institutions to improve their libraries, add Ph.D.'s to their faculties, and so on. This development, in conjunction with legal challenges to the gross disparities in what were supposedly separate but equal educational resources, accounted for the intense and sustained effort to upgrade the Negro colleges. After the United States Supreme Court handed down its landmark decision *Missouri ex rel. Gaines* v. *Canada* (305 U.S. 337) in 1938, the working conditions of Negro scholars were improved somewhat as the Negro schools were encouraged (for political rather than educational reasons) to add graduate programs, and were pressured to approximate more closely the external conditions of white schools. Although none of these added pressures resulted in equality of educational resources for either students or faculty, they did, on the whole, force some slight improvement in the position of Negro scholars. As a consequence, for a few institutions in particular, the period 1930-1945 was extraordinarily productive.

Atlanta, Fisk, and Howard (the latter not directly affected by policy changes of the SACSS, but by the decision of the federal government in 1928 to legalize its congressional appropriations and support a "twenty-year development plan") in these new circumstances attracted the overwhelming majority of the "second generation" of Negro scholars actively engaged in research. More than 80 per cent of all Negro Ph.D.'s in 1936, for example, were employed by Atlanta, Fisk, and Howard, and the latter had by far the largest concentration of Negro Ph.D.'s anywhere in the United States (and the world).[48]

A change of policy on Negro colleges by the philanthropic foundations also contributed to what appears in retrospect to be a "golden age" of scholarship for some of these institutions.[49] In the late 1920's two of the powerful foundations that had played a crucial role in determining the fate of Negro colleges, the Julius Rosenwald Fund and the General Education Board of the Rockefeller Foundation, developed a plan to create, in Edwin Embree's words, "at four centers, strategically placed throughout the South, institutions of the highest standards which are thus able to offer careers to distinguished Negro scholars and to prepare the potential leaders of the race." The centers were in Georgia (the Atlanta University system), Louisiana (Dillard University and Flint Goodrich Hospital in New Orleans), Tennessee (Fisk University and Meharry Medical College in Nashville), and the District of Columbia (Howard University's four undergraduate colleges and the four professional schools).[50] Since white schools still excluded Negro scholars (only three Negro Ph.D.'s were employed by white universities in 1936), the increased number of Negro Ph.D.'s, combined with the substantial change in the fortunes of the three leading Negro institutions, produced the first real opportunity for some Negro scholars to work in even a second-class university environment.[51] At first it appeared that Atlanta University, under the leadership of President John Hope, would become the principal center of Negro scholarship in the humanities and social sciences because of the presence of W. E. B. Du Bois and the group of scholars recruited to Atlanta like Mercer Cook (romance languages), Rayford W. Logan (history), Frank M. Snowden (classics), William H. Dean (economics), and Ira Reid (sociology). But the death of President Hope in 1936, the lack of an adequate system of tenure, retirement benefits, and faculty independence, combined with the stifling and vicious atmosphere of Georgia racism, made Atlanta less attractive than Howard, where President Mordecai Johnson had succeeded in substantially augmenting financial resources to support a more diversified and intellectually distinguished faculty than ever before in its history.[52] An indication of the degree to which Howard became the leading center of research and writing by Negro scholars in the 1930's is the composition of the graduate council of the Graduate School in 1934, which included, for example, Ralph J. Bunche (political science), Charles Eaton Burch (English), E. Franklin Frazier (sociology), Abram L. Harris (economics), Ernest E. Just (zoology), Alain L. Locke (philosophy), Charles H. Thompson (education), and Charles H. Wesley (history).

It is of course impossible to review adequately the research and publication of the Howard group, but a few examples will illustrate the main lines of development. One general observation that should be made first is that although race was the major preoccupation of these scholars, with a few exceptions like Burch, who was a specialist on the work of Daniel Defoe, no "school" of Negro scholarship developed. Indeed, on the whole they were methodologically conservative and generally reflected the dominant trends of American scholarship. The only point of sharp difference with their white counterparts was on the question of race. They reacted to the enormous body of scholarly literature designed to show that Negroes "had no history," had less intelligence than whites, were uneducable, and so forth.

An important catalytic element in this period was the *Journal of Negro Education*, founded by Charles H. Thompson in 1932. In its first issue, the editor said that the *Journal* was intended to "stimulate the collection, and facilitate the dissemination of facts about the education of Negroes," to "present discussions involving critical appraisals of the proposals and practices relating to the education of Negroes," and, finally, "to stimulate and sponsor investigations of problems incident to the education of Negroes."[53] In reference to the research objective, Thompson said that "it should be pointed out here that leadership in the investigation of the problems incident to the education of Negroes should be assumed to a greater extent by Negro educators. This has not been true to a greater extent, heretofore, because the average Negro student who has taken the pains to get research training, and, in many cases, a research degree, finds his research tendencies so dulled by the routine of 'school keeping' and by the fact that there is no ready and sympathetic outlet for the publications of the results of his investigations that it takes a considerable amount of stimulation to overcome the inertia and discouragement produced by this combination of circumstances."[54]

During the thirty years of his editorship Thompson not only provided a "ready and sympathetic outlet" for publications of research, but made the *Journal of Negro Education* into the most potent continuing critique of the public policy of segregation. An early emphasis was on highlighting the inequities in support of white and Negro education, which worsened in the first third of the twentieth century, and did not begin to improve until the legal challenges of the 1930's. Thompson pointed out that in those states maintaining separate school systems, in 1900 the disparity in per capita educational expenditures for the two racial groups was 60 per cent in favor of the whites; by 1930 the disparity had increased to 253 per cent.[55] His editorials were shrewd assessments of the changing tides of public policy and the internal developments of Negro institutions. He was critical of the low standards of most Negro schools, writing in 1946, for example, that one-half of the faculty in Negro colleges were deficient in graduate training in their fields, and commenting on the "intellectual decay" that was prevalent in the Negro college.[56] On the other hand he was critical of the often whimsical management practices of the Negro college presidents, and urged adoption of national standards of rank and tenure for faculties, something rare in most Negro institutions until relatively recent years.[57] But the most significant contribution was the publication of the annual *Yearbook* of the *Journal*, which included comprehensive studies of a wide range of problems related to Negro life (volume 8 on *The Position of the Negro in the American Social Order* is a particularly distinguished example). For many years the *Journal* was the best single source of information about the status of segregated schools and shifts in the legal strategies adopted to destroy segregation, and it was common for the *Journal* to publish articles like "The Present Status of the Negro Separate School as Defined by Court Decisions" or "Types of Potentially Favorable Court Cases Relative to the Separate School." Thompson also published a steady stream of research by Howard

H. Long, Martin D. Jenkins, and others on the question of the intelligence of Negroes and on intelligence testing which exposed the distortions of white psychologists and educators.[58] Because of the lack of adequate opportunity to publish articles in most of the best known journals, Negro scholars often published articles in the *Journal of Negro Education* not strictly related to "Negro education," like "Negro Character as Seen by White Authors," by Sterling Brown, the great Howard University literary critic, poet, and teacher. In addition a number of the *Yearbooks* were devoted to subjects broader than the *Journal's* name would suggest, such as the 1946 study of "The Problem of Education in Dependent Territories," with articles by Ralph E. Turner on imperialism, the system of international trusteeship by Rayford W. Logan, and "Colonies and Moral Responsibility" by W. E. B. Du Bois. Thompson also recognized the significance of "policy research," virtually all of which was done by whites before the *Journal of Negro Education* began its work in this area. In January 1936, for example, the *Journal* published an important series of articles on the New Deal and the race question, social planning, economic development, socialism, and communism by W. E. B. Du Bois, Norman Thomas, A. Philip Randolph, Ralph J. Bunche, and others. What one could call the "policy research nucleus" at Howard—Thompson, Bunche, Harris, Frazier, and Logan—was very active in criticizing public policy as well as the strategies adopted by various Negro groups.[59]

The best example of the mobilization of policy research at this time was The Howard Law School, where Professors Charles H. Houston, William H. Hastie, James M. Nabrit, Jr., Leon A. Ransom, George E. C. Hayes, and their students like Thurgood Marshall, Robert L. Carter, and Spottswood Robinson, III, pursued an unremitting attack on the legal foundations of segregation.[60] The Howard Law School's legal research on civil rights probably had a greater impact on American life than the research activities of any other Negro scholars.

Parallel to their work was the research and writing of a growing cadre in the social sciences. In history, the number of works by Negro scholars providing a corrective to the dominant view began to increase steadily. A few examples are *Negro Labor in the United States, 1850-1925* (1927) and *The Collapse of the Confederacy* (1938) by Charles H. Wesley (at Howard, 1913-1942); *The Diplomatic Relations of the United States with Haiti,*

1776-1891 (1941), *The African Mandates in World Politics* (1948) and *The Negro in American Life and Thought: The Nadir, 1877-1901* (1954) by Rayford W. Logan (at Virginia Union, 1925-1930; Atlanta, 1933-1935; and Howard since 1938); *The Negro in the Civil War* (1953), *The Negro in the American Revolution* (1961), and *Lincoln and the Negro* (1962) by Benjamin Quarles (at Dillard University, 1939-1953; Morgan State College since 1953); *The Free Negro in North Carolina* (1943), *From Slavery to Freedom: A History of American Negroes* (1947), and *The Militant South, 1800-1861* (1956) by John Hope Franklin (at Fisk, 1936-1937; St. Augustine's College, 1939-1943; North Carolina College for Negroes, 1943-1947; Howard University 1947-1956; Brooklyn College, 1956-1964; and the University of Chicago since 1964). Wesley, Logan, Quarles, and Franklin have been the best known of the Negro historians, but of course there are a number of others who made contributions to American scholarship but cannot be discussed here.

In sociology the most distinguished Negro scholar was E. Franklin Frazier, research professor in the Department of Social Science at Fisk University, 1931-1934, and professor of sociology at Howard, 1934-1962. His books and articles were a major contribution to the "scientific" study of race relations, particularly the social process by which Negro social institutions developed and interacted with the larger American society. The crude rationalizations of the subordinate status of Negroes in American life which dominated American sociology in Frazier's early years were virtually unremembered by the time death put an end to his work in 1962. Among his notable books were *The Negro Family in Chicago* (1932), *The Negro Family in the United States* (1939), *The Negro in the United States* (1949), *Bourgeoisie Noire* (1955), and *Race and Culture Contacts in the Modern World* (1957). Of his Negro contemporaries, Frazier probably received the most recognition from his white colleagues as reflected in his election as president of the American Sociological Society in 1948, and chief of the Division of Applied Social Sciences, UNESCO, Paris, 1951-1953.

The work in applied social science by George Edmund Haynes and Charles S. Johnson and his associates at Fisk was also extremely important in ridding American scholarship of some of its racist excesses. Johnson was director of social science at Fisk from 1928 to 1948 when he became the university's first Negro president.

His research at Fisk was more collaborative than Frazier's at Howard, and for many years his Race Relations Institutes were interracial oases in a sahara of southern bigotry and propaganda on race. Among Johnson's many books were *The Negro in American Civilization* (1930), *The Shadow of the Plantation* (1934), *The Collapse of Cotton Tenancy* (1935), and *Patterns of Negro Segregation* (1943).[61]

There were other Negro sociologists writing important articles and books, but few of them were able to secure positions which provided resources for research. And evidence mounted in the 1930's and 1940's that white philanthropy was reluctant to encourage research by Negroes, particularly in the social sciences. It appeared that virtually all of the well-prepared Negro social scientists had views considered too radical on the race question. Money was committed to Negro institutions in the hope of maintaining social peace; therefore vague programs to improve "race relations" were funded while serious research by competent Negroes literally starved for funds. In a revealing commentary on the situation, Ralph Bunche, at the time one of the forceful Young Turks in the social science division at Howard, wrote:

> Negro scholars even more completely than white, are subject to the munificence of the controlling wealthy groups in the population. Negro institutions of higher learning, particularly, are the inevitable puppets of white philanthropy. Obviously, therefore, whatever reorganization and reorientation of "Negro Education" is to be contemplated, must meet the full approval of these controlling interests. It is hardly to be expected that under such conditions "Negro Education" could ever direct itself to really effective solutions for the problems of the masses of working-class Negroes. The interests of those who contribute so much to the support of Negro education demand that the masses of Negroes remain what they now are—a handy and docile labor supply from which additional profits can be wrung, some minute share of which will in turn find its way to the support of "Negro Education" . . . Schools like Hampton and Tuskegee train Negroes in craftsmanship but make no effort to give them any industrial or social orientation . . . In fact, most Negro schools tread very lightly in the purely academic fields of the social sciences. They cannot afford to take the risk of losing their financial support.[62]

In the 1930's Negro scholars in the social sciences were still looked upon as "dangerous," especially if they were competent. The peculiar ambivalence, if not hostility, of foundations at that time is illustrated by the politics surrounding the organization and execution of the Carnegie Foundation's comprehensive survey of the "Negro problem" under the direction of Gunnar Myrdal. A similarly painful story was the death of the *Encyclopedia of the Negro,* which was to be edited by W. E. B. Du Bois and Guy B. Johnson, one of the most ambitious projects involving a substantial number of Negro scholars, though white scholars like Howard Odum, Robert E. Park, and Guy B. Johnson were involved, presumably to give "balance" to the encyclopedia. The project, conceived by Du Bois as early as 1909, was formally incorporated in 1932 by James H. Dillard, W. E. B. Du Bois, Charles S. Johnson, Mordecai W. Johnson, Waldo G. Leland, and Anson Phelps Stokes. After years of work a *Preparatory Volume of the Encyclopedia of the Negro* appeared in 1946 with contributions by Du Bois, Guy Johnson, L. D. Reddick, and Rayford W. Logan. Some controversy exists about the precise reason for the refusal of the foundations to support this project which included many of the most distinguished scholars on the subject, but one white anthropologist has claimed that his word alone was sufficient to "kill the encyclopedia," some indication of how scholarship reflected race relations in general.[63]

Despite these handicaps the research productivity of the Negro historians, sociologists, and economists in the 1930's is surprising, especially when the small number of Negro Ph.D.'s at that time is considered. In 1936, for example, there were only nine in history, fifteen in sociology, and five in economics.[64] As a group it is fair to say that Negro scholars made a substantial contribution to the rational study of race, and were pioneers in interracial cooperation among scholars in meetings at Atlanta, Fisk, and Howard, and in journals like the *Journal of Negro History,* the *Journal of Negro Education,* and *Phylon: The Atlanta University Review of Race and Culture.* The studies of Ellis O. Knox also reveal that for the fifteen-year period 1932-1947, about 85 per cent of the 2,535 M.A. theses and 359 Ph.D. dissertations on Negro subjects accepted by American universities were done by Negroes,[65] some indication of how neglected the field was in those years, since Negro graduate students and professors were greatly underrepresented in higher education in general.

Nevertheless, on the whole the isolation imposed by segregation was a powerful deterrent to sustained research and writing by Negro scholars and the hardship on scientists was even greater than for those in the humanities or social sciences because of the high cost of laboratories. Margaret Walker's memorable lines "the struggle staggers us/for bread, for pride, for simple dignity," are not an inappropriate characterization of the situation of Negro scholars no matter how distinguished in the era of hard-edged segregation.

It is easy to forget now just how segregation operated as a powerful deterrent to sustained research or writing.[66] In the South, Negro scholars were almost universally barred from libraries, from white university laboratories, and from meetings of local chapters of learned societies. Farther north, in Washington, D.C., for example, even the meetings and dinners of a national organization like Phi Beta Kappa were closed to Negro members, most of whom were Howard University faculty who had been inducted at New England colleges and universities.[67] In the *Twenty-fifth Anniversary Report* (June 1933) of the Harvard Class of 1908, Alain Locke (Ph.D. 1918, Harvard) wrote the following poignant lines to his classmates after outlining his career since his years as a Rhodes Scholar at Oxford (1907-1910) and graduate student at the University of Berlin (1910-1911): "One thing to be regretted has been the comparative isolation that separates Negro life and institutions from even academic and cultural interests at large; but I have done what I could in an interpretative way to bridge some of these barriers."[68]

A much better illustration however was the career of Ernest Everett Just (Ph.D. 1916, University of Chicago), the most distinguished (and probably most frustrated) Negro scientist in America. After a brilliant undergraduate career at Dartmouth College (A.B., Phi Beta Kappa, 1907) he began in 1909 his graduate training at the Marine Biological Laboratory at Woods Hole, Massachusetts, where he was to conduct research every summer until 1930, with the exception of two years. At the Marine Biological Laboratory Just was to become in Frank Lillie's words "more widely acquainted with the embryological resources of the marine fauna than probably any other person."[69] Just's fifty papers on fertilization and cellular physiology brought him international recognition, but that was not sufficient to escape the trap of color in the United States. As Lillie, his mentor at the University of Chicago, put it, "Just's scientific career was a constant struggle for opportunity for research, the breath of his life. He was condemned by race to remain attached to a Negro institution unfitted by means and tradition to give full opportunity to ambitions such as his."[70]

One of the things that made Howard unfit was its dictatorial president for thirty-four years (1926-1960), Mordecai W. Johnson, who, typically, succeeded in minimizing Just's opportunities for research at Howard. When Just secured research funds through the National Research Council, Julius Rosenwald, the General Education Board, and the Carnegie Corporation, there ensued power struggles in which the president sought to control the expenditure of the funds.[71] In his later years Just worked for short periods at the Kaiser Wilhelm Institut für Biologie in Berlin, at the University of Paris, and the Naples Zoological Station. The most comprehensive statement of Just's pioneering research methods and findings are in his two books, *Basic Methods for Experiments in Eggs of Marine Animals* (1939) and *The Biology of the Cell Surface* (1939). "An element of tragedy," Lillie said,

> ran through all Just's scientific career due to the limitations imposed by being a Negro in America, to which he could make no lasting psychological adjustment in spite of earnest efforts on his part. The numerous grants for research did not compensate for failure to receive an appointment in one of the large universities or research institutes. He felt this as a social stigma, and hence unjust to a scientist of his recognized standing . . . That a man of his ability, scientific devotion, and of such strong personal loyalties as he gave and received, should have been warped in the land of his birth must remain a matter for regret.[72]

One consequence of his experience was that Just discouraged students from pursuing a career in science, pointing to his own bitter disappointment as illustrative of how race determined opportunity and access to well-equipped laboratories.[73] E. P. Lyons, dean of the University of Minnesota Medical School, summarized the conflict between racism and merit in American academic life when he discussed Just's self-exile to Europe after his rebuffs from the Rockefeller Institute. "The greatest problem in American biology," he said,

> is Professor Just. He properly belongs to an institution like Rockefeller, and he was the most logical candidate to take the place of Jacques Loeb when he died, but the Rockefeller Foundation, spending millions of dollars to combat disease internationally, couldn't summon enough courage to solve an inter-racial problem. By its example it could have set a precedent to follow that science knows no race nor creed. What it actually did was only catering to old prejudices in spite of its presumed internationalism.[74]

The case of Professor Just is noteworthy for several reasons. First, it illustrates that at least until 1940, no amount of distinction in research was sufficient for a Negro scholar to be offered the superior research advantages of white institutions, and they were as a result condemned to work in institutions on the whole unsympathetic to their work. Perhaps equally important, Just's career showed the extent to which prevailing white attitudes about stereotypes of Negroes determined the American reputation of Negro scientists. Just believed in freedom of inquiry and racial equality, and his very existence was a challenge to racist contentions about the scientific ability of Negroes. Just's manner and mien did not conform to the prevailing white idea of what a Negro scientist should be like. On the other hand, George Washington Carver, who never published a research paper in any of the standard journals, had what was considered a proper demeanor, that of a kindly, pious old man who "knew his place" around white folks. As a humble agronomist he seemed to put whites at ease, and his mystical, anti-scientific approach to his work—"talking to the flowers" he called it—was quaint and acceptable. As a result, Carver is the best-known Negro scientist, just as Booker T. Washington was the best known Negro "educator," while Just or President John Hope are much less known. The examples could be considerably multiplied. The entomologist Charles H. Turner won an international reputation based on a steady output of research articles published in leading journals but was ignored in the United States and forced by American racial circumstances to teach biology at Sumner High School in St. Louis.[75] In physics, Fisk University's Elmer S. Imes's work on infrared spectra of the hydrogen halides, or Herman Branson's (Howard) research on radioactive isotopes and negative ions in the mass spectra of the methylamines[76] are only the best known examples of the distinguished research done by Negro scientists. In chemistry the most productive research done by Negroes was concentrated overwhelmingly for many years at Howard University under the leadership of Percy L. Julian (physostigmine and cortisone), R. Percy Barnes (alpha and beta diketones), and others.[77] It is important to note the relationship between resources and research in this connection.

As part of President Franklin D. Roosevelt's political program with respect to Negroes, the federal government's financial commitment to Howard University, especially its building program, increased tremendously under the leadership of Harold Ickes, secretary of the Department of the Interior which was responsible at that time for administering Howard's federal appropriation. Howard was a vital symbol of "Negro progress" under the New Deal, and one which cost Roosevelt very little politically in the South since it did not alter federal policy on segregation. Roosevelt himself dedicated Howard's new chemistry building on

October 26, 1936.[78] Whatever the motives involved, this was the first time that a Negro institution had received more than a million dollars for a science facility, and for many years Howard's science facilities were the best available to Negro scientists in universities. At other Negro institutions, science received a low priority in development plans, and only in the last twenty years has there been a change in policy. It is interesting to note that American industry dropped its bars to Negro scientists long before white universities. As early as 1940 there were three hundred Negro research chemists in industry.

The best known Negro industrial scientists have been James Parsons, director of research at the Duriron Company of Dayton, Ohio; Lloyd A. Hall, chief chemist of the Griffith Laboratories of Chicago; W. Lincoln Hawkins of Bell Telephone Laboratories; and William G. Haynes of the Union Pacific Railroad.[79] Charles R. Drew, the distinguished surgeon and serologist, remarked that Negroes who were employed in industrial research were especially fortunate because they did not "have to spend long years during [their] most creative period teaching in second rate institutions, which for the most part, have been totally ill-equipped for the carrying-on of productive research."[80]

In fairness to Negro colleges in the South, however, it should be pointed out that until relatively recent years, even in the white southern state universities, which had an overwhelming advantage over the Negro institutions in terms of financial support (though less than northern or western universities), achievements in scientific research were low. As one observer commented in the early 1940's about white southern institutions:

> The sort of scientific training which our students must have cannot be provided by second-rate institutions, and it has been repeatedly shown that we have relatively few institutions in the South which could, by any stretch of the imagination be regarded as approaching the status of first-rate universities. It is doubtful, however, whether there is a single institution in the South that is giving adequate attention and support to the sciences . . . Few people actually realize how expensive graduate work in the sciences must inevitably be.[81]

In some respects, at least, the lack of support for research in Negro colleges has been a part of a regional pattern,[82] but that should not obscure the pernicious role of racism. The Hatch Act of 1887 established programs of scientific investigation and experimentation in land grant colleges and universities to make them research centers, but for half a century not one state supporting a Negro land grant college established an experiment station for the use of Negroes.[83] Only in the last decade, for example, have Negro land grant institutions received any funds from their states for research, despite the fact that the Second Morrill Act of 1890 required that where racially separate institutions were maintained "the funds received in such State or Territory be equitably divided."[84] The disparities in support, from state as well as federal sources, are shocking. The National Science Foundation has reported that in 1968 the white land grant colleges in states where there are dual institutions received $200 million from various federal agencies, roughly eleven times the amount (about $18 million) awarded to Negro land grant colleges. For example, Clemson of South Carolina received $5.8 million from the federal government while its Negro counterpart, South Carolina State, received $490,000. The *Civil Rights Digest* (Spring 1970) exposes the continuation of the long history of discrimination in this area with telling comparisons:

> The University of Georgia, with 10 times the enrollment of Fort Valley, received nearly 24 times as much Federal aid. The University of Florida with less than five times the enrollment of Florida A & M, received 24 times as much Federal aid. Virginia Polytechnic Institute, with only 1½ times the enrollment of Virginia State, received five times as much Federal aid. North Carolina State, with less than 3½ times the enrollment of North Carolina A & T received nearly nine times as much Federal aid.[85]

> Similarly the states themselves appropriate nine times as much money to support the white Land Grant institutions than their black counterparts. Georgia appropriated 20 times as much state aid, Texas more than eight times, for white schools. In no case was there an equitable distribution of funds based on enrollment.[86]

It is not surprising, in view of these gross inequities, that the state-supported Negro institutions are forced to commit nearly all of their resources to teaching, and very little to research. The privately supported Negro colleges in the South are even more hard pressed for funds as the costs of instruction have risen faster than their sources of support. Earl J. McGrath reported that in 1959-1960, for example, Negro institutions spent $15 per student for organized research, while the average of all higher institutions of education in the United States was $301 per student, or twenty times as much. Put another way, in 1959-1960, Negro colleges and universities accounted for 1.91 per cent of the total expenditures in higher education, but only thirteen hundredths of 1.0 per cent of the billion dollars spent that year for research.[87] Some of the responsibility for the failure of Negro schools to become at least modest centers for research rests on their administrations.

Charles H. Thompson observed that too many administrators of Negro colleges "mistake omnipotence for omniscience," and "assume that because final authority rests with them, ultimate wisdom does also," and, finally, "confuse educational dictatorship with educational leadership."[88] E. Franklin Frazier said flatly that the failure of Negro scholars to more productively study major problems in the social sciences was partly the fault of what he called the "ignorant administration of Negro schools which have refused the intelligent proposals of Negro scholars." "As long as 25 years ago," he continued,

> I pointed out that urbanization had changed the entire relationship of Negroes to American society and that comprehensive and fundamental research should be done on Negroes in cities. But those Negroes who have controlled the destiny of Negro intellectuals ignored this and even today no Negro college or university is concerned with this fundamental problem.[89]

Similarly the shortsightedness of these institutions in not supporting, at least at Howard and several other institutions, a university press is startling. In the period of Howard's greatest research productivity, white university presses or private publishers had to be relied upon for publication opportunities. (The deceptively named "Negro Universities Press" is unrelated to Negro institutions and is a subsidiary of Greenwood Press.)

New Trends and Prospects for the Future

It has been clear that broad social and political changes in American society have had a greater impact on the fortunes of Negro colleges and their faculties than any purely internal efforts. Thus, changes in the general group status of Negroes created by urbanization, the gradual acquisition of political leverage, and the altered position of the United States as a world power, have had a profound impact on Negro scholars and their opportunities. After the Second World War, the gathering momentum of the movement to desegregate higher education gradually destroyed the basis for the upsurge of quality that marked the previous twenty years.

While it is true that in 1946 Robert Maynard Hutchins reported strong opposition to the appointment of Negroes to the faculty of the University of Chicago, regarded as a "liberal" university, there was nevertheless a slow erosion of racial barriers in higher education.[90]

Since some of the first Negroes to break these barriers were naturally among the top Negro scholars (like Allison Davis who left Dillard for Chicago, Abram L. Harris who left Howard for Chicago, and John Hope Franklin who left Howard for Brooklyn) and the supply was small, token desegregation was sufficient to slowly erode the small but productive clusters of research scholars in Negro schools. Segregation had produced the situation where superior men were consigned to schools inferior in facilities and encouragement of research, no matter how commendable their commitment to provide a sound education to Negro undergraduates. By the late 1950's and 1960's token desegregation had been accelerated by the impact of the "black revolution," especially the black studies explosion, and there has been heated discussion about a "black brain drain." There are numerous indications that the leading institutions of the "segregation era" have become enfeebled. The once high quality of journals like the *Journal of Negro History,* the *Journal of Negro Education,* and *Phylon* has declined precipitously in recent years and no Negro institution now publishes a really first-class scholarly journal. A number of distinguished scholars remained in Negro institutions during this period, but in virtually every case their retirement left their departments bereft of recognized scholars and many younger men were being recruited to white institutions.

There has been a countermovement away from tokenism, easily misunderstood and much maligned by older Negro scholars sensitive to its exaggeration and rhetorical excesses. High levels of racial tension in society have usually produced an acute awareness of the difficulty of existing in a "double environment," the white world and the separate black social world. The conflict between racial and national loyalties has been a persistent theme. As long ago as 1897 Du Bois asked:

What, after all, am I? Am I an American or am I a Negro? Can I be both? Or is it my duty to cease to be a Negro as soon as possible and be an American? If I strive as a Negro am I not perpetuating the very cleft that threatens and separates black and white America? . . . It is such incessant self-questioning and the hesitation that arises from it, that is making the present period a time of vacillation and contradiction for the American Negro; combined race responsibility is shirked, race enterprises languish, and the best blood, the best talent, the best energy of the Negro people cannot be marshalled to do the bidding of the race. They stand back to make room for every rascal and demagogue who chooses to cloak his selfish deviltry under the veil of race pride . . . Have we in America a distinct mission as a race . . . or is self-obliteration the highest end to which Negro blood dare aspire?[91]

The emergence of "black consciousness" on Negro campuses in the last five years is easily the most dramatic change in their institutional life and in the way some faculty and students regard themselves. As much a commitment to a way of life and a cluster of values as a point of view, black consciousness is the most widespread attempt to achieve an intellectual and cultural position designed to overcome the vicious heritage of racism in America. Because of the powerful psychological dimension to the movement and its rejection *en bloc* of whites, it has been a source of alarm to the leadership of Negro colleges, who realize all too clearly how dependent they are on white institutions for support. Unlike their predecessors, who despite the costs involved sought to achieve academic acceptance on white terms, many of the younger black academics reject white definitions of their situation. There is a growing disposition to challenge not only the methods of scholarship, but also its values and objectives as defined by white scholars. Many conservatives who shout cries of alarm at the dangers of this movement often forget the scandal of how American scholarship has rarely lived up to its ideals of objectivity or neutrality in matters relating to race. Unfortunately it is too late in the day and the record too blemished to feign horror at the idea that scholarship is impossible in an atmosphere overwhelmed by political and social struggle. There are increasing numbers of young black professors who see their main goal as contributing to the liberation of their people rather than acceptance by white scholars in their disciplines.

Wide differences of opinion exist, dividing principally on two questions: whether racial justice is possible in the United States, and whether it is possible to reject so-called "white standards" of scholarship without destroying all standards. There are also real differences about what the colleges should be, some arguing for them to become social and ideological centers for "liberation" in a political sense, while others insist that a college's real contribution to liberation must remain on the level of research and writing. One of the chief spokesmen for black consciousness, Nathan Hare, has written that "The black scholar can no longer afford to ape the allegedly 'value-free' approach of white scholarship. He must reject absolutely the notion that it is 'not professional' ever to become emotional, that it is somehow improper to be 'bitter' as a black man, that emotion and reason are mutually exclusive . . . The black scholar must develop new and appropriate norms and values, new institutional structures, and in order to be effective in this regard, he must also develop and be guided by a new ideology."[92]

So far, no Negro college has agreed to support the new "black scholarship" for a variety of obvious as well as subtle reasons. Quite apart from the racial issue, many doubt that anything remotely resembling scholarship as understood in the United States can be produced by researchers whose work is dominated by an ideology. The work of white scholars on race reviewed earlier in this essay was of course also dominated by an ideology, white supremacy, and no one can doubt it who has really taken the pains to read G. Stanley Hall or Howard Odum. But for all that, and it is quite a lot indeed, no institution outside of the South, with the possible exception of Princeton under Woodrow Wilson, ever made a clear commitment to white supremacy as an ideology guiding institutional development. Nevertheless, it is likely that a growing number of black social scientists, tired of the ambiguities, evasions, and hypocrisies inherently a part of the present situation, will find the position of Abd-al Hakimu Ibn Alkalimat (Gerald McWorter) persuasive. He has written that:

> Many black social scientists seemingly have not really known the extent to which science is inevitably a handservant to ideology, a tool for people to shape if not create, reality . . . we need a revolutionary ideology that reflects the utility of a black social analysis, the inevitable correctness of African prophecy of black gods creating a new man and the immortality of communal love as the basis for a commitment to kill and die for the liberation of all black people. In other words we need to get this shit on, and for that we need a revolutionary script for the terrible black drama of cosmic forces that we're about to rain down on these pitiful ofays.[93]

It is likely that there will be more adherents to a kind of cultural nationalism in black institutions rather than to any serious effort to launch revolution in theory or fact from colleges. Like all deeply felt movements, such a nationalism has great potential for destroying any possibility of genuinely critical (that is, also self-critical) intellectual centers in black institutions. The shrill stridency of many of the propagandists of blackness seems to confirm Ralph Ellison's prophetic dismay with Americans (white and black) who have an appetite for "that intellectual abandon, that lack of restraint, which seizes those who regard blackness as an absolute and who see in it a release from the complications of the real world."[94]

It remains to be seen whether black consciousness will be another of the tragic detours taken by Negro educators. Just as the earlier movements of moral uplift, character building, and industrial education were permeated by assumptions that Negroes were not ready for serious intellectual work, there is a subtle and of course unarticulated racist assumption in some of the black consciousness position that critical reason is for whites and visceral rage is for blacks. It is not surprising that some whites, including powerful foundations, support a position which confirms the hoary view of the Negro as a surly savage incapable of genuine thought, research, or scholarship. Many whites are apparently titillated by the spectacle of black college teachers posturing as hysterical prophets of doom, just as white New Yorkers once delighted in the antiwhite plays of LeRoi Jones (Ameer Baraka). Black studies programs, growing originally out of a legitimate need to correct the distortions and omissions of WASP curricula, have become in many instances special colonies within white universities for the containment of angry blacks—the Trojan horse again. The foundations have so far been prepared to subsidize these programs, often on the flimsiest grounds, and still persist in viewing black universities as service schools which ought not to try to develop sound standards of intellectual achievement and scholarship. Whether serious scholarship by Negroes will survive this decade will depend, in the end, on the extent to which racism can be disentangled from our conceptions of the human purposes of education and scholarship.

I wish to thank the following persons for consenting to be interviewed on various aspects of Negro education: Charles H. Thompson, Rayford W. Logan, Charles H. Wesley, Elsie M. Lewis, M. Wharton Young, Louis A. Hansborough, Carroll L. Miller, James M. Nabrit, Jr.

I am especially indebted to Herman R. Branson for important data on Negro scientists, and to Dorothy B. Porter for many sources on scholarship by American Negroes, and to Rayford W. Logan for information about Atlanta University and the *Encyclopedia of the Negro*. None are of course responsible in any way for any errors or interpretations in the essay.

References

1. See Edward Shils's discussion of psychological aspects of Asian and African scholars similar to those affecting Negro scholars in America in his article "Color, the Universal Intellectual Community, and the Afro-Asian Intellectual," *Dædalus* (Spring 1967), pp. 279-295. An example of the "peripheral" character of Negroes in American academic life is the still frequently heard complaint that even after years of rigorous and productive scholarship Negro scholars remain the "invisible men" of their profession. Except for one or two notable exceptions, they rarely, if ever, are invited to present papers to the national meetings of their professional organizations, despite the "high regard" some of their work is supposed to enjoy. It is not unusual for their work to be omitted from consideration entirely, behavior Americans usually believe a monopoly of Soviet historians. In John Higham, Leonard Krieger, and Felix Gilbert, *History* (Englewood Cliffs, N. J.: Prentice-Hall, 1965), W. E. B. Du Bois, Carter G. Woodson, Rayford W. Logan, and Benjamin Quarles are not mentioned once, and although there is discussion of the *Catholic Historical Review* (begun in 1916) and the "incipient professionalization of Catholic historiography under the auspices of the Catholic University of America" (p. 34), there is total silence about Woodson's founding of the Association for the Study of Negro Life and History in 1915, the establishment of the *Journal of Negro History* in 1916, and the "incipient professionalization" of historical writing about Negroes in the United States. "To be wholly overlooked," John Adams once said, "and to know it, are intolerable. If Crusoe on his island had the library of Alexandria, and a certainty that he should never again see the face of man, would he ever open a volume?" John Adams, *Works*, VI (Boston, 1851), 239-240.

2. John Hope Franklin, "The Dilemma of the American Negro Scholar," in Herbert Hill, ed., *Soon One Morning* (New York: Alfred A. Knopf, 1963), pp. 62-76.

3. Although Negroes are now overwhelmingly urban dwellers, it is clear that the peasant heritage is still very powerful. Hardly a unique phenomenon, the anguished isolation of intellectuals in peasant cultures has been the subject of wide study. See, for example, Richard Pipes, ed., *The Russian Intelligentsia* (New York: Columbia University Press, 1961) and Edward Shils, "The Culture of the Indian Intellectual," *Sewanee Review*, 67 (1959), 239-261, 401-421.

4. *Annual Report of the Freedmen's Aid Society of the M. E. Church* (1868), p. 14.

5. An illustration of the impact of the defeat of Reconstruction on the higher education of Negroes was the spectacle of William H. Councill, president of the State Normal School at Huntsville, Alabama, and Booker T. Washington's rival, insisting on trying to have none but ex-Confederate officers on his board of trustees, whose views on the education of the Negro are not difficult to imagine. Councill said, for exam-

ple, that "When the old, gray-haired veterans who followed General Lee's tattered banners to Appomattox shall have passed away, the Negro's best friends shall have gone, for the Negro got more out of slavery than they did." Quoted in Horace Mann Bond, "The Influence of Personalities on the Public Education of Negroes in Alabama, I," *Journal of Negro Education,* 6 (January 1937), 24-26.

6. Cited in Bond, "The Influence of Personalities on the Public Education of Negroes in Alabama, I," p. 24.

7. D. O. W. Holmes, *Evolution of the Negro College* (New York: Columbia University Press, 1934), p. 13.

8. Horace Mann Bond, *The Education of the Negro in the American Social Order* (New York: Prentice-Hall, 1934), p. 149.

9. Bond, "The Influence of Personalities on the Public Education of Negroes in Alabama, I," p. 23.

10. See Emmett J. Scott, "Twenty Years After: An Appraisal of Booker T. Washington," *Journal of Negro Education,* 5 (October 1936), 543-554.

11. See Lionel B. Fraser, "The Dilemma of Our Colleges and Universities," *Opportunity: Journal of Negro Life,* 15 (May 1937), 167-171.

12. Charles H. McCord, *The American Negro as a Dependent, Defective and Delinquent* (Nashville: Benson Printing Company, 1914), p. 124.

13. *Ibid.,* pp. 42-44.

14. G. Stanley Hall, a warm supporter of Washington's supine acceptance of disfranchisement in return for vocational education, said, "For myself, I doubt if any educational institution in the world's history ever showed in those who attend from year to year greater progress along so many lines—dress, manners, intelligence, morals, health—than is seen in the pupils of Tuskegee." Hall did demur from Washington's opposition to higher education, however. "The only modification," he said, "of Mr. Washington's programme that seems needed is that which Professor Du Bois pleads for, namely, opportunity for all the higher cultural elements of education to every Negro who can take it and make use of it." *Proceedings of the Massachusetts Historical Society,* 2d ser., 19 (Boston, 1905), 105-106.

15. McCord, *The American Negro,* pp. 66-68.

16. For a fuller discussion of industrial education see Henry Allen Bullock, *A History of Negro Education in the South from 1619 to the Present* (Cambridge, Mass.: Harvard University Press, 1967), pp. 167-193.

17. Sterling A. Brown, *The Negro in American Fiction* (Washington, D. C.: The Associates in Negro Folk Education, 1937), p. 54.

18. See Kelly Miller, "Negro Education and the Depression," *Journal of Negro Education,* 2 (January 1933), 1-4.

19. See Kelly Miller, "Howard: The National Negro University," in Alain Locke, ed., *The New Negro: An Interpretation* (New York: Albert and Charles Boni, 1925), p. 314.

20. Quoted in Horace Mann Bond, "The Influence of Personalities on the Public Education of Negroes in Alabama, II," *Journal of Negro Education,* 6 (April 1937), 174.

21. Rayford W. Logan, *The Negro in the United States,* vol. I, *A History to 1945—From Slavery to Second-Class Citizenship* (New York: Van Nostrand Reinhold Co., 1970), p. 66.

22. The first American Negro to earn a Ph.D. was Patrick Francis Healy, S.J., who received the degree from the University of Louvain in 1865. He joined the faculty of Georgetown University in 1867, and was president of the university from 1873 to 1882. Healy's career, however, was atypical in virtually every respect, and no other American Negro Catholic has since had a similar career. See Albert S. Foley, S.J., *God's Men of Color* (New York: Farrar, Strauss, & Co., 1955), pp. 23-31.

23. William A. Dunning, *Reconstruction: Political and Economic* (New York: Harper and Brothers, 1907), p. 212.

24. See Richard Hofstadter, *Social Darwinism in American Thought* (Boston: Beacon Press, 1955), chaps. 3, 4, and 9.

25. G. Stanley Hall, "A Few Results of Recent Scientific Study of the Negro in America," *Proceedings of the Massachusetts Historical Society,* 2d ser., 19 (1905), 95-107. It is especially interesting to note that when Hall returned to the United States from Germany in 1872 he applied for a position on the faculty at Howard, saying that he had "strong preference" for the university. It is not known why he was not hired, but this change in point of view about Negroes may be an index of how powerful a change in public opinion had been wrought by the "New South" propagandists and their northern allies. See the facsimile of Hall's letter of March 16, 1872, in Walter Dyson, *Howard University: The Capstone of Negro Education, A History, 1867-1940* (Washington, D. C.: Howard University, 1941). On page 104 of the *Proceedings* Hall writes, "For myself, an abolitionist both by conviction and descent, I wish to confess my error of opinion in those days." It seems from his comments, page 105, that Booker Washington influenced his change of mind.

26. See, for example, Robert Bennett Bean, "Some Racial Peculiarities of the Negro Brain," *American Journal of Anatomy,* 5 (September 1906), 353-432; Marion J. Mayo, *The Mental Capacity of the American Negro* (New York: Science Press, 1913); and George Oscar Ferguson, *The Psychology of the Negro: An Experimental Study* (New York: Science Press, 1916).

27. Albert Bushnell Hart, *The Southern South* (New York: Appleton and Company, 1912), p. 104.

28. See Rayford W. Logan, *Howard University: The First Hundred Years, 1867-1967* (New York: New York University Press, 1969), pp. 242-243, 309, 634. Even more perplexing is the fact that Hart made his 1912 statement after serving as adviser to W. E. B. Du Bois during his graduate work at Harvard. Hart highly praised Du Bois' work, and according to Du Bois, who was always sensitive to any racial slight, he was "one of Hart's favorite pupils." See Francis L. Broderick, "The Academic Training of W. E. B. Du Bois," *Journal of Negro Education,* 27 (Winter 1958), 10-16, and W. E. B. Du Bois, *Dusk of Dawn: An Essay Toward an Autobiography of a Race Concept* (New York: Harcourt, Brace & World, Inc., 1940), p. 38.

29. Howard W. Odum, *American Sociology: The Story of Sociology in the United States Through 1950* (New York: Longmans, Green, 1951), pp. 154-155.

30. *Ibid.*, pp. 38-41.

31. *Ibid.*, p. 41.

32. *Ibid.*, p. 188.

33. Dorothy B. Porter, "The Organized Educational Activities of Negro Literary Societies, 1828-1846," *Journal of Negro Education,* 5 (October 1936), 565.

34. A recent history of the American Negro Academy is an unpublished 1966 M.A. thesis by Mignon Miller, "The American Negro Academy: An Intellectual Movement During the Era of Negro Disfranchisement, 1897-1924," in the Negro Collection of the Howard University Library.

35. See William Simmons, *Men of Mark, Eminent, Progressive and Rising* (Cleveland: Rewell & Co., 1887), pp. 530-535.

36. See W. E. B. Du Bois, "Of Alexander Crummell," in his *Souls of Black Folk* (Chicago: A. C. McClurg & Co., 1903), pp. 215-227.

37. Du Bois, *Dusk of Dawn,* p. 58.

38. For a contemporary scholar's appraisal of *The Philadelphia Negro,* see E. Digby Baltzell's analytical introduction to the 1968 Schocken Books reprint. E. Franklin Frazier, whose own work *The Negro Family in Chicago* is very highly regarded, said of *The Philadelphia Negro* that "Nothing better has ever been done in the United States on a Negro community." See E. Franklin Frazier, "The Role of the Social Scientist in the Negro College," in Robert E. Martin, ed., *The Civil War in Perspective: Papers Contributed to the Twenty-Fourth Annual Conference of the Division of the Social Sciences,* Howard University, 1961, pp. 9-18.

39. Du Bois, *Dusk of Dawn,* p. 62.

40. Du Bois, *Darkwater: Voices from Within the Veil* (New York: Harcourt, Brace and Howe, 1920), p. 21.

41. Du Bois, *Dusk of Dawn,* p. 94.

42. When Du Bois returned to Atlanta the departments of economics and sociology were combined, but for most of the period 1933-1944 he was professor of sociology.

43. Du Bois, *Black Reconstruction* (New York: Harcourt, Brace and Company, 1935), pp. 726-727.

44. See *Berea College* v. *Kentucky,* 211 U. S. 26 (1908), in which the United States Supreme Court upheld *Berea College* v. *Commonwealth* 123 Ky. App. Ct. 209 S.W. 623 (1906).

45. Harry W. Greene, "Sixty Years of Doctorates Conferred Upon Negroes," *Journal of Negro Education,* 6 (January 1937), 30-37.

46. Harry W. Greene, *Holders of Doctorates Among American Negroes* (Boston: Meador Co., 1946). Greene must be used with care. Of the 393 persons listed as Negro Ph.D.'s, at least two, Samuel Strong and Herbert Aptheker, are white, and one, V[ishnu] V. Oak, an East Indian.

47. See Charles H. Thompson, "Why a Class B College?" *Journal of Negro Education,* 2 (October 1933), 427-431.

48. Greene, "Sixty Years of Doctorates Conferred Upon Negroes," p. 35.

49. For a discussion of the philanthropies concerned with Negro education see Ullin W. Leavell, "Trends of Philanthropy in Negro Education," *Journal of Negro Education,* 2 (January 1933), 38-52.

50. Edwin R. Embree, *Julius Rosenwald Fund, Review of Two Decades, 1917-1936* (Chicago, 1936).

51. For the impact of this policy on Howard see Logan, *Howard University,* pp. 223-224, 257-258, 265-266, 370, and Dyson, *Howard University,* pp. 291, 294, 321, and 440.

52. For the data on Atlanta University I am indebted to Dr. Rayford W. Logan, head of its Department of History, 1933-1938. See also, Clarence A. Bacote, *The Story of Atlanta University: A Century of Service, 1865-1965* (Atlanta: Atlanta University, 1969).

53. An indication of the need for the *Journal of Negro Education* was that the two most influential policy shaping studies of Negro education were done by whites. At least one of them, Thomas Jesse Jones, was suspected by many Negro scholars of being an enemy of the higher intellectual aspirations of the race. The two studies were: Thomas Jesse Jones, *Negro Education: A Study of the Private and Higher Schools for Colored People in the United States,* 2 vols. (Washington, D. C.: U. S. Government Printing Office, 1917) and Arthur J. Klein, *Survey of Negro Colleges and Universities* (Washington, D. C.: U. S. Government Printing Office, 1929). For the impact of these studies see Walter Crosby Ells, "Results of Surveys of Negro Colleges and Universities," *Journal of Negro Education,* 4 (October 1935), 476-481.

54. Charles H. Thompson, "Why a Journal of Negro Education?" *Journal of Negro Education,* 1 (April 1932), 2.

55. Charles H. Thompson, "Court Action the Only Reasonable Alternative to Reducing Immediate Abuses of the Negro Separate School," *Journal of Negro Education,* 4 (July 1935), 419-434.

56. Charles H. Thompson, "Editorial Comment," *Journal of Negro Education,* 16 (Winter 1947), 1-9.

57. See C. H. Thompson, "Rank, Tenure and Retirement of Teachers in Negro Colleges," *Journal of Negro Education,* 10 (April 1941), 139-150.

58. See the 1934 *Yearbook,* "The Physical and Mental Abilities of the American Negro," and the first ten volumes of the *Journal.*

59. See, for example, Ralph J. Bunche, "A Critical Analysis of the Tactics and Programs of Minority Groups," *Journal of Negro Education,* 4 (July 1935), 308-320. The constituency for such research was very small, since most Negroes associated with institutions like colleges and churches were hostile to an analytical approach, favoring instead rhetoric about "human relations" and "brotherhood." The Marxist orientation of some of this work was dropped by most of the group by the mid-1940's, at least in print.

60. Interview in August 1970 with James M. Nabrit, Jr. See also Charles H. Thompson, "Progress in the Elimination of Discrimination in White and Negro Teachers Salaries," *Journal of Negro Education,* 9 (January 1940), 1-4.

61. See Elmer A. Carter, "Charles S. Johnson," *Opportunity: Journal of Negro Life,* 15 (February 1937).

62. Ralph J. Bunche, "Education in Black and White," *Journal of Negro Education,* 5 (July 1936), 356.

63. See the "preparatory volume" published by the Phelps-Stokes Fund in 1946. I have secured details about the "killing of the project" from Rayford W. Logan.

64. Greene, "Sixty Years of Doctorates Conferred Upon Negroes," p. 34.

65. Ellis O. Knox, "The Negro as a Subject of University Research in 1946," *Journal of Negro Education,* 16 (Spring 1947), 180-189.

66. It should be noted, however, for analytical purposes that the other large grouping of "special colleges" in the United States—the Roman Catholic institutions—were perhaps even more intellectually isolated than Negro colleges, since their faculties were trained for the most part in Catholic institutions. Negro college faculties were more isolated socially, but since no Negro graduate school offered a Ph.D. prior to 1958, they were trained in "mainstream" universities. Despite the many obvious differences, however, it is useful to compare Catholic and Negro colleges and universities, because it becomes clear that in a great many instances low standards of

academic performance are the products of poverty, provincialism, and the expectation that education can serve an indefinite number of purposes.

67. Perceptive Negro educators recognized the peril of provincialism very early. John Hope, president of Morehouse College, said in November 1919 on the occasion of the inauguration of J. Stanley Durkee as president of Howard University that he had a great fear of intellectual isolation. See Inaugural Program of J. Stanley Durkee, President of Howard University, November 12, 1919, p. 36.

68. Page 456 of the *Report* (privately printed, 1933).

69. Frank R. Lillie, "Ernest Everett Just," *Science,* 95 (January 2, 1942), 10.

70. *Ibid.,* p. 11.

71. Interview in June 1970 with M. Wharton Young, professor of neuroanatomy at Howard University. See also Logan, *Howard University,* pp. 348-350.

72. Lillie, "Ernest Everett Just," p. 11.

73. See Ben Karpman, "Ernest Everett Just," *Journal of Nervous and Mental Disease* (February 1943), p. 253.

74. Quoted in Karpman, "Ernest Everett Just," p. 252. See also S. Milton Nabrit, "Ernest E. Just," *Phylon,* 7 (second quarter, 1946), 121-125.

75. Herman R. Branson, "The Negro Scientist: His Sociological Background, His Record of Achievement and His Potential" in Julius H. Taylor, ed., *The Negro in Science* (Baltimore: Morgan State College Press, 1955), pp. 5-6.

76. See Alexander Rich, ed., *Structural Chemistry and Molecular Biology: A Volume Dedicated to Linus Pauling by His Students, Colleagues and Friends* (San Francisco: W. H. Freeman and Company, 1968).

77. See Charles R. Drew, "Negro Scholars in Scientific Research," *Journal of Negro History,* 35 (April 1950), 135-149.

78. See Dyson, *Howard University,* p. 358 and photograph opposite page 74.

79. See Herman Branson, "The Negro and Scientific Research," *Negro History Bulletin,* 15 (April 1952), 131-137, and Drew, "Negro Scholars," p. 142.

80. Drew, "Negro Scholars," p. 142.

81. Quoted in Branson, "The Negro and Scientific Research," p. 133.

82. According to Branson, "The South has only one college, Charleston, in the first 50 liberal arts colleges throughout the country selected for high productivity of scientists. Among Roe's 64 mature scientists of outstanding achievement only 4 were from southern states. More significant . . . is Bello's finding that of the 104 outstanding young scientists under forty, only three are located in the South" (in Taylor, ed., *The Negro in Science,* p. 4).

83. See John W. Davis, "The Negro Land-Grant College," *Journal of Negro Education,* 2 (July 1933), 312-328.

84. See Herbert O. Reid and James M. Nabrit, Jr., "Remedies Under Statutes Granting Federal Aid to Land Grant Colleges," *Journal of Negro Education,* 17 (Summer 1948), 410-425.

85. William Payne, "Forgotten . . . But Not Gone: The Negro Land Grant Colleges," *Civil Rights Digest,* 3 (Spring 1970), 15; see table, p. 16.

86. *Ibid.,* pp. 15, 17.

87. Earl J. McGrath, *The Predominantly Negro Colleges and Universities in Transition* (New York: Teachers College, Columbia University, 1965), p. 108.

88. Charles H. Thompson, "Control and Administration of the Negro College," *Journal of Educational Sociology,* 19 (April 1946), p. 494.

89. E. Franklin Frazier, "The Failure of the Negro Intellectual," *Negro Digest,* 11 (February 1962), 32-33.

90. Horace Mann Bond quotes Hutchins in "The Negro Scholar and Professional in America," John P. Davis, ed., *American Negro Reference Book* (Englewood Cliffs, N. J.: Prentice-Hall, 1966), p. 554.

91. W. E. B. Du Bois, *The Conservation of Races* (Washington, D. C.: The American Negro Academy, 1897), p. 11.

92. Nathan Hare, "The Challenges of a Black Scholar," *The Black Scholar,* 1 (December 1969), 61-62 and throughout.

93. Abd-al Hakimu Ibn Alkalimat (Gerald McWorter), "The Ideology of Black Social Science," *The Black Scholar,* 1 (December 1969), 28, 35, and throughout.

94. Ralph Ellison, *Shadow and Act* (New York: Random House, Inc., 1964), p. 128.

PATRICIA ROBERTS HARRIS

The Negro College and Its Community

MOST NEGRO colleges were founded after the Civil War and the adoption of the Thirteenth, Fourteenth, and Fifteenth Amendments giving apparent citizenship to former slaves and other black persons. The few Negro colleges founded before the Civil War, as well as those established later, owed their existence to exclusionary practices of white institutions of higher learning and to the failure of primary and secondary institutions to prepare blacks for admission to the small number of white colleges that even in that period were prepared to admit the literate black man. The Negro college has always been a response to the peculiar relationship of the black man to the total American community. In a society in which blacks were the mudsill of the depressed southern agrarian economy, and the unskilled among the American proletariat of the North, it is remarkable that institutions were formed to provide "higher education" for blacks.

However, the requirement, partly moral and partly legal, that some education be provided for the new freedman made it clear that a source had to be found for teachers of these free men. The highly romanticized picture of the plantation mistress teaching Topsie to read was no longer even marginally credible when Topsie was a sharecropper instead of a slave immediately accessible to the big house.

The earliest of the black colleges staffed themselves with a significant number of not badly educated northern missionaries who came to bring education and salvation to the black institutions while their sisters and cousins went to Africa and Hawaii. In many instances the rigor of being a white educator of blacks in a southern community dedicated to maintaining the separation and superior-subordinate status of the races was even more dangerous and isolating than a similar role in Africa or in the South Seas. In these colleges, with their white missionary teachers presided over by white minister-missionaries, there was an additional dimension not usually found in overseas missions: the presence of educated blacks who joined the white missionaries as nominal equals and teachers of the black students. Despite the inhospitality of white education to aspiring black students, there were indeed blacks who had received an education. These men and women provided the nucleus of a group supported and nurtured during the last century by Negro colleges, the black intellectuals.

The impact of institutions with educated blacks and concerned whites on their immediate communities was significant. The presence in any location of an institution dedicated to the education of America's most dependent and disadvantaged minority was an anomaly that has never been fully appreciated. Concentration on the intellectual needs of people whose intellectual foundations had been deliberately ignored and whose capability for such activity had been deliberately negated by intensive and continuing propaganda made the Negro college a curiosity wherever found. For the white community, these institutions were twofold curiosities, referred to by the polite as the "colored" college and by the not so polite as the "nigger" college. By their presence they raised the question of whether the judgment of the absence of Negro intellectuality was a true one and gave rise to interesting adjustments and toleration by the white community. In community after community in which the titles of Mr., Miss, and Mrs. were denied blacks and in which given names were the customary means of address by whites to blacks, new accommodations were made for the staff of the colored college. Although the Mr. and Mrs. titles would be denied until the 1960's in many communities, titles of professor, doctor, and reverend were given to those who were members of the black academic community. It is, however, an interesting assessment of the low status of education generally in this country that professor and doctor would be given more readily as titles than Mr. and Miss, a condition that could not exist, for example, in Europe where the title professor carries the highest status and doctor comes just below it. Nevertheless, this grudging respect was a beginning of recognition that some status other than that of menial could be accorded to members of the black community. In addition, the existence of such institutions, especially in southern communities, was of help to the local economy, and while association with the staff of these colleges was shunned by most local residents, purveying of food, furnishings, and other services provided significant income for white entrepreneurs in these communities. The black teachers and administrators, although paid salaries below those of their white counterparts, were among the most affluent members of the black community and consequently a source of income to businessmen, white and black alike.

The interest of northern philanthropies provided for many of the black colleges' contacts with the outside world that would not have otherwise been available to either the white or black community. Many small towns heard the singing of Roland Hayes and Dorothy Maynor and participated in lecture series with national figures with whom they would have had no association had there not been a Negro college in the community. In addition, in many of these communities the black and white community members could sit together in the same room, although often in segregated sections, as they participated in these events. In community after community, the Negro college was the one place in which whites and blacks could sit down at a meal together (usually unpublicized) to discuss problems of race and other community concerns that cut across racial lines, but for which the public institutions provided no place for joint discussions.

When there was a need for representative blacks to deal with problems which the white community recognized as requiring black participation, the Negro college was often a source of such representation. However, the Negro college had no monopoly on providing such representation since the local undertaker or other businessman might be better known to the selecting white.

The most significant role of the black college in serving the Negro community was that of providing a glimpse of life as it might be to a racial minority relegated to the lowest rung of the nation's economic and social ladder. Although American life has never been conspicuously hospitable to the intellectual and the academician, the presence of some blacks in activities suggesting that brain as well as brawn resided inside black skins was an element that was useful in combatting the hopelessness now described as the absence of black pride. The characteristic American ambivalence toward intellectuality was also to be found, in abundance, among blacks. The low remuneration of college teachers, the disrespect shown by ignorant whites, and the high status accorded the businessman all contributed in some degree to the denigration of the black academician. The primacy of the black college president and his business manager in college policy-making and in community status was a reflection of the general American hostility to the intellectual. On the other hand, with notable exceptions in places such as Atlanta, Durham, and Birmingham, the black businessman never achieved in his community the reverence accorded to his white counterpart, probably because he was, whether undertaker or druggist, a small businessman whose influence in terms of service and employment of others was limited. The not so limited black college was, by contrast, usually a major black community employer, and, through its graduates, consistently adding to its constituency.

Through the production of this constituency, the black college created a community, the middle-class black community. Whatever may have been the objective competence of the graduates of black colleges when tested against median performances of white college graduates, the alumni of black colleges became the new black bourgeoisie. The creation and replenishment of an entire community was the most significant role played by the Negro college.

Although E. Franklin Frazier, through his accurate but incomplete description, has given the black middle class a bad name, the existence of this group is largely due to the existence of the Negro college. Most of the members of the black bourgeoisie are the graduates of black colleges. As teachers in the elementary and secondary schools of the South and of northern segregated systems, these graduates provided not only literacy for their students, but also a vision of the possibility of life-styles other than those provided by contact with white employers. That this life-style was in fact the same life-style as that of their white counterparts (which is the element Frazier failed to make clear) was of little significance. What was significant was the creation of a black middle class which could make black aspiration to move into middle-class life-style patterns viable.

From this black middle class, created by the black college, came the core of the leadership that changed the status of blacks in the United States. Although W. E. B. Du Bois was the product of the best that white academies had to offer, Booker T. Washington was the product of a black college. Regardless of the merits of the Washington-Du Bois debate, most blacks would take Booker T. Washington's route to education even as they chose Du Bois' route to equality. From Martin Luther King to Stokely Carmichael, spokesmen for the black community have been recruited from among graduates of black colleges.

Thus, it is probable that the greatest community contribution of the Negro college has been the creation of a community. Although it has been fashionable in the last quarter century to decry all bourgeois elements as decadent, the reality is that the changes wrought in the status of American blacks were due almost entirely to the efforts of the black middle class. The middle-class product of Negro colleges—physicians, dentists, lawyers, and ministers (admittedly not all college graduates)—supported and encouraged others to support civil rights activities. Largely independent of the white community, they could serve the cause of civil rights in relative safety.

Less independent were the elementary and secondary schoolteacher products of the black colleges, who were subject to the whims of white administrators and school boards well aware of the incongruity of their support of a growing black bourgeoisie, and, consequently, suspicious of their black teachers. The black public schoolteachers and administrators were, therefore, more cautious in assuming leadership roles than were the independent black professionals.

Nonetheless, the black professionals and teachers had found another community institution at the black college—the Negro fraternity and sorority. Some of these fraternities and sororities were founded on predominantly white campuses, but all achieved their psychological and philosophical comfort in chapters established during the twenties on Negro college campuses. Although the activities on the campus were disturbingly like those of the white fraternities during the Scott Fitzgerald era, there was a difference in the alumni activity. Activity in black college fraternities and sororities did not cease upon graduation, nor was it converted into mere symbolic identification at periodic smokers and rushing activities. The black college graduate (and many who were not graduated) maintained a relationship to the fraternal society, and these institutions became the major vehicle for black middle-class entertainment and community service activity.

The first volunteer Mississippi health program for Negroes was the product of a sorority founded at a Negro college, and the first civil rights lobby in Washington was established by the same group. Early attention by the alumni members of black Greek letter college based fraternities and sororities to guidance of Negro youth in career preparation and career choices raised the aspiration level of black youngsters across the country. Greek letter fraternities and sororities based on black college campuses provided for the development of organizational techniques and leadership. Several successful contemporary black politicians learned their political skills in the black fraternities and sororities.

In addition, the tiny black middle-class community extended its influence by the use of the college based fraternity and sorority to establish communication among graduates of the several black institutions. The black college graduate was surprisingly mobile and there were frequently too few graduates of individual institutions in most cities to enable these graduates to establish alumni associations of any size or significance. The most active alumni association, bringing together graduates of several institutions, was the Greek letter fraternity.

Through the national meetings of these Greek letter societies, members living throughout the country met brothers and sorors from other institutions. One fraternity's national meeting was a regular gathering place for a large number of the presidents of Negro colleges, who were fraternity members. Another group seemed to have a monopoly on professional civil rights activists, and the regular national meetings of that group tended to have a subculture of concern for the life of the civil rights movement. Still another group provided the base for recruitment of volunteers and staff of major integrated social welfare agencies.

In short, the college based fraternity and sorority provided a national community for the black middle class. This national community was fed by and could not have existed without the black college.

Another unheralded but important contribution of the black college was the provision of respectable elementary and college preparatory education. The, at best, casual and, at worst, nonexistent public education for Negroes led to the establishment of "academies" to provide the precollege education not otherwise available. Many older educated black Americans from the South secured their early education at these black college-related elementary and secondary academies. Although these academies have now largely disappeared, there are still "laboratory" schools, allegedly for the purpose of training teachers, but also useful in providing faculty and other middle-class children with higher quality education than is available in the public school system.

Extension service programs located at black schools have also provided adult education services of various kinds, and almost every black college has for years been swarming in the summer with elementary and secondary schoolteachers in special teacher workshops. A few, although not so many as might have, provided late afternoon and evening classes for teachers who wished salary augmenting credits for additional coursework.

Although few people believed that Lillian Smith's Nonnie had any real life counterpart, the home economics department of at least one Negro college had the reputation of providing excellent cooks for all the town resident millionaires (of whom there were several), thereby providing another (though not respected) aspect of service of which the white community approved.

Almost all of the community service of the Negro college flowed from the performance of traditional tutorial tasks, and not from conscious concern for discovery of ways in which the corporate university community—students, faculty, administrators, and governing board—could serve the community.

Although the administrators and faculties would deny it, most black colleges and universities, like their white counterparts, were dragged into conscious community related activities by their students. There are, of course, notable exceptions, usually the consequence of the presence of unusual individuals, such as Dean Gomillion at Tuskegee, and Presidents Mays and Clements of the Atlanta University system, who have made infinitely varied contributions to the political life of their communities. Despite these exceptions, black colleges lived in the midst not only of deeply segregated communities, but also within obviously impoverished and degraded black communities with inadequate or nonexistent community services, and with health and crime problems of great magnitude, without making significant contributions designed to change these conditions. The role of students in ending the segregation is well known. Equally well known in some circles was the opposition of some black college leadership to the student sit-ins.

The same ambivalence existed about service to the local community. Faced with limitations of resources that prevented effective emulation of Harvard and Yale, administrators had serious reservations about diverting funds from traditional academic activity to community service. Accustomed to thinking of extra-classroom activity only in terms of extracurricular or field service, the demand of students that institutional resources in addition to student activities fees be committed to off-campus, nonclassroom needs initially was met with little sympathy and with even less action on the part of black administrators. Seldom did the contiguous black community demand additional community services from the Negro college, because that community had a sense of the tenuous hold of the college on the financial support it had, and had little wish to jeopardize future funding by diverting it to innovative uses.

Despite activities of white institutions to change their surrounding neighborhoods, there was practically no emulation of these efforts by black colleges. The reason was probably that white institutional community change activities were seldom, if ever, altruistic, but almost always for the purpose of protecting well-defined interests of the institution, such as providing faculty housing, avoiding lower-class encroachment and crime, building new classrooms, improving campus aesthetics, or for all of these reasons. Community change sponsored by the white college, therefore, had little to do with community welfare. The Negro college had neither the need nor the funds for "urban renewal" and usually perceived no need to change the surrounding community.

Today the Negro college is in the difficult position of deciding whether its continued existence is consonant with developments in the white and black community. With the demise of legally enforced segregation in education, and with the establishment of community colleges, the role of the Negro college has been the subject of reevaluation. One of the major concerns has been that of the service to the community rendered by the Negro college.

With the expansion of employment opportunities, and the greater visibility of blacks in leadership roles, the Negro college has lost its primacy as the exemplar of the capacity of blacks to achieve and maintain middle-class status and intellectuality. In addition, radical black militants and many whites deny the validity of middle-class attitudes and aspirations, particularly for blacks. Intellectuality, always a shaky concept in the United States, is questioned by those who would elevate feeling and intuition above attempts at rationality. Thus, the derivative role of the Negro colleges of reassuring the black community that it could have intellectual aspirations, and of demonstrating to the white community black capacity to realize these aspirations, is under attack.

Added to this attack has been the legitimate concern of many that it is difficult to justify the continued existence of institutions established and maintained to cope with legalized segregation. The refusal of black educational leadership to deal with this question is a reflection of their recognition of the tenuous hold of American blacks on the mainstream, middle-class benefits of the society. Consequently, black leadership today is unanimous in insisting upon retaining black colleges which have over a century validated the potential of blacks to enter the mainstream. The defense of the educational role of the Negro college is buttressed by a fear on the part of blacks that they will be relegated to a permanent minority status in all institutions, with neither right nor opportunity to acquire and utilize major leadership skills. As a result, the black college will continue to exist.

It is in allaying fears and in providing security in assuming leadership roles that these Negro colleges should seek their future community role. Although all institutions of higher learning are in a financial bind today, the Negro college has always had and will probably always have fewer funds than needed to meet the requirements of its students. Therefore, expansive programs of urban renewal, or social welfare, with their attendant demand for highly trained personnel, should not be the goal of black colleges, even if funding can be found for them.

Instead, the community service of the Negro college should be an extension of the service provided in the past. The community service programs of the Negro college should be designed to discover and train individuals with the ability to evaluate and change their own environments. Some kind of credit or certification ought to be provided in order to convince participants that the activity is not just busy work.

The activity with and for the community should continue to be essentially tutorial, but with a wide range of subject matter. The initial area of concern of Negro colleges should be the resurrection of black history for the community it serves. Such offerings would reassure black students not certain of the acceptance of blackness by their administrators and teachers. Presentation of the history of the black man in the United States is essential to providing an acceptance by blacks of the fact that they are not aliens in a land which they have inhabited for over three centuries. Provision of this service to the community requires no exotic personnel or course preparation, but instead utilizes existing staff and provides that staff with association with nonacademic residents of the community.

In addition, skill inculcation, not unlike the traditional extension service course, could be provided by utilizing skills already available on any black college campus. English composition, mathematics, sewing, cooking, and interior decorating may not be revolutionary, but they meet the needs of workers and homemakers.

For the would-be revolutionary, courses that provide a theoretical framework for analyzing the community and for diagnosing its political ills need not be called Sociology I or Government I, but could be called by such titles as "The Nature of Social Exploitation" or "Diagramming the Power Structure." The community service provided by offering such courses is a rational framework for beginning to deal with social problems. The success of such an approach is attested to by such enterprises as worker education schools in the thirties and forties.

The major community contribution of the black college will be the training of secure leadership that will assume responsibility for engineering social change. If the Negro colleges of today can produce hundreds of Edward Brookes, Thurgood Marshalls, Kenneth Clarks, Anita Allens, or Elizabeth Koontzes, the community will be well served.

This is not to say that the black college has no nontutorial community service role. Part of the creation of concerned leadership is the inculcation of community action skills early in the lives of the political leaders. Students of black colleges represent an underutilized community service resource. The old rah-rah activity of black college campuses is disappearing, and now is the time to make certain that it is not replaced by sterile "rapping" and soul music. Instead, the energies of black students ought to be channeled by black teachers and administrators toward the college community. Deans of men and deans of women should divest themselves of their anachronistic custodial roles and become deans for community service. Direction of students into community activity in which they can be useful is a role that ought to be assumed by the black college.

The absence of recreation for black youth in almost all communities is notorious. The imagination and creativity of black students should be used in devising and providing recreation for black youngsters of all ages. Resourceful teachers of education could augment their courses by advising students on how to establish and maintain preschool activities for underprivileged students. Careful planning of course schedules might well permit establishment of student day-care centers. There are enough examples of college student led tutorial activity directed to elementary and secondary students to encourage such activity on every campus. Use of the institution's physical plant for all of these activities will make the resources of gymnasia, auditoria, classrooms, and campuses available to what is essentially a deprived community. Such carefully thought through community service, with leadership and coordination from the institution, would enure to the benefit of the students' education and to the quality of American life.

Thus innovation as well as continuation of traditional activities can enhance the already significant service of the black college to its community. It must be recognized by the black colleges themselves and by the educational community at large that the black college, no matter what its location, is engaged in the creation of a community as well as the service of a community. The community served by a black college always extends beyond its geographic location because of the significant incremental value of the production of additional members of a black educated class. If the black college did no more than increase the number of literate, competent black citizens, its community contribution would be mammoth. It is a bonus that extended community service improves the ability of the institution to minister to its students by sharpening their skills, and by sharpening the skills of their teachers. With the limited resources available to black education, it is fortunate that the properly primary concern of these institutions for increasing their students' competence need not be sacrificed even as the needs of the institutions' local neighbors are being met.

The changes in the relationship of black institutions of higher learning to their white counterparts are more apparent than real, and will have little effect on the Negro college's community role. Although there are increasing contacts between black and white institutions, these are not unique, having existed in some degree prior to the outlawing of legally enforced segregation. The out-migration of whites from communities in the South which in the days of legally segregated schools had black and white housing in the same neighborhood, coupled with the increased hostility of black students in black institutions to including whites in their programming, will result in the continuation of the constituency of the black college in essentially the form it has always had.

The permissible period of projection of race relations in the United States is the shortest of any that could be made, as the experience of the sixties demonstrates. Nonetheless, when the constituency of the Negro college changes, it will no longer be a Negro college. Such a change of constituency cannot be perceived on today's horizon, and the community of the Negro college, with a few possible exceptions in areas with small black population, will continue to be the community of the descendants of Negro slaves. To serve the needs of this community is to fill a void not filled to date by anyone else.

MACK H. JONES

The Responsibility of the Black College to the Black Community: Then and Now

BLACK COLLEGES have been roundly excoriated by diverse elements[1] for defaulting on their responsibilities to the larger black community. There are those who argue that black colleges have been too elitist and have not given proper deference to the opinions and judgments of the masses, while others have criticized them for failing to take the initiative in giving these same masses sufficient guidance and leadership. Some have inveighed against them for failing to approximate the role attributed to major white colleges in American society as a whole, while others have vehemently denounced them for slavishly aping such institutions. These criticisms, along with myriad others repeatedly leveled at black colleges, obviously have some bases in fact. Black colleges have not completely fulfilled their responsibilities to the larger black community. However, much of the criticism suggests a profound misunderstanding of the relationship between institutions of higher learning and their sponsoring communities in general and an even more skewed perception of the place of black colleges in American society. Indeed, the critics themselves are often inconsistent, criticizing black colleges for not being "good" American colleges on the one hand and for not meeting their special responsibilities to the black community on the other.[2]

Such specious analysis is a function of the fact that much of the discussion of the role and responsibilities of black colleges rushes pell-mell toward evaluation before giving sufficient attention to the societal context within which they are obliged to function. Fundamental questions and their implications for the role performance of black colleges go begging—questions such as: Who decided that black colleges should be established and what purposes did they have in mind? How did these purposes affect the recruitment of faculty and administrative personnel, the composition of the student body, and the structure of curricula? And, in turn, how have all of these factors, singly and cumulatively, influenced the historical relationship between the black college and the larger black community? It is not so much that those writing about black colleges are unaware of the importance of these questions, for they are almost invariably alluded to in a prefatory manner. However, with the preface out of the way analysis usually proceeds with little or no deference being given to them.[3]

The fact of the matter is that since their inception black colleges have had built-in antithetical goals and objectives. The white community, as is always the case with groups enjoying superordinate status in a society, has sought to maintain its position of dominance at the expense of blacks, while the latter have sought to achieve equal status,[4] and both have sought to use the black college as an instrument in their struggle. This assumption must be the focal point of any intelligent discussion of the success of the black college in meeting its responsibility to the larger black community, and it is with this thought in mind that this essay will attempt to assess the past performance of traditionally black colleges and to suggest the nature of their contemporary responsibilities to their communities.

It is my contention that when black colleges were founded in the aftermath of emancipation their major responsibility was grounded in the conditions of the black community at the time. They were charged with developing a cadre of blacks who could challenge and overcome immediate threats to the survival of the black community while working simultaneously for equal status in American society. Contrary to popular sentiment, I contend that black colleges, collectively, met this responsibility. They were instrumental in developing among blacks in North America all of the skills necessary not only to survive but also to build a black nation as well. Since, however, the fulfillment of this responsibility has not brought about equality of status as black pioneers had expected, but rather a heightening of white oppression, black colleges are faced with new responsibilities to their communities. It is now their task to create a new political consciousness among blacks that will lead to a commonly shared ideological network or world view which, in turn, will facilitate an understanding of the black predicament in an *international context.* Such an ideology would disabuse its holders of the many counterrevolutionary values which now impede the black struggle, define their friends and enemies, and order the priorities of the black diaspora in America. This task requires a radical restructuring of black colleges as we know them.[5]

The phrase "responsibility of the black college to the larger black community" should not be interpreted to mean two separate and distinct entities, even though much of the discussion about college-community relations suggests as much. The relationship is more of an organic one. The college, like myriad other institutions, is established by the community to perform certain functions deemed essential to its survival. The community, one must remember, is the sum total of the infinite patterns of goal directed activities of its members acting both as individuals and as constituents of groups and institutions. Thus the college is simply one of many specialized institutions having a number of community defined functions, some primary, others secondary or even tertiary. The major responsibility of the college to the larger community, like all other community institutions, is to perform well those primary functions for which it was established. If it fails to perform adequately its primary tasks, then its involvement in secondary and tertiary matters will likely be inconsequential or even counterproductive.

It is appropriate, then, to begin by asking what, in general, are the primary responsibilities of colleges to their communities? For what purposes are institutions of higher learning established? Essentially such institutions have always had as their primary purpose reinforcing the legitimacy of the prevailing regime as defined by those of power and wealth, predisposing subjects toward supportive behavior, and preparing students to assume productive positions in the community within the constraints imposed by the regime. That is the overriding purpose of higher education in every society —imparting to the students socially useful skills and sociopolitical consciousness which will lead them to choose to employ their acquired skills in a fashion consistent with the basic values of the regime. I am using the term regime to mean

> all of those arrangements that regulate the way in which demands put into the system are settled and the way in which decisions are put into effect. They are the so-called rules of the game, in the light of which actions by members of the system are legitimated and accepted by the bulk of the members as authoritative.[6]

The forces determining the content of the regime, it is true, are not likely to be monolithic, but rather a mosaic reflecting the eternal struggle for dominance between and among competing interests. Nevertheless, there will be basic societal values, an ideological network, within whose constraints the behavior of its members will be expected to fall.

Institutions of higher learning, along with other socialization agents, are responsible for insuring that patterns of behavior dictated by the regime are accepted as legitimate. For example, the ideal product of the South African university system would accept the legitimacy of apartheid and his Russian counterpart would show similar deference toward scientific socialism; the Tanzanian student would accept the behavior code implied in the Arusha Declaration and the ideal American product would accept the constraints of capitalism grounded in white supremacy as legitimate.

In societies where sizable minorities exist in more or less separate and identifiable communities and are singled out for deferential and unequal treatment by the dominant element, educational institutions serving the former will be characterized by dual and conflicting purposes. The dominant community, in the absence of genuine pluralism, will use its superior power to influence the structure of these institutions such that they serve to reinforce the existing order, that is, their position of dominance at the expense of the minority community. The latter, on the other hand, will try to structure educational institutions serving them such that they are supportive of their struggle for liberation. These opposing forces may be referred to as the dirty worker[7] function at one pole and the liberation vehicle at the other.

In societies in which a group or groups are subjugated by others there exist a number of individuals and institutions who are hired or who hire themselves to administer, contain, and control the members of the group being dominated. These are the dirty workers; they earn their livelihood by keeping the subjugated in their place as defined by the existing regime. Dirty workers who are recruited from both the oppressed and oppressor communities include, among others, policemen, real estate brokers, slumlords, social workers, rapacious neighborhood merchants, loan sharks, and in some instances teachers and clergymen. Dirty workers, consistent with the will of the dominant community, tend to perform their roles in a fashion which maintains the subordinate status of the oppressed community, though this is done not so much by centralized conspiratorial design as by a common perception of reality which dictates a network of normative assumptions about the nature and worth of minority group members and about the kind of treatment and respect to which they are entitled. Acceptance of these assumptions is reinforced by judicious manipulation of rewards and punishment by those elements with direct material interest in maintaining the status quo.

Liberation vehicle, of course, refers to institutions which accept as their primary function promoting and supporting those changes in the regime advocated by members of the oppressed community.

These conflicting purposes, as I have already asserted, are clearly evident in the history of black colleges in the United States and herein lies much of the confusion and contradiction regarding their effectiveness in serving the larger black community. When black colleges were founded in the wake of the Civil War, the dirty worker syndrome was doubtless the dominant factor. To be sure, some of the founders and their philanthropic benefactors had benevolent intentions[8] and it would be uncharitable and historically inaccurate to suggest that they were engaged solely in Machiavellian techniques to maintain white dominance. Nevertheless, it cannot be gainsaid that the white community was more concerned with making blacks useful workers and consumers for American capitalism than it was with black liberation. Black colleges were structured not only to work within the constraints of American capitalism and racism but to reinforce their legitimacy as well.

Thus, efforts to assay the performance of black colleges in meeting their responsibilities to their community must take into account the salient conditions of the black community, the general goals toward which it tended, and the extent to which these goals challenged the dirty worker syndrome, for the effectiveness of black colleges in meeting their responsibilities depended upon the interplay of these factors. The conditions of the black community during the later decades of the nineteenth century when the first black colleges were founded were dire indeed. Blacks were largely illiterate, impoverished political subjects without political rights, whose claim to citizenship and, indeed, membership in the human family were questioned by the society in which they lived. The notion that they were inherently inferior and therefore uneducable was widely accepted. The responsibility of the black college was grounded in these abysmal conditions; it was charged with obviating them by serving as one of the primary vehicles for developing a cadre of black leaders in all walks of life who could move the community in its chosen direction. That direction, historical evidence suggests, was toward equal status within American society, although there was measurable support for the concept of an independent black society.

W. E. B. Du Bois, in the light of these historical circumstances, reduced the responsibilities of the black college to the community to four basic missions. These missions, which may be utilized to assess their historical record, are:

1. Establishing the principle that higher education should be made available to blacks;
2. Defending the principle of racial equality by combatting national and international doctrines to the contrary;
3. Establishing freedom of Negro colleges to decide what they would teach and to whom it would be taught;
4. Promoting democracy and social power for black people by working for enfranchisement and gradual acquisition of political power.[9]

On the other hand, elements from the white community moving from the dirty worker perspective had other objectives for the black college in mind. They stressed the acquisition of vocational skills at the expense of liberal education and under their influence curricula were studiously structured to omit courses and activities which dealt realistically with the black predicament in America. The accommodationist philosophy of persons such as Booker T. Washington was warmly supported by the white community, while that of his rivals was condemned.[10] Every effort was made to insure that black students acquired a political consciousness which would lead them to accept their subordinate position in society. The social sciences and humanities celebrated Euro-American rather than African-Afro-American experiences. Indeed, it is reported that at one point Atlanta University, a school that leaned toward the liberation vehicle end of the continuum, was admonished to cut back on its efforts to reflect the African experience and to give more attention to "standard" European oriented subjects.[11] White opposition to black colleges as instruments for social equality was practically unanimous. In some cases, even whites teaching on black campuses demanded separate dining facilities.

Thus, one can see that the missions implied by Du Bois ran diametrically counter to the preferences of those sharing the dirty worker perspective. Recalling the inviolability of the old aphorism that the piper's patron has a disproportionate voice in tune selection, one can understand the dilemma of the colleges caught between these conflicting forces.

Nevertheless, by the mid-1950's black colleges, in spite of these constraints, had made considerable progress in satisfying the responsibilities enumerated by Du Bois. To be sure, many administrators accepted almost completely the role of dirty worker and such administrators still exist in alarming numbers.[12] However, others refused to accept such a role and supported, in varying degrees, programs and policies implied in Du Bois' categories. For example, as early as 1887 Atlanta University publicly challenged dirty worker pressure[13] and continued throughout the next several decades to support the struggle for equal rights. During the 1920's agitation on black campuses for equal rights continued.[14] Similarly, the civil rights movement of the 1950's and 1960's was largely a product of the ferment on black campuses.

It is true, of course, that administrative authorities, most notably presidents, publicly opposed the involvement of their schools in the liberation struggle and expelled hundreds of black students and fired scores of faculty members for their civil rights activities.[15] However, to assess the efforts of the colleges solely on the disposition of their administrators is to make the mistake of saying that they, the administrators, are in fact the colleges. The college, to the contrary, is a composite of students, faculty, and administrators, with students the most important of the three. Thus, for example, in assessing the efficaciousness of, say, Southern University in Baton Rouge, the fact that students led the liberation movement there is more important than the fact that then President Felton Clark expelled sixteen students for their involvement. Similarly, the contribution of Howard University lies in the fact that students struggled throughout the mid- and late 1960's to advance the cause of the black nation and not in the fact that the administration clung tenaciously to its role as dirty worker.

To say that black colleges have met the responsibilities entrusted to them at their inception is not to exonerate their contemporary successors from criticism, because the conditions under which African-Americans live have changed, the responsibilities of the colleges have changed commensurately, and black colleges have not moved to meet these new responsibilities. Instead they continue to operate according to the prescriptions of Du Bois' now obsolete missions. While it is impossible to say precisely when these new responsibilities evolved, it seems fair to say that by the mid-1950's the missions enumerated by Du Bois had been fulfilled and it had become obvious that a new age had dawned.

At this juncture it is appropriate to ask exactly what happened to render obsolete the historical missions of black colleges and to usher in an era of new responsibilities. Essentially, as suggested earlier, it was the successful execution of a number of tasks implied in the earlier mission, the concomitant failure of these changes to bring about substantive changes in the black predicament, the resulting heightened intensity of the black struggle, and the repressive response by the white nation. The new mission of the black college is grounded in the synthesis of these developments. Let us elaborate.

To begin, propositions that blacks are educable and that higher education should be made available to them have been firmly established and doctrines of racial inferiority have been debunked (in spite of efforts to resurrect them). Impediments to the franchise and formal political participation also have been largely overcome. However, the realization of these objectives has not led to substantive changes in the lives of black people, *but rather it has demonstrated that their oppression is not an aberration in the system but an essential condition of the system itself, and that therefore accession to black demands for equal status requires radical restructuring of America's socioeconomic and political systems—a restructuring which makes demands both materially and psychologically on every American subject and which has profound implications for the role of the United States as the enforcer of European hegemony over colored peoples of the world.* Both the black and white communities have begun to recognize these truths and to act accordingly. *These reactions constitute the new conditions under which the black community lives and structure the nature and content of the contemporary responsibilities of black colleges to their communities.*

The white community, both governments and individuals, has indicated that it lacks the will and resolve to restructure itself in a fashion consistent with black demands. A series of euphemisms have been coined to enshroud this development in respectability—white backlash, silent majority, reverse racism, middle American, forgotten American, and so on. In the context of black-white relations they all mean the same thing: Stop nigger you have gone far enough.

You have become a threat to my superordinate position and if you do not desist I am prepared to visit severe punishment upon you, including the ultimate sanction, organized violence. As one black college president said, this climate is conducive to genocide.[16] The blatant repression of black people by law enforcement agencies in places such as Chicago,[17] Augusta,[18] Orangeburg,[19] Jackson,[20] Houstion,[21] and Detroit[22] are cases in point.

The major responsibility of the black college to the larger black community in the face of these ominous developments is to interpret them to the black nation with a view to creating a universally accepted perception of the black predicament and providing a catalyst for serious discussion of the goals, both long and short term, of black people and of the most expeditious means for their realization. Of course, the colleges would continue to impart to their students specialized skills such as engineering, accounting, medicine, psychology, and so on. These skills would be imparted, however, in a different political context. Contrary to the apologists of "pure science," all knowledge is imparted in a political context, and in the United States that context is white nationalism.

How does the black college move to meet this responsibility? It must begin by accepting the black predicament as the central concept around which everything else at the college revolves. As Du Bois argued as early as 1933,[23] the Negro problem "has got to be" the center of the black college if it is to meet its responsibility to the black community.

> Starting with present conditions and using the facts and the knowledge of the present situation of American Negroes, the Negro university expands toward the possession and the conquest of all knowledge. It seeks from a beginning of the history of the Negro in America and in Africa to interpret all history; from a beginning of social development among Negro slaves and freedmen in America and Negro tribes and kingdoms in Africa, to understand the social development of all mankind in all ages. It seeks to teach modern science of matter and life from the surroundings and habits and aptitudes of American Negroes and thus lead up to understanding of life and matter in the universe.[24]

To meet the conditions implied in Du Bois' exegesis present black colleges must radically restructure both curricular and extracurricular activities. Social sciences, humanities and the arts, and education curricula must be recast so that the beginning of all analysis is Africa and the problems of black people living in America; all other knowledge must be interpreted from that very beginning. For example, the history of African people would replace the course in Western civilization as the lodestar for historical analysis; political science courses would be concerned with acquiring and manipulating power to produce radical change rather than with maintaining a stable commonwealth; similarly, sciences and technical subjects would be taught in a political context growing out of the problems of black people; extracurricular activities would be grounded in the experience of African people with their struggle against Euro-American exploitation being the focal point.

The products of colleges making such revisions would be radically different from present ones. Completely disabused of dirty worker inclinations they would see clearly and understand fully the true position of blacks in American society and the prescriptive implications of that position for a normative assessment of international political movements. The incompatability of their interest—liberation—and that of American capitalism grounded in white supremacy—exploitation—would be obvious. They would be impervious to the calls of that legion of diversionary pied pipers: black capitalism, soul power, Philadelphia Plans, poverty panaceas, and so forth. They would recognize them for what they are and act accordingly. From this new perspective a sustaining ideology would automatically flower, an ideology that would accentuate peoplehood among Africans throughout the diaspora. It would define both their allies and enemies, order their priorities, and etch in the contours of the future they envision for their progeny.

A number of black institutions have already begun to move in this direction. Malcolm X Liberation University located in Durham and Greensboro, North Carolina, The Center for Revolutionary Art and the Institute of the Black World both based in Atlanta, Georgia, and the Center for African Education in Washington, D.C., are all moving from the perspective suggested in this paper. However, these organizations reach only a small number of black students. Black colleges, on the other hand, still train approximately one-half of all blacks who enter college, including perhaps a majority of prospective primary and secondary school teachers who will serve the black community. The possibilities are enormous. Black colleges have the power to remake the political consciousness of the black student and ultimately of the black nation. That is their primary responsibility to the larger black community. If it is met, secondary responsibilities such as working with community organizations, participating in community politics, providing staff assistance for community leaders, and so on will take care of themselves. If the colleges do not meet their primary responsibility, their secondary involvement, as suggested earlier, will be of little consequence anyway.

References

1. Critics, to cite a few, include such unlikely bedfellows as Nathan Hare, an accomplished black sociologist and one of the leading intellectuals in the black liberation struggle; Lionel Newsom, who is now president of a black college; William Carson, a white former marine colonel whose interest in guerrilla warfare and counterinsurrectionary strategy led him to write a book on black students; Christopher Jencks and David Riesman, two white scholars with solid Establishment credentials; and Bernard Harleton, a black teacher at a white college. See Nathan Hare's "Legacy of Paternalism," *Saturday Review* (July 20, 1968), "Behind Black College Revolt," *Ebony* (August 1967), and "Final Reflections on a Negro College: A Case Study," *Negro Digest* (March 1968); Riesman and Jencks, "The American Negro College," *Harvard Educational Review,* 37 (1967), 3-60; Carson, *Promise or Peril: The Black College Student in America* (New York: W. W. Norton, 1970); Commission on Higher Education in the South, *The Negro and Higher Education in the South* (Atlanta: Southern Regional Education Board, 1967) (President Newsom was closely associated with drafting this document); Bernard Harleston, "Higher Education for Negroes," *Atlantic Monthly* (November 1965).

2. The Riesman-Jencks and Harleston articles cited in the preceding note are replete with such inconsistencies. The careful reader will also notice similar ambivalencies in the Southern Regional Education Board publication and in Nathan Hare's analysis, though on a more limited scale.

3. To borrow a phrase from Malcolm X, such analysis makes the victim the criminal.

4. For further discussion of this theme see my "A Frame of Reference for Black Politics," in Lenneal J. Henderson, Jr., ed., *Black Political Life in the United States: A Fist as the Pendulum* (San Francisco: Chandler Publishing Company, forthcoming).

5. For one scholar's views on what a restructured black college would look like see Gerald McWorter, "The Nature and Needs of the Black University," *Negro Digest* (March 1968).

6. David Easton, "The Analysis of Political Systems," in Roy Macridis and Bernard Brown, eds., *Comparative Politics* (Homewood, Ill.: Dorsey, 1964), p. 97.

7. For further discussion of the dirty worker syndrome in black-white rela-

tions see my "The Kerner Commission: Errors and Omissions," in Philip Meranto, ed., *The Kerner Report Revisited,* University of Illinois Bulletin (June 1, 1970). See also Frank Joyce, "Racism in the United States," in Priscilla Long, ed., *The New Left* (Boston: Porter Sergeant, 1969).

8. For a thorough history of black education including the role of white benefactors see Henry A. Bullock, *A History of Negro Education in the South* (Cambridge, Mass.: Harvard University Press, 1967).

9. W. E. B. Du Bois, "The Cultural Mission of Atlanta University," *Phylon,* 3 (1942), reprinted in Meyer Weinberg, ed., *W. E. B. Du Bois: A Reader* (New York: Harper and Row, 1970).

10. For a brief yet instructive discussion on this point see Robert H. Brisbane, *The Black Vanguard* (Valley Forge: Judson Press, 1970), pp. 101-111.

11. Reported to me by Professor Richard Barksdale, Dean of Arts and Sciences, Atlanta University.

12. For a frank statement by one college president embracing his role as dirty worker see the remarks attributed to the president of Mississippi Valley College in "Black Students Challenge the Order at Mississippi Valley State," *New York Times,* May 25, 1970.

13. See Clarence Bacote, *The Story of Atlanta University* (Princeton: Princeton University Press, 1969), pp. 86-102; also Du Bois, "The Cultural Mission."

14. Brisbane, *The Black Vanguard.*

15. The author was twice so honored, being expelled as a student in 1960 and fired seven years later for his "civil rights" activities.

16. "Atlanta University Position Paper on Race and Violence in the United States," read by President Thomas Jarrett at his press conference, May 25, 1970. See story in *Atlanta Constitution,* May 26, 1970.

17. Chicago police, according to a federal grand jury report, fired indiscriminately into quarters occupied by members of the Black Panther party killing two of the occupants. A *New York Times* editorial called it a police "shoot-in" rather than a shoot-out. See "Excerpts from Grand Jury's Report," *New York Times,* May 16, 1970; and editorial, *ibid.,* May 18, 1970.

18. Police shot six unarmed black males in the back during racial disturbances in Augusta, Georgia. See "3 Augusta Victims Not Rioters?" *Atlanta Constitution,* May 18, 1970, p. 4B.

19. Police wantonly fired into a crowd of fleeing black students on the campus of South Carolina State College in February 1967 killing three and injuring twenty-seven others. Although nine highway patrolmen were charged in the deaths, they were quickly acquitted by a jury of their peers after deliberating ninety minutes. See *New York Times,* May 28, 1968, p. 1.

20. Highway patrolmen fired indiscriminately into a crowd of black students on the Jackson State campus killing two and injuring numerous others.

21. In May 1967, Houston police fired hundreds of rounds into an occupied male dormitory before charging the building, arresting every male occupant, and maliciously destroying the students' personal effects. For story and substantiating photographs see *The Informer* (Houston, Texas), May 20, 1967; see also *New York Times,* May 18, 1967, and *Houston Post,* May 19, 1967.

22. During racial disturbances in Detroit in May 1967, a group of black citizens were terrorized in a local motel before two were viciously slain by police authorities who were, of course, acquitted. See "Was Justice Done in the Algiers Motel Incident?" *New York Times,* March 1, 1970, p. 10E.

23. W. E. B. Du Bois, "The Negro College," in Weinberg, ed., *Du Bois,* p. 178.

24. *Ibid.,* p. 181.

ELIAS BLAKE, JR.

Future Leadership Roles for Predominantly Black Colleges and Universities in American Higher Education

A GREAT deal of attention has always been paid to quantitative analyses of the future of predominantly black colleges. These analyses of student growth possibilities, of sources of income and how much of it is needed, of the probabilities of new sources developing are necessary and important. The quantitative data in this essay, however, are in a sense introductory to its main theme: a consideration in detail of some unique educational program directions that give black colleges a natural advantage in their development. There is in this essay an assumption that as these schools move into the second hundred years their role must be diversified. They will continue to be of critical importance to the future of black Americans, but in a different way; they must develop some uniqueness in supporting a truly pluralistic society. Differences are not respected in America, despite its official rhetoric. At the same time, educational equity* will likely depend to a large extent on the expansion of the sizes of black colleges.

It is important, before dealing with the future of these colleges, to make concrete their importance. There is no doubt of their historical achievements, but rarely is any attempt made to restate what exactly that means in terms of American life.

Table 1, from Charles S. Johnson,[1] indicates clearly that the predominant contribution to education of black Americans in the period 1914-1936 was carried by the black colleges. (The interaction between these college graduates—plus thousands of others who completed high school on college campuses and in normal school—and the development of literacy has not been properly

* Meaning enrollment in proportion to the numbers in the population *and* the production of undergraduate, graduate, and professional degrees. Enrollment is not enough; outcomes must exist in graduates.

TABLE 1. Per Cent Distribution of Degrees Conferred on Negroes by Negro and Northern Institutions, 1914-1936

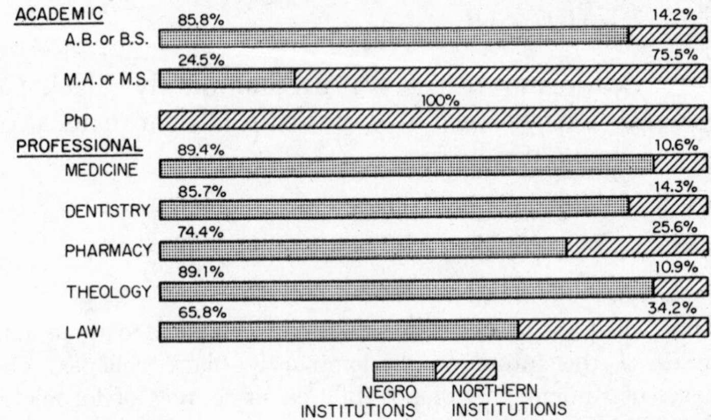

detailed. For example, from 1865 to 1930 a totally illiterate people advanced to slightly over 80 per cent literacy. Between 1890 and 1930 black literacy increased 93.8 per cent compared to 32 per cent for the southern region as a whole.[2])

Some more up-to-date estimates of a similar nature in 1968 indicate that thirty-two years later the pattern is still the same (see table 2). The estimate of four out of five baccalaureates awarded to blacks coming from predominantly black colleges could well be an underestimate, since the estimate for production of black graduates assigns about one black graduate out of a hundred

TABLE 2. Degrees Earned by Black Americans in Black and White Colleges and Universities, 1968

Degree	Black colleges	White colleges	Total
Bachelor's	17,242	4,458	21,700
	(79.5%)	(20.5%)	(100%)
Graduate and professional	2,756	2,819	5,575
	(49%)	(51%)	(100%)
Totals	19,998	7,277	27,275
	(73%)	(27%)	(100%)

SOURCE: John Egerton, *State Universities and Black Americans* (SERS, May 1969). Egerton found that 0.7 per cent of the baccalaureate degrees were earned by blacks in thirty-nine of the one hundred largest state universities. Public institutions give 61 per cent of all degrees. 0.7 per cent of 636,863 bachelor degrees awarded in America in 1968 is 4,458 degrees. He found 1.2 per cent of the graduate and professional degrees going to blacks. 1.2 per cent of 234,969 graduate degrees awarded in 1968 is 2,819 degrees. The national data on earned degrees comes from *Earned Degrees Conferred, 1967–68, Part A. Summary Data* (National Center for Educational Statistics, Department of Health, Education, and Welfare).

to every college in the country. The estimate also was made without subtracting the contribution of the black colleges from the total number of baccalaureate degrees.

These graduates from black colleges represent about 35 to 40 per cent of those who enter as freshmen, indicating serious problems in getting them through, since 50 to 55 per cent of those who enter nationally are graduated. Looking at the entering freshmen, one wonders if any other colleges could do as well. In a sample of fourteen colleges, public and private, the median income was $3,900 and from a third to half of the mothers and fathers were domestics and laborers with less than a high school education. Their freshman test performance was about one standard deviation below the norms for the nation, *except for a nonverbal test* on which they scored slightly above average.[3] More will be said later about unique possibilities for colleges dealing with such populations in building educational programs.

In earlier decades the students were probably poorer and even less well educated than in the late 1960's. Yet 74 per cent of a sample of about 1,000 black Americans with earned Ph.D.'s earned the baccalaureate in black colleges. In a sampling of 110 black state legislators from across the nation, 64 per cent attended black colleges. From a sample of eighty recent and current black federal officials (Civil Service and presidential appointees), 64 per cent were graduated from black colleges.[4]

It is a serious question of social policy and of morality when such schools are called anachronisms. These schools supported a grave social responsibility for the nation. It is of dubious morality for those who could have made different decisions in the past about allocating adequate resources to these schools to raise the issue of their survival. The morality of the treatment of these schools needs to be raised more often.

In the next decades, the magnitude of the numbers needed to give black Americans equity in higher education makes the predominantly black colleges indispensable. They are a source of spaces unlikely to be found elsewhere with the increasing competition for college places among whites.

According to the projections in table 3, 224,000 nonwhite freshmen should have enrolled in college in September 1970. The estimated enrollment is 114,975,* with about 45,000 enrolling in

* The American Council on Education reported 98,270 blacks in the entering freshman class of 1969 and 84,058 in the 1968 entering class. Assuming

TABLE 3. Projected Equal Enrollment of Nonwhite Students in College Based on Per Cent of Nonwhite Youth in College Entrance Age Group

Year of entrance	Total enrollment (thousands)	Per cent of nonwhites	Number of nonwhites (thousands)	Nonwhite freshmen (thousands)	Nonwhite high school graduates (thousands)	Freshmen as per cent of high school graduates
1970	7,181	13.5	970	224	407	55
1972	7,925	13.5	1,070	246	437	56
1975	9,056	14.3	1,295	319	503	63
1978	10,033	15.1	1,515	330	561	59
1982	11,218	16.6	1,862	390	—	—

SOURCE: Elias Blake, Jr., "Background Paper on the Traditionally Negro College," *The Congressional Record* (May 11, 1970), p. E4093.

black colleges. An additional 100,000 freshmen would tax both black and white colleges in the areas where black Americans are concentrated, the South, east of the Mississippi River, and along the West Coast mainly in California. By 1975 the number of nonwhite freshmen should triple from the 1969 figure of about 100,000 to 319,000. In this context, the suggestion that freshman enrollments may be declining in some black colleges in 1969 should not become a trend. No available places should be left vacant anywhere. Private and public social policy should make certain this does not happen.

If 1.8 million nonwhites are to enroll by 1982, rapid expansion in the enrollment in black colleges is a necessity. If their enrollment tripled to 480,000 by 1982 (it was 160,000 in 1968), such a figure would be only 28 per cent of the total number of black youth in college. It seems somewhat unrealistic to talk about a diminishing role for predominantly black colleges that implies a withering away. If the society is responding as it ought to, the black colleges could triple in size while decreasing their total percentage of black youth enrolled in college.

Current constraints in higher education do not lead one to be optimistic that rapid enrollment increases will occur at the magnitude required to meet the projections in table 3. The kinds of constraints are:

1. *The conservatism of college faculties.* Their understanding

a similar increase from 1969 to 1970, one arrives at 114,975 as the probable number of black freshmen in the 1970 entering class. The 1968 data are from "The Black Students in American Colleges"; the 1969 data are from "National Norms for Entering Fall Freshmen—Fall 1969."

of the problems and willingness to teach a significant minority of less well prepared black youth is questionable. No historical precedents lead one to predict colleges will react any differently than the precollege schools to increased black enrollment. In elementary and secondary schools, a dramatic increase in the proportion of students requiring a higher quality of instruction has broken down the urban school systems. The public schools have never been hospitable to or particularly effective with low-income populations. The low skill requirements in the job market made it possible to absorb their dropouts in earlier decades; colleges never have served low-income groups. The process of deterioration of public education has not been reversed in any major areas of concentrated black population. Black graduates of the precollege system, many with passing grades at graduation, will press on the colleges. Not enough places in hospitable predominantly black colleges with a tradition of admission await them. College faculties in four-year or two-year colleges will be asked to adapt and create the needed programs to advance these black high school graduates. One can expect resistance to this, especially in four-year colleges and universities (and possible ineptness in two-year colleges) and increasing use of the same "disadvantaged" alibis of the public schools to avoid mastery of the problem.

2. *The junior college as a questionable alternative.* To date, their effect on equity (moving black youth toward degrees) is ambiguous. The attrition patterns are discouraging, as are the part-time enrollment patterns (52 per cent nationally). Added to that are de facto segregation trends in cities such as Chicago. Unequal and inadequate patterns of support for such segregated colleges may follow. "California has the most highly developed system of two-year community colleges . . . In 1967 freshmen comprised about 66 per cent of the full-time enrollment and sophomores 33 per cent . . . Thus about two out of three freshmen, who enter two-year colleges in California, do not return for the second year."[5]

3. *Fifty-three per cent of the black population still lives in the southern and border states.* Only the most sanguine appraisal of the desegregation process both in high schools and colleges would assume a rise in enrollment equal to the projections in table 3. One of the important questions is whether the *quality* of the desegregation process in the high schools is doing damage to college aspirations of black youth. Certainly placing the future of black seniors in the hands of white counselors runs the risk of

creating the northern pattern: discouragement from going to college and assignment to nonacademic tracks.

4. *Competition for four-year and two-year college places by a higher proportion of white high school seniors.* A safe prediction is the intensification of the issue of how to go about enrolling more black youth. Large numbers will not be well prepared, thus requiring special efforts *inside* the colleges similar to those in predominantly black colleges. Such a volatile political issue in terms of philosophy and expense is likely to create more rather than less conflict. Already, major national higher education associations oppose the targeting of federal financial aid, other than guaranteed loans, to low-income youth exclusively. More resistance is building to targeting the current programs on colleges with high proportions of low-income youth. The natural constituency of higher education is families in the \$8,000 to \$20,000 range. Blacks are almost all below the \$10,000 level.

These four constraints point to the need for more rather than fewer colleges and universities functioning as predominantly black colleges have done historically. Compensatory programs or specially designed first year programs *after admission* seem the only realistic alternatives. Historically, the building of "special" or "new" structures for new populations (vocational-technical high schools of the past or community colleges of the present) has been ineffective for black youth, mainly because the commitment of educators who run these systems is always mitigated by the racial and class biases pervasive in American life.

The need for more colleges that have the approach to higher education of predominantly black colleges and the large number of enrollees anticipated would seem to demand a greater role for these colleges in the next thirty to fifty years. Predominantly white institutions, whether in religion, labor, business, politics, or education, resist large infusions of blacks. Generally, breaks occur between national leaders who call for equality and local and regional followers over attempts at so-called enlightened social policies designed to bring equity. This has been seen in unions, churches, and industries. Educators are no better; they too are products of the racism in American life. Tokenism is the result of these breaks, with a desire to wait for "natural processes" of upgraded education to create a more "qualified" pool. Higher education will talk a better game, but its performance is subject to the same constraints as any other essentially conservative institution.

A rational social policy, then, builds on strength or potential strength and protects existing resources rather than gambling the future of educational equity on new and untried developments. A strengthened future for predominantly black colleges is, therefore, the wisest and most pragmatic national policy for the public and private sector to follow. To assume the success of predominantly white higher education in dealing with a new problem is indeed foolhardy. The current conflicts with small numbers of blacks cannot be expected to diminish with sharp increases in numbers. The conflicts will move to more fundamental issues bearing on whether, given "standards" for higher education, larger numbers ought to be enrolled or whether they can be admitted at all *in large numbers,* given their unequal preparation.

Without rising enrollments in black colleges undergirded with adequate resources for instruction, the constraints listed above could result in a growth curve of graduates that is too slow and risky for the health of the American social fabric. In 1968, 7.6 million nonwhites between the ages of five and seventeen were in the population; 6.2 million nonwhites were in the deteriorated public school system.[6] As of September 1970, about 200,000 nonwhite potential college freshmen out of the 1969-1970 graduating classes did not go to college. We are certain that three to four out of ten entrants into black colleges (with largely poor preparation) will take degrees. We know nothing about black students in nonblack colleges and their performance.

If, indeed, there is a rational social policy toward predominantly black colleges, their importance should increase dramatically even if their share of the total black enrollment declines. They should be the leading exemplars of how one builds programs that take in and hold through graduation very large numbers of black high school seniors. Such a role will be crucial because only the most sanguine (or irrational) observer would doubt the possibility that predominantly white colleges, two-year and four-year, North and South, will do very badly at adjusting to this new problem. Handsome resources have not protected some of our most prestigious institutions from showing themselves insensitive, inept, frightened, and confused about dealing with small numbers of black students.

The question then should be *what kind* of stronger and better supported future will there be for predominantly black colleges, since they are the society's social insurance that increased enrollments will in fact mean a sharply increased number of graduates. If the number of graduates from black colleges declines, then the over-all *rate* of increase in graduates could well be slowed.

A second reason the question should be what kind of stronger future for the predominantly black college is a basic need for survival of a black controlled institutional life. Though the question has been moot to this point because of the absence of choices, when and if the choice is real there must be black run and controlled institutions in education, in religion, in business and industry, and in politics. If there is truly respect for diversity, then there must be a significant number of these colleges appropriate to the needs of whatever proportion of 22 million black Americans desire them. It is doubtful whether many white or black educators envision first-rate, well-endowed universities dominated by black faculty and administrators and enrolling an overwhelming majority of black students. The subtle racism in integrationist circles can acknowledge one or two as a theoretical possibility but not say ten or twelve first-rate universities with fifty other solid institutions.

The following part of this essay tries to deal with the issue of what kind of future there is for black colleges in terms of programs and uniqueness of direction. After all, the private and public policy-makers can insure the existence of all or almost none of the predominantly black colleges. A combination of public and private resources over a decade can insure the future of these schools if some other kinds of schools get significantly fewer resources out of increasing allocations. That is the choice which has never been made. The private philanthropic sector could show leadership by making black colleges their major direction of support for a decade, with other sectors of higher education a lesser priority.

What Kind of Predominantly Black College?

The questions of quality, vision, and imagination were not raised in the previous section. The following proposals will assume that for predominantly black colleges not to strike new directions as a subset of colleges is to be accessories before the fact of their own social murder. Such things as social murder are of questionable intellectual validity, to be sure, but intrusive forces, which control money (foundations) and legal theories (the Justice Department), do not always respect the necessity for black controlled institutions. That is clear in the sorry spectacle of the

"Justice" Department's standing powerless while enforcement of the "law" allows "desegregation" to show open contempt for predesegregation achievements of black schools in academic and extracurricular matters and to allow the humiliation of black educational leadership all across the South.

The reported policies of major foundations predicated on the assumption that rapid development of enrollment of blacks in white colleges is to be supported with more resources than previously niggardly supported black colleges is another example. These are not benign factors; they are aggressive policies that must be counterattacked with more than counterrhetoric.

The strongest counterattack is to put forward serious, detailed blueprints for radical and significant educational change. Note the use of the word blueprint. It takes into account the question of resources not now available for quality programs. To breathe life into any blueprint, faculty commitment is an absolute requirement. Faculties in predominantly black colleges are not any less or any more conservative than other college faculties. Without strong leadership it may be that such conservatism will allow the loss by default of an opportunity for national leadership.

As will be implied in the following proposals, to shake faculties away from the conventional wisdom will take collective action among the colleges. If some of the things suggested here are successful in attracting money, attention, and prestige, a genuine reform movement can survive and have impact on the American civilization.

Rational and Creative Instructional Designs for Undergraduates

Much of American undergraduate education is irrational and based on unproved hypotheses. It is developed on a priori bases growing out of collective faculty experience uncritically evaluated. Not even what is known about incoming freshmen in any way informs how they are treated in first year programs. Teachers of the lowest status and least experience are used on students at the point of their greatest need and susceptibility to influence: the first semester of the freshman year. The need for black colleges not to follow this model is intensified by the proportion of their freshmen who arrive with high motivation but spotty academic preparation. Let us take some of the conventional wisdom and indicate how it might well be illogical for purposes of building programs for freshman academic survival. Conventional wisdom: *If students have academic weaknesses, place them in special classes designed to overcome their weaknesses before inducting them into a rigorous and intellectually demanding program.*

Given what one learns about students as they enter, this may be counterproductive and only the strongest students (in academic and ego strength) will survive. Survey data from a group of fourteen colleges[7] revealed the following data replicated over two years, 1968 and 1969, with 2,400 students. In response to an item, "Everytime I try to get ahead I get stopped," 41 per cent agreed or were not sure; on another item, "Sometimes I feel I just can't learn," 42 per cent gave the same responses; in response to "People like me have more problems succeeding," 54 per cent agreed or were not sure. In terms of self-perceptions in English, only 9 per cent viewed themselves as below average in the expression of ideas and 7 per cent in knowledge of English.

What then is the likely effect on students of a program that in its structure affirms the pessimistic view they hold and tells them initially they are below average in areas such as English where they perceive themselves as having strength? Add to this new and unfamiliar surroundings and the conventional wisdom should be questioned. A program should be designed with challenging intellectual content, which also works on language skills and grants full college credit. Both of these things can be done if proper attention is paid to sequencing of materials, teaching style, and content of materials. The course, say in English, can grow out of student interests as a bridge to standard content.

An example, from a course sequence which attempts to do just that, may help. The materials used total only thirty-six pages, with excerpts from Thoreau's *Civil Disobedience;* "Crito" in *The Last Days of Socrates;* Adin Ballou in Leo Tolstoy's *The Kingdom of God Is from Within You* (the catechism of nonresistance); LeRoi Jones's "What Does Non-Violence Mean?" from *Home,* a collection of essays; Ralph Ellison's "That Same Pain, That Same Pleasure" and "The World and the Jug" from *Shadow and Act;* Martin Luther King's "Letter from a Birmingham Jail"; and Gwendolyn Brooks's "A Bronzeville Mother Loiters in Mississippi Meanwhile a Mississippi Mother Burns Bacon."[8]

The theme of the materials is responsibility—that is, to the state (Thoreau, Socrates, Ballou)—and man's obligation to obey or disobey unjust laws (Jones, King). The students must read silently, read aloud, dramatize, defend dramatizations, write answers to the writers with which they agree or disagree. They must determine how to get emotional effects and make a satirical point, and must closely study texts to verify and justify their points of view. A sound recording, *The Hand Is on the Gate,* with the Brooks's poem included, is also used, plus documentary photographs such as in *The Movement* with text by Lorraine Hansberry. To do individual final assignments, the student must go further than the excerpts. The question is always: How do you make language do things, spoken and written?

Certainly one can see the attempt to immerse the student in language—language about important ideas, written by important intellectual figures, concerning issues deeply felt. Even these materials can be stilted and dryed up with pedantry and the teachers' verbal overkill. A style of restraint is needed. Students reactions and ideas are sought until they feel they too have important comments to make, and their own experience is used to inform and extend those of the intellectuals they are reading.

Why would this be successful?

1. Good teachers prefer to teach ideas rather than grammar and topic sentences. Nomenclature bores teachers and students and results in mutual frustration.

2. Contemporary materials, much of it by black Americans, is juxtaposed with conventional materials (Jimmy Smith's jazz version and Leonard Bernstein's versions of "Peter and the Wolf" in a study of style, with student defense and analysis of choice; Smith tends to be preferred).

3. If the teaching style allows the validity of the student's experiences to help him understand responsibility, expression is in more volume with less pressure.

4. The writing assignment conceived of as punishment or a chore diminishes; ideas become as important as the absence of errors; diminishing of errors to zero over sterile prose is a pyrrhic victory for teacher and student.

The uniqueness of the above slice of educational thinking rests in the fact that very little of it is found on any large scale anywhere except in the writing of critics of education. Predominantly black colleges that can, despite handicaps of students, institute a high proportion of such classes will make the question of future versus no future absurd except to willfully biased observers. Few colleges in America would view, even as a remote possibility, use of the kind of work described above with "disadvantaged" freshmen, particularly since it is superior to what is happening to "advantaged" freshmen. The materials were created in a combined curriculum development and teacher development program in twenty black colleges since 1967. If these developments can take hold, then the more dramatic ideas in the following section are not without possibilities.

The reasoned approach can be applied to other problems. The distribution of too few students in science and mathematics is a serious problem. Why not, then, design first year courses that undercut fears of science and mathematics. In the same surveys where 9 per cent of the students perceived themselves as below average in English, 28 per cent viewed themselves as below average in mathematics (only 18 per cent above average). Rather than a first professional course in mathematics, chemistry, biology, or physics, why not a first year recruiting course designed to convince a larger share of undergraduates they can do science and mathematics as a major? The need for numbers in this area demands a better ratio between the sizes of introductory courses and the number of graduates three years later.

The major job in freeing up action on the ideas above is involvement of faculty in a nondefensive, nonthreatened way. Colleges that work out these problems will have some success, *assuming there is a basic social policy to support these colleges with significant new pools of money.* As American higher education wrestles with educating larger numbers of black youth, such colleges will be a key to avoiding the predictable responses: "Maybe they ought not to be here, given their preparation," or "We made a genuine effort but the attrition was so great it raises a question about the efficiency and use of resources." The future of the education of black Americans, as far as policy and practice are concerned, will then reside in the black academic community where a long-term commitment is more likely, undistracted by initiatives in pollution control and ecology unrelated to black and poor people.

New Knowledge and a New Future for Predominantly Black Colleges

A college or university does more than create a program of instruction for undergraduates. That program must be infused with the intellectual work of some part of a faculty which is original and new. The choices that faculties make will determine the true greatness of any subset of black colleges. There must be areas of knowledge in which great universities are ascendant. They set the standards of excellence, and their teaching role up through the graduate level creates new and highly respected intellectual circles.

To approach conventional specialties in conventional ways is to be excellent with no distinctiveness. It extends the approach to intellectual life in America's university community which claims a kind of amorality and valueless search for truth. Where a choice is made *not* to deal with certain intellectual areas, a value has been expressed. The prestige associated with high accomplishments and accolades by peers accrues to the area of study. As it becomes important, other areas become less important. Predominantly black colleges must:

1. Create new areas of knowledge and an intellectual peerage among themselves that generates new questions about American culture and civilization as currently presented by American scholarship.
2. Try to approach science and technology from a new perspective, that of applied science and its relationship to solutions to the physical and spiritual problems of racial and class bias (extending into the international sphere ultimately).
3. Create the necessary rituals, celebrations, and traditions which signal respect for and preservation of the historical record and accomplishments of black men in America in the areas of both individual achievement and mass cultural infusion.

The concrete ideas presented below are operational programs of knowledge development to which men can turn today and tomorrow. *They are not programs that encompass the entire activity of a college or university. Quite conventional curricula could exist side-by-side with these kinds of activities. Student choices would be free.* This view, however, does maintain that for black colleges and universities to exist for as long as America exists, they must challenge and change its intellectual landscape and some of its assumptions about itself as a culture. The universities must in fact create the need for their existence.

A personal comment before proceeding. I have had great difficulty in deciding to set down some of the following ideas at all. My fear is that the best ideas will be developed rapidly into comprehensive programs by already rich universities with faculties teaching one course and having time to do so. Another fear is that the black professionals, who now newly reside on the campuses of major white universities, will be the instrument for this occurring. Intellectual competition, to be sure, is open and free. When, however, one is uncertain, as I am, of the basic commitment to the development of these black colleges by any power segment of the society, free and open only means unfair advantage for those now in the best competitive position.

A fear about the internal academic community in predominantly black colleges is the other half of my concern. The programs of knowledge development require breaking new ground. This means proceeding according to one's own values and conviction of rightness. This means proceeding without the support of eminent graduate colleges and their learned professors. It means on the other hand a return to the traditions set by Carter Woodson, W. E. B. Du Bois, and Alain Locke. The responsibility for generating starts I put squarely in the offices of the presidents and deans. They must encourage and reward those who would initiate new ideas; they must sometimes find those on their faculties who may not now be of long experience, of high reputation, or of great influence and persuade them it is worthwhile to try new things, to design unusual small-scale research, and to pursue research that has no precedent or history before they start it.

Arbitrarily, the areas of knowledge development have been divided into: Aesthetics, Social-Political Institutions, and Scientific-Technical Development. Under these rubrics, most of the conventional disciplines can be classified. Hopefully, these classifications will generate new combinations.

Aesthetics

The area of aesthetics covers generally the areas of music, literature, and art, those areas which usually are pervasive in so-called general education programs. What is called aesthetics affirms that great civilizations existed and by their products do we know them. The focus in a predominantly black college should be on the American civilization. The Western and European base of much of our cultural criticism and apprisal may well be running out of intelligibility as an organizing principle.

The standard dictionary definition of aesthetics is: "A branch of philosophy dealing with the nature of the beautiful and with judgments concerning beauty and the description of artistic phenomena and aesthetic experience by means of other sciences (as psychology, sociology, history, ethnology)." The term is used here because of its emphasis on beauty. Judgments in that arena have caused black people in America a great many trials and tribulations and still trouble them greatly. Beautiful shades into the higher reaches of judgments of what is good. It is beyond excellent; it approaches the sublime.

Good art, music, and literature are the expressions of those values. There are deep conflicts in American life around these issues that have clearly affected the intellectual life of the university. Pathology and aberration have been the organizing principles in the study of black life, not beauty—but more about that in the Social Institutions area. Things created out of the life and being of black Americans can be beautiful even when they conflict sharply with the art, music, and literature of the Western, European academy. They can and must be accorded their rightful place.

The emphasis in the area of aesthetics should be on music. This is an area of undisputed black ascendancy in American life and in the history of the world. This discussion takes the view that jazz is a new music, a new idiom, as are its folk roots in the slave and peasant culture of the American South. A new music is a major cultural contribution in the history of any civilization. Beyond that, more than the study of music as music is implied here. One must deal with the uses of and the impact of music in the institutional life of black Americans. The rhythms affect views of language and its use in poetry and literature. Much of Langston Hughes's poetry, for example, cannot be read well without a sense of jazz rhythms. Though the church has fallen into disrepute among younger black intellectuals, more understanding is needed of the uses of music in the traditional black church. A cryptic and suggestive list of other areas of new knowledge are:

1. Better and more complex studies of rhythm in Afro-American music.* A provocative statement by Martin Williams puts the issue well: "No, it does no damage [to] my belief in the equality of men, I trust, to conclude that Negroes as a race have a rhythmic genius that is not like that of other races and to concede

* Jazz, blues, gospel, spirituals, rhythm and blues of authentic quality performed by their originators.

that this genius has found a unique expression in the United States."[9] Recent studies have indicated that the rhythmic complexity of Afro-American music is rather simple compared to its original African model. It is now clear that the polyrhythms of African music are outside the conception of rhythm in Western music.[10] Collaborations should be pursued between skilled African musicians and skilled Afro-American musicians. These should be *players* (soloists) as opposed to composers or musicologists because the rhythmic invention in Afro-American music is richest at that level. Recordings of the interchanges can be the raw material for new musical developments by players and composers.

2. Better studies of blue tonality in Afro-American music, which should lead to the design of new instruments. The blue notes are not in the Western scale, though they are notated as flatted thirds and sevenths. The pitch varies widely and becomes in fact a variety of tones as sung and played by Afro-American musicians. The piano, the basal instrument, cannot articulate blue tonality very well. The tones are not there. A new piano that allows more expressiveness of blue tonality should be designed. In essence this new piano would acknowledge the expansion of the Western scale by black Americans. Musicians and engineers could collaborate on this and other instruments. The electrified instrumentation of much of psychedelic rock music is designed to create blue tonality but rather badly, to my ears. Amplification is no substitute for skill and craftsmanship. The two above areas of new knowledge will be moving, then, into an Afro-American music with new scales, new notations, and new meters. The universities can train and develop the musicians.

3. Compositional extensions of the solo work of gifted jazz virtuosi such as Charles Parker, John Birks Gillespie, John Coltrane, and Art Tatum. The increasing number of gifted composers, such as Oliver Nelson, Quincy Jones, David Baker, and Roger Dickerson, should be given time and resources to experiment with the solos using instrumentation up through a full orchestra. One could envision: variations on the solo from the theme "Giant Steps" by John Coltrane for a sixteen-piece orchestra.

4. More in-depth studies of the dominance of Afro-American music in American culture and in the larger Western world. The appellation "popular" music does not decrease the brute fact of the dominance that now approaches half a century and now spans generations. Those adults who reject rock and roll hark back

to the swing era of Benny Goodman, Glenn Miller, and Tommy Dorsey. Same music, different era. It is a serious question as to why this strain of music overrode other ethnic strains, despite its regional origin (the South) and its suppression in a "race" market for thirty years. What is it about this music is one question that has been superficially approached; the deeper question of *why* is not much discussed. One provocative hypothesis is that, in terms of evoking human responsiveness, the root music of the multiple African cultures is superior to that of the Western cultures. It could well be that the negative view of man as sinful mortal held by the church in the early development of Western "serious" music fatally flawed its expression of human emotions.

5. Study of the rituals and traditions surrounding listening to music. Afro-American music, if one uses the traditional black church as the model, requires a kind of involvement that is difficult to resist. In the church the rhythmic and tonal (blue tonality) intensity, when at their height, create almost involuntary participatory acts. Only those whose cultural values about church behavior amount to a prejudice can resist the joining in. Participatory listening is contrary to Western rituals, in which one must stay outside the composers' and performers' music. A hand clap or exclamation is not allowable even at the height of emotional expression (unless it comes at the end). In the black church and later in secular performances, the audience is integral; it adds rhythmic propulsion by clapping; it punctuates phrases by cries or shouts. Yet, there is a respect for the performer's artistry. At the dramatic moments there is a still, dead, pregnant silence. Music as a functional part of man's experience and expression is at stake here. Is the Western concert ritual in any way superior? Is music that requires fifteen to twenty to thirty minutes of dead silence and complete cerebral attentiveness the highest form of musical development? The music is after all for man, a complex organism of great expressiveness. Should he be immobile and passive?

6. More exact studies of the relationships between Afro-American speech and Afro-American music. Field studies, which pin down some of the glib hypotheses, are needed. If the studies are successful, they open up a fertile arena, especially for poets, for more complex work. The idiomatic phrasings of Afro-Americans associated with music need analysis. Their passage into wide usage needs more explanation. Tell it like it is/ hang-up/ coolit/

strung out/ his bag is/ dig. Is it the rhythm, the imagery? Why are they so attractive to the media?

7. The need consciously to begin collecting manuscripts and musical sketches of major contemporary musicians and to acquire their papers when they retire or pass on. This is a highly competitive business, yet one would think that a university doing some of the things listed above would have an edge. How they relate to these figures in terms of recognitions, awards, and honorary degrees will be a factor too. It would be interesting to see how many honorary doctorates Duke Ellington has from black colleges and universities or how many events have been scheduled in his honor in recent times. Amassing complete collections of recordings would also be a way for a university to gain advantage—with competition for, say, the works of Duke Ellington, John Coltrane, Louis Armstrong, and so on. A single university that acquired the musical estates of both Louis Armstrong and Duke Ellington would become a mecca for serious scholars on American music.

Why this area is called aesthetics is most clearly seen in 4 and 5. In a way, music most clearly etches the conflicts in cultural values that must be resolved if black Americans are to be unrestricted personalities on their own terms. Clearly, musicians of standard training cannot hold to the conventional standards of excellence and embrace the work of some of the greatest Afro-American musicians as excellent. In this context one is raising the issue of the values by which one judges art, music, and literature and how they enlarge life. That is the business of a university.

A broader view is needed, then, of aesthetic judgments in American life. It will be a healthier, more robust society for that development. Universities that are involved in the development of a new music and new views of artistic expression and communication are assured of stature. The fact that existing models of the alternatives are taken from black America gives the black college or university an inherent advantage. If the scholarship is productive, general education programs in all higher education would have quite different emphases by the year 2000. The cultural life of the campuses would have a wider range of sources. Most major American universities could well be involved at some level in dealing with the evolving developments in American culture deriving from predominantly black universities.

The predominantly black university must create the rituals which celebrate greatness. Annual events that recognize excellence in the areas of research and scholarship must be instituted. If there is true artistry in a Mahalia Jackson (and there is), some university should have a Mahalia Jackson chair of voice. There should be a Langston Hughes prize for poetry. There should be an Ellington school of music. There should be Martin Luther King or Malcolm X prizes for oratory or speaker of the year awards for consistent platform brilliance. These prizes need not necessarily be annual; true excellence is not always an annual event. Universities, through these events and occasions, establish public traditions extending beyond the peerage of the university scholars.

A deeper problem for American higher education is that, in my view, its culturally based scholarship is too much turned toward Europe, Greece, and Rome. It is questionable whether those civilizations any longer enlighten youth about the incredibly complex American experience. It does not speak to the paradox of the Black Panthers, George Wallace, and John Lindsay all taking the Declaration of Independence as source for their posture. Those civilizations are hard put to clarify deep racism in a country with supposedly protected personal freedoms and poverty in the midst of affluence when lesser nations have no slums, better medical systems, and social welfare programs. An American, whatever that is, is unlike traditional Western nation groups; he has often paid a frightful price for being Italian or Jewish or Irish before becoming an American—even to forsaking his father's name.

The black American, despite his treatment, has not only survived, but has seen expression of his experience in music, in speech, in the use of his body in dance and locomotion come to dominance. A predominantly black university must recognize that out of that experience, then, may be something that speaks to all Americans and affirms their being.

> Jazz is the music of a people who have been told they are unworthy . . . feeling unworthy is fundamental to 20th Century man who . . . is in danger of losing his old goals or has lost them already. But the music involves the discovery of one's worthiness from within. And it is thus an experience men of many races and many circumstances have responded to.[11]

The predominantly black colleges sit filled with vital young people who still live the experience out of which jazz comes. If they look closely at the other aesthetic expressions of that experience, they may find the key to the redirection of American civilization.

Social-Political Institutions

By a conscious act, the social scientists in the black university should put a moratorium on the study of pathology. If recent history is any precedent, that will continue to be done by white social scientists. A first study might be an analysis of the personalities and personal-social development of white men who spend their careers cataloguing the results of racism on the lives of black Americans. As implied under aesthetics, there is more to the lives of black Americans than powerlessness, frustrations, illegitimacy, crime, low educational achievement, and on and on. The flaw in all of this research is that it gives no basis for what one must do to work on one's problems. The pinnacle of negative research was reached in Kenneth Clark's *Dark Ghetto.* It mercilessly dissected the largest and most complex urban community of black men in the world. At the end, one cannot quite decide whether Clark believes in any possibilities of improvement for the future. Obviously, judging from his involvements, he does. But on the level of looking for signs of how to proceed one must conclude all the brilliance of his analysis left that issue essentially untouched.

We had no leaders with power, no strategies for change about which he was hopeful. To get power, I presume we need planning, systematic and rational, with a research base. The ghetto, because of its treatment by white America, is an enemy to this alternative because it has "a primitive hostility to the creative use of human intelligence."[12] Again a weak solution: "planning" and pessimism about its success.

The new areas of knowledge must proceed away from the Clark approach and look closely for patterns of strength and success and survival, despite the fact that these patterns are not modal. To find solutions it makes sense to study solutions. To infer solutions from a study of pathology has failed again and again. Millions of black Americans are not suffering from pathology. Under the same conditions that destroy and demoralize their peers, they hold their families together—families filled with love—they send their children to school, and these children do not drop out, they go to college. We may find in more studies of these areas of black life solid hypotheses about building the mass movement so badly needed. Some research for new knowledge is needed in the following areas:

The Family

1. The strengths and detailed functioning of *the extended family* needs attention. When it works, it works quite well in saving children from a harsh life without parents, uncles, aunts, grandmothers, older sisters. At Howard University, for example, in 1961 a match between the name of the parent or guardian and the name of the students revealed that in about 25 per cent of the cases the guardian or parent had a different name from that of the student. What are the supports? What are the motivations, the psychology of these families?

2. The matriarchy should be revisited. Some women seemed quite successful at creating strong, resourceful men. How is this done? What are the characteristics of this matriarchy? How does it differ from those where the males do seem to be hurt? In our surveys at ISE,[13] 27 per cent of the freshmen marked "mother only" as the person lived with and another 9 per cent marked "other," most of whom were also females. The males should be isolated and they and their families studied.

3. What are the roots of militancy and activism in the black family? In terms of leadership, we need to know more about its development within the family.

4. When one looks at families that have the same characteristics and one produces school achievers and the other does not, what are the differences? Teachers have many hypotheses but no real knowledge.

5. The answers to such questions have the seeds for adult education programs dealing with young mothers and fathers, mothers without husbands, and even college students prior to graduation. Stronger families are useful regardless of the political strategies.

The Church

Lately, the church is seen as a dysfunctional institution by some younger black intellectuals. It is, however, a powerful force in the lives of the black Americans the same young intellectuals need for political power. The large independent churches should get special attention. What are the mechanisms for holding the network of classes, clubs, and teams together; how does one rise to leadership; what are the reward systems in the month-to-month detail work that must be done? One may learn a great deal about the motivational roots for a mass movement here. For example, at a large independent church in Washington, D. C., forty-seven "team captains" were listed to perform functions in planning for an anniversary of the church. Millions of dollars have been raised; there is a nursery school and a start on a new half-million dollar addition to the church. One may argue about the uselessness of such a church for black liberation, but it is a functioning, living social organism that meets many needs of its constituents. No black social scientist knows how or why it works in terms of empirical research and analysis.

Education

Can one identify successful black youth in high schools in terms of grades, when they are at the same time not "nice" in the conventional sense of liked by teachers? One is looking for the genesis of assertiveness combined with achievement. Where are highly successful all black high schools in terms of drop-outs, college-going rates, and gainful employment upon graduation? Are they all schools of middle-income black families? A detailed study of four basically low-income schools would be invaluable: one in the urban North, one in the urban South, one in the rural South, one in a small northern town (an all black rural northern school would be extremely difficult to find). How do the students perceive such a school? How do they perceive the elementary and junior high schools from which they come?

The long-range goal of such research is to begin to construct strategies that can strengthen the internal institutional life of black communities. In the long run, agents of change would work on two levels, the larger political level and the school-by-school, neighborhood-by-neighborhood level. Social scientists cannot tell anyone how to apply their findings, but the findings would at least deal in positive factors.

Politics

On another level, more sophisticated analyses of alternatives for political strategies need to be studied. The false dichotomies of integration, separation, segregation take up too much time. Some black social scientists should set the task of looking at possible futures for black Americans without using any of the labels. There should, instead, be careful studies of population trends, political attitudes, institutional reactions to changes in location (schools, real estate, jobs, churches), kinds of people who leave black low-income concentrations for white middle-income concentrations, those who go to black middle-income areas, and common special interests with other groups, and from these studies a series of probabilities could be developed. These would not be definitive but would certainly raise the level of dialogue above its current primitive level. The models should include what the cities would look like with maximum concentrations of blacks in them in the year 2000 versus maximum dispersal patterns. What are the legal alternatives to the current pattern of federal to state to city funding of transportation, education, and law inforcement? Can black controlled nonprofit public corporations be set up and federally funded to deal independently with services such as transportation, housing codes, and garbage collection in the ghettos?

On another level, solid work should be done on the relationship between social science and solutions to human problems. Given the dynamism in social relationships, the model for the social scientists should be small units—a school, a neighborhood—and they should deal with them without attempts to generalize. Over a year ten skilled psychologists might change one hundred schools, if their discipline has any validity in the real world. Yet no basic generalizations might occur. In a decade more might well be accomplished than from the grand hypotheses of a Daniel Moynihan or a Kenneth Clark.

A university can do other things, but it would be on the frontier if it were in any of these areas in a substantive way. The techniques developed and what is learned is not limited to black Americans, though its primary and initial relevance is to them.

Scientific-Technical Development

Some basic work needs to be done in the philosophy of science or the ethics of science. Basic questions need to be raised about the Western model of rationality. Aristotle's *Organon,* may have been missing a *source* of premises in the logic of life as it moves in the universe among planets and animals. Man's intelligence has enabled him to rip through any such limitation, if it did exist. We may be on a course dictated by a rationality devoid of human qualities. Could it be true that the mind as master of the body makes mind the ultimate destroyer of the body? A particularly interesting exposition of an alternate view of logic is found in the book *Muntu* by Janheinz Jahn. He points out that in African philosophy there was a "coherence or compatibility among all the disciplines. A medical theory, e.g., which contradicted a theological conclusion was absurd and vice versa." It was impossible to separate science, religion, land law, social theory, and philosophy. There is a provocative discussion of medicine men and healing by magic and double blind studies using placebos in scientific experiments. Jahn points out a significant percentage of cures from placebos that even the physician thought was medication. He then raises the question of the "magic" component in modern medicine. He does not argue that modern medicine is not superior, but that there should probably be an intentional combination of medication and "magic" for most effective results.[14]

For scholars wishing to pursue non-Western models in more detail without the Western biases, significant new ground can be broken. Science has clearly been irrational in some of its applications if consonance with life was a criterion for a larger rationality. New cultural value systems dealing with these issues need development and elaboration. Some generations of scientists trained in universities under the sway of a new ethics and logic of science might make a difference in the history of the world and its survival time.

On an operational level more data are needed on:

1. A study should be made of the eating patterns of young pregnant mothers, including the social milieu of eating.

2. How can the diet of babies be improved in the constraints of infrequent medical advice and insufficient funds?

3. Can nutrition and health in the ghetto be improved through additives to popular food stuffs, in carry-outs, and in small grocery shops? Can the chicken and barbecue places which dot the ghetto be a positive force in nutrition, *without* changing the diet?

4. Teams of nutritionists, marketing experts, and legal experts should collaborate on how to popularize, say, a new high protein soft drink aimed at young children or a new kind of ice cream truck with subsidized lower prices and diet-balancing ice cream.

5. Teams of engineers, construction experts, and labor market experts should work on low-cost housing using nonunion labor.

6. Architects, media experts, advertising experts, and educators should collaborate on designing schools to maximize useful sensory inputs for learning.

These are all applied areas, to be sure, but basic or pure science questions should soon intrude themselves into the work of universities operating in these areas. Centers are needed with a long-term, undeviating attention to the problems suggested by the items listed above.

As one reviews the proposals, their potential is matched only by the general absence of widespread interest in them in the academic world. The latter problem is enormous because it requires schools, not now respected, to strike off into areas in which there are few training pools. Are these issues related to what black youth must do to succeed in America? The last question will be used as a final point.

Nothing precludes what any undergraduate learns under major professors in these new areas from being used in the most conventional ways. What will hold the best students is intellectual excitement. Large numbers of students will undoubtedly ignore those parts of the university or college where some of these activities occur. The deeper issue is that the educative impact of knowing that black men are in charge of areas of knowledge for the entire society is incalculable and all positive. To be in the environment of a place where studies are being made by black scholars which shake and rattle the conventional wisdom will infuse youth with new visions of their roles in American life. The fact that the laboratory and source of invention is within the experiences and problems of black Americans will stop forever the doubts, the anxiety, the uncertainty about much of the black experience.

The kinds of leadership roles projected for predominantly black colleges and universities lead to the redirection of American civilization away from its predominantly white, northern European base to a multiracial, pluralistic civilization. Racism is a major flaw in the four-hundred-year rise of American civilization. The human values expressed in America's ideals and their cultural extensions excluded black people in their inception—and ultimately all nonwhites in practice. The issue of black people as people is still unresolved and a negative symptom of what the future may hold is seen in the racial distributions of the cities and suburbs in the North and South.

A new mission of some predominantly black colleges and universities can be to make the human and cultural values of this entire civilization reflect an emphasis more hospitable to black Americans. As race has been a dominant theme in America's past and present, so should the artistic, literary, and scientific contribution of black intellectuals be a dominant force in its future. The future of the world may well depend on the American civilization producing a generation capable of accepting the humanity and ascendancy of nonwhite people. Black people are the best hope for influencing the civilization in that direction; their colleges and universities should start now to consider their role in the reshaping of America as a civilization.

REFERENCES

1. Charles S. Johnson, *The Negro College Graduate* (Chapel Hill: University of North Carolina Press, 1936), p. 18.

2. Henry A. Bullock, *A History of Negro Education in the South* (New York: Praeger, 1970), pp. 171-172.

3. The Institute for Services to Education (ISE) surveys produced these data. The income data agree largely with those of the American Council on Education on the black college student. The income distribution is slightly lower. In my view, the ACE data are not weighted enough in terms of the large state schools which enroll 60 per cent of the students.

4. Elias Blake, Jr., "Background Paper on the Traditionally Negro College," *The Congressional Record* (May 11, 1970), p. E4091.

5. Robert H. Berls, "Higher Education Opportunity and Achievement in the United States," in *Economics and Financing of Higher Education in the United States,* Joint Economic Committee, Congress of the United States (Washington, D. C.: Government Printing Office, 1969), pp. 164-165.

6. *Preprimary Enrollment of Children Under Six,* National Center on Educational Statistics and School Enrollment, October 1968, U. S. Bureau of the Census, p. 20, no. 190, Table I.

7. The fourteen colleges enroll 40,000 students, seven public and seven private. The surveys were done in the Thirteen College Curriculum Program from which much of the thinking on instructional design comes. The colleges are: Alabama A. and M., Bennett, Bishop, Clark, Florida A. and M., Jackson State, Lincoln, Mary Holmes, Norfolk State, North Carolina A. and T., Southern, Talladega, Tennessee A. and I., and Voorhees.

8. From "Ideas and Their Expression," in the English unit, *Responsibility,* designed cooperatively by teachers from black colleges and the Institute for Services to Education.

9. Martin Williams, *The Jazz Tradition* (New York: Oxford University Press, 1970), pp. 7-8.

10. See Gunther Schuller's *Early Jazz, Its Roots and Musical Development,* I (New York: Oxford University Press, 1968). He indicates the most careful notations of African rhythms by Western musicians were incorrect because the polyrhythms were additive and did not even start and stop at agreed upon intervals (6, 8, 12 bars). The music is polyrhythmic and polymetric simultaneously. The basic point is that Western rhythmic concepts cannot be used in this case. Yet a variant does exist in Afro-American playing and singing styles, which is also difficult to notate.

11. Williams, *The Jazz Tradition,* p. 15.

12. Kenneth Clark, *Dark Ghetto* (New York: Harper and Row, 1965), p. 212.

13. See note 3 above.

14. Janhienz Jahn, *Muntu* (New York: Grove Press, 1961), pp. 96-97.

CONRAD K. HARPER

The Legal Status of the Black College

THE TERM "Negro or black colleges and universities" usually refers to institutions established for blacks shortly before and after the Civil War. Although some of these institutions were publicly controlled, most were privately supported by church groups.[1] These institutions now enroll more than 150,000 black students or more than a third of all black college students in the country.[2] Today presumably most of the approximately 123 predominantly black junior colleges, colleges, and universities receive substantial governmental financial support.[3] This fact arguably makes them subject to constitutional requirements barring racial segregation.[4] Even those which receive entirely private funds nonetheless may be required to be non-racially discriminatory either because they benefit from indirect public support such as tax exemptions or because their private nature must yield to the public interest in non-racial discrimination.

The legal status of black colleges as racially identifiable institutions must be seen against the background of general legal requirements regarding racial discrimination in educational facilities. The assumption here is that the legal status of black colleges can be no different, in the main, from that of white colleges even where one of the following rationales is adopted: (1) the black college offering a traditional curriculum is so necessary to the black community that white youth otherwise qualified for admission have no right to attend such a college; or (2) the black college is legally distinguishable as offering a different type of curriculum which is both legitimate and explains blacks' primary interest in it. The first rationale seems unlikely to withstand judicial scrutiny; the second may nonetheless entitle a white youth or professor of appropriate intellectual stature to nondiscriminatory treatment. The second rationale provides, however, a possible legal justification for black colleges and black studies programs.

Although many of the charters of black colleges did not explicitly exclude whites, all were founded at a time when applicable state law in most states required racial segregation in public schools or in other spheres.[5] The federal government approved separate-but-equal land grant colleges in the Agricultural and Mechanical College Act of 1890.[6] The likely and often realized result even today is that a majority of black colleges have all black student bodies.[7]

Public Colleges

In 1899, three years after *Plessy* v. *Ferguson*,[8] the Supreme Court upheld a Georgia school board's closing a black public high school on the grounds of claimed financial hardship although the white public high school remained open.[9] Nine years later, in 1908, the Supreme Court sustained a Kentucky statute forbidding colleges from simultaneously offering education to blacks and whites.[10] In so doing, the Supreme Court necessarily determined that a state could regulate the admissions policies of a private college.[11] In 1927 the Supreme Court approved the Mississippi practice of classifying a child of Chinese descent as ineligible to attend white public schools.[12] But in a quartet of decisions from 1938 to 1950, the Supreme Court held (1) blacks must be admitted to white graduate schools where no black school was immediately available in the state; (2) upon admission blacks could not be segregated; and (3) all aspects of education, including intangibles, must be equal in racially separate institutions.[13] Following the *Brown* decisions,[14] the short step of outlawing segregation in public higher education was quickly taken.[15] As a matter of federal constitutional law, therefore, it is now settled that race cannot be the organizing principle of public education.

It is sometimes suggested that many predominantly black or predominantly white public colleges have their racial composition largely as a result of segregated housing patterns. Thus it is expected that Federal City College in Washington, D.C., and some campuses of Chicago City Junior College are predominantly black,[16] while the University of North Dakota is predominantly white. Even in an ethnically diverse setting, a municipal university, such as the City University of New York, often may not reflect the ethnic group distribution in the city.[17] These facts bear an obvious resemblance to the theory of de facto segregation which asserts public elementary and secondary school officials have no constitutional responsibility for racially segregated schools resulting from neighborhood school zones.[18] Where it is shown such racially segregated housing results in part from governmentally required and encouraged housing segregation, however, school officials may well have a duty to take affirmative action to assure desegregated schools.[19] Public colleges may similarly be required to change their recruitment and admissions policies to counteract a historic pattern of segregation. A federal district court in Tennessee recently required affirmative acts by the state, in addition to an open door policy administered in good faith, where the racial composition of state colleges remained virtually the same.[20] The Office of Civil Rights of the Department of Health, Education and Welfare has also ordered five states, including Pennsylvania and Maryland, to desegregate their colleges or lose federal financial assistance.[21]

Private Colleges Having No Church Affiliation

A majority of the 123 predominantly black colleges are not controlled by religious denominations.[22] But of the 72 private black colleges, 56 list a church affiliation.[23] While some question might be raised as to the degree of denominational control, for purposes of discussion, private colleges having no church affiliation are treated in the following paragraphs in order that the issue of religious control can be put in proper perspective in the next section.

Many black colleges are private in form but receive such substantial governmental funds that they probably would be deemed public for purposes of the constitution's guarantee of equal protection of the laws. While one federal appellate court declined to determine whether Howard University was subject to the Bill of Rights because it receives over half of its annual operating budget from Congress,[24] another federal court has expressly held that white private segregated schools cannot constitutionally receive state subsidies.[25] The 1964 Civil Rights Act explicitly prohibits racial discrimination by recipients of most types of federal funds,[26] presumably including colleges aided by the National Defense Education Act of 1958 and the Higher Education Facilities Act of 1963.[27] Furthermore, in the areas of discrimination in private hospitals and privately owned public accommodations, governmental financial support of an otherwise private establishment has been a significant factor in outlawing segregation in such establishments.[28] Even nonobvious state involvement in a facility, such as the substitution of private trustees for public officials, may not insulate the facility from constitutional prohibitions where there is no definitive showing of complete state disengagement from the facility.[29]

Federal law explicitly exempts private clubs from the prohibition of racial discrimination in places of public accommodation[30] and housing.[31] The employment provisions of the 1964 Civil Rights Act do not apply to educational institutions.[32] But any private black college claiming the right to discriminate racially will doubtless face at least the same stringent judicial scrutiny of its private nature accorded to allegedly private clubs.[33]

Even a bona fide private college receiving no public funds may be subject to the restraints of the Thirteenth Amendment and the 1866 Civil Rights Act where it plausibly can be shown that the refusal to admit a student or hire a faculty member is on racial grounds akin to a "badge of slavery." The Supreme Court recently applied somewhat similar reasoning in barring racial discrimination in a private park.[34] If it is assumed that education is a vital public function, the state may be required to assure no racial discrimination even in privately operated colleges.[35] In addition, on at least two occasions white private colleges have successfully challenged racially restrictive charters and in one of the cases the state was barred from attempting to enforce racially restrictive requirements.[36]

Private schools receive, in effect, federal and state subsidies from certain tax benefits, especially the exemption from income tax and the corresponding income tax deduction given to a school's donor.[37] Other tax benefits may include exemptions from social security taxes and federal excise taxes.[38] In 1967 the Internal Revenue Service issued a news release barring tax deductible contributions and tax exemptions to segregated schools where the schools' involvement with a state or political subdivision was unconstitutional or illegal under federal law.[39] Apparently in response to a federal court order outlawing tax exemptions and deductible contributions to segregated schools,[40] the Internal Revenue Service has taken a similar position recently[41] but tax exemptions have been granted to segregated white southern schools in the last few years.[42] Although tax benefits alone have not been found sufficient to hold a private institution to constitutional prohibitions on racial discrimination,[43] it is likely that the structure of such an institution is in large part conditioned by the provisions of the tax exemptions.[44] In these circumstances, government is involved in the institution in a most meaningful way, that is, by influencing organizational structure and facilitating economic support. It has even been suggested that while a private segregated school might have insufficient governmental ties for court-ordered desegregation, a tax exemption might nonetheless be denied.[45] Apparently the reasoning would be that government is under no compulsion to support, by tax benefits, a segregated institution.[46] This reasoning might be further strengthened if it were concluded that (1) segregated schools are, by that fact alone, not organized for exclusively educational purposes; (2) such schools serve private and not public interests; (3) the national policy against racial segregation is paramount; and (4) a tax exemption is a grant of federal financial assistance subject to the requirement of no racial discrimination under the 1964 Civil Rights Act.[47]

Private Colleges Having Church Affiliations

A private college otherwise subject to constitutional restraints on racial discrimination might claim that its church affiliation erects a First Amendment shield against interference in its racial policies. More particularly, such a college might contend that a governmental requirement of desegregation is a law respecting an establishment of religion or an abridgement of the free exercise of religion. Where members of a church are of different races, there would appear to be no First Amendment bar to compelling a college not to discriminate racially as between members. Where a church either has no racial minorities as members or excludes such minorities from membership, a more difficult question is presented. If the church-affiliated college has admitted non-church members as students then the college should not be permitted to discriminate racially in admitting non-church members. Where the college has admitted only church members and, therefore, no minorities, the basic issue becomes: will the constitution permit a racially exclusive religious group to restrict student enrollment only to co-religionists? The answer is not clear.

On the one hand it is said the government cannot legitimately determine whether a religion is bona fide except for a cursory examination of creed and belief.[48] From this proposition it is further suggested the government has no right to vary the religious and racial composition of a college where religious homogeneity is deemed crucial for pedagogy.[49] On the other hand it is said a school or college has primarily a nonreligious purpose so that constitutional protections for religion need not be extended to such activities.[50] An emerging answer to this problem may lie in the notion that the state may require desegregation of all nonpublic schools, including parochial schools, when otherwise the general welfare may be endangered by an overwhelmingly black public school population and an overwhelmingly white private school population.[51] At least two states, Massachusetts and New York, have explicitly prohibited racially discriminatory admissions policies by sectarian colleges in selecting members of their religious group.[52]

The Future of Black Colleges

Insofar as the organizing principle of a black college today is the color of its students and faculty, it would appear to be a legal anomaly because the general trend of the law has been to desegregate educational institutions. It should be said, however, that there is little if any evidence of white students and faculty who are barred from black colleges because of race. While there have been isolated instances of a private educational institution's successfully excluding an applicant on racial grounds even after 1954,[53] it is probably fair to say that most private educational institutions and all public ones are subject to constitutional commands of desegregation. But courts ought to be wary of wholesale college desegregation where blacks may choose a black college for reasons of racial pride and cultural enrichment.[54] Furthermore, the continued identity of a black college may be exceedingly helpful in attracting students who otherwise might fail to obtain any higher education. This is especially important if it is recognized that black colleges will remain a major avenue for black higher education.[55] In addition, black colleges have served and are likely to continue serving as major repositories of institutional power in the black community and as significant sources for trained blacks. In this sense a black college might be analogized to state scholarships intended to aid minorities commonly known to suffer many disadvantages.[56] Recent developments have, however, centered on black control of institutions and curriculum changes.

The current movement toward decentralized public elementary and secondary schools[57]—where, for example, the parents of Harlem children gain some control over school management in their community—can be seen as a healthy development of community consciousness and confidence. Moreover, the continued existence of racially separate schools makes it appropriate for those directly affected to exercise some authority over the schools. A similar theory might be offered for predominantly black control of any college having a predominantly black enrollment. But the argument for community control is often not put racially but geographically. Harlem residents need a voice in school administration, it is said, not because they are black and the schools are black, but because they live in the area served by the schools.

An obvious reason for stressing the geographic argument is that a racial rationale is legally suspect. Aside from black junior colleges, most black colleges are unlikely, however, to have a plausible geographic argument since many of them have students from several states and other countries rather than from a compact area contiguous to the college. In these circumstances, the law is likely to legitimate the predominantly black college only insofar as it offers a nonracial *raison d'être*. Since geography cannot be relied upon for legitimacy, curriculum might be an attractive alternative. This is particularly true where the curriculum emphasizes the study and analysis of the experience of blacks here and abroad.[58]

An inquiry of this magnitude necessarily involves an examination of social, political, cultural, and economic forces from the particular perspective of those denied, on racial grounds, full measure of reward for their status and talents.[59] Institutions focusing on this type of inquiry presumably will attract a substantial black enrollment. But the need to give traditional curriculum subjects may preclude the establishment of an entire college devoted to such an inquiry. Rather, the future may be charted by the growth of specialized, postgraduate establishments such as the Institute of the Black World in Atlanta. Similarly, the growth of black studies programs in various colleges[60] may be analogized to the specialized institutes of regional studies at various universities. It should be assumed, however, that such institutions would be legally required to give nonracial consideration to any student or faculty member of any race having suitable interests and qualifications.

Black colleges today and for years hence are legally defensible largely in instrumental terms: that is, these colleges perform the valuable service of providing an education to students who otherwise probably would not be aided. Such colleges also perform the important political and social role of husbanding black institutional power while training a significant proportion of the blacks who receive a college education. The black college or institute, as it may emerge in the future, will likely retain these functions and perhaps be legally justified as a racially identifiable entity on the additional ground of offering a unique curriculum.

REFERENCES

1. Dwight O. W. Holmes, *The Evolution of the Negro College* (New York: Teachers College, Columbia University, 1934), pp. 67-149, 187-189, 192-194.

2. Carnegie Commission on Higher Education, *From Isolation to Mainstream: Problems of the Colleges Founded for Negroes* (February 1971), p. 14.

3. Earl J. McGrath, *The Predominantly Negro Colleges and Universities in Transition* (New York: Teachers College, Columbia University, 1965), pp. 21, 27, 180-181. The assumption that most black colleges receive governmental financial support is my own based upon McGrath's data showing slightly more than half of the $81 million received by the colleges in 1959-1960 was from governmental sources. Governmental spending for education has increased dramatically since 1959-1960.

4. There is, of course, considerable force to the position that voluntary separation by blacks is appropriate in certain circumstances and is very different from white-enforced segregation of blacks. See Lerone Bennett, Jr., "Liberation," *Ebony,* 25 (August 1970), 36–43. But in the current status of legal doctrine, this view—while politically and philosophically critical—would not legally justify an all-black college which was otherwise subject to the constitutional proscription of racial segregation.

5. The relevant statutory and judicial sources are cited and summarized in the Appendix to the Supplemental Brief for the United States on Reargument, *Brown* v. *Board of Education,* 347 U.S. 483 (1954).

6. 26 Stat. 417 (1890); now codified in part as 7 U.S.C. § 323 (1964).

7. McGrath, *The Predominantly Negro Colleges,* p. 14.

8. 163 U.S. 537 (1896).

9. *Cumming* v. *Richmond County Board of Education,* 175 U.S. 528 (1899).

10. *Berea College* v. *Kentucky,* 211 U.S. 45 (1908).

11. A. Miller, "Racial Discrimination and Private Schools," *Minnesota Law Review,* 41 (1957), 145, 158.

12. *Gong Lum* v. *Rice,* 275 U.S. 78 (1927).

13. *Missouri ex rel. Gaines* v. *Canada,* 305 U.S. 337 (1938); *Sipuel* v. *Oklahoma State Regents,* 332 U.S. 631 (1948); *Sweatt* v. *Painter,* 339 U.S. 629 (1950); *McLaurin* v. *Oklahoma State Regents,* 339 U.S. 637 (1950). See also the earlier case, *Univ. of Maryland* v. *Murray,* 169 Md. 478, 182 Atl. 590 (1936).

14. *Brown* v. *Board of Education,* 347 U.S. 483 (1954); 349 U.S. 294 (1955).

15. For example, *Frasier* v. *Board of Trustees of the University of North Carolina,* 134 F. Supp. 589 (M.D.N.C. 1955), *aff'd.,* 350 U.S. 979 (1956). See Jack Greenberg, *Race Relations and American Law* (New York: Columbia University Press, 1959), pp. 40, 260-267.

16. McGrath, *The Predominantly Negro Colleges,* p. 13, refers to Chicago City Junior College.

17. Note, "Integration of Higher Education in the South," *Columbia Law Review,* 69 (1969), 112, 123, n. 72.

18. For example, *Bell* v. *School City of Gary, Ind.,* 324 F. 2d 209 (7th Cir. 1963), *cert. denied,* 377 U.S. 924 (1964). The de facto segregation issue has never been authoritatively treated by the Supreme Court.

19. *Brewer* v. *School Board of City of Norfolk, Va.,* 397 F. 2d 37, 41-42 (4th Cir. 1968).

20. *Sanders* v. *Ellington,* 288 F. Supp. 937 (M.D. Tenn. 1968); but see *Alabama State Teachers Assoc.* v. *Alabama Public School and College Authority,* 289 F. Supp. 784 (M.D. Ala. 1968).

21. *New York Times,* March 11, 1969, p. 44 (city ed.).

22. McGrath, *The Predominantly Negro Colleges,* p. 19.

23. *Ibid.*

24. *Greene* v. *Howard University,* 412 F. 2d 1128, 1131, n. 2 (D.C. Cir. 1969); accord, *Grossner* v. *Trustees of Columbia Univ.,* 287 F. Supp. 535, 544-549 (S.D.N.Y. 1968).

25. *Poindexter* v. *Louisiana Financial Assistance Comm'n.,* 275 F. Supp. 833 (E.D. La. 1967) (3-judge court), *aff'd. per curiam,* 389 U.S. 571 (1968); see *Kerr* v. *Enoch Pratt Free Library,* 149 F. 2d 212 (4th Cir.), *cert. denied,* 326 U.S. 721 (1945).

26. 78 Stat. 252, 42 U.S.C. § 2000d (1970).

27. Statutory citations may be found in Note, "Federal Tax Benefits to Segregated Private Schools," *Columbia Law Review,* 68 (1968), 922, 935-936, n. 79. A question not treated in the text is whether a black student's receipt of a government scholarship would impose desegregation requirements on his college. Such requirements would presumably apply where the scholarship was under the National Defense Education Act because the college in effect is an agent of the federal government in disbursing scholarship funds. See 20 U.S.C.A. § 424 (1969). As such, the college is very much like other private institutions whose governmental financial involvement requires the application of constitutional norms. See n. 28 below.

28. For example, *Simkins* v. *Moses H. Cone Memorial Hospital,* 323 F. 2d 959 (4th Cir. 1963), *cert. denied,* 376 U.S. 938 (1964) (hospital); *Burton* v. *Wilmington Parking Authority,* 365 U.S. 715 (1961) (restaurant); *Derrington* v. *Plummer,* 240 F. 2d 922 (5th Cir. 1956), *cert. denied sub nom. Casey* v. *Plummer,* 353 U.S. 924 (1957) (cafeteria).

29. *Evans* v. *Newton,* 382 U.S. 296 (1966) (park); *Pennsylvania* v. *Brown,* 392 F. 2d 120 (3d Cir.) (en banc), *cert. denied,* 391 U.S. 921 (1968) (Girard College).

30. Civil Rights Act of 1964, 78 Stat. 243, 42 U.S.C. § 2000a (e) (1970).

31. Fair Housing Act of 1968, 82 Stat. 84, 42 U.S.C. § 3607 (1970).

32. 78 Stat. 255, 42 U.S.C. § 2000e-1 (1970).

33. For example, *Wright* v. *The Cork Club,* 315 F. Supp. 1143 (S.D. Tex. 1970), *appeal pending* (5th Cir.); *Daniel* v. *Paul,* 395 U.S. 298 (1969).

34. *Sullivan* v. *Little Hunting Park,* 396 U.S. 229 (1969).

35. See *Guillory* v. *Administrator of Tulane Univ.,* 203 F. Supp. 855, 858-859 (E.D. La. 1962), *vacated on rehearing,* 207 F. Supp. 554 (E.D. La.), *aff'd.* 306 F. 2d 489 (5th Cir. 1962); Note, "The Wall of Racial Separation: The Role of Private and Parochial Schools in Racial Integration," *New York University Law Review,* 43 (1968), 514, 522-525, 528-530, 533, which discusses elementary and secondary schools.

36. *Sweet Briar Institute* v. *Button,* 280 F. Supp. 312 (W.D. Va. 1967) (3-judge court); *William Marsh Rice Univ.* v. *Carr,* 9 Race Rel. L. Rep. 613 (Harris Cy. Tex. Dist. Ct., 1964), *aff'd. sub nom. Coffee* v. *William Marsh Rice Univ.,* 408 S.W. 2d 269 (Tex. Civ. App. 1966).

37. Int. Rev. Code of 1954, §§ 170(b) (1), 170 (b) (2), 501(c) (3).

38. Int. Rev. Code of 1954, § 4294; 42 U.S.C. § 410 (a) (8) (B) (1964).

39. IRS News Release, August 2, 1967, 7 CCH 1967 Stand. Fed. Tax Rep. ¶ 6734.

40. *Green* v. *Kennedy,* 309 F. Supp. 1127 (D.D.C. 1970) (3-judge court).

41. *New York Times,* August 20, 1970, p. 1 (late city ed.); *ibid.,* September 12, 1970, p. 12 (late city ed.); *ibid.,* October 6, 1970, p. 31 (late city ed.).

42. *New York Times,* August 3, 1967, p. 24.

43. *Guillory* v. *Administrators of Tulane Univ.,* 212 F. Supp. 674 (E.D. La. 1962).

44. Note, "Federal Tax Benefits to Segregated Private Schools," *Columbia Law Review,* 68 (1968), 922, 930-931.

45. J. Allen, Note, "The Tax Exempt Status of Segregated Schools," *Tax Law Review,* 24 (1969), 409, 419; cf. *Walz* v. *Tax Comm'n. of City of New York,* 397 U.S. 664 (1970), holding that city tax exemptions for religious organizations do not abridge the First Amendment.

46. See R. Weil, Note, "Tax Exemptions for Racial Discrimination in Education," *Tax Law Review,* 23 (1968), 399, 407, n. 31, discussing the 1949 denial of a tax exemption of the Armstrong Trust apparently because the Trust propagated the doctrine of white supremacy; Rev. Rul. 67-325, 1967 *Int. Rev. Bull.* No. 40, p. 7, denying deductibility of contributions to and tax exempt status of segregated recreational facilities.

47. Allen, "The Tax Exempt Status" pp. 409, 424-431; Civil Rights Act of 1964, 78 Stat. 252, 42 U.S.C. § 2000d (1970).

48. *United States* v. *Ballard,* 322 U.S. 78 (1944).

49. See R. Power, "The Racially Discriminatory Charitable Trust: A Suggested Treatment," *St. Louis University Law Journal,* 9 (1965), 478, 499.

50. *Ibid.,* pp. 499-500.

51. Note, "The Wall of Separation: The Role of Private and Parochial Schools in Racial Integration," *New York University Law Review,* 43 (1968), 514, 533.

52. Mass. Ann. Laws, ch. 151C §§ 1-2 (1965); N.Y. Educ. Law § 313 (McKinney 1969). See also Note, "Federal Tax Benefits to Segregated Private Schools," *Columbia Law Review,* 68 (1968), 922, 948, n. 130.

53. For example, *Reed* v. *Hollywood Professional School,* 338 P. 2d 633 (Cal. Super. Ct. 1959).

54. *Harvard Law Review,* 82 (1969), 1757, 1760-1761.

55. McGrath, *The Predominantly Negro Colleges,* pp. 3-4.

56. See Note, "Constitutionality of Restricted Scholarships," *New York University Law Review,* 33 (1958), 604, 608; R. Power, "The Racially Discriminatory Charitable Trust: A Suggested Treatment," *St. Louis University Law Journal,* 9 (1965), 478, 494.

57. For example, N.Y. Educ. Law §§ 2590-2590n (McKinney Supp. 1969).

58. See Vincent Harding, "Toward the Black University," *Ebony,* 25 (August 1970), 156-159; *Statement of Purpose and Program, Fall, 1969,* Institute of the Black World, Martin Luther King, Jr., Memorial Center (Atlanta, n.d.), pp. 1-5.

59. At least one black scholar has stated an appropriate black curriculum cannot be created today because the necessary research has not been done. Gerald A. McWorter, "Deck the Ivy Racist Halls: The Case of Black Studies," in Armstead L. Robinson and others, eds., *Black Studies in the University: A Symposium* (New Haven: Yale University Press, 1969), p. 68.

60. See, for example, the issue of the *Journal of Negro Education,* 39 (Summer 1970), devoted to "Black Studies in American Education."

WINFRED L. GODWIN

Southern State Governments and Higher Education for Negroes

It is clear today that the future quality of American life will be determined in great measure by the success—or failure—of the national effort to insure the equality of all citizens in terms of opportunity, justice, and the law. It is equally clear that education must play a central role in this national effort, and that education beyond the high school will prove crucial as a means of preparing young Negro men and women for fuller participation in the professional, economic, social, and governmental life of the nation.

Implicit in the goal of equal opportunity are two objectives: (1) insuring that opportunities for higher education are equally available to all citizens, subject only to the limitations of their individual interests and abilities, and (2) completing the transition from the South's dual system of higher education to a unitary system providing, without discrimination, for the needs of all citizens, black and white. While the second of these objectives is essentially regional, both are of great national significance and require serious attention from all sectors and sections of the nation and its academic community.

Still, however strong the national concern and however necessary federal funds and programs, states now are primarily responsible for higher education. The actions of states, therefore, will determine to a great extent the quantity and quality of higher educational opportunities available to Negroes.

Southern state governments, especially, bear a heavy responsibility, in view of the historic dualism at all levels of education. In 1968 an estimated 12,000,000 blacks resided in the region,[1] including some 820,000 of college-age population. Of these, only 20 per cent were enrolled in postsecondary institutions, compared with 40 per cent of the southern white college-age population.

This inequity in opportunity is not new; its causes are rooted deep in the region's history of economic underdevelopment and racial politics. What is new in much of the region is a keener awareness that this condition is intolerable, as well as increased concern about how to correct it.

Until recently, the South's traditional black colleges provided the only effective opportunity young Negroes had to enter post-secondary education. For most of their existence, these institutions have been operated as a tolerated, though largely ignored and undernourished part of the region's biracial society. Working with meager resources and with students largely from segregated schools, the black colleges supplied the black community with teachers, ministers, and other professionals, whose ranks provided the major black spokesmen to the society at large.

While the 1954 Supreme Court school desegregation decision somewhat quickened the pace of desegregation in higher education, public concern and state governmental actions centered on the decision's meaning for public elementary and secondary education. It was another decade before the mounting civil rights movement, black student militancy, and a series of national and regional studies of black colleges aroused widespread public attention to the black colleges.

Most recently, as federal concern for compliance with civil rights legislation turned to higher education, various southern states have been directed "to disestablish past patterns of segregation," "to dismantle the dual system of higher education," to eliminate "the racial identifiability of all institutions." These directives suggest a variety of perceptions of what integration in higher education means. Nevertheless, as a result most states have been examining more closely their roles in providing higher educational opportunity to black citizens, in the black college and elsewhere.[2] It is important to note that for a number of states this increased federal attention to civil rights compliance in higher education served primarily to accelerate efforts under way at state and regional levels to cope more effectively with higher educational needs of black citizens.

At this writing no federal court or agency has defined clearly what a unitary system of higher education is or how it can be developed. Indeed, the limited consideration of the matter in federal courts has only served to offer contradictory notions of what compliance in higher education is. For our purposes here, we define a unitary system in higher education as one in which all of a state's teaching, research, and service resources are utilized for all its citizens without racial discrimination in admissions, staffing, financial support, or any other phase of the educational enterprise.[3]

In a unitary system, institutions which are predominantly white will increasingly serve larger numbers of blacks, and traditionally black colleges will be assisted in developing broader roles and attracting additional white students. Especially for black institutions the unitary system concept recognizes the need for an identity based on pride in past accomplishments and dignity in new contributions to total state programs. Black institutions will not operate as "separate but equal," but neither will their planning and partnership with other institutions require that they repudiate efforts which have been meaningful and which may be adapted to contemporary needs.

We may identify a unitary system in several ways:

The necessary planning process will provide for black involvement and participation in decision-making. Persons of both races will be involved in this statewide planning process and be representative of both policy and operational levels.

Cooperative planning among institutions will focus on statewide needs of all citizens. Institutions serve diverse constituencies with both special and common concerns. The institutions are obliged to respond to the legitimate interests of these groups. Within the total system, access to various postsecondary educational experiences will be provided for all these groups.

Maximum use will be made of all available and projected higher educational facilities. Campus facilities will be considered in terms of interinstitutional use and—where possible—joint research and/or service operations will be located in existing facilities. Neighboring institutions which have been traditionally white or black will coordinate their academic programs to utilize space where it exists rather than seek new space.

Institutions will make extensive use of faculty exchange and joint appointments. This includes the identification of faculty in highly specialized disciplines, the inclusion of appropriate and qualified faculty in joint research projects, and the availability of specialized courses through systematic programs of student and faculty exchange.

Institutional roles will consider the unique characteristics of each institution in the total system. Many institutions offer majors in the same academic fields—teacher education at the undergraduate level, for example. However, specialities can be based on an institution's unique ability to assemble instructional, research, and service capabilities. Thus the traditionally Negro institutions can provide, through teaching, training, and other means, special competence in the educational problems of the economically and educationally disadvantaged at all educational levels.

The location of institutions and their proximity to each other will be factors in determining role and scope responsibilities. Public institutions in every state are in locales ranging from rural to urban settings, which serve as indices of student needs and program potentials. In some places public senior institutions are near community colleges or vocational/technical schools. In several southern cities traditionally Negro and predominantly white institutions are within walking distance of each other. With proper planning, advantage will be taken of this proximity in developing each institution's programs and in building cooperative programs.

In expanding its system of higher education into any locale—by creating new institutions or branches of existing ones—a state will recognize the resources available through an existing institution. If the existing institution is a traditionally Negro public college, expansion will be accomplished in such a way that dualism will not be perpetuated or restored.

There are formidable problems, of course, in making these ideas operational. While no state has achieved a unitary system in these terms, there is considerable agreement in a number of states with the objectives expressed.

The role of the black college in an integrating society is of major interest. There is little disposition among white or black leadership to close, phase out, or merge public black colleges in the South. Undoubtedly, a variety of conflicting motives account for this situation, but there are quite practical reasons as well. These institutions enroll almost half of the blacks in college in the South. Most are modest in size, but even the smallest could probably muster sufficient political support to assure survival. More important, there is a growing understanding that in a pluralistic society the ending of officially sanctioned discrimination neither satisfies the black community's desire for identity and greater self-determination nor ends the public responsibility to improve opportunities for blacks.

There is perhaps a greater general appreciation today in the South among blacks and whites than elsewhere of the potential in black colleges. It is widely agreed that the traditionally black college will continue for some time to provide the major college opportunity for large numbers of blacks. The plain fact is that public elementary and secondary education is not yet preparing black students for college entrance in proportion to their numbers. Of course, the desegregation of public schools has only begun. Also, the effort to compensate for economic, cultural, and educational deprivation in the preschool years has not had time to produce major changes in college readiness—and probably will not for some time. Schools in impoverished rural areas and inner-city ghettos are still groping for solutions to problems of uncertain magnitude and depth. For this reason, the traditionally Negro colleges will provide for many students who do not gain admission elsewhere. Otherwise, higher education will bar a shockingly high percentage of Negro citizens, many of them possessing unmeasured potential for advanced education. But if one of the most frequently cited justifications for the black college is its expertise in educating the disadvantaged—and most state leaders readily accept the proposition—it is equally important to recognize that assigning traditionally Negro institutions a permanent role as teachers of the unprepared would doom the entire enterprise.

In most states, fortunately, leaders recognize that provisions must be made to raise standards at these colleges, to expand opportunities for Negro students at other institutions, to improve means of gauging student potential, and to develop programs of high quality in special fields, including black studies in the indigenous setting, which will attract more nonblack students to black campuses. It is most urgent that black college leadership, both administrators and faculty, become increasingly concerned with identifying new roles which their institutions may appropriately fulfill within the total context of a state's postsecondary offerings.

Despite decades of benign neglect, most states have been substantially increasing financial support of public black colleges. (It is not the public black college that is on the ragged edge of economic survival.) In most states officials readily acknowledge that black institutions need better financial support in order to remedy accumulated deficiencies and gradually to gain a broader constituency. Most states have either equalized faculty salaries between black and white institutions or are moving to do so. But additional support for other purposes is almost uniformly needed. Generally, states appear sympathetic to providing supplementary funding to meet specific needs. One state higher education agency head reflected this when he said, "I am quite skeptical of just adding some faculty members or adding a certain number of dollars to an institution's budget, based on the estimated proportions of disadvantaged students enrolled there. I would like to see a more specific commitment from the institution that it would develop and operate programs which would be effective in reducing some of the learning disabilities that students have."

To help both state and institutional leaders focus on specific, realistic financial steps that should be taken, a regional task force in the South, including black and white legislators, has recommended to states and private sources that special funding be provided black colleges to:

—support special guided studies programs for disadvantaged students,
—augment faculty salaries,
—reduce teaching loads so faculty will be able to devote more time to working with students individually,
—increase funds for student financial aid, which is now identified by some black presidents as their number one need,
—provide a full range of administrative services including improved student counseling, sharpened internal management, updated programs to prepare students for new career opportunities, improved recruiting, admission, and placement services,
—overcome deficiencies in library resources, laboratory equipment, and such instructional aids as computers and other programmed learning devices.[4]

Several states have responded to the need for "catch-up" funds at the black institutions. North Carolina appropriated $1,000,000 for 1967-1969 and $1,300,000 for 1969-1971 to the state board of higher education as additional allocations for the five black public institutions. Approximately $2,000,000 has been requested for the

1971-1973 biennium to expand their effort. The Florida board of regents has approved a differential factor in allocating funds to Florida A. and M. University in support of compensatory programs there. The Mississippi legislature made a special appropriation of $600,000 to Mississippi Valley State College in 1968 to strengthen the faculty and improve library facilities. In 1970 the general assembly of Tennessee created a joint legislative commission to examine special financial needs of black institutions. The commission has presented its report on Tennessee State University and offered ten recommendations relating to finances.

Special funding is needed to help, but administrators and faculties will determine whether necessary curriculum renovation occurs in the black colleges. Generally speaking, curricula are not changing as rapidly as career opportunities are opening to blacks.[5] Aside from the traditional inertia characteristic of most institutions in curriculum matters, many faculty and administrators in the black institutions are primarily concerned with bringing basic academic programs up to their concept of adequate quality. When twelve predominantly black colleges were recently given financial and other encouragement to make curricula revisions and changes, most chose their freshman studies programs or their general curricula. Only about a fourth of the group made changes in response to new vocational opportunities for black students. In most states black college programs do not reflect the rapidly growing community college programs. State planning and coordinating agencies are increasingly concerned with the articulation of these two types of institutions, as well as with duplication of programs between senior institutions that is an inheritance of a racially dual system. State coordinating boards and institutions, left as free as possible from both localized political and academic vested interests, can plan for elimination of duplication in a manner educationally beneficial to both students and institutions. This has occurred in some instances, and, with appropriate sensitivity to black feelings that integration has usually been a one-way street, sound and equitable interinstitutional arrangements can be completed in many instances. Indeed, a major avenue to developing a unitary system in higher education is through creation of new kinds of cooperative relationships between predominantly black and white campuses located in proximity, relationships in which:

—the benefits flow in both directions, replacing the older con-

cept of superior-inferior relationships with an equal partnership,
—the goals are educationally significant and not limited to exchange of faculty and students for appearance's sake,
—the traditionally Negro institutions have increased opportunities to serve the entire community even as black students have additional opportunities in white institutions,
—there is provision for integrative experiences rather than for mere desegregating experiences as students and faculty of institutions work together to accomplish specific educational objectives.

Such relationships are emerging, some with state encouragement, and some quietly and without public attention.

Some black institutions understandably have been apprehensive over the establishment of new senior campuses in their localities. Federal court suits have ensued in Alabama and Tennessee and others may well come, with the ultimate legal resolution uncertain. In each of these cases, a new campus is being established as a component unit of a multicampus state university, and in each instance the governance of public higher education is such that state-level considerations have been subordinated to the expanding university's special interests and wishes. In Tennessee, however, the price for the new campus was a court order for a state plan which would assure elimination of the historic dual structure. Thus state-level considerations inevitably will arise when the expansion of "desegregated" public higher education suggests the possibility of perpetuating the historic isolation of the black colleges.

A contrasting approach is represented in North Carolina where a coordinated transition is under way for transfer of the predominantly white land-grant university's degree-granting branch to the responsibility of the neighboring public black institution.

As important as the needs of the traditional black colleges are, and as necessary as it is for states to help them serve more effectively in a slowly integrating society, states will substantially increase the degree of postsecondary opportunities for blacks by further integration of the predominantly white institutions and especially by relying considerably more on the community college. Black enrollment in senior white institutions is still relatively small—only about 2 per cent of total enrollments in both public and private sectors. Some major white universities are making sincere efforts to overcome the effect of white-oriented admission requirements that have barred most blacks; none have been encouraged to adopt admission quotas for blacks. While white universities are more sophisticated than they were two or three years ago about the special measures required for substantial black enrollments, their leaders have not been notably successful in obtaining the necessary financial resources for needed student aid, black faculty, and special programs in both counseling and curriculum. Considerably more effort is needed to secure understanding by state governmental leaders of the importance of providing such resources. The great difficulties of many prestigious institutions across the nation in providing adequately for successful black student experience has made this a more formidable task.

States are strongly encouraging maximum utilization of the community college. This is not surprising when one observes that the relatively poorer South has invested heavily in the public two-year college in the last twenty years as a promising way to erase its long-standing lag in post-high school attendance. Since 1948 the number of such institutions has almost tripled, and their enrollments have increased some sixfold. In the most rapidly growing and prosperous states of the region they are, as elsewhere, the chief means of providing mass higher education.

Community college systems in the region are not being developed as dumping grounds for blacks or as ways to impose a "ceiling for black educational attainment." Governors, legislators, and state higher education boards have been more willing than most educational leaders to promote the two-year institution on evidence that, more than any other factor, it significantly increases enrollments in postsecondary programs at low costs to students and supporting governments. But it is also apparent that for many black students the community college has serious deficiencies: programs and standards too oriented to middle-class white culture, the stigma associated with remedial programs, lack of career counseling, and inadequacy in preparing seriously disadvantaged students for continued work toward the baccalaureate. Nonetheless, blacks in several states are enrolling in community colleges in increasing numbers. In Florida almost a third of the blacks enrolled in postsecondary programs are in community colleges, and the proportion in the region at large appears to be between 15 and 20 per cent. In Dallas 36 per cent of the Negro high school graduates sampled in a recent study went to college and 34 per cent of that group enrolled in a local community college. In Fort Worth the corresponding figures were 43 per cent and 51 per cent. As the community colleges become more sensitive to black needs and more convenient and economically accessible to the bulk of the black population, they will be the most significant gateway to better opportunity for the masses of young blacks.

The progressive development of unified higher education systems in which blacks have truly equal opportunities will require more than piecemeal efforts to deal with the various institutional types in a state. As suggested earlier, then, there is serious need in most southern states for more conscious, specific plans for systematic steps toward a unitary scheme, with detailed provisions for:

—the admission of larger numbers of black students to previously segregated institutions,
—further opportunities for low-cost, readily accessible post-high school education, primarily through community junior colleges, for the bulk of black students,
—the strengthening of curriculum, instruction, administration, student services, and learning resources at the traditionally Negro universities and colleges, whose students will still include sizable numbers with real but often unproved promise,
—the substantial increase in black students entering graduate and professional programs through provision of state aid to qualified applicants,
—the restudy of roles for all institutions within a state—traditionally black and traditionally white—so that a coordinated and comprehensive single system may be developed during transition from the dual system of the past.

These plans need to go beyond the current effort to secure compliance at the institutional level with civil rights legislation to the longer-range considerations of how a state's total postsecondary system is employed to equalize opportunity. In Florida, for example, a legislatively created committee has recently prepared a comprehensive plan that can be expected to have an important impact on post-high school education in the state. The plan includes specific related recommendations for meeting needs of blacks in all postsecondary programs—vocational schools, community colleges, private and public black and white universities.[6] As such, it is impressive support for the compliance plan submitted by the state university system.

The Outlook

The South is not one undifferentiated region. Political, economic, and social characteristics vary, sometimes substantially, between the border states, the upper South, the deep South, and the Southwest. It is difficult therefore to generalize, but some forecasting about state governments and black colleges and black higher educational opportunity is nevertheless offered.

First and foremost, states will expand their efforts, albeit at quite variable rates, to create unitary higher education systems, including improvements in existing black colleges and in extension of opportunity for blacks in other types of institutions. This will happen as part of a continuing effort in southern states since World War II to improve all of higher education and erase the long-standing regional lag. That effort has had some success. College attendance has increased greatly. Impressive community college systems have been created, and in Florida, North Carolina, Texas, Maryland, and Virginia (and there are others) community college boards are making extensive efforts to recruit and to serve the needs of increasing numbers of blacks and other minority students. Graduate education has grown considerably, and in some instances, with distinction. College and university appropriations have grown to 14 per cent of state revenues as public leaders have touted higher education as a strong stimulant to economic growth. While higher education will find it increasingly difficult to enlarge its share of state funds, there is little reason to assume that it will yield its gains. Texas, Georgia, and North Carolina are but three southern states giving serious attention to the possibility of state financial aid to private colleges. It is quite possible that these and other states will develop modest aid programs, as South Carolina has done recently. State aid to private institutions already exists in selected graduate and professional fields. In addition, there is growing recognition that plans for the expansion of public higher education must take into account more fully the programs and resources of private institutions. Despite occasional suggestions that some of the poorer private black colleges convert to state control, no state is likely to accept such offers. To do so would only add to the difficulties and confusions accrued from the historic dual system which most are now seeking to resolve.

Every southern state now has some state-level mechanism for planning and coordinating, if not always governing, the development of public higher education. While these agencies are not necessarily the best or only means available at this time through which states can prepare plans for racially unitary systems, and while all of them need to give more systematic attention to the matter, some have already shown far more concern for the complex problems of creating racially unified systems than have many institutional and state leaders. They are surely the best long-term bets to assure orderly progress toward such systems. Their influence and authority will continue to grow in most states, and consistent with the history of higher education planning and coordination, their efforts will strengthen the less favored institutions and generally relate total available resources more effectively to total state needs. They do need the presence of more black staff and board members to strengthen their efforts on behalf of black higher education. Georgia has a new black vice-chancellor for its state board of regents and Virginia has a new black member on its state council for public higher education. Such appointments will increase, and at a faster pace where blacks aggressively seek them.

Generally speaking, state higher education agencies, as well as institutional governing boards and concerned state officials, can be considerably assisted by forthright and specific proposals and plans from black leadership—administrators, faculties, students—especially in regard to new institutional roles and programs. The need for vigorous black input may appear to some more obvious than the opportunity, but the opportunity is real and great, and is a greater challenge than black leaders have had. It is abundantly clear that frustrated and angry young blacks will continue to demand greater public responsiveness to their higher education needs, including additional efforts by the black college to reflect the black experience more clearly in its programs and services. But there is also evidence that increasingly they will be listened to and their ideas seriously considered. In short, public higher educational opportunities for blacks will be significantly influenced by the extent of skillful and aggressive initiative on the part of black administrators, faculties, and students in advancing specific proposals for improving those opportunities. But those proposals must range beyond mere preservation of the status quo or increased support for present and past programs of the black college. At a time when our society is beginning to discuss new structures and options in higher education the urgent needs of blacks must be considered in the broadest possible context, not only in terms of the traditional black college.

A number of other factors will help determine the pace and effectiveness of steps toward unitary systems. More perceptive and supportive federal policies and actions are essential. To date, the federal approach to compliance in too many instances has reflected uncertainty and confusion over objectives and procedures. Thus one high state official in Maryland responded to federal rejection of the state's compliance plan by saying, "There is a vast difference . . . between desegregation . . . and elimination of racial identifiability . . . Desegregation is sound public policy, is supported by the language of Title VI [of the Civil Rights Act], and is attainable in reasonable measure at most of our institutions. In my opinion, the elimination of historic racial identifiability is *not* an essential element of successful desegregation, is *not* covered—or even suggested—by the language of Title VI, and is of questionable merit as public policy."

In addition to a clear and firm commitment to assuring compliance, there are other more important ways, direct and indirect, in which the federal government can exert great influence. For example, the extent and form of student financial assistance will have major, direct impact on the number of blacks entering post-high school education. The federal government, not the states, will chiefly determine how much assistance will be available. The federal government can and should provide additional financial support for black institutions, both through existing and new programs, for example, support for planning curriculum change in light of new career opportunity for blacks, with sufficient support to institute the changes as they are identified. It is especially important that the federal government provide substantial long-term funding to encourage the growth of cooperative programs in which traditionally black and white institutions in proximity, on an equal partnership basis, coordinate their instructional resources to serve the total population. And it should do so in a way that will increase the support from state and private sources. In many less direct but fundamental ways—programs to reduce poverty and unemployment, to improve housing, and to assist public school systems, to cite a few—the federal government will in large measure determine the long-range economic and political ability of blacks to participate more fully in unified higher education programs.

The growing political power of blacks in the region is the soundest reason to believe that higher education opportunities for blacks will improve. Since the Voting Rights Act of 1965 black registrants have increased dramatically in the deep South. Excluding the border states, the number of southern Negro registered voters increased eightfold between 1960 and 1969. One immediate result has been a remarkable growth in the number of elected black officials—legislators, mayors, councilmen, school board members, law enforcement officials, and so on. The Georgia legislature, for example, includes fifteen blacks, and new black legislators have been elected in Alabama and South Carolina. There is every likelihood that black voter registration will continue to grow. Reapportionment under the 1970 census will further enhance black political power in many areas. That power promises no millennium for southern Negroes, but it has already had significant impact in many places. Depending on the issues and where and how it is applied, black political power will undoubtedly have increasing influence on the Negro's role in southern society. It is already visible and real in urban Atlanta and in rural Alabama and Mississippi as well.

The continued growth of black political power will mean, among other things, an increased voice for blacks in supporting, planning, and operating higher educational systems. Black state legislators are already showing active interest in the problems of higher education for blacks, as in Tennessee, where they succeeded over some opposition in getting a legislative committee established—with a black majority—to study special financial needs of the black colleges. The first black was recently appointed to the University of Maryland board of regents. Blacks are being appointed to institution boards in Arkansas, Virginia, and other states. Virginia has its first black on the state board of education and on the state council for public higher education. Others will be named elsewhere to state boards responsible for governing and/or planning and coordinating public higher education. And if it is certain that they will not have easy answers for the stubborn problems that are the legacy of segregation, it is equally certain that their long-denied exercise of responsibility holds promise that the South may yet remold its institutions to serve all the people.

Many a "new day" has been proclaimed in the South, and it is doubtful that one is now at hand, given the current mood of many blacks and whites. But there is an emerging generation of new, young political leaders, white and black, in Arkansas, Georgia, Florida, the Carolinas, Tennessee, Virginia, and elsewhere. The new South Carolina governor said at his inauguration: "We can and we shall in the next four years eliminate from our government any vestige of discrimination because of race, creed, sex, religion or any other barrier to fairness for all citizens. We pledge to minority groups no special status other than full-fledged responsibility in a government that is totally color blind. The politics of race and divisiveness have been soundly repudiated in South Carolina."

The new governor of Georgia stated: "At the end of a long campaign, I believe I know our people as well as anyone. Based on this knowledge of Georgians, north and south, rural and urban, liberal and conservative, I say to you quite frankly that the time for racial discrimination is over. Our people have already made this major and difficult decision, but we cannot underestimate the challenge of hundreds of minor decisions yet to be made. Our inherent human charity and our religious beliefs will be taxed to the limit. No poor, rural, weak or black person should ever have to bear the additional burden of being deprived of the opportunity of an education, a job, or simple justice."

In his first few days, the governor persuaded the black vice-president of Georgia's second largest public university (predominantly white) to take a leave of absence and serve as one of the three members of the state board of pardons and paroles.

And so the search continues for ways through which white and black leadership can work together for a better lot for the southern black. In working toward that end, however, in which the importance of more and better higher education for blacks is so central and obvious, it is likely that the vision and vigor of black political and educational leaders especially will be the critical factor.

REFERENCES

1. The region here is defined as the fourteen member states of the Southern Regional Education Board: Alabama, Arkansas, Florida, Georgia, Kentucky, Louisiana, Maryland, Mississippi, North Carolina, South Carolina, Tennessee, Texas, Virginia, and West Virginia.

2. This essay is concerned primarily with public higher education.

3. This characterization of a unitary system is based on a staff document of the Southern Regional Education Board, May 1970.

4. *Special Financial Needs of Traditionally Negro Colleges,* Southern Regional Education Board, 1969.

5. For additional discussion of needed changes, see *New Careers and Curriculum Change,* Southern Regional Education Board, 1968.

6. *Florida Post-High School Education: A Comprehensive Plan for the 70's,* Select Council on Post-High School Education, Tallahassee, Florida, 1970.

TOBE JOHNSON

The Black College as System

PAST STUDIES of black colleges have contributed little of positive worth to the development of black higher education in the United States. This is true even when the studies have been "funded and guided by organizations and individuals sincerely interested in advancing the cause of higher education among black Americans."[1] Accordingly, the most significant outcomes of such studies have probably been two: first, to confirm the negative biases of white publics about these schools—and more generally about black people—and second, to force black college personnel and their constituents into a defensive rather than a positive posture about the equality of the black college. Because of these negative consequences, some black college administrators and faculty have concluded that there should be a moratorium for a generation on these studies. I tend to support the "no further studies position," and therefore am ambivalent about the present essay. Like Polyanna, however, I am always overwhelmed by the positive prospects of an opportunity, and I write this analysis for whatever positive contribution it might make to the desperate struggle of black colleges for survival. Were I less sanguine in predisposition, I would doubtless take my cue from W. E. B. Du Bois' metaphor of the blacks imprisoned in the cave, behind the plate glass window.

A preliminary note is in order about the methodology used in making this analysis. This is an *interpretive* essay rather than one based on a collection of empirical data about black colleges. It is a reflective effort to distill the main characteristics of these 120-odd institutions and to say something about the etiology of these characteristics without a careful examination of the individual schools that make up the total. Given the dynamics of the black consciousness movement and its on-campus manifestations during the past four years, it would have been desirable to present a more refined analysis of the differential impact of the movement on the various schools since it might permanently alter their character. Yet, because these manifestations of the movement are still in the embryonic stage at the majority of schools, perhaps no great loss of understanding will be occasioned by the present approach, rather than a more empirical one. Finally, for those wishing to understand my orientation toward the black colleges, I would describe it as supportive and evaluative—evaluative because understanding rather than self-deception and fantasy are essential to the renewal of these institutions by and for black people.

Analytically, we might look at the internal processes of the black college as a system involving several subsystems or components which interact to produce an output, in this instance the black college graduate. The essence of a system is the interrelationship and interdependency of its component parts. The major parts of the system of a college are the administration, faculty, and students who interact, primarily around the curriculum, to produce the graduate. Yet the quality of the interaction process, of the curriculum, is also a function of a number of other factors, one of the most important of these being the resources available to the institution to attract faculty, students, and, ultimately, to design and implement the curriculum. When we talk about resources, however, we must look outside the black college to the supersystem: those institutions and persons who control the resources these colleges need to continue to exist. For the black colleges are in the main penurious, and their well-being depends largely on their ability to demonstrate to the potential benefactors in the supersystem—for example, the national foundations, federal and state governments, nonprofit private corporations—that the schools are worthy of their support. Convincing these mostly white potential benefactors of the worthiness of these institutions is, as black college administrators know all too well, not always an easy task.

One cannot understand fully the characteristics of black colleges by concentrating solely on their internal dynamics. Rather, one must be aware of the nature of the interrelationships between the colleges and the supersystem. Nor should this awareness be limited to the matter of how the schools obtain the resources necessary for their existence. The black college has historically been affected and conditioned in all of its dimensions by the outside world—from the academic question of its accreditation to the primeval question of its very physical existence in some hostile communities. Indeed, the black college as an institution is largely a product of the constraints imposed upon it by the supersystem.

Although the basic characteristics of black colleges probably evolved as an adaptation to an often hostile supersystem, the adaptation once in process has had significantly enduring implications for the ongoing internal life of these colleges. Expressed somewhat differently, adaptation is a conditioning as well as a survival process; thus even though some of the more primitive and obviously hostile pressures from the supersystem abated in recent years, some of these institutions continued to function more or less as they did in the past. Such continuity in behavior is perhaps predictable in the absence of strong antipodal pressures from the outside, or of the occurrence of certain critical events within the institution itself which could produce a modification of its characteristics (for example, turnover in leadership).

Having postulated the dependency relationship of the black colleges to the external world, and having suggested that this relationship has had long-term consequences for the nature of these institutions, I return now to the initial analytical model proposed. No systematic effort will be made to examine the external forces which impinge upon the schools; these will be considered only when it is necessary to relate them causally to the internal dynamics of the colleges. We will begin our examination of the black college by looking at how it has been administered historically.

Regardless of the kind of black college one examined in the past—private, state, church-related or not—it is readily apparent that the basic operating decisions of the institution were in the hands of the president. Although there was, and remains, a wide spectrum of presidential behavior—from the modern Bledsoe model at Mississippi Vocational College to the enlightened approaches of some of the younger presidents—the fact remains that the ultimate locus of authority on campus is the presidency.

Most of the older black college presidents probably resemble the autocratic officials who presided at the prestigious white schools during the nineteenth century. Yet, despite the fact that authority on many of the white campuses became diffused and formally collegiate many years ago, this has tended not to occur on the black campuses where the president has more often than not remained in full control of the institution.[2] The reason why this is so remains to be explained definitively. The hypothesis of this essay is that the president, serving as the mediator between the college and the threatening environment, found it necessary to consolidate and maintain personal control over his organization. This hypothesis is consistent with the more general hypothesis that the more hostile and threatening the environment, the easier it is to legitimate the centralization of power within a threatened institution. And since black colleges from their inception have always been confronted by a hostile or nonsupportive environment, it can be argued that strong personal authority was essential to their survival. This, perhaps, would be even more true in the case of the state universities where the president found it necessary constantly to reassure the often bigoted legislators and boards of regents that the institution, under his steadying stewardship, was immune to unsettling social and economic views and activities. Symbolically, this was the meaning of the behavior of one black state college president, who, as late as 1962, continued to maintain a secret dining room on his campus for white regents and legislators, with whom he never dined.

While it is possible that presidential behavior such as that was a function of the survival needs of the institution as these presidents interpreted it, it does not necessarily follow that their authoritarian tendencies would disappear when the environment became less threatening. This, of course, may well be true of all patterned behavior which continues even after the reason for it no longer exists.

Besides the purely survival aspect of the president's autocratic role, there is also a somewhat different order of presidential behavior which has had the same consequence on the campuses as authoritarianism but whose etiology is even less obvious. That is paternalism. Very strong currents of this ran through the administration of some of the most able black presidents. The paternalistic president, like most whites, assumed that the black faculty members, even if capable of making sound educational and administrative decisions, were not responsible enough to execute them without close presidential supervision. Thus, such presidents would spend valuable time investigating the minute details of task execution—even menial activities which one might well have expected custodial and maintenance staffs to execute without such prestigious oversight.

The appointment and budgetary processes were the basic means by which the presidents controlled their institutions. Except perhaps at the larger state schools where it was impossible for the president to hire every prospective teacher, the responsibility for making faculty appointments was in the hands of the chief executive. Indeed, some presidents considered the recruitment of personnel a basic part of their job. (A corollary of the power to hire personnel, of course, is the authority to fire.) As for the budgetary process, even today genuine academic and departmental budgets are virtually nonexistent in black colleges. Although the budgetary process in most nonprofit institutions is seldom rational in the sense that every penny allocated is expected to produce the best possible result for the institution and is instead based on the relative bargaining strength of the claimants for each dollar, budgetary allocations at most black schools are not even subject to bargaining. Budgets at these schools are made by the chief executive in conjunction with his chief fiscal officer and, rarely, the dean.

Placing this behavior in a broader social perspective, however, it must be acknowledged that the presidents seldom have been sufficiently certain of what funds would be available the ensuing year to make the projections implied by the budgetary concept. The effectiveness of a budget plan as an operating statement of the allocation of funds over a projected period is to an extent nullified by extreme uncertainty with respect to the availability of funds.

Presidentialism, as LeMelle and LeMelle term presidential autocracy, has been the dominant characteristic of many of the black colleges.[3] The remarkable uniformity of style of governance, across institutional types and through time, suggests that it sprang from deeply grounded societal and cultural forces, and as such is not primarily attributable to the personality characteristics of those holding the office. I am not implying here, however, that the role requirements of the historical black college presidency would not tend to favor one personality type rather than another. Obviously, an accommodative type personality would fit the requirements of the office better than a militant type. Yet, apart from the consideration of whether it would have been possible for the latter type to be appointed to the office, especially in the state schools, the constraints of the role probably would have produced the presidential behavior patterns we have discussed, regardless of idiosyncratic personality differences. This point is emphasized because it forces us to try to locate the source of presidentialism in the social structure rather than ascribing it to the character of the men who have presided over the black schools.

What have been the consequences for the black colleges of presidentialism as a style of leadership? The answer to this question presupposes some knowledge of the characteristics of these schools. Probably the most obvious characteristic of most of the black schools is their conservatism except on the question of racial integration. On this issue, of course, they have been the most progressive—and often the only progressive—forces in their locale. The conservatism of black institutions was one of the characteristics which David Riesman and Christopher Jencks singled out in their treatise on the *Academic Revolution*, and which, more recently, was documented by two black scholars, Samuel Nabrit and Julius Scott, Jr., in their *Inventory of Academic Leadership*. "Conservatism" as a general concept refers to the tendency of persons or institutions to preserve that which is established and to oppose change and innovation. Three dimensions of conservatism that have characterized black colleges will be examined in this essay: (1) their "low risk" orientation which tends to discourage innovation and controversial ideas; (2) their low incentives and even dis-incentives to individual initiative and creativity of faculty and staff; and (3) their tendency to reinforce the authoritarian-submissive behavior of faculty, staff, and students. Another significant characteristic associated with presidentialism, though it cannot properly be labeled "conservatism," is excessive jealousy and competition among faculty and staff for presidential favor.

It should be clear that I am *not* postulating that the presidents deliberately set out to accomplish the results or consequences enumerated above. Indeed, I could argue that, most of the time, the presidents were striving consciously to promote and protect the interests of their school in the context of a nonsupportive, if not always hostile, environment. I could further argue that the governance processes at these schools simply reinforced the pressures from the outside world which tended to cow the blacks associated with these schools, particularly in the rural South. What I *am* suggesting, in terms of the three dimensions of conservatism, is that there were institutional "costs" or consequences associated with presidentialism. The consequences are what Robert Merton called the latent functions of a social practice, such functions being defined as the consequences of a practice which is neither intended nor recognized.[4]

Although the over-all orientation and tone in most black schools are set largely by the presidents, the faculty's contribution to the educational outputs of these institutions cannot be discounted. It would follow from what has been said previously in this essay that the more autocratic and domineering the president, the more the school's character, including its academic program, is likely to reflect his influence. But even the most omnipotent president cannot directly intervene in the ongoing, day-to-day classroom interactions between faculty and students, even if he wished to. For the irreducible role of the college faculty member is to teach, and this function alone assures that the faculty—at least as a collectivity—will significantly influence the internal processes of the institution.

Yet acknowledgment of faculty influence in the system, particularly with respect to the educational program, should not lead us to forget the meta-influence of the president. This overarching influence is based on his authority to hire and fire, to reward and punish, to determine budgetary priorities, and to influence the basic value structure and orientation of the school. Thus as we examine the internal faculty processes in the following sections, we will want to keep in mind the motif of presidential dominance.

Recruitment and Selection

Faculty recruitment at all but a few black colleges is based on two elemental desiderata: (1) the need for faculty to teach the courses offered, and (2) the need for a sufficient number of persons with advanced degrees to meet the accreditation requirements of the regional accrediting agencies. The first desiderata must be met if the institution is to operate at all, and most black schools manage to meet it, though in many instances this not only involves some faculty members teaching out of their specialities, but also requires a smaller number to teach subjects only remotely related to the areas of their advanced degrees. In general, the poorer a school, the more likely this is to happen. The second desideratum, however, poses the more insistent—and in some instances, insurmountable—problem for most of these schools: recruiting and retaining sufficient personnel with masters' and Ph.D. degrees to meet the minimum standards of the Southern Association of Colleges and Schools, the accrediting agency in the region where most black schools are located.

Historically, it has not been too difficult for the better-known schools like those in the Atlanta University Center, Fisk, Howard, and Tuskegee to attract black Ph.D.'s because they provided the best employment opportunities. (Someone has observed that the course of American history—certainly Afro-American history—and higher education might have been different had Harvard seen fit to employ the brilliant Du Bois.) Most of the outstanding black scholars, both those born in the North and those born in the South, taught at these institutions at one time or another between 1920 and 1960. Because these schools graduated most of the students who subsequently took doctors' degrees, they were in a somewhat privileged competitive position in securing the young graduate's services. Some astute presidents exploited this cycling process, and in so doing provided their schools with a continuous source of talent as well as inspiring the students to complete their graduate work.

Nevertheless, even the more fortunate black colleges have not been able consistently to employ a sufficient number of black faculty to meet the Southern Association's accreditation requirement. For example, in the thirty-six United Negro College Fund Schools, approximately 28 per cent of the black faculty have earned doctor's degrees. The Association requires 30 per cent for accreditation, and this means that at least 2 per cent of the doctorates necessary for good standing with the Association must be provided by nonblacks.[5] Consequently, the black college faculties are the only faculties in the country which are multiracial and multiethnic in more than a token sense. Not only were the northern white missionaries instrumental in establishing the schools after the Civil War, they also made up the bulk of the teachers for over a quarter of a century. (Southern Jim Crow laws, of course, prevented whites from teaching at the black state schools until de jure segregation was ended by United States Supreme Court decisions.)

The multiracial composition of the faculties on black campuses does not necessarily imply cosmopolitanism. And it is not patent that the nonblack presence on these campuses has always been in the best interests of black educational development. Carter G. Woodson thought that the white missionaries had "more enthusiasm than knowledge," although he felt that they should be "honor [ed] as a martyred throng."[6] The positive contribution of many of the southern whites who succeeded the missionaries on some black campuses is subject even more to negative questioning. Woodson recounted a number of experiences as a teacher on such campuses. On one campus, the "white women connected with the institution would bow to him in patronizing fashion when on campus, but elsewhere they did not see him."[7] On another, the white president entertained blacks only in the students' dining room, never in his home. And on a third campus, the white president refused to permit the students to enter his front door. Woodson concluded from these experiences that "Negroes trained under such conditions without protest become downright cowards, and in life will continue as slaves in spite of their nominal emancipation."[8]

The quality of the nonblack teachers varies among the different black schools. On many campuses, these teachers are all too often political refugees who neither understand the culture nor speak the language intelligibly; retired professors whose energy level does not always measure up to their awesome responsibilities; and wives of professors who are comfortably employed at neighboring white schools. On the other hand, some of the nationally better-known black schools, like Morehouse College in Atlanta, have been quite fortunate in the quality of white teachers they have attracted in recent years. Morehouse, for example, attracted a number of reasonably mobile young white faculty members during the past ten years who contributed significantly to the development of the physics, psychology, and English departments at the college. These young people brought with them some strange and exciting new ideas from such places as Berkeley, MIT, and the Peace Corps. They also brought a not inconsiderable capacity for work, which leavened the impact of their ideas. Largely because of their own career orientations, but sometimes because of black faculty hostility or indifference toward them, however, these types do not tend to remain indefinitely on black campuses.

In the past few years, black teachers, especially those with Ph. D. degrees, have been operating in a seller's market. Consequently, teachers who heretofore could find employment only at black schools now have a broader range of alternatives, including private industry, government, the big foundations, as well as white academia. These new opportunities for black faculty are the crux of the faculty "brain drain," which some theorists of black education are lamenting. Although the dimensions of this drain are not yet clear, its long-run implications would seem to threaten the very existence of these schools, particularly if they should prove to be unable to compete for the ever-declining percentage of black Ph. D.'s coming out of the graduate schools. Thus when the black brain drain is juxtaposed with the white Ph.D. glut, it seems rather clear that the black administrators increasingly will be faced with the dilemma of meeting the price its most mobile black faculty members can command, or of employing less-sought-after, and therefore less expensive whites.

Faculty Opportunity: Growth, Development, Self-Actualization

By comparison with the black student, very little is known about the black faculty member. While it is true that relatively hard statistical data, such as age, advanced degrees, disciplines, and so forth are available, nevertheless, little or no systematic information about the basic determinants and dynamics of faculty behavior—cognitions, attitudes, values, and motivation—exist. The rudimentary state of knowledge about these dynamics is illustrated (unintentionally) by Riesman and Jencks, in their largely anecdotal study of the black college. Particularly vivid is their parenthetical description of a black dean at a leading black college who admitted that his head itched when he talked with whites because he was forced to play the "darky" role with them as a child.[9] As responsible social scientists, of course, the authors should have been "wary of the seductive but logically weak tendency to attribute validity to an idea on the basis of seemingly compelling, and perhaps esoteric, anecdotes from real life."[10] Nevertheless, they were not—so serious and responsible research remains to be done in this area. The present essay cannot pretend to do what needs to be done; the effort here is a more modest one designed to delineate the contextual dimensions of faculty opportunity and behavior.

Analyses of faculty responses to a question designed to elicit their ranking of the "Importance of various areas of responsibility" and the activities they are doing "Less than I want" suggest that black teachers do not differ significantly from white faculty, on white campuses, about their preferred activities and responsibilities.[11] (The table below summarizes the response of the Morehouse College faculty to these questions in 1967.) Nevertheless, with the exception of Morehouse, these analyses indicate considerable divergence between faculty responsibilities and activities, ideally, and what teachers actually do as measured by their responses to the "Less than I want" question. Assuming that the preference ranking is "real" rather than an artifact of the questionnaire, it would seem to follow that in most black schools there is a serious discrepancy between the ideal and the real, between what teachers say they want to do and what they in fact are able to do. How can this discrepancy be accounted for and what are its consequences for the schools?

Areas of Faculty Activity and Responsibility

	% say important or very important	Rank[a]	% say "Less than I want"	Rank[a]
Teaching in area of academic specialization	74	(1)	30	(7)
Research	60	(2)	72	(1½)
Student advising	53	(3)	23	(8)
Professional meetings	51	(4½)	47	(3)
Writing	51	(4½)	72	(1½)
Tutorials and other one-to-one student contacts	45	(6)	42	(5)
Cross disciplinary teaching	28	(7)	43	(4)
Administrative responsibility	21	(8)	6	(10)
Team teaching	17	(9½)	34	(6)
Faculty committee	17	(9½)	8	(9)

[a] The rank of two tied scores is indicated by assigning them identical mixed numbers. For example, the rank order tie between the responses to the professional meetings question and the writing question is handled by assigning 4½ to both. That is, they account for ranks four and five between them. See the discussion of rank order correlation coefficients in Benton J. Underwood and others, *Elementary Statistics* (New York: Appleton-Century-Crofts, 1954), pp. 155–156.

Perhaps a useful way to deal with the discrepancy is to resort to the systems model. In doing so, however, it should be kept in mind that the model is an analytical or heuristic contrivance to facilitate our thinking about the interaction processes producing the target behavior outcomes; it is *not* a snapshot of reality. We have seen above that the black college is extremely vulnerable to the supersystem, and that this system has determined the very nature of these schools. Indeed, as Riesman and Jencks remind us, these schools were "for the most part financed by white philanthropists, controlled by white boards of trustees, initially administered by white presidents, and largely staffed by white faculty."[12] Black colleges, then, are extremely open systems. Our interest is in the interplay between the supersystemic and internal systemic factors that affect black faculty opportunities for growth, development, and self-actualization.

LeMelle and LeMelle have recently set forth a number of factors which they feel have retarded black faculty development.[13] The authors do not use the systems terminology, but the factors they describe can be so translated. The supersystemic constraints historically have been:

1. Little support for blacks wishing to attend graduate schools.
2. The racist character of the graduate schools which prevented and/or deterred more blacks from attending them.
3. The historical barriers erected against blacks in the professional associations.
4. The lack of enthusiasm among publishing houses for black publications.
5. The lack of financial support for blacks who wanted to do research.

Given this racist obstacle course that blacks had to run in order to earn the doctor's degree or to become scholars, it is understandable why such a small number did. From a different perspective, however, the *miracle* might well be that as many blacks as did achieved these distinctions, for besides these obstacles there were a whole range of constraints within the schools themselves which mitigated against the development of black faculty.

An examination of the internal system of most black schools gives additional insight into the reasons for the discrepancy between the stated preferences of black faculty and their actual activities. If we use the five top-ranked preferred activities in the table to represent the activities black faculty would like to engage in, it is possible to demonstrate that they tend to be incompatible with many of the survival needs of the schools. Thus the desire to teach in one's area of specialization often has to give way to the schools' need for faculty members to offer instruction, not only across the board in their subject fields, but sometimes outside that field. Furthermore, the necessity for remedial teaching further reduces the opportunity for some faculty to offer specialized courses in their area of interest. Again, the teacher's desire to do research, to write, and to engage in other scholarly pursuits tends to run afoul the school's requirement that he teach a *minimum* of twelve hours or its equivalent, which possibly could involve up to twelve or more preparations a week. Finally, the teacher's realization of his desire to attend professional meetings depends upon whether the school has funds for this. Such funds, of course, are not always available.

The rewards and satisfactions that faculty ideally could achieve by spending their time doing the five things they preferred to do can be called intrinsic job satisfaction and rewards. Such rewards and satisfactions relate to the teacher's achievement, advancement, recognition, and status.[14] These satisfactions are generic, and theoretically at least can accrue to anyone, black or white, whatever his job. On the basis of the meager evidence presented here, one might tentatively conclude that many black teachers do not receive significant intrinsic satisfaction from their work.

There is a second kind of satisfaction and reward related to one's job that might be considered here. This is extrinsic, and it is a function of the person's relationship to his work environment—co-workers, supervisors—on the one hand, and the conditions of his work—including pay, security, policy—on the other.[15] Applying the concept of extrinsic satisfaction and rewards to the work situation of many black faculty members, it would appear that they receive only minimal rewards from their work. For example, working conditions in black colleges are notoriously poor; secretarial and other support services tend to be bad or nonexistent, and the bureaucracy—despite the diminutive size of many of the schools—tends to be unbelievably rigid, and, hence, frustrating. Presidentialism, of course, tends to be the dominant method of decision-making. This may be modified on some campuses to the extent that senior faculty members are more or less influential in the decision-making process. (In this, black schools are no different from Harvard, Berkeley, Columbia, and so forth.) As for remuneration it is also well known that the salaries at the black private colleges are well below the national level. The disparity is especially acute at the level of associate and full professor.

What have been the consequences for the black colleges of the large number of dis-incentives with which it presents its teachers? No definitive answer to this question can be given here, but the work of Daniel Bell (*The Reform of General Education*) and Riesman and Jencks possibly provide us with some clues. These writers assert that college and university teaching has become a profession in which the most able teachers are cosmopolitans rather than locals. That is, they are upward mobile, striving for the best possible university position they can find. Their achievements and mobility are models of the meritocracy which Michel Crozier described. Harvard, Columbia, Yale, and Princeton—schools to which they aspire to teach—are considered national rather than regional or local educational establishments. As we have seen, however, such mobility was not possible for even the most meritorious black scholar. Thus mobility in the Riesman sense until very recently had no meaning for blacks. Instead, many black teachers tended to perceive mobility largely in terms of salary increases rather than the prestige of institutions. For example, among the state schools in the Southwest, this mobility as remuneration involved a complex exchange of faculty among several schools. The basis of the exchange was the availability of increased salary at the exchange institution which the faculty member could not obtain at his present institution, though his qualifications were identical with the teacher who would be recruited to fill his position. This point underlines the fact that the most significant rewards and hence inducements at many of the black colleges have been financial, although the salaries have been below the national average. In Maslow's hierachy of goals and values,[16] such inducements rank relatively low. And it does not seem to include the enthusiasm and the devotion to work associated with "higher" motivational factors, such as ego, and the need for self-actualization.[17] To summarize, the internal system at many black colleges: (1) does not provide sufficient incentive for development and self-actualization of many teachers, and (2) tends to produce a "local" or provincial orientation among most of the faculty.

What are the implications of this analysis? A starting point is a recent statement by Lerone Bennett that "there has never been a greater need for [black colleges than exists today] and that if [such colleges] did not exist they would have to be invented."[18] I share Bennett's value-fact sentiments. In the light of the existential conditions of most black colleges, however, our position logically leads to the basic question of how can these institutions achieve the twin goals of liberating and educating black people which Bennett feels are the reasons for their existence? The answer, clearly, is that most of these schools must undergo profound renewal before they can even hope to accomplish this mission. Yet the chances are poor that such renewal will be forthcoming without substantial positive support from the supersystem.

REFERENCES

1. Tilden J. LeMelle and Wilbert J. LeMelle, *The Black College* (New York: Frederick A. Praeger, 1969), pp. 21-22.
2. The exponential growth in the size of the university and its increased complexity, which is a function both of its greater size and of specialization, can account for a substantial part of the diffusion of authority in the large university. But the colleague pattern of authority developed also in many small liberal arts colleges which do not possess these attributes.
3. LeMelle and LeMelle, *The Black College,* pp. 88ff.
4. Robert K. Merton, *Social Theory and Social Structure,* rev. ed. (Glencoe, Ill.: The Free Press, 1957), p. 63.
5. This is the minimum aggregate percentage, of course; the percentage is substantially higher than this at most of the schools.
6. Carter G. Woodson, *The Mis-education of the Negro* (Washington, D. C.: The Associated Publishers, Inc., 1933), p. 26.
7. *Ibid.*, p. 27.
8. *Ibid.*
9. David Riesman and Christopher Jencks, *The Academic Revolution* (Garden City, N. Y.: Doubleday and Company, 1968), p. 409.
10. Robert C. Carson, *Interaction Concepts of Personality* (Chicago: Aldine, 1969), p. 5.
11. I chaired the Morehouse College Institutional Self-Study in 1967-1968. Since then, as a consultant to the Southern Association of Colleges and Schools, I have worked closely with several colleges doing institutional self-studies. Thus I have had an opportunity to observe first-hand the organization and operation of a number of black colleges in the southern region.
12. Riesman and Jencks, *The Academic Revolution,* p. 418.
13. LeMelle and LeMelle, *The Black College,* pp. 19-20.
14. Freemont James Lyden, "Motivation and the Civil Services," *Public Administration Review,* 30 (May-June 1970), 297-298.
15. *Ibid.*
16. A. H. Maslow, *Motivation and Personality* (New York: Harper and Row, 1954), esp. pp. 80-106.
17. The tentativeness of this hypothesis must be underscored. At least one empirical study has found that pay can act *either* as "motivator (when related to performance) or as a hygiene (when related to seniority and other extrinsic factors)." Lyden, "Motivation and the Civil Services," p. 297.
18. Lerone Bennett, Founders' Day Convocation Address, Morehouse College, February 18, 1971.

THOMAS F. PETTIGREW

The Role of Whites in the Black College of the Future

Do WHITES have a significant role to play in the future of predominantly black institutions of higher learning? A simple "yes," or "no," or "sometimes" is meaningless in answering such a query. A rounded answer must emerge from a consideration of both the mission and the future of black colleges in the broader context of American race relations as a whole.

The Mission(s) of Black Colleges and Universities

Other essays in this volume consider this topic in greater depth, but any discussion of the future contributions that white Americans can make must obviously begin here. To talk first of mission is not to be confused, of course, with seeking a justification for the existence of black colleges, which do not require justification any more than other American colleges. But it is to make clear what some of the goals and functions of these institutions have been and could be.

We must base our thinking on two healthy realities which were emphasized at the Conference on Negro Colleges held by *Dædalus* in March of 1969:[1] variety and change. One cannot intelligently speak of *the* mission of black colleges, for their variety and rate of change demand a discussion of a range of missions. Indeed, even the definition of black colleges is made difficult today by the rise of such predominantly black public institutions in northern central cities as Federal City College in Washington, D. C. For the purposes of this essay we shall confine our discussion largely to the 120-odd traditionally black institutions centered in but not confined to the South. Yet even with this group the variety has long been great, ranging from Fisk, Howard, and the Atlanta complex all the way to struggling Morris College in Sumter, South Carolina. And there is every reason to expect that this diversity will continue to increase.

Moreover, black colleges, like white colleges, are currently undergoing considerable change. The structures, faculties, students, and curricula are all subject to thorough review; consequently, some of the historic missions of these institutions may not and should not be missions of the future. But these institutions cannot be understood today without a look backward to their past missions and accomplishments.

First, black centers of higher learning are responsible in part for the emergence of an articulate black middle class in America. In many ways, it can be argued that race relations in the United States —crisis-ridden as they are—are still better than what the nation deserves on the basis of the past treatment of blacks in this country. Racism and its attendant system of unremitting white supremacy, for instance, has traditionally aimed at preventing the development of a significant black middle class. Yet within the past generation the black American middle class has expanded rapidly.

The rate of this expansion depends obviously on one's definition of "middle class." If we accept the modest definition of middle class as a family with an annual income of $8,000 or more (in constant 1968 dollars), then approximately 4 per cent of nonwhite families in 1948, 10 per cent in 1958, and 32 per cent in 1968 qualified.[2] Similar trends emerge when we adopt educational or occupational definitions of middle class. Hence, if our definition includes only white-collar members of the labor force, then the nonwhite middle class grew from 16 to 26 per cent from 1960 to 1969.[3] Or if our definition more realistically includes craftsmen and foremen as well as white-collar workers, then the nonwhite middle class grew from 22 to 35 per cent from 1960 to 1969.[4] At any rate, by a variety of rough census definitions the black middle class has become almost a third of the group.

There are many reasons for this remarkable expansion, but certainly one important factor in this growth of the middle class is the unique contribution of predominantly black colleges. Their graduates, for instance, probably account for four-fifths or more of all black college graduates alive today.[5] Of course, the black middle class is often as maligned these days as institutions of higher learning in general and black institutions of higher learning in particular. The severest black criticism of both the black middle class and the black college emanates from the black middle class itself—a phenomenon hardly unique to black Americans. Yet caste barriers will never be abolished in the United States as long as caste and class are highly confounded. That is, a black America that is overwhelmingly poor and untrained could never mount the protest and achieve the societal alterations necessary to overthrow the rooted system of institutional racism. Witness the fact that most of the protest leaders of recent years—ranging the spectrum from Whitney Young to Stokely Carmichael—are products of middle-class homes and college educations. Note, too, that these leaders are usually the products of the black college—Young from Kentucky State, Martin Luther King from Morehouse, Carmichael from Howard, and so on.[6] Nor was it coincidence that the new confrontation militancy of the 1960's emanated from students at North Carolina A. and T.

One of the most striking examples of this fulfillment of a protest mission was provided by the late Charles Hamilton Houston, the unsung giant of civil rights law in the first half of this century. An honor graduate of the Harvard Law School, Houston began teaching at the Howard Law School in 1924 and became its associate dean in 1929. Here he rigorously trained an entire generation of the nation's finest civil rights lawyers as part of his broader strategy for challenging the vaunted "separate but equal" legal doctrine. The most famous of these products is Associate Justice Thurgood Marshall. Houston was also appointed the first special counsel of the National Association for the Advancement of Colored People in 1935. The remarkable series of legal victories in civil rights over the past thirty-five years directly stem from the efforts of the brilliant Houston and his base at the law school of Howard University.

In addition, black centers of higher learning have served as repositories for data and materials vitally connected with the black experience in the United States. Today the emphases on black culture and the black experience constitute an intellectual and ideological vogue. But neither received emphasis during the many lean years that these institutions continued their unrewarded efforts. Two examples of invaluable resources illustrate the point. The Amistad Race Relations Center, formerly at Fisk and now at Dillard, has for a half-century accumulated a collection that no serious student of black American cultural history can ignore. And the Department of Records and Research at Tuskegee Institute has painstakingly gathered and collated data on such critical racial phenomena as lynching. Indeed, the Tuskegee data on lynching go back to 1882 and constitute the only such source known to me. Similarly, the renewed interest in black American ties with Africa has long been pursued by these same institutions before it was in style. For example, St. Clair Drake has pointed out Tuskegee's early involvement with Africa, including advisory missions to Togoland in 1900 and the Sudan in 1906, active help for the financial difficulties of Liberia in 1910, and President Booker T. Washington's active role as vice-president of the Congo Reform Association.[7] In turn, missionaries of all denominations sent African students to attend black colleges and universities, in particular Howard, Hampton, Tuskegee, Lincoln, Wilberforce, Fisk, and the Atlanta complex.[8] These activities were without doubt an important factor in the rise of African nationalism.[9]

The missions of the black college over the past century, then, have ranged widely from producing an articulate black middle class and concerted protest for change to serving as cultural repositories and links to Africa. Yet the fundamental mission has been to offer advanced educational opportunities to millions of talented black youth who were essentially denied such opportunities elsewhere. Given the inferior and segregated primary and secondary schools that the South and the nation have typically provided these youth before they reached college age, this basic mission has necessarily entailed considerable remedial training—a grueling, expensive task that is assigned only scant prestige in college circles. But looked at differently, this remedial role may well have been the single most important function of the black colleges. Educational institutions have the peculiar tradition of rating themselves by the quality and achievements of their graduates apart from what the students bring to the college to begin with. Thus, more to the point would be an input-output, "value-added" analysis of what colleges actually provide their graduates which they otherwise would not have possessed. With this more realistic standard of evaluation, it would not be surprising if many black colleges have long surpassed Ivy League schools in their value-added contributions to their students.

But as the *Dædalus* conference in 1969 made abundantly clear, this fundamental mission is shifting. The critical tasks in regard to the black middle class, protest, black culture, and Africa remain; but the select role as the dominant source of education for black Americans is drawing to a close. As black studies programs spring up, black enrollments rise dramatically, and black faculty are eagerly sought at predominantly white colleges throughout the nation, the very identity and existence of the 120 black colleges and universities come into question. And as Daniel Thompson has pointed out, this revolution is complicated further by the fact that higher education generally is undergoing sharp change on non-racial as well as racial matters. "If the other colleges would remain stable, we could define our position relative to theirs," observed Thompson at the *Dædalus* conference; "but by the time we have done that the other colleges have changed radically."[10] We cannot overlook, then, that our discussion of the black college must be seen as a segment of a wider domain that is currently in the midst of extreme flux.

These sweeping changes of the last five or six years generate understandable fears expressed at the *Dædalus* conference and elsewhere that a process of "creaming" may take place. Predominantly white colleges may seek out only the most highly qualified black students and faculty, leaving remedial education as an even greater focus of black colleges. Worse, many fear that the black studies programs on such campuses as Harvard and Stanford will attract funds away from similar programs in black institutions. Obviously, these fears are not imaginary; but the situation is still very much in flux, though terms such as "brain drain" are already being used by the media.[11] At least some predominantly white colleges have attempted to enroll only the most disadvantaged blacks;[12] many of the most eminent faculty members of the black colleges have tended to resist the lures of wealthy northern colleges; and the tight "economies" of the Nixon years have severely limited funds for black studies programs in both white and black colleges. Yet these dangers are realistic, and we shall return to them.

The Future of Black Colleges

The shifting character of their most fundamental mission naturally raises concern as to the future(s) of black colleges. Once again, the great range of these institutions and the vast differences in the situations in which they find themselves guarantees an array of future outcomes for the 120 black colleges. But all of them are affected by the current changes in the education of black Americans; and all of them must secure, in Talcott Parsons' words, a "balance between identity and participation."[13] "Identity, in some sense, always involves an aspect of separateness," Parsons argued at the *Dædalus* conference, "but not an absolute separateness."

Participation, by contrast, requires by definition access to and experience with the rest of society. Black studies programs accentuate identity, culture, and pride; but, as Sir Arthur Lewis has bluntly pointed out,[14] black economic advances in American society require competence in basic and specialized skills that have a direct payoff in effective participation in the American market place. How can black colleges in the future achieve effective resolutions to this tension? In the past, despite imposed segregation, argue their critics, these colleges have slighted identity concerns in favor of training for participation on a "white" basis; now, goes the demand, more attention must be provided such matters as black culture and pride. One interpretation of the often heated but unusually interesting discussions of the *Dædalus* conference in 1969 was that they revolved almost completely around this issue.

Note that this issue is more subtle and complex than a simple conflict between racial separation and integration.[15] From the perspective of many white-controlled mass media, the black community is caught up in a major debate between separation and integration with a growing tide of blacks opting for the former. Indeed, a significant shift in the militant stance and rhetoric has occurred during the late 1960's, but the tension is far more accurately described in Parsons' terms of a "balance between identity and participation." In a real sense, integration has not failed in America for it remains to be tried as a national policy. Many blacks of all ages sense this; many feel that the nation failed integration rather than integration failed the nation. Influential black opinion turned in the late 1960's from integration as the primary goal to other goals—group power, culture, identity, integrity, and pride. Only a relatively small segment of blacks see these goals as conflicting with integration. Indeed, it is a fact that strictly separatist solutions for the black ghettos of urban America have been most elaborately and enthusiastically advanced not by black writers but by such popular white writers as Joseph Alsop, the newspaper columnist, and William H. Ferry, formerly of the Center for the Study of Democratic Institutions.[16]

Even the terms "separatist" and "integrationist" that make sense for white Americans necessarily must shift meaning when applied to black Americans. Given the national events that have occurred during their short lives, it is not surprising that a growing number of young blacks regard racial integration less as an evil than as irrelevant to their preoccupations. They often call for *selective* separatism of one or more aspects of their lives while also demanding their rights of entry into the society's principal institutions. It is no accident that the most outspoken members of this faction are college students in predominantly white universities.

Through some white eyes, this behavior seems highly inconsistent; it looks as if they talk separation and act integration. But actually the inconsistency is often, though not always, more apparent than real. Consistent with the new emphasis upon power and pride, these young blacks are attempting to define their situation for themselves with particular attention to group autonomy. They are generally as opposed to imposed separatism as blacks of past generations, and they reject other imposed doctrines as well. And for many of them, integration appears imposed by "white liberals." "Why is it that you white liberals only insist on *racial* integration," they often ask, "when separation by class and ethnicity is a widespread fact of American life? Why is it no one gets upset by Italian separatism or Jewish separatism, only black separatism?" That the imposed separation of blacks in America is qualitatively different and more vast than that practiced against or by any other sizable American minority, that integration as a doctrine was a creation not of white liberals but of their own fathers and grandfathers—these answers to the young blacks' insistent question are intellectually sound. But such responses do not relate to the feelings that undergird the question, for they ignore the positive functions of the new emphasis which excite many young black Americans today.

The positive functions of the new militancy and ideology are exciting precisely because they go to the heart of many young blacks' personal feelings. If the new ideology's analysis of power at the societal level is incomplete, its analysis of racial self-hate at the individual level is right on the mark. Its attention to positive identity and "black is beautiful" is needed and important. Indeed, the abrupt shift from "Negro" to "black" is an integral part of this movement. Many members of older generations would have taken offense at being called black; it was considered a slur. But in facing the issue squarely, young blacks desire to be called by the previously forbidden term in order to externalize the matter and convert it into a positive label. The fact that the historical justification sometimes cited for the shift is thin at best is not the point.[17] The important consideration is psychological, and on this ground there is every reason to believe that the change is healthy.

The significant point is that the new thrust of black youth and its emphasis upon identity does not require absolute racial separation either of individuals or institutions. Repeated surveys of the racial opinions of black adults throughout the nation suggest that the heralded generation gap is not as great among blacks as has sometimes been thought.[18] Hence, on the basis of their extensive 1968 survey for the Kerner Riot Commission of black residents in fifteen major cities, Angus Campbell and Howard Schuman conclude:

> Separatism appeals to from five to eighteen per cent of the Negro sample, depending on the question, with the largest appeal involving black ownership of stores and black administration of schools in Negro neighborhoods, and the smallest appeal the rejection of whites as friends or in other informal contacts. Even on questions having the largest appeal, however, more than three-quarters of the Negro sample indicate a clear preference for integration. Moreover, the reasons given by respondents for their choices suggest that the desire for integration is not simply a practical wish for better material facilities, but represents a commitment to principles of nondiscrimination and racial harmony.[19]

Young men prove to be the most forthright separatists, but even here the percentages of men aged sixteen to nineteen who were separatists ranged only from 11 to 28. An interesting interaction between type of separatism and educational level of the respondent appears in Campbell and Schuman's data. Among the twenty- to thirty-nine-year-olds, college graduates tended to be more separatist in those realms where their training gives them a vested interest in competition-free positions—black-owned stores for black neighborhoods, black teachers in mostly-black schools. The poorly educated were most likely to believe that whites should be discouraged from taking part in civil rights organizations and to agree that "Negroes should have nothing to do with whites if they can help it" and that "there should be a separate black nation here."[20]

But if separatism draws little favorable response even in the most politicized ghettos, positive aspects of cultural pluralism attract wide interest. For example, 42 per cent endorse the statement that "Negro schoolchildren should study an African language." And this interest seems rather general across age, sex, and education categories. Campbell and Schuman regard this as evidence of a broadly supported attempt "to emphasize black consciousness *without* rejection of whites . . . A substantial number of Negroes want *both* integration and black identity."[21]

When viewed historically, this preferred combination of black consciousness without separation is not a new position for black Americans. It was, for example, their dominant response to the large-scale movement of Marcus Garvey in the 1920's. Garvey, a West Indian, stressed pride in Africa and black beauty and successfully mounted a mass movement throughout the urban ghettos of the day, but his famous "back to Africa" separatist appeals were largely ignored as irrelevant.

The tension between "identity and participation," then, appears far more relevant to the future of black colleges than the more often discussed tension between separatism and integration. And it is within this same context that black studies programs on both predominantly black and white campuses might best be evaluated. The functions for such programs are straightforward. Basically they will, one hopes, provide a long overdue intellectual corrective for America's self-image as a one-ninth black nation. At their best, these programs can serve an identity and cultural function for black students while also eroding the racist perspective of white students. To eliminate white participation in such programs, as has been the aim in a few places, constitutes a blatant violation of Adam Powell's Title VI of the 1964 Civil Rights Act; but, more important, such restriction would thwart much of its value. One cannot accept the Kerner Commission's cogent and pointed indictment of white racism as the core of America's race problem and then turn and limit the power of effective means of combatting white racism. Actually, these points are widely recognized and only isolated instances of uniracial programs are to be found.

Effective black studies programs, like urban studies centers, could also serve as important academic models for (1) more socially relevant work of an (2) interdisciplinary nature. Many of our campuses in the United States today, white and black alike, offer painfully few such models. And students of both races are rightfully demanding them. Once again, however, a delicate balance must be achieved and maintained. "Relevance" is a tricky matter, for the same pragmatic value orientation of American society that demands "practical" research and solutions "that work" also leads to a deep suspicion of "experts" and academics. Rigor combined with relevance, then, becomes a necessary if difficult goal. As an interdisciplinary model, black studies are uniquely well situated. Not only does it necessarily have one foot in the humanities and another in the social sciences, but it requires a multidisciplinary approach within each of these areas.

Together with the clear need and rationale for black studies programs, we must also consider the threats to them that have arisen. On many predominantly white campuses, black studies programs were originally organized either as a patronizing gesture to black students or as a begrudging response to intense internal and external pressure. With such beginnings, would it be surprising if they fail later for lack of resources? Just as serious is the danger that black studies programs on these campuses will be exploited and structured as a ghetto of their own, academic appendages aimed at diverting pressure for racial change in the regular structure of the traditionally white college. Thus, with black America the focus of the new program, the need to consider it in regular courses not listed under the program is often seen as reduced. Likewise, with the hiring of black staff for the program, the need to hire black staff in other programs and departments is also seen as reduced. One could easily get the impression from the recent hiring patterns of black teachers for formerly all-white institutions that competent black specialists in fields other than black studies do not exist.

Further threats to the viability of black studies programs are posed by both ideological pressures and its current faddishness. In some schools, black studies have been urged as merely a campus power and propaganda device by a particular campus clique with limited interest in basic scholarship. From this view, the programs could serve as prestigious platforms to further particular ideologies—not the first time, to be sure, such attempts have been made on American campuses. Finally, it is clear that the faddish nature of the programs over the last few years has severely strained available talent and consequently limited the development of the programs. This situation has motivated most of the raids on black institutions for outstanding black faculty; unfortunately, it has not led to the more rational and useful practices of trading visiting professorships, joint classes and programs, and other cooperative measures which we shall discuss shortly.

Such a listing of the advantages of and dangers to black studies programs strongly suggests that a differentiation of services and emphases will have to take place among the programs; and it is here that possibilities for employing black studies programs as an invaluable bond between predominantly black and white colleges arise. Since these programs cannot achieve high standards in all aspects of such a broad field, they will have to specialize and to coordinate their activities across campuses. Some have already begun to focus primarily on humanistic elements of the black experience; others on social science elements. Some on largely black campuses focus primarily on identity issues for black students; others on largely white campuses place more stress upon the consequences and myths of white racism for both black and white students. The shortage of staff, funding problems for all of higher education, and efforts to keep them from becoming isolated academic ghettos all combine to ensure that universities and colleges throughout the nation will have to begin utilizing this natural differentiation efficiently by the sharing of students, faculty members, and materials. Much the same could be argued, of course, for many components of higher education, but here again black studies programs could lead the way as a positive model.

The varied futures of black colleges, then, will revolve around the balance needed "between identity and participation." In seeking a viable balance, their further development of identity emphases will coincide with similar attempts by other colleges to develop from scratch effective black studies programs. These programs, as we have seen, meet real needs and could offer important structural models for academia; yet their viability is threatened by real dangers. It would appear, however, that links between these differentiating programs across campuses could maximize their benefits while reducing the dangers to their development. And not incidentally, the ties across predominantly black and white colleges derived from cooperation in black studies would involve near-equality of effort in a way that the paternalistic "adoption" during the 1960's of black colleges in the South by famous universities in the North did not and could not possess. If anything, the black colleges would typically constitute the prime resource in black studies coordination; and, perhaps, this fact could serve as a bargaining point for coordination in other areas where the largely white college might be the prime resource. Precisely such a healthy collaboration between Morgan State and the University of Pennsylvania was reported on by Martin Jenkins at the *Dædalus* conference.[22]

Finally, in attempting to visualize the future of private black colleges in concrete terms, one is tempted to make comparisons with the nation's many Roman Catholic colleges. Talcott Parsons and Michael Winston raised the analogy at the 1969 Conference on Negro Colleges but pointed out the differences: the Catholic colleges tended to impose their own separatism upon themselves, and this for some years entailed greater intellectual but less social separatism than that imposed on black colleges.[23] Yet it is revealing and suggestive to witness the truly massive changes which Roman Catholic higher education has undergone in recent years. The shortage of funds and a general upgrading has forced a few smaller institutions to close and many more to merge. And the larger Catholic institutions have become increasingly less isolated and more in contact with the non-Catholic portion of the academic world. Some of them now have significant and rising percentages of non-Catholic faculty members and students, especially in the social sciences.

What, then, might one guess for the future of private black colleges? A few of the most financially precarious may well have to shut their doors. Yet the rapidly rising black demands for a college education suggest that mergers, even among these marginal institutions, will be more typical, just as with small Roman Catholic colleges. It seems doubtful, however, that any of these squeezed institutions will follow Kenneth Clark's interesting suggestion some years ago that some of them might convert themselves into top-quality preparatory schools. Public black colleges will also be merged in numerous instances, particularly the smaller ones. Sometimes in the border states and Middle South, economics will even dictate the merger of black and white schools. And a few public black colleges may begin to lose their racial identity as white enrollment increases; indeed, this trend would have already occurred in Virginia, Tennessee, and other southern states if their alertly racist legislatures had not acted quickly to establish new state higher educational facilities snugly near such long-established black institutions as Virginia State College and Tennessee A. and I. in order to divert the interest of local white commuter students.[24]

Experimentation with new alternatives to the "identity-participation" dilemma will result in new diversity. However, both private and public institutions are limited in their options in this regard, the private schools by tightening financial strains and the public schools by conservative state and federal legislatures. At any rate, it appears fairly certain that black colleges, private and public, will become more, not less, diverse and range from an almost exclusive emphasis upon the participation pole to an equally exclusive emphasis upon the identity pole. The latter model has been outlined by Vincent Harding and Stephen Henderson in *Ebony*;[25] and it may be followed most completely by almost totally black public colleges now emerging in the largest central cities with significant black populations in the less-resistant North.

Finally, a crude projection of student size is in order. Some observers seem to think the constituency for black colleges will slowly disappear as blacks are increasingly enrolled in formerly all-white colleges. But I seriously doubt this possibility in this century. Though the percentages are in some dispute, it appears that the percentage of black students in college who are enrolled in black institutions has declined from about 80 in 1950 to roughly 35 in 1970, and it may well decline to 30 per cent or lower by 1980. Yet the absolute numbers of blacks in largely black colleges have not declined over these years and may well rise dramatically in the seventies with the addition of the new public and largely black colleges such as Federal City College. The reason both of these trends can go on simultaneously is obviously that the total base of black college students is rising rapidly. Black America is young and getting younger. Half of all blacks in the nation today are below twenty-two years of age, and the black birth rate did not begin to level out until about 1957. But even more significant is the rapid rise in the percentage of college-age blacks who are now getting the opportunity of attending an institution of higher learning. Short of a longer and more devastating economic recession than we have already experienced, this percentage should continue to rise dramatically, reaching perhaps 25 per cent by 1980 or so. Consequently, neither predominantly black nor predominantly white colleges will lack for black students during the next decade, though the great bulk of this increase in black college attendance will be absorbed by public institutions with lower tuitions and the possibilities for inexpensive commuting.

The Role of Whites

From this particular perspective of the missions and futures of black colleges, a number of points follow regarding the role of whites in black colleges of the future. Virtually all of these points fit neatly under the guiding rubric suggested at the *Dædalus* conference by Matthew Holden: "options for modifying the constraints on black institutions."[26]

Financial support. The chief constraint on black institutions of higher learning, as numerous essays in this volume make abundantly clear, is financial. This has been a continuing fact throughout their century of existence, and it applies with special force to private colleges. Major private support from white Americans is clearly necessary in the future, though it must come in forms as well as amounts that are substantially different from the past. The days of ultimate white control derived from meager support should have ended long ago, but vestiges of it conspicuously remain.[27] Black college boards composed largely of wealthy or church-appointed whites which meet regularly in the North almost a thousand miles from the campus obviously provide their own type of "constraint on the options of black colleges." In this regard, the increasing dependence of private colleges, black and white, on foundation aid rather than individual philanthropists and church boards has represented an improvement if not an unmixed blessing.

Yet private white contributions, even if they were to somehow take a significant leap upwards, will never provide a solid financial base for black or white private colleges and universities. Higher education in general and private schools in particular, of course, are currently undergoing a severe economic crisis. And there is no hope in sight short of a new federal approach to underwriting a significant share of the cost of higher education. I am sanguine enough to believe that such a new approach will eventually be adopted out of necessity once the Vietnam war mercifully sputters to a close and releases at least some funds for domestic initiatives while alleviating the nation's latest anti-intellectual reaction to campus unrest.

Consequently, the most important role that concerned whites can play regarding the finances of the black college is, in my opinion, as informal lobbyists for shaping future federal programs for higher education in ways that will make them especially significant for black institutions. The small federal program conceived in the 1960's for "developing institutions," for example, had an unusually important impact for many black colleges. Conferees at the *Dædalus* meeting in 1969 were not at all certain just what federal aid package for colleges would be particularly beneficial for black institutions. There was some sentiment that only direct funds to colleges would help, rather than direct funds to students, on the expectation that supported black students would overwhelmingly choose predominantly white institutions.[28] Such an assumption seems at least questionable. In part, its accuracy depends on just how attractive current reforms at black colleges will prove to be to potential students. But we should at least obtain data on what the college choices at the undergraduate level have been in recent years of black veterans who utilize "the G. I. bill-of-rights." Such information is important, for it seems politically likely that the Congress will want to divide future aid between grants to colleges and to students. And we cannot overlook that on the average black college students are in far greater need of aid than white college students, a fact that leads to both a higher drop-out rate and longer degree periods for blacks.

Similarly, support at the state legislative level for realistic appropriations to predominantly black public colleges is also critical, a task that becomes at least possible as the number of black and liberal white legislators in southern states begins to attain the size of a significant minority. Pressure, judicial and otherwise, needs to be focused, too, at preventing many of these legislatures from dissipating state monies for higher education in order to build new public facilities near established black institutions.

Cross-campus cooperation. Throughout this essay we have noted the urgent need for cross-campus cooperation—in facilities, faculty, students, and programs. And we observed that the emergence of black studies programs makes genuine partnership between primarily black and white institutions possible now in contrast to the often patronizing arrangements of the past. This condition is critical, for much of the past resistance to such cross-racial cooperation came from imperious white educators who saw little in it for themselves and distrusting black educators who remembered the indecorous failures of previous minimal efforts in this direction.[29]

But how likely is such cross-campus cooperation? It seems that the 1970's will witness a general tightening of resources for higher education across the board. And in all truth, we now operate a highly inefficient *system* of higher education in this country. Thus, the time may be near at hand when the structural foundations for fruitful cross-campus cooperation can be laid. The financial savings and upgraded offerings made possible by such arrangements could greatly benefit colleges and universities of all types. But there would be additional racial benefits of cooperative schemes in faculty and student exchanges. Indeed, nothing short of extensive faculty exchanges such as called for by Vincent Harding and others can begin to handle even temporarily the critical shortage of black Ph.D.'s. As Alex Poinsett points out, both black and white college administrators are placed in difficult positions by the present squeezed black faculty market.[30] On the one hand, the predominantly black college administrator keenly resents the raiding of his faculty by white institutions offering far more than his pressed budget allows. On the other hand, the predominantly white college administrator is pressed by his own black students to hire black faculty at once; if he succeeds, he is accused of unethical raiding of the supply of academicians for black colleges. Obviously, the only long-term way out of this dilemma is to increase greatly the supply of black Ph.D.'s. In the meantime, however, faculty trading rather than raiding seems to be the fairest arrangement.

Cross-campus cooperation could be made even more likely if governmental and foundation funding systematically offered incentives for it. The basic social psychological model for generating cooperation between two competing parties is to have a third party offer new resources which are attainable only through cooperation. There is no reason to believe that the same model could not be effectively applied here. The efficient use of tax and philanthropic dollars demands joint programs and facilities across campuses of all descriptions, and such joint activities would have important and positive racial implications for southern colleges, black and white. The vital criterion, however, of such programs must be absolute equality of the partner institutions in the relevant decision-making.

Increasing the supply of black Ph.D.'s. Whites have an especially important role to play in vastly increasing the number of first-rate black Ph.D.'s in America. As we have seen, such an increase would benefit both black and white colleges. Obvious as this need is, the data on the subject to date are not encouraging. One survey indicates that in 1967-1968 only 1.75 per cent of the total enrollment in graduate schools of arts and sciences was black.[31] And only 0.78 per cent of all Ph.D.'s awarded by these schools since 1964 went to blacks. There are indications of a small increase in the graduate enrollment of blacks within the last year or so, but a small increase is not enough. The Ford Foundation has estimated that the number of blacks enrolled in graduate schools must increase seven times and the annual output of new black Ph.D.'s must increase fifteen times to produce a ratio of scholars equaling the black ratio in the national population.[32]

Such a dramatic increase is not going to happen under present structural arrangements. Thus, one major graduate school in the Northeast has begun giving full scholarships to every black applicant who is accepted for admission by his department, an expensive arrangement that cannot be managed but for a small minority of white acceptances. True, its black enrollment has gone up, but the increase does not approach that called for by the Ford Foundation. A key problem is attracting black applications, particularly from predominantly black campuses. This fact suggests that formalized ties between a black college's undergraduate program and a predominantly white college's graduate program might be established in order to encourage plans and applications for graduate training. Faculty exchanges would help here, too; and so would undergraduate student exchanges, summer programs at the graduate school between the junior and senior years, and the knowledge of guaranteed financial aid if accepted. A number of these programs exist now here and there. But what is being suggested here is a new structural arrangement whereby a particular graduate school links itself directly with one or more black college undergraduate programs, with the arrangement including a variety of opportunities for the black undergraduate to become acquainted with the graduate school, its offerings, teachers, and financial opportunities.[33]

A final word. This section has emphasized three domains in which whites can play critically useful roles for black colleges and universities of the future: financial support, cross-campus cooperation, and increasing the supply of black Ph.D.'s. There are many other roles whites can play effectively, of course, especially as teachers and students at the institutions themselves. Direct participation by whites at a number of black schools may, however, become more difficult.[34] But the important point is that the critical roles for whites should not be in the domain of governance. To use the key phrases coined at the 1969 *Dædalus* Conference on Negro Colleges, concerned whites must work "to modify the constraints on black institutions" so that they might achieve their own effective "balances between identity and participation."

References

1. Proceedings of the Conference on Negro Colleges, March 6-7, 1969, American Academy of Arts and Sciences, Boston, Massachusetts; hereafter referred to as Proceedings.

2. U. S. Departments of Labor and Commerce, *The Social and Economic Status of Negroes in the United States, 1969* (Washington, D. C.: U. S. Government Printing Office, 1970), p. 17. "Nonwhite" is the strangely negative category of the U. S. Census which includes in addition to blacks such other non-Caucasian groups as Indian-, Chinese-, and Japanese-Americans. Blacks constitute 92 per cent of the category, but other nonwhites collectively are somewhat more advantaged, especially the Japanese-Americans, whose median education and income levels are now higher than those of white Americans. Consequently, it is a useful rule of thumb to correct nonwhite figures by adjusting them a few percentage points in the direction of disadvantage. For example, when 32 per cent of nonwhite families in 1968 have at least an $8,000 annual income, then the black American percentage is probably about 30.

3. *Ibid.*, p. 41.

4. *Ibid.*

5. According to recent data collected by Elias Blake, Jr., of the Institute for Services to Education in Washington, D. C., almost 80 per cent of black A.B. degree winners took their work in predominantly black institutions as recently as 1968. Blake also estimated that three-fourths of all black Ph.D.'s in the nation did their undergraduate work at these institutions. Alex Poinsett, "The 'Brain Drain' at Negro Colleges," *Ebony*, 25 (October 1970), 74-82.

6. Interestingly, the typical pattern of many of these leaders was to receive graduate training at a predominantly white institution following their undergraduate work at a black institution—for example, Young at the University of Minnesota, King at Boston University, McKissick at the University of North Carolina.

7. St. Clair Drake, "Negro Americans and the African Interest," in J. P. Davis, ed., *The American Negro Reference Book* (Englewood Cliffs, N. J.: Prentice-Hall, 1966), pp. 681-682.

8. *Ibid.*, p. 669.

9. *Ibid.* As an example, Drake cites John Chilembwe, an African minister who attended a black Baptist college in Virginia and later led the Nyasaland uprising of 1915.

10. Proceedings, p. 11.

11. Poinsett, "The 'Brain Drain.'"

12. The enrollment of just prosperous or just poor students is an ill-advised policy for any college, black or white. The Ivy League university which accepted only disadvantaged blacks and systematically excluded equally disadvantaged whites as well as advantaged blacks has witnessed the greatest student dissatisfaction over the program and the most violence.

13. Proceedings, p. 76.

14. W. Arthur Lewis, "The Road to the Top Is Through Higher Education—Not Black Studies," in R. W. Mack, ed., *Prejudice and Race Relations* (Chicago: Quadrangle, 1970), pp. 242-254.

15. For a fuller treatment of this critical point, see T. F. Pettigrew, *Racially Separate or Together?* (New York: McGraw-Hill, 1971), chap. 12.

16. J. Alsop, "No More Nonsense About Ghetto Education!" *New Republic*, 157 (July 22, 1967), 18-23, and "Ghetto Schools," *New Republic*, 157 (November 18, 1967), 18-23. For answers to these articles, see R. Schwartz, T. Pettigrew, and M. Smith, "Fake Panaceas for Ghetto Education," *New Republic*, 157 (September 23, 1967), 16-19, and "Is Desegregation Impractical?" *New Republic*, 157 (January 6, 1968), 27-29. W. H. Ferry, "Black Colonies: A Modest Proposal," *The Center Magazine*, 1 (January

1968), 74-76. Ferry even proposes that "black colonies" be formally established in American central cities, complete with treaties enacted with the federal government. The position of black militants is in sharp contrast to this; they complain of having a colonial status now and do not consider it a desirable state of affairs.

17. Some insist that "Negro" was the slave term, but actually "Negro" and "black" were both frequently used in slave documents. Critics argue that the true skin color of black Americans is basically brown and not black, and thus the term is inappropriate. But "white" Americans are seldom white either. Besides, "Negro" is merely the Spanish term for "black." Consequently, the importance of the term "black" is basically psychological.

18. W. Brink and L. Harris, *The Negro Revolution in America* (New York: Simon and Schuster, 1964); W. Brink and L. Harris, *Black and White: A Study of U. S. Racial Attitudes Today* (New York: Simon and Schuster, 1967); P. Meyer, *A Survey of Attitudes of Detroit Negroes after the Riot of 1967* (Detroit, Mich.: Detroit Urban League, 1968); P. Meyer, "Miami Negroes: A Study in Depth," *The Miami Herald,* 1968; and Center for Urban Education, "Survey of the Residents of Bedford-Stuyvesant," unpublished paper, 1968.

19. A. Campbell and H. Schuman, "Racial Attitudes in Fifteen American Cities," in The National Advisory Commission on Civil Disorders, *Supplemental Studies* (Washington, D. C.: U. S. Government Printing Office, 1968), p. 5.

20. *Ibid.,* p. 19.

21. *Ibid.,* p. 6.

22. Proceedings, pp. 83-84.

23. Father Greeley has pointed out an interesting disadvantage of this isolation which may have in time its black analog. When an array of separatist professional institutions (for example, a Catholic Lawyers Guild and Catholic sociological, historical, and psychological societies) are organized, a potential "mobility trap" comes into being. This trap entails rapid mobility for talented leaders and professionals within the ethnic group at the high cost of cutting themselves off from less certain but more significant mobility in the wider society. Andrew M. Greeley, *Why Can't They Be Like Us?* (New York: Institute of Human Relations Press, 1969), pp. 29-30.

24. A suit was brought in federal court in Nashville against this practice in Tennessee.

25. Vincent Harding, "Toward the Black University," *Ebony,* 25 (August 1970), 156-159; and Stephen Henderson, "Toward a Black University," *Ebony,* 25 (September 1970), 108-114.

26. Proceedings, p. 93.

27. Samuel Nabrit supplied some remarkable examples of this phenomenon from his study of the governance of black colleges. He described one group of colleges which are dominated by one religious denomination but which receives from the denomination only $15,000 each on the average. *Ibid.*, p. 47.

28. *Ibid.*, pp. 103-111.

29. Thus, when in 1967 I called for cooperation between black and white colleges in the South, a veteran black educator rejected the possibility because "of the 'master-slave' psychology and thinking which dominate the overwhelming majority of Southern white colleges." T. F. Pettigrew, "A Social Psychological View of the Predominantly Negro College," *Journal of Negro Education*, 32 (Summer 1967), 274-285; and Charles H. Thompson, "The Higher Education of Negro Americans: Prospects and Programs—A Critical Summary," *Journal of Negro Education*, 32 (Summer 1967), 295-314.

30. Poinsett, "The 'Brain Drain.'"

31. *Ibid.*, p. 76.

32. *Ibid.*

33. Safeguards would be required to ensure that these facilitating arrangements did not act to limit individual choice of graduate school by discouraging application to what might constitute for many individuals more appropriate graduate schools.

34. Some of the black spokesmen who would emphasize identity functions of black colleges to the virtual exclusion of participation functions often express a desire to rid the institutions of whites entirely. Such action, of course, constitutes a violation of Title VI of the 1964 Civil Rights Act, for Civil Rights Acts do not apply only to whites and predominantly white institutions.

ST. CLAIR DRAKE

The Black University in the American Social Order

In Brief Biographical Retrospect

MY EARLIEST memories of a black college involve an episode fifty-six years ago—half a century after the Civil War and two years before the United States entered World War I. My father had taken me, a four-year-old, with him on a visit to his alma mater, the school that had fashioned him into a preacher and my mother into a schoolteacher—Virginia Theological Seminary and College at Lynchburg. He had come there as a young immigrant from Barbados; my mother had come across the mountains from Staunton in the Shenandoah Valley. I remember that visit because some enterprising young student preachers let me play with the yardstick, tape, and cloth in the tailorshop they were running to finance their education. Years later I watched black Baptists giving suppers and begging "to keep Seminary alive." Union University was the white Baptists' gift to Negroes. Seminary was *theirs.* It is still alive, impecunious and struggling. They refuse to let it die. Freedom Fighters in Central Africa know more about Seminary than do black Americans, for John Chilembwe, who led the Nyasaland rising against the British in 1915, and was hanged for it, was a Seminary graduate. (His death ended plans for a Pan-African business corporation he and Afro-American Baptists had incorporated.)

By 1923, I was attending Booker T. Washington High School in Staunton, not a very good one compared to the Stonewall Jackson High School several blocks away; in fact, it had only been in existence two years. Prior to that, a few black children who got beyond elementary school went "off to boarding school"—to Hampton, Virginia State, or Virginia Seminary, usually. In 1927, I left for Hampton. It had a college by then. I was introduced to the black protest during my first month there. The students presented sixty-four demands, struck, and closed the institution down. Hampton was never the same after that. I was a student delegate to Tuskegee's Fiftieth Anniversary ceremonies, and remember my shock at finding that Dorothy Hall was reserved for white guests only! I was graduated into a depression in 1931 at the age of twenty with a B.S. Hampton was in transition from trade school to college in those days, but between New England-type schoolmarms and a couple of brilliant black professors I received a good liberal education plus training to teach high school. I also absorbed the "service to the race" values and learned to appreciate Negro history, music, and folklore. It never occurred to me that what I was getting was "inferior." That summer I visited at least thirty black institutions as a Quaker Peace Caravaner, having been recruited by an elderly white female history teacher who was a member of the Society of Friends.

A year at a Quaker graduate center in Pennsylvania, three teaching at Christiansburg Normal and Industrial Institute in Virginia, and then to New Orleans as a research assistant to Allison Davis where he, Horace Mann Bond, Lawrence Reddick, Fred Hall, Randolph Edmunds, and other young black intellectuals *thought* they were laying the foundations for what would grow into a major university—Dillard—with generous foundation funding. I think their dreams were betrayed. Sufficient money never came through. But during 1935 and 1936 I saw what a good black college in the South could mean to ambitious young men and women. I also saw some pretty poor colleges in operation.

How I got into the University of Chicago as a graduate student in 1937 I don't know. They stamped UNACCREDITED on my Hampton transcript but let me in. They didn't make me take a Ph.B., either, as they usually made graduates from such schools do. Yet, I never felt handicapped there by having gone to Hampton.

I went back to Dillard to teach in 1941, where I was fired for supporting the students in a protest against Jim Crow on a city bus. Black student action had begun to stir that early.

After the war, I settled in for twenty-three years at Roosevelt University in Chicago, one of less than a half-dozen Negroes teaching at "white" institutions in 1946. I taught summer school at Lincoln in Pennsylvania twice, visited Lincoln in Missouri once, and spent some time at the University of Ghana and the University of Liberia. Between 1965 and 1970 I revisited Dillard twice and the Atlanta complex two or three times, spoke at Southern twice and Howard, Morgan, and Coppin once each, helped to install President Peebles at Jackson, and watched new black community colleges here and there in the North grow up. I now teach at Stanford University. After half a century of contact with them, I feel that black America still needs some of its black colleges and universities.

The origin and development of institutions of higher education for Negroes in the United States has been directly related to the existence of a system of slavery in the South from 1660 to 1865, and to the caste system that replaced it, as well as to the widespread existence of racial prejudice on the campuses of northern universities and colleges prior to the 1950's.* It has thus been part and parcel of what Gunnar Myrdal has analyzed

* The terms "Negro," "black," and "Afro-American" will be used interchangeably in this essay with no ideological connotations, but with full awareness that "black" is the term that expresses the current militant mood.

as "An American Dilemma." With the dissolution of the caste system in the South as a result of the civil rights movement and the concurrent change in the racial policies of northern colleges and universities, a reassessment of the functions of black institutions of higher education has been taking place. The future of what is now called the "*predominantly* Negro college" will be organically related to the changing structure of race relations within the context of changes taking place in the American social order. A brief review of the past may throw the present and the future into more meaningful perspective.

The Formative Period: 1850-1920[1]

From the early nineteenth century onward, some Afro-Americans were determined to secure college and university training, and some white Americans assisted them in securing it. By the middle of the century a few score individuals had graduated from colleges and professional schools in the North or in England or Liberia. By 1900, there were at least 2,500 living college graduates—about one for every 3,600 Negroes. The tiny pre-Civil War group of college-trained Afro-Americans tried to use its knowledge and skill for both personal satisfaction and "race leadership," while the abolitionists used the educated Negroes as Exhibit A's. When, in 1854, the first institution was established specifically to provide "higher education" for black Americans it was sited near a terminal of the Underground Railroad in Pennsylvania. Its stated purpose was to produce leaders for the nearly 4,000,000 Afro-Americans in the United States, only 500,000 of whom were not enslaved, as well as to train teachers and preachers for the newly established Republic of Liberia in West Africa. Thus, Ashmun Institute, which became Lincoln University in 1863, was functionally related to the domestic and international dimensions of crucial problems then facing the Black World. The initiative, however, was not in the hands of representatives of black people. White abolitionists and missionary-minded church people had decided what *they* thought was good for Africans and Afro-Americans and had put *their* zeal and money into an institution to realize *their* objectives. Indeed, Lincoln University was never entrusted to the hands of a black president until Horace Mann Bond began his twelve-year tenure in 1950. He was eventually replaced by a white president selected by an interracial board of trustees, responsive in the final analysis to the wishes of the white Presbyterian founders, not to black alumni or to the black public. The board has set a goal of making Lincoln coeducational and integrated.

The founders of Lincoln may have been paternalistic but they never had any doubt about the ability of black men to master the standard liberal arts curriculum of the day. By 1900, Lincoln had graduated over six hundred men (five times more than any of the thirty-three other black degree-granting institutions then in existence). They had been subjected to a heavy dose of Greek, Latin, and the Holy Scriptures, but had also been exposed to "Great Events of World History," "McCosh's Logic," "higher grammar and analysis," elementary sociology and political economy, as well as some algebra, geometry, trigonometry, geology, chemistry, physiology, and psychology.

Two years after Lincoln was founded, the Cincinnati Conference of the Methodist Church (white), in response to the desires of an enterprising free black community in the northern state that had the most severe laws of any against free Negroes, established a college bearing the name of the great English abolitionist, Wilberforce. A black denomination, the African Methodist Episcopal Church, purchased the assets of the institution in 1863, and brought into being the first black-controlled college in the United States. Although it could never attract the kind of financial resources that became available to Lincoln, black people of all denominations treasured Wilberforce as "our own." Its curriculum, however, was essentially the same as that of Lincoln (with astronomy added). It had a total of only 120 graduates to match Lincoln's 600 by 1899, but already it had provided his first teaching opportunity for black America's outstanding young scholar, W. E. B. Du Bois. Wilberforce still exists, having survived a schismatic crisis that led to the founding of Central State College (for Negroes) nearby. Central State, now becoming integrated, has grown to an extent that Wilberforce never could without subsidy from the state or from white philanthropists. Proudly independent, Wilberforce has recently announced an extensive modernization program.

The emancipation of slaves in the South during and after the Civil War stimulated the establishment of a multipurpose agency by the federal government, the Bureau of Freedmen, Refugees and Abandoned Lands. One of the first activities of the Freedmen's Bureau was to establish elementary schools and "academies" in cooperation with various church boards. An educational infrastructure was quickly created that could prepare enough students for pursuing a "higher education" to justify establishing additional "universities." Within thirty-five years after the end of the war the African Methodist Episcopal Church was operating three institutions in addition to Wilberforce—Allen University in South Carolina, Paul Quinn College in North Carolina, and Morris Brown College in Atlanta, Georgia. The black Baptists had established Benedict College in South Carolina, while Livingstone College in North Carolina was being supported by the African Methodist Episcopal Church, Zion. These Negro denominations had missions in Africa and they brought over some students to study side-by-side with Afro-Americans, although the main thrust of their work was toward turning out leaders for American Negroes. A Pan-African perspective has always been an integral part of the value-cluster of private black institutions. In 1895, Atlanta University convened a conference on Africa and in 1912 Tuskegee was host to an International Negro Conference. This interest deepened with the emergence of over thirty-five independent African states during the 1960's. It still remains strong at some black colleges.

At the turn of the century, in addition to the institutions controlled by black denominations, white church boards were operating twenty institutions that granted degrees. Those that proved to have the greatest growth potential were three supported by the American Missionary Association (Congregationalist): Fisk in Tennessee, Talledega in Alabama, and Atlanta University, as well as two other Atlanta schools, Clark (Methodist Episcopal) and the Atlanta Baptist College (renamed Morehouse later). Most of these church institutions received some support from the Freedmen's Bureau, which also established Howard University in 1868 as a school open to people of all races. By 1900, Arkansas, Virginia, Georgia, and Mississippi were each supporting one degree-granting institution for Negroes—thus keeping them away from other state colleges while at the same time exerting some control over the content of black higher education. The legislatures that held the purse strings were frankly racist. The thirty-one southern institutions of higher education for Negroes had an enrollment of about 750 students pursuing degree courses in 1900, and had graduated close to 1,500 individuals since the freeing of the slaves. These were only slightly over half of the Afro-American college graduates in existence, however, since some northern schools had hesitantly and reluctantly embarked upon a policy of highly selective admissions of a few Negroes.

The Fifth Conference for the Study of the Negro Problem, meeting at Atlanta University in May of 1900—only thirty-five years after slavery was legally outlawed—considered a report on "The College Bred Negro" prepared by the corresponding secretary of the conference, the young black Harvard-trained intellectual, W. E. B. Du Bois. Full of faith in Science and Progress, and convinced in those days that the Truth would set men free, teaching sociology and carrying on research at Atlanta, Du Bois was objective and honest as well as optimistic. It was his considered judgment that not more than 350 of the 750 students then taking college subjects in the thirty-one black institutions had entered with an adequate precollege education if judged by the standards of the smaller New England colleges. Howard, Fisk, Atlanta, and Wilberforce had attracted the best prepared group. But Du Bois was not worried about low entrance standards. He took it for granted that each freshman class would be better prepared than the preceding one as the level of secondary training rose. Most of the colleges were dealing with this problem by having a preparatory school—an academy—on the campus. It was the worth of the final product to the black community that concerned him. Du Bois' study pointed out that about half of all the 2,500 college graduates were employed as teachers, about 17 per cent were preachers, at least 6 per cent were physicians and dentists, and about 5 per cent were lawyers. Another 3 or 4 per cent were in business, with a similar proportion in government service. This college-trained elite group formed the growing point for that Talented Tenth which Du Bois felt was absolutely necessary to supply leadership to black communities and to the national community in a world dominated by white men. They were needed, too, he felt to temper the ethos of crass materialism that dominated the epoch and to which he feared black people might succumb. Commenting on his statistics Du Bois said, "The figures illustrate vividly the function of the college-bred Negro. He is, as he ought to be, the group leader, the man who sets the ideals of the community where he lives, directs its thoughts and heads its social movements. It need hardly be argued that the Negro people need social leadership more than most groups; they have no traditions to fall back upon, no long established customs, no strong family ties, no well-defined social classes. All these things must be slowly and painfully evolved."[2]

Education and money were the key counters in the climbing game that characterized the white class system. Denial of both to the ex-slaves was crucial to the maintenance of a caste system in the South. Naturally, all black leaders placed the rapid expansion of elementary and secondary schooling in first place as the basic strategy for weakening the caste system over the long pull and for developing a parallel class system among Negroes in the process. Du Bois felt that it was "in the furnishing of teachers that the Negro college has found its peculiar functions" and went on to defend that institution: "To furnish five millions and more of ignorant people with teachers of their own race and blood in one generation was not only a very difficult undertaking but a very important one . . . It brought the masses of blacks in contact with modern civilization, made black men the leaders of their communities and trainers of the new generation. In this work college-bred Negroes were first teachers, then teachers of teachers . . . teachers whose training has not been merely for breadwinning but also for human culture."[3] The bulk of the teachers, of course, were less highly trained individuals—the products of rapidly mushrooming "academies" and normal schools which sometimes bore the label "college" or "university" as an optimistic hope of what they would be in the future, but did not yet attempt college work or grant degrees. They all taught Christian virtues and middle-class values in addition to the three R's and some breadwinning skills. But black graduates did participate in training these teachers, sharing the task with white men and women. It was as "success models," however, that black college graduates probably had their greatest effect on Negro youth.

Du Bois' dream of half-a-hundred black schools attaining full university status and producing a black Talented Tenth was never realized. During the last twenty years of the nineteenth century the matter was settled as to what kind of education was deemed "best" for most ex-slaves and as to how limited financial resources would be allocated. Northern church boards continued to support colleges that provided a theologically-tinged liberal arts education, and some of these had both "academies" and divinity schools attached to them. They came closest to Du Bois' model, though he would have preferred a far more secularized education. The black churches continued to operate similar institutions. But a group of northern industrialists who were interested in a stable, conflict-free New South, with a literate industrious black and white labor force, threw its support behind institutions that stressed Booker T. Washington's concept of "industrial education." Institutions concerned with developing a Talented Tenth became the stepchildren of the philanthropists; the Tuskegee-Hampton approach dominated the education of black people in the South until after World War I. Hampton and Tuskegee, not Howard, Fisk, and Atlanta, secured the large endowment funds and the money needed for rapid physical expansion.

The Era of "Southern Liberalism": 1920-1945

From the post-Reconstruction period until the 1960's—for more than eighty years—Negro-white relations in the South were controlled by a system of color-caste that had its origins in post-slavery plantation agriculture and survived as an anachronism. Educational theory and practice had to be accommodated to this all-embracing system of separation, subordination, and black powerlessness. Since it contradicted the basic value system of the nation as well as the norms of a relatively open class system, the Supreme Court, in 1896, gave official sanction to a compromise formula, the doctrine of "separate but equal." Southern "liberals" seized upon this principle as a sanction for their efforts to weaken gradually the system of color-caste in political, economic, and public sectors, while preserving segregation in the areas of more intimate social participation, that is, to bring it into line with northern practices. The first step, however, was to accept the legality of segregation in the educational system but to insist upon making it "equal." Black educators had no choice but to accept the terms as set by *southern* liberals, especially since the northern philanthropists accepted them. Booker T. Washington became the most eloquent defender of "separate but equal" as a realistic "southern strategy," without ever sanctioning it for the North or committing himself to the idea that it was an eternal verity for the South.

Washington elaborated a pragmatic first-things-first approach toward equality within a framework of separateness. Conceding the need for a few college graduates, he insisted that the bulk of resources allocated for Negro education by private philanthropy and southern state governments should be given to improving schools that were providing elementary education, teacher training, and instruction in agriculture and crafts. These should also stress "character training" sanctioned by religion and emphasizing thrift, sobriety, sexual restraint, and temporary absention from politics and total abstinence from "agitation." He visualized a large black middle class gradually emerging in the South that would include owners of homes and farms, successful artisans, farmers, and businessmen, all providing their children with varied types of education in the future. Washington was convinced that this middle class would eventually win the respect of its influential white neighbors, "the better-class whites," who would, someday, recruit black individuals into the upper echelons of business, industry, and government on their merit—so long as it remained very clear that Negroes had no desire to be included in their churches, voluntary associations, or families. He believed that segregation and discrimination in public places would disappear in the process.

Washington became the adviser to an impressive group of wealthy men who included Negro education among their other much more extensive philanthropies, men such as Andrew Carnegie, John D. Rockefeller, and the railway magnate, William Baldwin. Washington became so influential that W. E. B. Du Bois complained bitterly about the power of what he called the Tuskegee Machine. Washington extended the deeply rooted Pan-African interest by sending teams to the Anglo-Egyptian Sudan and German Togoland in 1905 and 1906 to teach cotton growing and by convening an international conference of Negroes at Tuskegee in 1912. He also managed to interest the Phelps-Stokes family in these international extensions of the Hampton-Tuskegee idea.[4] Before his death in 1915, the Phelps-Stokes Fund was also emerging as the major research component in a foundation complex concerned with education in the South: the General Education Board (Rockefeller), the Slater Fund, and the Anna Jeanes Fund. Two years after Washington's death, the Julius

Rosenwald Fund was established to give greater effectiveness to the philanthropies of one of the great black leader's most devoted admirers who had decided to concentrate his efforts upon improving Negro education in the South.

These foundations made it possible for a group of enlightened southerners to secure posts that freed them from roles in regional institutions so that they could cooperate with black educators in the task of moving a caste system in the direction of "separate but equal." During the early stages of World War I, the Phelps-Stokes Fund planned and carried out a comprehensive survey of Negro education which leaned heavily upon advice from liberal southern white educators and churchmen. The Welsh-American secretary of the fund, Thomas Jesse Jones, prepared the report which was released in 1917 by the U.S. Bureau of Education in two volumes entitled *Negro Education.* While the report was being readied for publication, a massive migration of Negroes to the North began and it did not slacken until over a million black people had emigrated during a five-year period. Northern industrialists had encouraged some movement of this type since the early 1900's in order to secure strikebreakers, but now they needed a mass of labor to fill the gap created by a cessation of immigration from Europe.

The great exodus strengthened the hand of southern liberals, since they could argue to the conservatives that all of their plantation labor might walk away if caste controls were not relaxed. This point was used to reinforce the recommendations of the Phelps-Stokes report:

(1) Immediate improvement of public schools for Negroes by increased financial contributions from southern municipal, county, and state governments.

(2) Strengthening of industrial and agricultural education at black state institutions, particularly in land-grant colleges (Morrill Act funds were available).

(3) Improved teacher training programs and movement toward payment of equal salaries for black and white teachers with equal training.

(4) Revision of college and university curricula away from traditional liberal arts models, especially those that emphasized the classics, with increased attention to the natural and social sciences.

(5) Elimination of inefficient private black institutions, particu-

larly those that called themselves "colleges" and "universities" but were doing substandard work and did not have the facilities to merit foundation support.

(6) Close coordination of the activities of all foundations and church boards involved in Negro education.

(7) Closer association of southern white educators and governmental officials in planning the future of Negro education.

Du Bois probably spoke for a wide segment of black college graduates when he reviewed the report in *Crisis* and commented that "Thinking Negroes . . . will regard the Jones Report, despite its many praiseworthy features, as a dangerous and in many respects unfortunate publication."[5] What was very disturbing was the implication that most black colleges were inferior and the emphasis upon allotting a greater role to white southerners in decision-making about the fate of black institutions and the philosophy that should guide educational development. Few black people trusted southern liberalism. Yet, no matter what some black leaders thought about it, the Phelps-Stokes report became the charter for black education in the South. Administrators of state institutions and the Hampton-Tuskegee partisans welcomed it.

Implementation of the Phelps-Stokes recommendations was delayed temporarily due to the entry of the United States into World War I. Then, after the war, new factors were at work that forced a reformulation of southern liberalism, added new dimensions to the meaning of equality, and made the concept of "separate" less rigid. The war had heightened race consciousness among black people everywhere and generated a determination—even in the South—to demand substantial changes in the system of race relations. The most dramatic evidence of the changed temper of the black masses was the worldwide positive response, between 1920 and 1927, to the charismatic Jamaican leader, Marcus Garvey, and his Universal Negro Improvement Association. The UNIA stressed racial pride, racial loyalty, and international solidarity of black people to be expressed through the building of black economic, political, commercial, and educational institutions. The movement established its own Liberty University in Virginia, in addition to the Black Star Steamship Company and a Negro Factories League. Liberty Halls sprang up in southern cities as well as in the North. Simultaneously, black writers, artists, and poets produced the Harlem Renaissance and the New Negro movement, while the Association for the Study of Negro Life and History, founded in 1915, began to extend its activities to black schools and churches all over the South.

These currents of heightened race consciousness had a profound effect upon students and teachers in southern schools, forcing administrators and planners to take into account their attitudes and actions—or what they suspected their attitudes to be. The international Communist movement, too, was beginning to speak of its "Negro work" in the United States. Southern white liberals thus gained new leverage when trying to convince reluctant white politicians and community leaders that something *had* to be done "for the nigras" if future trouble was to be avoided. Soon after the race riots during the summer of 1919, a Southern Commission on Interracial Cooperation was established in Atlanta by a white Methodist minister and some of the northern foundations helped to fund it. Black leaders were able to emphasize the fact that the New Negro would never tolerate any cooperation that seemed to be either a "sellout" or that put their leaders in an undignified or demeaning position, and the first small breaks in social equality taboos appeared as black and white leaders began to meet, and even eat, together out of the public eye. But, it was the action of students in black colleges that forced southern liberalism to reorient itself.

Accepting the Phelps-Stokes report as a preliminary working document, the leading black educators, between 1920 and 1925, emphasized those portions of it that stressed the point that industrial education offered no panacea in a period of rapidly changing technology and that even Tuskegee and Hampton should add degree-granting courses. They carried their point, too, that if secondary school systems were to be strengthened as planned, more, not fewer, college graduates were needed as teachers. This led to pressure for improvement of the quality of education in state-supported colleges through greater expenditures upon libraries and laboratories. The Julius Rosenwald Fund not only provided fellowships for teachers to do graduate work, but also took on the task of stimulating the construction of elementary and secondary schools throughout the South, scoring a remarkable success. By 1925, staff and students in black institutions were both larger and more sophisticated.

Between 1925 and 1930, black students forced the pace of

change in areas of greatest concern to them. It had been customary for graduates of black colleges to go North for graduate studies and they often had to repeat a year or two of their college work. Now, a dual demand emanated from the ranks of alumni and students that this handicap be removed by bringing black colleges and universities up to the level where they could be accredited by the regional association and that some M.A. and Ph.D. work be offered at more black institutions. Determined resistance, too, emerged to white dominance of the academic hierarchy—too few black department chairmen, deans, and college presidents in black schools. Of even greater import to students was the continued authoritarian supervision of their personal lives by both white and colored teachers and administrators who were trying to press them into a nineteenth-century Puritan New England mold that frowned on dancing and card playing and that insisted upon excessive chaperoning because it was assumed that extraordinary measures were required to overcome the inborn propensity of black people to succumb to sexual temptation or to be frivolous. A series of strikes erupted between 1925 and 1928 at Hampton, Howard, and Fisk, with black students demanding fundamental changes.[6] Despite the heavy hand with which these student protests were suppressed, extensive reforms were set in motion. Yet progress was very slow. On the eve of the depression, Du Bois was writing:

> Provision for undergraduate college work for Negroes is gradually being provided for—at larger colleges like Howard, Fisk, Virginia State, Virginia Union, Wiley, Talladega and others; and Hampton and Tuskegee and the land-grant colleges; at many state and private colleges in the North where discrimination is not prohibitive . . .
>
> For professional training we have two medical and dental schools, one law school, and several theological seminaries—a meager list, supplemented by white schools where discrimination is widespread . . .
>
> But for graduate study we must with few exceptions depend upon Northern institutions. Most of these institutions are quietly doing everything they can to discourage and exclude Negro students . . . But the man who needs encouragement and lacks funds and yet has the mental equipment will be lost to the race and the world, unless we have a graduate school in the South . . .
>
> Here then are the fields open to Atlanta University if it receives, as now seems probable, adequate and uncircumscribed endowment. The old heads of the General Education Board who believed in the Baptist faith, white supremacy and industrial training for Negroes are gradually being gathered to their fathers.[7]

Backed up by judicious foundation financing, southern liberals were able to outmaneuver racist and reactionary legislatures and local authorities and to expand and improve the "colored" sector of a dual elementary school system between 1925 and 1945, as well as to provide for extension of public secondary schools. Black colleges were, thus, freed from the necessity of running academies to prep a group of entrants and could widen the social class base of their recruitment. When the Phelps-Stokes Fund report was published in 1917 there were twenty-eight publicly-supported institutions in the South giving some type of college level work exclusively for Negroes, in which 1,053 college students were enrolled along with 7,861 doing elementary and high school work. Expenditures on these state colleges for Negroes increased from $150,000 annually in 1917 to $6,000,000 in 1949.

In 1917 there were 625 private institutions in which most of the students were doing work in academies or trade schools, but in which 1,588 students were carrying some college level work. Not one of these colleges and universities—private or public—was accredited by a regional or national association![8] From the mid-twenties until the outbreak of World War II the transfer of decision-making for the private institutions was taking place from church boards to philanthropic foundations, and the pressure was on to "rationalize" Negro higher education, as a result of which the total number of black colleges and universities was reduced from 653 in 1917 to 105 in 1949. College enrollment, however, went up from 2,641 to over 60,000 in this thirty-two-year period. Selected small church-related institutions were pressured and enticed into merging to form foundation-funded secular institutions, while others were helped to secure state subsidy or to be taken over by the state. In 1944, a United Negro College Fund was established to coordinate appeals to the public for twenty-seven private institutions that had won accreditation from regional bodies. Another forty were left to struggle to survive without official approval or organized philanthropic sanction, in the hope that most of them would disappear. *Of the 105 institutions existing in 1949 only Fisk, Howard, Talladega, and North Carolina State College for Negroes were accredited by the Association of American Universities!*[9]

Yet, at all levels, measured by any conventional indices, black higher education had improved between 1925 and 1950, including the strengthening of the elementary and secondary infrastructure. The improvement had been accomplished by a trade-off within the framework of southern liberalism in which northern philanthropists and southern officials had the final word, with black educators serving as advisers, brokers, and sometimes as justifiers to the black public. The basic understanding was that the concept of "separate" would not be challenged. Du Bois assailed the terms of the unwritten contract until the mid-thirties, when, in the depths of the depression, he wrote a famous article, "Does the Negro Need Separate Schools?" in which he said "the answer, to my mind, is perfectly clear. They are needed just so far as they are necessary for the proper education of the Negro race . . . if we recognize the present attitude of white America toward black America, then the Negro not only needs the vast majority of these schools (nearly 2,000,000 students being taught by about 48,000 Negro teachers in the South), but it is a grave question if in the near future he will not need more such schools . . . instead of our schools being simply separate schools forced on us by grim necessity they can become centers of a new and beautiful effort at human education which may easily lead and guide the world in many important and valuable aspects . . . Sympathy, Knowledge and the Truth, outweigh all that the mixed school can offer." In 1942, he expanded this theme in an article on "The Cultural Missions of Atlanta University."[10] What Du Bois was saying nearly thirty years ago is being reiterated today by black Americans who feel that liberation not integration is the pressing need of the hour for black Americans, since American society is still essentially racist.

While Du Bois was shifting toward the position that separate institutions had functional utility even if they were financially weak and not always fully accredited, the director of the Rosenwald Fund, Edwin Embree, was making a frank and honest appraisal of "the discrepancies still existing between white and Negro college education":

In proportion to population, four times as many whites as Negroes have had some college education.

No Negro institution in the seventeen segregated states and the District of Columbia offers work leading to the doctorate degree and only eight Negro state colleges give work toward the master's degree.

No state institution provides to Negroes an opportunity for professional training in medicine, dentistry or pharmacy. Other fields largely ignored are engineering, law, social service and library science.

Twelve states have established out-of-state scholarship funds for the advanced or professional education of Negroes but this is an extralegal expedient and in every case is financially far from a reasonable substitute.
A number of states have attempted to establish certain graduate and professional work in a publicly supported state institution, but present efforts in this direction are strikingly feeble in comparison with the need.
A few states have admitted Negroes to their universities and there are indications that this could be done in a number of others without much difficulty.[11]

Du Bois' prescription was a combination of massive aid to private institutions by the foundations and a fight for increased state aid to black state colleges. The director of the fund that had worked most diligently to make separate education truly equal over a thirty-year period, however, was emphasizing another dimension of the problem:

The Negro does not receive educational opportunity equal to white students of the same community in any separate school system . . . Recent Supreme Court decisions have ruled that the states must adhere to their own constitutional provisions by giving the same facilities to Negroes as those available to whites. *Past experience, however, proves that this is impossible under a segregated system. Equality of educational opportunity will be fully realized only when segregation is outlawed.*[12]

Five years after Embree wrote these words, in 1954, the Supreme Court ruled that enforced segregation in public schools was unconstitutional. In 1962, it required federal troops to enroll one student in the University of Mississippi! Sixteen years after that decision an attempt was still being made to transform dual school systems into unitary systems in the South. By this time a substantial number of Negroes were taking essentially the same position that Du Bois was advising in 1942, phrasing it: "Neither integration nor separation, but *liberation,* is the issue, and the two approaches are not mutually exclusive."

The Desegregation Decade: 1955-1964

Although it took northern philanthropists and southern liberals over fifty years to realize that a philosophy of "separate but equal" could not be realized so long as a caste system controlled the economic and political life of the South, one decade was enough to convince black Americans that legal desegregation of public educational institutions was only a first step toward assuring relevant quality education for Negroes in the region. They were led to reexamine the concept of integration in all of its ramifications relating to education generally and higher education in particular—to assess its utility if viewed not as an end in itself, but in relation to the crucial problems of identity and empowerment confronting the black minority in the region and the nation.

The mass movement against discrimination and segregation in the South began in the mid-fifties, but the initial successful challenges were in the field of higher education, and professors and students of the law school of Howard University played an important role in the legal strategy. Suits were filed in the upper South during the thirties, with support from the NAACP, to gain access to state institutions offering graduate and professional training. Virginia and Maryland attempted to avoid a restructuring of their institutions by providing out-of-state fellowships for the few black students demanding entry to "white" universities. Then, in 1935, the Maryland Supreme Court ruled that failure to provide a separate law school necessitated the admission of a black litigant to the University of Maryland Law School. In 1938, when Missouri opted for out-of-state subsidy in the case of Lloyd Gaines who had applied for admission to the law school, the U. S. Supreme Court ruled that this type of maneuver was a denial of "equal protection" for black citizens. Missouri proceeded to set up a separate law school at a Negro state college. "Protection" was made equal but the quality of the educational experience was not. One spin-off from this decision, however, was acceleration of planning for offering graduate and professional work in some black state institutions. A decade after the Gaines case, the Supreme Court ordered the University of Oklahoma to admit Ada Sipuel to the University of Oklahoma Law School because it had failed to provide a separate black one. Texas, in the meantime, hastily set up a law school in a basement to try to keep Herman Sweatt out of the University of Texas Law School. In 1950, the Supreme Court ruled that this kind of separateness was not equal, and for the first time in history ordered a black student's admission to a southern white educational institution.[13]

The victory in the Sweatt case established a principle but it was obvious that entry into southern graduate and professional schools was going to be a case-by-case, state-by-state, agonizingly slow process. While approving of the court victories, black college presidents, naturally, used the situation to gain support for inaugurating and strengthening graduate and professional work at their own institutions. There had long been considerable resentment among college-trained Negroes over the unwillingness of foundations and private philanthropists to build up even one outstanding black university or to turn the medical schools at Howard and Meharry into major research and teaching institutions. They had watched Tulane grow while Dillard, dubbed a "university" and named for a white Virginia liberal, after a foundation-sponsored shotgun wedding of Straight College and New Orleans University, was given only enough aid to become a fairly good liberal arts college. Atlanta eventually received a financial shot-in-the-arm, but no sensitive black person can avoid asking, even today, why, with obvious need throughout the South, its social work school has never been able to realize the dreams that E. Franklin Frazier, Forrester Washington, and Whitney Young must have dreamed for it. No integration of black students into white graduate schools will ever be accepted as a substitute for developing graduate and professional schools at *some* "predominantly Negro" institutions into departments of national and international distinction. To do less is to betray the promises of 116 years of institutional development and to imply that "only white can be right."

While southern graduate and professional schools were accepting a token registration of black students to avoid court action, and some states were increasing their aid to black state institutions, the NAACP was directing its attention to challenging segregation in the elementary and high school sectors. The great victory came in 1954, although it is important to note that Topeka, Kansas, as well as Summerton, South Carolina, was in the dock. This decision knocked the last legal props from under segregated public school systems. The Desegregation Decade had begun. By 1965, however, black people everywhere were asking whether all the efforts of the lawyers and the incredible courage of those southern kids who risked the jeers and the blows to enter white schools had been worth it. An incredibly small proportion of black students had been integrated after fifteen years. They were asking the question, too, of whether losses in terms of teachers' jobs, symbolic names on school buildings, and self-determination within specific black elementary and high schools justified the meager gains from desegregation. By

1970, when the federal administration was claiming to make the final assault on dual school systems—but was really blowing hot and cold—some black students were actually protesting against being sent from a James Weldon Johnson High School with Crispus Attucks' picture on the wall to a Stonewall Jackson High School with the Confederate flag flying. They were asking why desegregation could not work both ways if we are to have integration. Black college presidents had been asking that same question about their institutions for a decade. Where two-way integration was tried at elementary and secondary school levels, however, southern white parents of the middle class often began to look for private schools. The problem of working out the meanings in the concept "unitary school system" becomes a priority task for the seventies.

Black southerners did not choose school desegregation as the issue on which to join battle in the 1950's. That issue was picked by the NAACP and a small group of white liberals, North and South. The black lower-middle class chose an issue where its dignity and comfort were at issue every day—segregation in public transportation. The Montgomery bus boycott not only launched an assault upon the caste system but also showed the power of black institutions in mobilizing for black solidarity. Churches became the citadels from which the "troops" sallied forth to nonviolent battle and the Southern Christian Leadership Conference extended the area of operations and institutionalized this type of action under the leadership of a young minister, Martin Luther King, who received a first-class undergraduate education at a black college and took his Ph.D. from a predominantly white one.

Five years after the adults had moved against the system, black college students chose *their* issue—lunch counters and restaurants—and they launched the sit-in movement out of which the Student Non-Violent Coordinating Committee (SNCC) emerged. The Committee on Racial Equality (CORE) selected bus stations and a wide range of other situations as targets. Black college campuses now became centers of resistance alongside churches, posing problems for administrators of state institutions, but with limited sanctuary provided by some of the private ones. Miles and Tougaloo became symbols of militancy. The first student killed, however, was murdered in the town of Tuskegee and the campus became the scene of actions that reversed the Booker T. Washington tradition.[14] The best students from the best black institutions from the highest status families were in the forefront of the Movement.[15] Black institutions have assumed such a historic significance that the present generation of students will resist their being integrated out of existence.

By 1964, the political apparatus—not buses and lunch counters—was becoming the primary focus of attention for both adults and young people in the southern movement. They radicalized a campus tradition already in existence, for Professor Ira De A. Reid at Atlanta had begun campaigns for voter registration in Georgia in the thirties and Professor Charles G. Gomillion at Tuskegee had played a similar role in Alabama.[16] During the summer of 1964, black students along with their white allies selected the hard core bastion of resistance to political empowerment—Mississippi—aiding local leaders in a massive registration drive. Freedom Fighters, black and white, died together that summer in Mississippi. It was inevitable that desegregation and integration would take on new dimensions of meaning once the conquest of political power became the issue. The questions would inevitably be raised of just how and with whom integration within the political system could and should take place, and how much integration works to the advantage of specific black communities or to black people as a whole. The Democratic Convention of 1964 was a disillusioning experience for the young activists. The Black Power upsurge came in the aftermath.

The Black Power Upsurge: 1965-1970

While the Movement in the South was trying to bring a black electorate into existence during the summer of 1964, the opening move in a distinctively northern ghetto type of action occurred with attacks on white institutions of control and exploitation operating in black neighborhoods of Rochester, Philadelphia, and Harlem. The next year was a traumatic one for militant black youth. Their hero, Malcolm X, was assassinated. The attempt of SNCC to lead a black party to power in Lowndes County, Alabama, was frustrated. Watts exploded to the cry of "Burn, Baby, Burn." For adults in the Movement, however, the Voting Rights Act of 1965 was seen as a supremely important victory. 1966 was the year in which the great debate began,

"Which way? Integration or pursuit of Black Power?" Then, in 1967 the first Black Power Conference met in Newark shortly after the inner city had gone up in flames, during what has gone down in history as the hottest of hot summers. This became the year, too, in which armed resistance to the local police was being widely discussed by southern black students. The next year, 1968, the year of the martyrdom of Martin Luther King, signalized the end of an era. The slogan of "any means necessary" became increasingly popular with ghetto youth leaders and their street following, while black college students utilized the occasion of King's murder to use aggressive non-violent tactics on the campus to demand curriculum reconstruction in the direction of emphasis upon greater relevance to "the black condition" and to insist upon participation in the planning and administration of their education. At Orangeburg, Houston, and Jackson armed confrontations occurred between black students and the police.[17] The black student movement was only a specialized variant of a general student movement breaking out all over the world.

The Black Power upsurge had both its violent and non-violent manifestations. At one extreme were quite conservative proponents of black capitalism (sanctioned by philanthropic foundations and the federal government). At this pole, too, lay all of those who were concerned with maximizing political mobilization for achieving gains "within the system." At the other extreme were small groups of black nationalists in local areas of the North toying with the idea of urban guerilla warfare. The continuum of attitudes toward separatism ranged from the separatist exclusivism of the Black Muslims and the Republic of New Africa to those who believed that black people should "define themselves for themselves" and "get themselves together," but also form mutually rewarding coalitions with selected groups of whites. This was not only the majority position among black Americans, but was also the stand taken by the most highly publicized group devoted to "any means necessary," the Black Panthers. Their slogan, "Power to the People," had a Marxist meaning merged with Biblical symbols, power to *all* "the people" who are "oppressed" in "Babylon" (that is, the United States).

What all proponents of Black Power had in common was a refusal to designate integration as a goal or to make a programmatic issue of it. For them "taking care of business" should assume priority over all else, and by 1970, a formulation was taking shape, "Not integration or separation is the goal, but black *liberation.*" There was a tendency to stress local task-oriented nonideological issues which could unite blacks across ideological lines—community control of schools and the police, mobilization behind candidates in specific electoral contests, direct action for jobs in the construction industry, protests by welfare recipients, participation in Model Cities planning, tutoring projects, and so forth. Increasingly, black students have sought involvement in these off-campus activities after winning a "power base" on the campuses.

A concept of functional unity became prevalent based on a philosophy of "wisdom is justified of all her children." (Rev. Ralph Abernathy spoke at murdered Panther Fred Hampton's funeral and the Rev. Jesse Jackson has had the Blackstone Rangers in his Chicago picket lines against construction workers.) Black students, on the whole, have been concerned to bridge what they consider the gap between the "black bourgeoisie" and the black masses, to present a "black united front" for group development.

The "reparations" movement, dramatically initiated by James Forman in 1970 with a stated goal of "black empowerment," illustrates the temper of young black people occupying roles in Establishment institutions, since black ministers within white churches used the leverage of Forman's Black Manifesto as pressure upon their own denominations. The proliferation of black caucuses in national academic associations and social work agencies is another case in point.

Caste, Class, and Structural Change

The pursuit of Black Power has been accorded legitimacy by various important segments of the white Establishment—including the Ford Foundation and the White House. This seeming paradox is one aspect of the uniquely American race relations situation. The civil rights movement and the Black Power upsurge were closely related to ecological, demographic, and occupational changes taking place over a twenty-five-year period. The two social movements had an important feedback effect on these processes, and their impact on the South was so fundamental that the use of the term "revolutionary" to describe them is not mere rhetoric. The caste system was smashed and the transition toward an ethnic-class system similar to that in the North began. In such a system, ethnic solidarities persist in family and associational structures by custom *not* law, while relatively free competition and participation prevail in the economic and political systems. Some individuals, in time, move out into the nonethnic social class system.[18] The most significant changes in the North involved a massive increase in the number of black Americans employed in white-collar occupations and in the number of people in training for such occupational roles, but there was no change there in the structure of the basic economic or social system. Also, patterns of residential segregation already present were intensified.

In all regions, occupational changes resulted in an enlargement of the black middle class, while accelerated recruitment into colleges from low-income families had profound implications for Negro middle-class life-styles of the future. However, differences between conditions in the South, the West, and the Midwest and North suggest that problems involving the higher education of Negroes vary significantly by region.

The trend toward movement of black Americans out of the South, that began early in the twentieth century with a trickle of strikebreakers, into the Midwest and Northeast became a massive exodus to those areas during World War I and the early twenties. Migration slackened during the depression, but spurted again during World War II, with the West Coast, as well as the Midwest and the Northeast, attracting black migrants. The drift continued and between 1950 and 1960, alone, the net migration of Negroes out of the South was 1,457,000 persons. Between 1940 and 1966, the net migration out was over three and a half million.[19] By 1970, the rate of migration was slowing down. *A basic demographic and ecological fact of American Negro life is that, despite the great dispersion during a fifty-year period, slightly over half of all black people still live within the fourteen states defined by the census as the South.*[20] Pressure to leave the region could be considerably less in the future since the caste system has been destroyed, the worst forms of rural exploitation have lessened, and increased urbanization and industrialism should offer more attractive job prospects. Booker T. Washington's "Let down your bucket where you are" may make more sense to black youth in the future than it has in the past. Yet, the median income of Negroes as compared with whites remains lowest in the South. *The primary role of black colleges and universities, the overwhelming ma-*

jority of which are in the South, may well turn out to be preparing the generation now growing up for maximizing opportunities for the economic and social development of black southerners. This was the role of such institutions in the transitional period after the Civil War. The South now faces its second Reconstruction.

The basic social problems of both the North and the South increasingly will be centered in the cities. The process of rapid urbanization has proceeded concurrently with the movement of Negroes to the North and West, with a resulting concentration in these regions of blacks in metropolitan areas. By 1960, 93 per cent of all Negroes in the North were living within Standard Metropolitan Statistical Areas and 67 per cent lived in the central cities of such areas. The South had experienced an urban drift, too, with 46 per cent of all Negroes living within metropolitan areas and 34 per cent in central cities.[21] Preliminary releases of 1970 census data indicate that urbanization of Negroes continued throughout the sixties. However, the very large nonurban population remaining means that southern black colleges and universities have responsibilities to a type of clientele for which Lincoln, Wilberforce, Central State (Ohio), and the new predominantly black community colleges in the North do not have to plan.

Within cities, North and South, black people are settled predominantly in enclaved communities and are bound together by a nexus of institutions interrelated by a system of social class that is, itself, a part of an ethnic subculture with an ethos that the culture-bearers describe by the term "soul." The Desegregation Decade did not result in any significant dispersion of Negroes within cities or into the suburbs, despite much talk and some action by northern white liberals to achieve "open occupancy" and integrated neighborhoods. The trend of white middle-class movement to the suburbs that began in the twenties was speeded up in the fifties and sixties for reasons only partly due to racial prejudice—desire for safe, clean, orderly neighborhoods with good schools; desire for "uncontaminated" middle-class enclaves; proximity to new industrial developments; lower tax rates; or preference for white *ethnic* communities of higher status than the inner city colonies. But deliberate flight from Negroes was a factor, too. By 1969, 55 per cent of the total black population of the United States was living in central cities as contrasted with only 26 per cent of the white population.[22] The suburban "rings" were virtually lily-white and their residents were determined to admit only a few token blacks selected from those of similar social class. Those Negroes who did enter the urban rings tended to form all-black suburbs. In the North, a few cities (including Newark and Gary) had become over 50 per cent black by 1969, as had the nation's capital. Demographers predicted more "black cities" to come. The South had numerous cities in which black residents were over a third of the population and by 1970, Atlanta had moved over the 50 per cent line. *More residential segregation not less is the prospect for the seventies.*[23]

For Negroes, the subjective aspect of the trend toward increasing concentration of black Americans within urban communities is complex. Ambivalence is evident in polls taken during the sixties, with a tendency toward acceptance of the predominantly black neighborhood by most black people not only as a fact of life, but also as opportunity to mobilize Black Power and to implement self-determination. There is certainly a widespread pragmatic first-things-first view that refuses to assign high priority to what seems like a useless and demeaning struggle to build integrated neighborhoods when there are urgent problems within black communities demanding concentrated attention.

The dimensions of inner city problems are indicated by the fact that, during the 1960's, between 50 and 70 per cent of all black families in large cities have been living in neighborhoods defined as poverty areas.[24] Within such areas in the North, male unemployment rates have fluctuated between 10 and 20 per cent during the sixties, subemployment between 25 and 35 per cent, and the per cent of families with female heads between 20 and 40 per cent.[25] Despite high morbidity and mortality rates, the net reproduction rates remain high. Although sometimes expressing fear of genocide from whites, the "wretched of the earth" in these ghettos refuse to commit suicide.[26] Black ghettos have been differentiating slightly into slum and nonslum neighborhoods during the 1960-1970 decade, but the proportion of families *above* the poverty line who live in poverty areas has stayed around 60 per cent.[27] More affluent families have not been able to move out. This status inconsistency is one of the obvious reasons why lower-middle class blacks tend to identify vicariously with violent militants, even when they do not participate in their actions. Trapped in these ghettos, those who have experienced economic mobility are inclined to support in varied ways their kinsmen and neighbors who are trying to transform the ghetto.[28] They tend to view the community colleges in their midst—predominantly black in many cases—as instruments in this struggle.

Changes in the occupational structure that occurred between 1945 and 1960 speeded up the differentiation of most black communities into two segments: one involving a half to two-thirds of the population that was getting ahead; the other being a segment left behind.[29] This widening gulf is at the root of fundamental differences in outlook about the present and future that emerge within all large black communities. Failure to recognize the explosive potential of the resentment created by this cleavage or attempts to divert attention from it by emphasizing black progress, as the federal government was doing during the late sixties, will have disastrous consequences. Neither benign neglect nor repressive measures can cope with black communities where from a quarter to a half of the population has repudiated the philosophy of enduring poverty without protest.[30] The Negroes below the poverty line have not only seen whites raising their standard of living, but there have been enough dramatic gains by black people over a quarter of a century to both fuel resentment and to generate confidence that victories and breakthroughs are possible in the future, and, thus, to motivate and sustain continued efforts to break down occupational barriers. Educators and social workers face the problem of trying to channel some of the optimism into sustained efforts at obtaining formal training. Only a national commitment of financial resources on a vast scale and planned conversion of industry to peacetime production with assured employment can lend credibility to the effort in the eyes of black youth.

The basic motivation to secure education beyond the elementary level lies in the fact that it increases the chances of securing a type of job that can increase purchasing power (although there are obviously status implications, too). For a quarter of a century—until the recent recession—black Americans like white Americans were participating uncritically in the economic rewards flowing from an expanding war-fueled economy characterized by distribution techniques that produced a consumption oriented Affluent Society, one in which less than a fifth of the population now remains below a poverty line defined as between $3,000 and $5,000 in annual income for a family of four, depending on region and degree of urbanization. The socioeconomic pyramid within the black world reflects this long period of economic expansion. By 1968, one in five black families were in the $10,000-a-year-and-over income bracket. (Two in five white families were in this category.) During the previous six years the percentage of whites in this group had doubled; the percentage of blacks tripled. At the upper levels of this black 20 per cent were a scant 6 per cent receiving incomes of over $15,000 a year, and at the core of this group were the most successful of the college and university graduates—the doctors, lawyers, judges, dentists, college professors and administrators, business executives, and technicians who had "gone highest," as well as a group of entertainers, athletes, and various kinds of astute "hustlers."

Just below the top economic group, about a third of all black families were living a conventional American middle-class style of life (tinged with "soul") on annual family incomes of between $10,000 and $5,359 (the median for black families). A substantial proportion of these, though not all, had made it into this level by securing some education beyond high school. Many were continuing their education through courses taken in the evenings (and during the summers if they were teachers).

The source of income for most of the occupations at these higher paid levels (as at lower income levels) lies outside of the black community in mainstream businesses or in governmental agencies. The basic thrust of the civil rights movement was against discrimination in these areas and the gains that accrued were predominantly in the North. Young migrants from the South shared these gains. Throughout the 1960's, private industry, educational institutions, and philanthropic foundations were deliberately recruiting Negro professional, managerial, and technical personnel. This structural integration into roles at upper levels often began with tokenism, but it meant that black faces did begin to appear in contexts where they had never been seen before. Such initial breakthroughs opened up possibilities for future gains even if they were only token. Most of the members of the self-employed black professional group, on the other hand, depend upon a black clientele for their income as do black businessmen. Their interests, as well as idealism, lead them to support the ideology of black capitalism but they seldom have the illusion that black institutions can supply most of the employment needed for the black masses, and they tend to support all types of movements designed to raise the income level of the entire group.

The numerically large new increments to the black middle class between 1950 and 1970, however, were not in occupations that required college degrees, although the children of this group are oriented toward securing such training. Between 1960 and 1968 there was a net increase of over 900,000 nonwhite workers holding jobs that tended to have relatively good pay or high status. About 250,000 of these were secured in professional and managerial pursuits, but 280,000 were in clerical and sales work, 190,000 in the crafts, and 160,000 in manufacturing.[31] Most of the young people who moved into the white-collar sector did not, of course, enter the highest paid and more prestigious occupations, but *continued a trend that began between 1950 and 1960 when the number of Negroes in clerical and sales work rose by 81 per cent compared with a 31 per cent increase for Negroes in all occupational categories.* Between 1960 and 1964, the proportion of all black employed workers in the country doing white-collar work almost doubled, rising from 10.2 to 18.7 per cent. *By 1968, the basic occupational structure was one in which about one-fifth of all black males and nearly a third of all black women were doing some type of white-collar work.* These are occupations in which an investment in formal education has its payoff, and a previous generation of educated blacks supplies the role models.[32] For black males in the North the increase in white-collar employment between 1950 and 1960 was from 4.6 per cent of all employed black males to 11.0 per cent. The proportionate increase was about the same in the South but from a low base of 2.4 per cent to a meager 4.1 per cent.

The high gains in the North reflected both the vast expansion of the white-collar sector in American commerce and industry and the willingness of employers, under pressure, to alter entrenched patterns of discrimination and to hire Negroes for some of the jobs freed by the 10 per cent of white clerks and kindred workers who died or went on to better jobs during the 1950's. Black salesgirls, telephone, telegraph, and keypunch operators, and stockroom help are no longer a rarity. The low gains in the South meant that it was easier to integrate lunch counters than business offices, and that the economic system and governmental bureaucracies were not expanding at the same high rate as in the North. The idea of the need for black business to burgeon in order to "employ our own" has a very appealing ring to southern ears. The seventies will see either an expansion of white-collar employment for Negroes in the public and private sector or widespread social unrest, for black business alone cannot provide the response to the demand, and black youth will certainly make the demand.

Despite these massive changes, the black occupational pyramid for the nation was still an unbalanced one in 1968 as compared with that for the white population, and much of the imbalance was due to the lag in occupational upgrading in the South, especially with respect to girls and women (see table 1).

Table 1.
Basic Occupational Structure, by Race and Sex, 1968

	Male		*Female*	
	White	*Nonwhite*	*White*	*Nonwhite*
White collar	42.6	19.8	63.8	32.9
Blue collar	46.2	60.3	16.6	20.4
Service	6.1	14.8	18.0	45.6
Farming	5.1	5.1	1.6	1.1

SOURCE: Compiled from "Employed Persons by Major Occupation Group, Color and Sex," in Patricia Romero, ed., *In Black America, 1968: The Year of Awakening* (Washington, D. C.: United Publishing Corporation, 1969), pp. 516–518.

By 1969 an occupational structure had developed among Afro-Americans in which about 78 per cent of the males were in the labor force (as compared with 81 per cent of the white males) and 50 per cent of the females (as compared with 40 per cent of the white females). These were people at work or looking for work. At any given moment, about 3 or 4 per cent of the Negro men could not find jobs (as compared with about 2 per cent of the white men), and 5 or 6 per cent of the Negro women (as compared with 3 or 4 per cent of the white women).[33] In urban ghetto areas, intermittent employment and very low wages ran the subemployment rate up to between 30 and 40 per cent of all black workers. National unemployment rates for black teenagers had fluctuated from 1967 to 1969 between 25 and 30 per cent of those in the labor force. For whites it was less than 15 per cent. The able-bodied unemployed, the marginal workers, the aged and infirm formed the core of the 20 to 30 per cent of the black population below the poverty line.

Nearly all young black people, whether militant revolutionaries or conventional "climbers" accept it as axiomatic that education is mandatory for black liberation as well as personal advancement. Significant numbers of black youth took advantage of a variety of programs offered during the fifties and sixties for gaining more formal education.[34] The results reinforced the regular public school activities, and between 1960 and 1966 a historic situation was reversed. Within the twenty-five to thirty-four-year-old age-group, the median number of years of school completed was higher by 1966 for males than for females (see table 2). Both

Table 2.
Median Years of School Completed, 25–29-Year-Old Age-Group

	1960	*1966*
White females	12.3	12.5
White males	12.4	12.6
Nonwhite females	11.1	11.9
Nonwhite males	10.5	12.1

SOURCE: *Social and Economic Conditions of Negroes in the United States*, BLS Report No. 332, October 1967, p. 46; adapted from table, "Educational Attainment of Persons 25 to 29 Years Old, by Sex, 1960 and 1966."

sexes within this age-group were also closing the gap between themselves and whites of the same sex.

By 1969, nearly two-thirds of all black males and over half of all black females between twenty-five and thirty-four had received four years of high school education or more, and the change since 1960 for males was dramatic (see table 3).

Table 3.
Per Cent of Persons Age 25–29 with Four Years of High School or More

	1960	*1966*	*1969*
White females	65	74	77
White males	63	73	78
Nonwhite females	41	47	52
Nonwhite males	36	49	60

SOURCE: *The Social and Economic Status of Negroes in the United States, 1969*, BLS Report No. 375, p. 51; adapted from table, "Per Cent of Persons 25–29 Years Old Who Completed Four Years of High School or More, by Sex, 1960, 1966 and 1969."

The proportion of black men who had finished college almost doubled between 1960 and 1969, rising from 3.9 to 7.6 per cent. The proportion of women increased only slightly, however, although black women were closer to white women in proportion of college graduates than were black men to white men. The racial differential remained large for both sexes (see table 4).

For both males and females, although substantial upgrading in employment occurred between 1950 and 1970, the median

Table 4.
Per Cent of Persons Age 25–34 with Four Years of College or More

	1960	*1969*
White females	7.8	12.3
White males	15.7	20.2
Negro females	4.6	5.6
Negro males	3.9	7.6

SOURCE: *The Social and Economic Status of Negroes in the United States, 1969*, BLS Report No. 375, p. 52; adapted from table, "Percent of Population 25 to 34 Years Old Who Completed 4 Years of College or More, by Sex, 1960, 1966, and 1969."

income at various educational levels remained, as in the past, far from equal as between blacks and whites. The situation for males, particularly, had a discouraging effect upon those who had struggled hard to secure an education. It paid off, but not enough (see table 5). These differences reflected in part the substandard edu-

Table 5.
Median Income of Males, Age 25–54, by Educational Attainment, 1968

Amount of formal schooling	*White income*	*Negro income*
1 year of college or more	$10,149	$7,481
4 years of high school	8,154	5,801
1–3 years of high school	7,229	5,255
8 years of elementary school	6,452	4,499
Less than 8 years of elementary school	5,131	3,558

SOURCE: *The Social and Economic Status of Negroes in the United States, 1969*, BLS Report No. 375, p. 21.

cation Negroes had received in many neglected schools, both northern and southern; low salaries of Negro teachers and clergymen; and the high proportion of Negro professional men and businessmen depending for patronage upon the economically depressed Negro community. But the differences also reflected denial of opportunity to secure the better paid managerial and sales positions. *The average income of a nonwhite family with a male head who had finished high school was less than that of a white family whose male head had finished only eighth grade.* Yet black people of all age-levels continued to seek formal training while agitating for improvement of schools, and fighting for more and better white-collar jobs. The changes during the last half of the sixties were impressive, but students of race relations were more impressed by the still existing differentials.

As the seventies began, black women were facing special problems. *Almost two-thirds of the employed white women in*

1968 were doing some type of white-collar work, but less than a third of the black women were so employed. Despite the significant gains mentioned previously, this situation had not changed appreciably. Almost half of the black women were still in some type of service occupation. The depressed status of black women vis á vis white women is also reflected in the situation where about twice as many black women at all income levels carry the responsibility of serving as family heads, the percentage being over a third for all black women in the below-$5,000-a-year group, and over a half for women in that group with incomes of under $3,000 as compared with slightly over 25 per cent for white women (see table 6).

Table 6.
Per cent of Families With Female Heads, at Various Income Levels, 1968

Income	*Per cent of all white families*	*Per cent of all Negro families*
$15,000 and over	3.0	7.0
$10,000–14,999	4.0	9.0
$7,000–9,999	6.0	11.0
$5,000–6,999	12.0	22.0
$3,000–4,999	17.0	36.0
Under $3,000	27.0	56.0

SOURCE: *The Social and Economic Status of Negroes in the United States, 1969*, BLS Report No. 375, p. 73.

Most black children live in homes where both parents are present. Even within the low income group between $3,000 and $5,000 per year about half of all Negro children were living in families where both mother and father were present, although the proportion fell to 27 per cent in families with incomes of less than $3,000 per year (see table 7). There is little that educational institutions alone

Table 7.
Per cent of Unmarried Children under 18 Living With Both Parents, at Various Income Levels, 1969

Income	*White*	*Negro*
$15,000 and over	98.0	87.0
$10,000–14,999	97.0	88.0
$7,000–9,999	95.0	90.0
$5,000–6,999	88.0	78.0
$3,000–4,999	75.0	55.0
Under $3,000	49.0	27.0

SOURCE: *The Social and Economic Status of Negroes in the United States, 1969*, BLS Report No. 375, p. 75.

can do about the status of black women or the family itself. The structure of economic opportunity must be changed.

In June 1965 President Johnson delivered a speech at Howard University that elicited widespread criticism from Negro leaders. He seemed to be suggesting that all the major civil rights battles had been won and that the primary task for the future should be preparing Negroes to take advantage of new opportunities. He proposed that emphasis should be shifted to trying to reform and strengthen Negro family life in order to bring it closer to the achievement-supporting white middle-class model. He implied that the will of black Americans to aspire and their ability to compete may have been damaged. Negroes resented both what seemed like the President's advice to "cool" the militancy and his pointing of the finger at the Negro family rather than at racism as the root of black America's difficulties. When the knowledge became general that a white researcher in the Bureau of Labor had done the staff work for the speech, the "Moynihan Report" rather than the President became the target of their wrath. The memorandum was a propaganda document, designed to shock complacent Americans into action, not a work in social science, but it also had serious weaknesses of methodology and interpretation.[35] In criticizing Moynihan, however, one of his significant statements was usually overlooked, his observation that the "tangle of pathology" he was describing did *not* apply to at least half of the black Americans. This was a point he was to make again five years later when he became President Nixon's formal adviser on urban affairs and informal adviser on race relations. Using 1968 government statistics, he stressed the existence of a stable middle class which should be appealed to as a portion of "middle-America" in the implementation of a policy of "benign neglect" of black militant pressures and of the race problem as opposed to the poverty problem. Again the brickbats flew at Moynihan, but the *fact* of the existence of that new expanded middle class he hoped, with unrealistic naïveté, to wean away from the black protest movement was one of the most significant phenomena in black America. Indeed, the nonviolent civil rights movement between 1955 and 1965 had been an upsurge of the church-going southern black middle class and upward mobile youth in southern black colleges from all sections of the country. It was not the revolt of a psychologically alienated and defeated *Lumpenproletariat*. Those who won that revolt against the caste system of the South are now involved in consolidating their gains. But members of the black middle class—North and South—are also expressing increasing interest in finding ways to "pay their dues" for the privilege of enjoying what they gained by espousing the cause of those who have received no payoff from the victory in terms of an improved standard of living. The antipoverty campaigns of the Southern Christian Leadership Conference in the South and the founding of the Welfare Rights Organization are efforts by middle-class leaders to assist the people left behind to achieve gains within the system.

Structural changes have been altering the values of the black middle class. OEO units such as the Community Action Program created new roles in which the better organized personalities among the poor found themselves on committees that not only gave scope to their formerly unrecognized abilities but also brought them into relations with higher status individuals and incorporated them into the lower margins of the middle class. Government funded scholarship programs as well as talent scouts from private universities have brought a new breed of black student to the campus whose patterns of behavior are lower class. They retain loyalties to their kinsmen as well as speech styles and behavior codes that disturb and sometimes shock college administrators and teachers. They force acceptance of elements of "soul" from which the older middle class sought to escape. Many of them ridicule the reformism of those who are diligently trying to "pay their dues" and they call for Power to the People. Even if they are eventually "co-opted" by the educational Establishment, they will have altered the older black middle-class life-styles as they themselves graduate into that middle class. In this respect they are playing roles similar to those that white college youth are playing to alter the values of their social class system.

Sociologist William McCord and an interracial team of researchers, reporting on *Life-Styles in the Black Ghetto* (New York: W. W. Norton, 1969) for three urban communities studied in 1967 (Oakland, Houston, and Los Angeles), have pointed out, however, that about a third of the people in these communities might be defined as "stoics," neither impressed by the gains nor too hopeful of more to come, in addition to a smaller older group "stuck" below the poverty line whom they designated "the defeated." A solid middle-class core and a group of highly motivated youth from all strata constituted "the achievers." The people living life-styles with the most potential significance for social change, however, were two small predominantly youthful groups, "the revolutionaries" and the "rebels without a cause." Within the first of these youth groups, the research team included both the students at southern colleges who had been challenging the remnants of caste-controls and the out-of-school youth in the North and West—Black Panthers and black nationalists—who were trying to inject discipline and ideology into the situations of chronic ghetto discontent. The authors finished their research just before the black student movement erupted upon predominantly white campuses with demands for more black students, more black faculty, facilities to build black solidarity, black studies programs, better working conditions for black hired help, and sometimes separate dormitories. Since they wrote, too, the Black Panthers have become a neo-Marxist group optimistic about organizing what they like to call the black "lumpens" to play a "vanguard role" that the white proletariat is reluctant to play in making a socialist revolution. When McCord and his associates wrote, the Black Muslims were the most effective force in transforming some of the "rebels without a cause"—delinquents and criminals—into well-organized personalities with constructive middle-class goals. By 1970, the Panthers were most influential among this group—in prison and out—attempting to remold them into urban guerrillas. By 1971, Panther leaders were involved in factional fights, however, and black student leaders were trying to work out the implications of a slogan raised at a national conference on the campus of Atlanta University in 1970, "We are an African people." But black student emphasis upon nonrevolutionary local concerns remains strong.

This new breed of student is seeking instrumentalities for maintaining close ties with the masses of the black people. During the early sixties, students from black colleges in the South showed their willingness to risk physical attack and to go to jail in order to pull down the caste structure. During the late sixties, a militant minority was demanding curricular and administrative reconstitution and fighting the local police and state troopers in occasional on-campus and off-campus confrontations, but black student leadership is fragmented and uncertain as to next steps. The nonactivist majority has been groping for a way to express relevance to the black community—local and national. Administration and faculty in black colleges face an opportunity to provide them with training and organizational structure to help them solve that problem. American educational institutions have been functioning as training centers for Peace Corps volunteers to be sent abroad. Is it not possible that black institutions could provide a counterpart of VISTA (Volunteers in Service to America)—BLACK COMMUNITY DEVELOPMENT BRIGADES—utilizing OEO work-study funds during the academic year and finding subsidies for summer projects? This student generation should be helped to consolidate, during the seventies, the gains their older brothers and sisters fought for in the sixties.

New Values in the Making

The changing structure of race relations in the United States over the past two decades—the geographical regroupings, the incorporation of black people into new roles, and the enlargement of the black middle class—has also involved the creation of some new structural units in the total social system with roles filled by both blacks and whites, agencies concerned with enforcement of civil rights acts or compliance with antidiscrimination regulations, as well as commissions and committees such as the Urban Coalition or the Southern Education Foundation. Since neither intercultural education nor the proliferation of new structures has eliminated discrimination on the basis of race or brought full equality, new analyses using the concept of institutional racism have recently emerged.[36] Marxist and neo-Marxist analyses of racism and group subordination have found new organizational expression leading to demands for revolution instead of reform, a new social order instead of a patched-up old one. These structural changes have been, in part, a result of changes in values and have themselves generated further value-change.

The return of soldiers after World War II and the Korean war, the intervisiting between southern black folks and their friends and relatives in the North, the sense of race consciousness developed in black schools and black churches, the rise of new African and Caribbean nations—all of these factors created the atmosphere in which, when seamstress Rosa Parks challenged bus segregation in Montgomery in 1955, a Desegregation Decade could begin. That the young people in high school and in college eventually went into action was not surprising. What did surprise everybody was the fervor and discipline, accompanied by unity between leaders and loyalty to them, that was exhibited.

The most striking effect of the structural changes taking place in race relations and within the black community has been the creation of a sustained mood of optimism. Soundings of public opinion since 1966 reveal no significant change in the situation reported that year when a Harris poll found that from 65 to 75 per cent of the black respondents said "better" in answer to the question, "Do you think the attitude of white people about Negro rights will get better, worse, or stay about the same?" There was no variation between North and South and very little between rural and urban respondents, or by age group. *The lower-middle income group was most optimistic (75 per cent).* However, a panel of national community leaders was far less optimistic, only 59 per cent of them visualizing "better" prospects. Related to the optimism was a verbal display of group self-assurance. A question was posed: "Some people have said that since there are ten whites for every Negro in America, if it came to white against Negro, the Negroes would lose. Do you agree?" No more than a third of any of the groups sampled professed agreement that black people would lose! Rural southerners were *least* inclined to concede inability to win a showdown (20 per cent); lower-middle income northerners were most cautious in their estimate (33 per cent). Here again, leaders were most "realistic," with 61 per cent of them seeing defeat in any decisive confrontation. There were no significant age differences.[37] These comments were solicited when Black Power slogans were initially being raised. The "hot summer" of 1967 followed and then the assassination of Martin Luther King, Jr. Yet, the mood has been sustained. Whatever the actual power relations might be, it is obvious that two decades of successful struggle against caste in the South and for expanded economic opportunity in the North had diminished the sense of powerlessness among most black Americans. To use a British sportsmen's phrase, they felt they were on a "winning wicket."

The erosion of the sense of powerlessness has been accompanied by new orientations in the identity quest. During the 1950's E. Franklin Frazier, in *Black Bourgeoisie* (New York: The Free Press, 1957), excoriated the professional classes for trying to be carbon-copy whites, ignoring the fact that they not only always paid lip service to race pride, but also supplied leadership to the NAACP, the Urban League, and numerous organizations devoted to "racial uplift," including schools and colleges. Understandably, they rejected what they considered the coarser, ruder, more unsophisticated aspects of lower-class life, as all upper and upper-middle classes do everywhere. Even as Frazier wrote, however, Martin Luther King and his lower-middle-class followers were utilizing the religious manifestations of soul to forge the instrument of nonviolent coercive power that revolutionized southern life. They won partly because white southerners shared religious thought-styles and had behavior patterns in common with them, and partly because they were able to make *nonviolent* modes of protest acceptable throughout American society. Blacks who participated in the southern Movement tended to lose their identity problems in the course of the struggle.

During the early sixties, militant northern black youth began to challenge what they experienced as the devaluation of ghetto subculture and "negroidness," generally, by the white world that surrounded them. Vicarious identification with emergent African new nations stimulated the taking on of new identity symbols—African coiffures, dashikis, a smattering of Swahili, the assumption of African names, all secular correlates of what had already occurred within the ranks of the Black Muslims. Less serious minded young people were, at the same time, elaborating a virtual cult of "soul," including soul music and soul food. "Soul-brother" became the magic word that their elders in business scrawled on the windows for insurance when ghetto outbursts erupted. Negroes in the upper strata could not resist the penetration of their subculture by some elements of the "Afro" and "soul" complexes and found a new sense of group identity in the process—as well as new dimensions of enjoyment. It became easier for them to do so since the white world was selling "soul" for hard cash and was investing it with legitimacy and respectability, there being a market for it among whites as well as blacks. A serious attempt by the media after 1968 to project a more favorable image of black Americans reinforced both those who were proclaiming that "Black is beautiful" and those who saw value in making integration respectable. Whether they preferred Moms Mabley or Julia, Aretha Franklin or Sesame Street, Dick Gregory or Flip Wilson, black TV viewers could now gain new levels of satisfaction.

Televisions are ubiquitous in homes, restaurants, barber shops, and bars of black ghettos where opinion is crystallized. Probably no fact has been more important in value-attitude breakdown and reconstitution, and, perhaps, in affecting overt behavior with respect to race relations during the 1960's. Black Americans of all ages have watched a drama unfold in which The Race has been a participant—portrayed, interviewed, talked about. They have seen themselves in action as a collectivity, and have sometimes been able to see acquaintances, friends, or themselves on the screen before them, as well as a succession of culture heroes. Freshmen entering college in 1970 were nine or ten years old when the great March on Washington occurred in 1963 and Dr. King delivered his eloquent address on The Dream. They witnessed the burial of the nation's assassinated President that year and of the man they made *their* martyr, Malcolm X, two years later. They saw violence from southern whites at Selma and Philadelphia, Mississippi, and then Watts burning. It should not be surprising that some of them looted or cheered the looters, and perhaps threw a brick or a firebomb in one of the 139 cities where ghettos exploded in 1967, including Jackson, Natchez, Mobile, Birmingham, Columbia, Orangeburg, Nashville, Durham, and major Florida cities, as well as places with such names as Fruitville, Maryland, and Prattville, Alabama. Then in April 1968, northern high school students took to the streets shouting "The King is dead," and there were outburst in places as remote as Gaffney, Alabama, and Zebulon, Georgia. The current crop of freshmen were sophomores and juniors in high school when, just prior to, and in the wake of, King's death the media began to give constant coverage to the two "baddest niggers," both of them products of black colleges, Stokely Carmichael (Howard) and Rap Brown (Southern) and to blame them for armed confrontations on southern campuses (Orangeburg, Houston, Nashville, Jackson). The pictures of black students on the receiving end of white police power, but sometimes returning bullet for bullet as well as brick for bullet, must be deeply embedded in the nether-consciousness of this generation, with Jackson State, 1970, as the latest episode in an unfolding sequence of tragedies. What their attitudes are we can only guess, but it may be important to find out. Southern college students were exposed, via the media, to another college story, too, the black student movement on predominantly white campuses—usually nonviolent, but not always. All black students have seen soul politicalized and radicalized and some have been a part of the process, particularly the increasing number of those from low-income ghetto homes, the first generation of their families to attend college.

Newsweek in its "Report from Black America" issue of June 30, 1969, noted that "Southerners tend to be more hopeful than Northerners, Northerners more militant than Southerners—and Northern young people by far the angriest blacks of all . . . the poorest blacks are by and large the most conservative . . . both a sense of grievance and a taste for action actually rise with income and education." Within three years the proportion of all black Americans—not just young ones—who believed that "local police are harmful to Negroes" had risen from 33 to 46 per cent; those who felt draft laws were unfair to Negroes from 25 to 47 per cent; and strong opponents of the Vietnam war from 35 to 56 per cent. Of all segments of the American population, black Americans ranked highest in 1970 on sympathy for white student antiwar protestors.

Time's "Black America 1970" issue of April 6, 1970, reported that 77 per cent of all black Americans say "Keep up the pressure" and 59 per cent are prepared to sanction violence as a last resort. But new values had not eliminated the old ones. When asked, "How will blacks make *real* progress?" 92 per cent answered, "By electing more blacks to public office" and 93 per cent "By starting more black-owned businesses." But 97 per cent replied, "*By getting more blacks better educated.*"

Black Power Perspectives in the South

The development of higher education in the South during the 1970's will take place within the context of a social order in transition away from a caste-class system toward some not yet discernible new structuralization of race relations. The period bears some similarity to the 1920's and 1930's in that change in black colleges and universities was partly a response to an upsurge of militant race consciousness within the black middle class and among black students, and that active interest of federal government agencies with money to spend encouraged innovation. The most decisive new variables are a significant change in white southern attitudes toward Negroes and an increase in opportunities for Negroes to wield effective political power.

In the *Dædalus* study on "The Negro American" (Fall 1965 and Winter 1966), Paul Sheatsley noted that in 1965 over half the white southerners in a scientific poll said they thought Negroes were "just as intelligent as whites." Since in 1942 the proportion stood only at about 20 per cent, Sheatsley suggests that "The implications of this revolutionary change in attitudes toward Negro educability are far-reaching." A pro-integration scale developed by the National Opinion Research Council in 1963 revealed wide differences between the North and the South, but in both regions, scores for the age-group under forty-five were more "liberal" than those for older people and the higher the education level the least caste-bound the attitudes. There was strong evidence that attendance at integrated schools resulted in more favorable attitudes toward Negroes, a finding also noted among University of Alabama students by researchers in 1970.[38] By 1966, there was a general recognition in the South as well as the North that black citizens had legitimate grievances, but also a strong feeling that they were "trying to move too fast"—60 to 70 per cent of the respondents in the East and the Midwest, 75 per cent in the West, and 81 per cent in the South.[39] There is no evidence of any softening of this attitude during the past four years, but despite the tensions surrounding attempts to enforce school desegregation and vigorous political activity by Negroes, the degree of acceptance of change is more impressive than the ranting of die-hard reactionaries, episodes of racist police brutality, or isolated incidents of mob violence. The key decision-makers in industry and commerce, in some unions, in education, and in the churches of the upper and upper-middle classes, exhibit concrete evidence of the changed attitudes that the pollsters report. The behavior of elected officials, on the other hand, reflects the sentiments of their constituencies and the variations run the scale from the situation in Chapel Hill, North Carolina, where the mayor himself is black, to the blatantly racist situations in some rural counties in Alabama and Mississippi. Newly elected governors of Georgia and South Carolina were denouncing racism in 1971. Prospects for interracial cooperation and coalition formation, in many situations, are highly favorable. The rising educational level among southern whites increases the chances for joint activity of blacks and whites in dealing with southern problems.

The most widespread form that the Black Power upsurge has taken in the South is the attempt to maximize political power, although it has assumed the ghetto outburst form here and there, notably in a number of Florida cities sporadically since 1966 and in Augusta, Georgia, in 1970. Such expressions by alienated youth and frustrated low-income masses are inevitable on a wider scale if the pace of change in socioeconomic conditions is not accelerated. The SCLC, since 1968, has attempted in Charleston and Memphis to supply leadership to organized groups of black workers using traditional strike tactics. Black college students, too, since 1968 have not only used the nonviolent tactics characteristic of black students throughout the country, but a portion of them have been more prone to adopt tactics of "armed self-defense" than any other student groups in the country. The Voting Rights Act of 1965 strengthened the hands of all leaders with faith that problems can be solved "within the system" and they have elicited enthusiastic support from a wide sector of the black middle class. However, the election of Richard Nixon as President in 1968 and the coming to power of a Republican regime that spoke of a "southern strategy" added an element of unforeseen uncertainty (and anxiety) with which black political strategists have to cope during the early stages of the transition period away from the caste system. The concept of a "new Federalism" makes it imperative that black representatives find a place on decision-making committees and boards at municipal, county, and state levels to protect black interests, especially since the administration is in an economy minded as well as a "woo the South" mood. And this demands an organized electorate whose power can place representatives in these strategic positions.

The basic demographic constraint upon the exercise of Black Power in the South lies in the fact that although slightly more than half of the nation's Negro population lives in that area, the 12,000,000 or more individuals constitute only 20 per cent of a population of over 60,000,000. Inevitably, survival and progress depend upon the emergence of a new normative system which legitimizes interracial cooperation, devoid of any implication of caste relations. At the political level, a variety of forms of coalition politics must evolve. A viable social order will probably crystallize out in the form of a "new pluralism" that will reconcile the present seeming contradiction between ideologies of segregation and integration that now polarize segments of the population. The predominantly black colleges and universities have an important role to play in shaping such an emergent southern social system.

The dynamic younger portion of the Afro-American population conceptualizes the tasks of the future in terms of how to maximize what might be called the Black Power Potential (BPP) of 22,000,000 black people in the United States. An important fact to remember is that lack of a national numerical majority is offset by strategic geographical location. This was demonstrated in the northern and border states between 1920 and 1950 when Negro concentrations in a dozen cities proved to be the balance of power in national elections. Massed purchasing power in these cities also brought occasional victories in Don't Spend Your Money Where You Can't Work campaigns. The continuing concentration of black population in northern and western core cities of metropolitan regions opens up perspectives for varied forms of group action that sophisticated leaders will certainly exploit to the fullest. Despite the fact that black people constitute only one-fifth of the southern population, their ecological distribution suggests a significant Black Power Potential there, too. The proportions of Negro to white population *within* southern cities has always been high, but caste-restraints prior to the 1960's, except in isolated instances, prevented full realization of the latent power. Those constraints are now being broken. The problem of mobilizing political and economic resources is crucial in such larger cities where there have been increases in black population since 1960 (see table 8).

Table 8.
Per Cent Black Population, 1950, 1960, 1967, for Seven Southern Cities With Over 100,000 Negro Residents in 1960

City	*Negro population (1960)*	*Percentages*		
		1950	*1960*	*1967*
Atlanta	186,000	37	38	44
New Orleans	236,000	32	37	41
Baltimore	326,000	24	35	41
Memphis	184,000	37	37	40
St. Louis	214,000	18	29	37
Houston	215,000	21	23	22
Dallas	129,000	13	19	22

SOURCE: *The Social and Economic Status of Negroes in the United States*, BLS Report No. 375, 1969, p. 9.

Within the group of cities of 100,000 to 300,000 there were twenty-eight in which between 25,000 and 100,000 black people formed communities and constituted over 13 per cent of the population in 1960. Of the twenty-eight cities, twenty were southern. Table 9 arranges them in terms of their political potential using proportion black as an index.

The 40 per cent of the southern population that lives in rural

Table 9.
Assessment of Political Black Power Potential Based on 1960 Population, for a Selected Group of Cities

City	Negro population	Per cent Negro
Very high BPP		
Richmond, Va.	91,972	41.0
Jacksonville, Fla.	82,525	41.0
Gary, Ind.	69,123	38.0
Winston-Salem, N. C.	41,185	37.0
Nashville, Tenn.	64,570	37.0
Jackson, Miss.	51,556	36.0
Savannah, Ga.	53,035	35.0
Montgomery, Ala.	47,198	35.0
Portsmouth, Va.	39,290	35.0
Shreveport, La.	56,607	34.0
Newport News, Va.	38,700	34.0
High BPP		
Chattanooga, Tenn.	43,141	33.0
Mobile, Ala.	65,619	32.0
Baton Rouge, La.	45,475	30.0
Beaumont, Tex.	34,883	29.0
Charlotte, N. C.	56,248	28.0
Columbus, Ga.	31,208	26.0
Greensboro, N. C.	30,817	25.0
Moderately high BPP		
Little Rock, Ark.	25,286	23.0
Kansas City, Kan.	28,134	23.0
Camden, N. J.	27,463	23.0
Miami, Fla.	65,213	23.0
Trenton, N. J.	25,638	22.0
Dayton, O.	57,288	21.0
Youngstown, O.	31,677	19.0
Flint, Mich.	34,521	17.0
Jersey City, N. J.	36,692	14.0
Akron, O.	37,636	13.0

SOURCE: Special tabulation of population data by race for cities of 100,000 and over supplied to author by U. S. Bureau of the Census upon request.

areas is characterized by a variety of patterns of race relations ranging from the traditional plantation through mixed rural settlements to rural ghettos. There are still counties where blacks outnumber whites, although they are not so numerous as they were in the past. They assume great symbolic significance when Black Power wins them. In 1968, only four southern states had rural black majorities: Arkansas, Mississippi, North Carolina, and South Carolina.

Political participation can be conceived of as a right regardless of what kinds of ends political power serves. However, since the inauguration of the New Deal during the 1930's, disadvantaged groups—economic, ethnic, racial—have made "welfare politics" an integral part of American life. Public officials are held accountable by the people for using public funds to rectify inequities that have arisen from the operation of the private economic sector, reinforced by various kinds of ethnic and racial prejudices. The best of our contemporary politicians combine detailed knowledge of concrete problems that concern their constituencies with broad public service values. It is unlikely that black voting constituencies will tolerate a group of "co-opted" politicians who simply become a part of corrupt southern state machines taking their cut on deals, or local functionaries dispensing patronage to cliques and protecting rackets as they sometimes do in northern ghettos. To realize their aspirations black voters in the South will eventually force their leaders into being leaders of reform movements that will change the temper of politics in the South. They will create inevitably an atmosphere of increased tolerance. The instrumentality may be interracial rebel Democratic groups challenging the regulars, as in the case of Julian Bond's associates in Georgia, or a similar movement of the type Charles Evers is trying to build in Mississippi. Or it may, in some places, take the form of a separate black party that some of the militants visualize, and which assumed a moderate form in Alabama in 1970. In any event, it will demand a new type of socially conscious, well-informed political leader with competent administrative aids and research personnel. *It is out of black colleges and universities that such leadership is most likely to come.*

The leaders of the civil rights movement are now involved in consolidating gains won between 1964 and 1970 through the response of their followers to energetic voter registration and voter education projects. The enforcement of the Voting Rights Act of 1965 resulted in an increase in the number of elected officials from 70 to 385 in three years. By the end of 1969 there were 479.[40]

Aspiring black politicians and the newly enfranchised black voters throughout the Deep South are certainly not going to be satisfied with only local conquests since influence at the state level is crucial for the protection of black lives and property and for development of their school systems. Certainly, too, as awareness of the extent of Black Power during the Reconstruction period (when the two best senators Mississippi has ever had were black) becomes more general, election of some black congressmen will become a priority goal. And, coping with the problem of poverty demands greater federal attention. It is imperative that a new generation of white students in southern schools be exposed to the truth about Reconstruction: that it was an era in which Black Power was shared power, not an era of black domination; of social development, as well as some peculation and plundering.

The civil rights battle in the South could never have been won without a strong measure of support from the federal government. That support was assured because of the political power that had been built up between 1920 and 1965 in the black ghettos of the North. As black majorities inherit more and more decaying northern cities, they will need massive financial support from the federal government to prevent them from becoming scandalous slums whose decline will be blamed on blacks rather than long-term trends and on the flight of white population and industry that left them without an adequate tax base. It may well be that southern blacks will repay the debt to their kinsmen in the North by using *their* newly achieved political empowerment as pressure upon Washington to give effective support to the black metropolises in the North.

The New Pluralism and the Black University

In the final analysis the fate of publicly supported black institutions of higher learning in the South will be determined by the extent to which the black electorate is mobilized, Black Power consolidated, and coalitions formed that will provide adequate financing and a truly liberal environment for the educational enterprise in the South. The welfare of all the educational institutions as well as of all the people in the South would be best served by the emergence of a social structure in which three styles of life and types of institutions and associations can exist side-by-side with no invidious distinction drawn between them, and with free movement of individuals among them: all-black, all-white, and racially mixed. (A careful study of the racial and ethnic system in Hawaii and Puerto Rico could provide models for comparison.) Such a system replacing color-caste might be referred to as the "new pluralism."[41] The South actually seems to be moving with glacial slowness in this direction, but it is by no means a conflict-free, nonviolent process, or without its intellectual and ethical ambiguities and dilemmas. Racists use the slogan "freedom of choice" to mean something quite different from pluralism, and the working out of unitary school systems, if not monitored with vigilance, could crystallize institutional racism behind the rhetoric of integration.

Desegregation must precede the emergence of a new pluralistic pattern, but the outcome will also involve the prolonged process of gradual modification of hostile and prejudiced attitudes on the part of whites as well as the forcible containment of violence by racist minorities. Aggressive and violent black nationalism will diminish only to the extent that this process accelerates. Such a long-term process of reconditioning will be facilitated by various types of task-oriented interracial actions including campaigns to abolish poverty, to recast educational systems, and to improve public health. It will also involve trial and error approaches to coalition—often controversial—such as the sophisticated electoral politics of Atlanta, resulting in a black "vice-mayor" and school board chairman, the not yet successful political alliances in Mississippi, or the attempts to work out local agreements of the type Roy Innis of CORE was proposing to white opponents of school desegregation in Mobile in 1970 to provide for two school districts, one black with a white minority and one white with a black minority.

Seen as an ideal-type, a democratic pluralistic society would find a place within it for the expression of sentiments and actions ranging from separatist black nationalism to total integration—including intermarriage whenever any two people want to contract it. (Charles Evers, as mayor of Fayette, felt his experiment in local black municipal administration was in jeopardy when he had to face a case of mixed marriage on his official staff and he fired the couple. On the other hand, at least one private college in the Deep South accepted such a faculty marriage recently without disaster to the institution.) Many black intellectuals are now defining "*the* problem" as not being one of separation versus integration, but, rather, of how to achieve black *liberation*. The entire issue of *Ebony* for August 1970 was organized around a debate: "Which Way Black America? Separation? Integration? Liberation?" Lerone Bennett contributed the definitive article on "Integration-Separation Dilemma Is a False Issue."

Voluntary spatial separation may well be the deliberate choice of a small but significant minority. A 1964 poll revealed that nearly a quarter of the black respondents in the South answered "yes" to the question, "Do you think it would be a good idea to give American Negroes their own country and let them set up their own nation?" Of the 15 to 20 per cent in the North who gave the same response, some visualized the South as one area in which the nation should be established. This is an expression of a persistent Utopian dream among the peoples of the Black Diaspora of achieving black sovereignty upon lands where African blood, sweat, and tears once fell during the long centuries of slavery. When the Haitian revolutionaries proclaimed a republic in 1804 such sentiments were reinforced throughout the New World. Today, a half-dozen independent black nations exist in the Caribbean, and there have always been some leaders who have wanted to see black liberation take a similar form in North America. Realists, however, have always stressed the crucial difference between black majorities living on discretely bounded West Indian islands and a black minority enclaved by whites within the United States. The pragmatic black politicians of the Reconstruction period never considered either secession or autonomy. Ironically, the first detailed proposal for black sovereignty in North America came from a white group during the depression, the Communist party, which developed a concept of "self-determination for the Black Belt"—all of the contiguous southern counties with 50 per cent or more population. The party originally conceived of a socialist Black Belt Republic, then modified the concept to mean "autonomy," and finally left it completely open-ended. Virtually all Negro intellectuals ridiculed the idea of a Black Belt Republic, but we have no way of really knowing what the black sharecroppers and common laborers in the South thought about the idea, though "going North" was their usual liberation tactic.

Quite independently of any Communist influences, a black Chicago realtor during the thirties started an abortive Movement for a Forty-ninth State, while the Black Muslims later raised the demand for a territorial allotment to "The Lost Found Nation in the Wilderness of North America" as reparations. During the sixties a small young militant group formed the Republic of New Africa specifying five southern states in their reparations demand. When the frontier was still open the Muslims demand would not have seemed bizarre. The Mormons established the state of Deseret in Utah and the United States once defined Oklahoma as the Indian nation. *The establishment now of any all-black states, or an all-black South, is, of course, a Utopian fantasy, but a South containing scattered pockets of strongly consolidated black power cooperating with each other and coexisting with the surrounding white majority in whose institutions they share power is not.* The form of these pockets of Black Power might vary along a continuum from separatist black nationalist rural communities through counties with black majorities to black wards and precincts within multiracial cities.

Both the Black Muslims and the Republic of New Africa, by 1970, were stating short-term goals that fell short of their earlier Utopian visions—the establishment of agricultural communities composed of their members and producing commodities to be marketed in black-owned stores in urban communities. The Muslims are doing this on a very limited scale now. It does not seem unrealistic to visualize a situation in which, after black political control has been established in some counties where substantial black majorities exist, such communities could find the milieu in which to prosper that the Ku Klux Klan recently denied the Muslims in Alabama. If white American counties have been able to accommodate the Old Order Amish, Mennonite settlements, Indian reservations, the Hutterites, and now hippie communes, there is nothing outlandish in the prospect of black-controlled county governments letting peaceful, industrious, black communities "do *their* thing."

Some black southerners without any ideological commitment to black nationalism will want to combine to work out their problems using a well-tested institutional form—the cooperative. They find difficulty in trying to do so now, but an extension of Black Power might provide an encouraging environment. The Southwest Alabama Farmers Cooperative, composed of 2,000 poor black farmers, has been in existence since 1967. Governor George Wallace vetoed its OEO grant during its first year, and when his action was overridden in Washington, the Alabama congressmen immediately demanded an audit of SWAF's books. The maneuver failed, but when the cooperative began to truck out its cucumbers and okras to the market, state police held up the vehicles for "inspection" until the produce spoiled. Then, the state called in the FBI to investigate "misuse of federal funds." SWAF received a clean bill of health, but Governor Brewer vetoed the second installment of the OEO demonstration grant. When it came through despite the governor's opposition, he obtained a circuit court injunction, again charging misuse of funds. However, the organization survived all of the harassment, drawing upon over a million dollars in federal and private funds, astute legal assistance by friends, and the courage of its members to see it through the formative state. It did $172,000 worth of business in 1969. Whether SWAF continues to exist and prosper and expand depends upon the speed with which Alabama black voters can win enough influence at the state level to insure protection for it. Eight to ten other cooperatives of this type have sprung up here and there over the South, with three of them leasing land they hope to buy eventually, the others being composed of black landowners. Between forty-five and fifty small cooperatives representing about 15,000 members have organized a Federation of Southern Cooperatives to coordinate production and marketing of handicrafts, candy and bakery products, farm produce and timber, as well as buying clubs and grocery stores, and cooperative wholesales supplying gasoline, clothing, coal, and fish to themselves. The cooperative movement is ideally structured to facilitate racial and ethnic pluralism at the local level with membership of local cooperatives in state and regional bodies that are multiracial and multiethnic, the Central States Cooperative League being an example. In addition to all-black cooperatives, racially mixed units could emerge in local areas where it is feasible and farmers desire it. During the depression, members of the Southern Tenant Farmers Union conducted an interracial cotton producing cooperative in Bolivar County, Mississippi, the same county in which the all-Negro town of Mound Bayou was located. The white plantocracy was hostile to both communities. Black political power could have protected both.

Not all black farmers, of course, are interested in the cooperative movement. Some want assured access to credit and marketing facilities and governmental services so that they can take their chances as individuals or corporations on making profits from the large-scale mechanized capitalistic farming, lumbering, dairying, and ranching operations that will dominate the southern rural future. Many smaller landowners wish to combine some subsistence agriculture with employment in the new rural and semirural factory complexes that are beginning to appear in the South. Some of these will live in all-black rural concentrations. Others will be scattered among white farmers, functioning in the normal county setting, depending upon their own voting strength or upon the influence of regional and national black organizations to protect their interests. The experience of Macon County, Alabama, where Tuskegee is located, indicates how one such group has approached its problems through sharing political power with white residents rather than insisting upon complete black control. Greene County, Alabama, will be the test case of total black political control.

The all-black town that simply grew up naturally or that emerged by deliberate design is an old phenomenon in the South. The most highly publicized such communities have been Mound Bayou, Mississippi, and Boley, Oklahoma. In both cases as well as in the case of some forty-odd other communities that once existed in Oklahoma, lack of supporting political power elsewhere in the state left them open to intimidation and sometimes terror. They were also unable to attract the capital needed for growth. It is likely, however, that the number of all-black towns will increase in the future due to the operation of several processes:

(1) Flight of whites from small communities where blacks predominate as they assert their political strength. Charles Evers attempted to prevent this from happening after he was elected mayor of Fayette.

(2) Incorporation of present unincorporated black settlements. One that has recently been in the news is Roosevelt City, a suburb of Birmingham, Alabama. Such communities will need to attract both federal and private funds for economic and social development.

(3) Planned new towns of which the best known case is Soul City, projected as a prototype project in rural North Carolina by CORE's former director Floyd McKissick as one aspect of his scheme for "Black Business Development with Social Commitment to Black Communities." Federal planning under HUD is likely to result in some predominantly black integrated new towns.

All such rural and suburban black clusters will, of course, have growing commercial and associational ties with a wide range of institutions in urban communities where the centers of both Black Power and White Power are located. Insofar as black financial institutions in cities like Durham, New Orleans, and Atlanta concern themselves with these communities they will strengthen the nexus that binds the black population of the region together as an ethnic community without any necessary antiwhite or separatist implications.

The proportion of black southerners not living on farms is approaching two-thirds, and short of a wholesale reconstruction of rural life that is not likely to take place, the majority of the black population, and particularly of the younger segment, will be concentrated in the cities. The degree of ghettoization will continue to vary from city to city, but all communities will maintain a black institutional structure and social class system that relates them to the national black community. The race relations situation in southern cities is exceedingly fluid due to uncertainties surrounding the implementation of orders to desegregate the schools. A wide variety of patterns of accommodation exist but they are constantly changing. In 1963, 84 per cent of the black respondents in Atlanta and 79 per cent in Birmingham expressed a desire for integrated schools although a majority of southern black respondents were reported to have said they would prefer living in all-black neighborhoods if they could be sure they were physically kept up. The passage of seven years has shifted Negro attitudes sharply toward indifference or hostility to school integration in some communities though not in others. White responses have varied in relation to factors such as proportion of black fellow citizens involved, distributional patterns by social class, activity of racist politicians and organizations, type of influential white educational leadership, and actions of the federal government.

Polls taken during 1963 and 1966 revealed a high degree of optimism as to likelihood of favorable change in attitudes of whites. Experience with the school desegregation process has diminished the optimism. Other new variables have entered the picture too, among them increased action by teenage "rebels without a cause" and revolutionaries. The bridge-building process has been proceeding rapidly and diligently at the upper-middle- and upper-class leadership levels, but whether or not the new pluralism will replace caste relations within southern cities is going to depend upon what kind of relations are eventually defined between blacks and whites at blue-collar levels and among white-collar workers as black high school graduates demand their share of such jobs, particularly black women. Labor unions and professional and political associations will play a crucial part in developing and legitimizing new role relations between blacks and whites. To date they have not risen to the occasion, and black leaders may have to take the initiative by devising new institutional increments themselves to restructure black–white relations at this level. Julian Bond's attempt to build a progressive movement within the Georgia Democratic party and SCLC cooperation with unions as black workers continue to move into the textile industry may be straws in the wind.

The development of the new pluralism in the South is going to be influenced to a large extent by what happens over the next decade in the elementary and secondary schools. It is in this sector of the educational system that new forms of consciousness are developing from the varied experiences incident to new types of classroom situations. By 1968, the situation had moved to the point in Texas where nearly 40 per cent of the black public school students were in some sort of integrated situation, and between 20 and 30 per cent were in North Carolina, Virginia, Tennessee, Florida, and Arkansas. The proportion was less than 10 per cent in Louisiana, Alabama, and Mississippi, but somewhat higher in Georgia and South Carolina. Obviously, both white and black graduates from these situations will differ in some respects from those socialized in completely segregated situations, though precisely how we do not yet know. The current thrust toward unitary systems in the Deep South will speed the process of reconditioning youthful minds.

The institutions of higher learning will be supplying teachers, administrators, and consultants to the public schools, as well as being involved in curriculum reconstruction. They, not the parents and politicians, will have the strategic role in influencing the shaping of new attitudes and behavior patterns in race relations. *The predominantly black institutions will have a crucial role to play in the process of developing white responses in several ways:*

(1) By participating in the development of models of unitary state systems at the level of higher education. These systems will themselves express truly pluralistic values only if black institutions insist that they take this form, educating the educators as they interact with them.

(2) By providing learning experiences for black students in which they not only deal with their own identity problems and prepare themselves adequately for careers but also have an opportunity to participate in a variety of interracial situations, arriving at their own choices as to the degree of interracial contact they will incorporate into their adult life-styles. They will also be providing input into white student attitude formation. Some black students will reject such interracial contact unless it can be interpreted as "training" whites for participation in the coalitions needed for black liberation.

Black students are not, at the moment, in the mood for giving high priority to "educating white folks," although black administrators must put it high on the institutional agenda as a part of *their* roles of office. The major contribution black institutions will make to the emergence of a democratic pluralistic society, however, is through their contribution to the transformation of the *black* community from a disadvantaged, poverty-crippled segment of American society into a liberated ethnic group. This is not a task that predominantly white institutions can be expected to assume with the same devotion and insight that the predominantly black institutions can bring to the task. As Vincent Harding has phrased it in a recent article, in the special issue of *Ebony* referred to above, "If we are not for ourselves then who will be for us?" The young generation struggling for black self-determination will not accept training for "black liberation" from the faculty and students of predominantly white institutions because it does not think they are fitted for the role, nor should white institutions try to play it in this epoch of black empowerment. There are obviously areas of common concern to white and black students and scholars, but black southerners must determine how and in what roles they, as individuals, prefer to cooperate in dealing with the common problems. Some black educators and students as individuals will undoubtedly choose to focus upon broader nonracial issues such as research on environmental problems, traffic control, or general public administration, for instance, but for a predominantly black *institution* to allocate its limited resources to such problems is, I think, to abandon its historic role and to abdicate its functional position in the evolving pluralistic pattern. It may even be desirable to advise some students who wish training for more specialized fields of general service to secure it at other types of institutions (thus contributing to eventual integration, incidentally). Likewise it might be appropriate for some white students to be accepted into black institutions if they plan to work primarily on matters involving race relations so they can understand the black perspective.

There are two areas in which predominantly black institutions will concentrate some of their energies if they are responsive both to group needs and black student formulations of them:

(1) By providing, in addition to first-class career training for black students who will, on the whole, become a part of the black middle class after they graduate, opportunities to find satisfactory ways to "pay their dues" to black people who live other life-styles through making some courses available that have a community service thrust.

(2) By focusing the bulk of the research output and consultation services on problems relating to black liberation rather than to the military-industrial complex or purely theoretical concerns.

There has been considerable discussion in recent years about the need for a "black university" to achieve such goals. Sometimes the concept implies the strengthening of one or two existing institutions to the point that they will become the black equivalents of Harvard or Berkeley. The objective of building up one or two first class universities with internationally valued graduate and professional schools certainly should not be eliminated, but it is also possible to conceive of the black university as a loosely coordinated action-structure including *all* of the so-called predominantly Negro institutions, united by a common core of basic values and serving the black community through a deliberately thought-out functional division of labor. Vincent Harding, one of the most persuasive and eloquent advocates of the black university concept, has, himself, said in the *Ebony* article, "whether a new place or a renewed institution or a complex of institutions [it] involves an attempt to break with the long established familiar patterns of white domination and control over black higher education. This includes areas of curriculum, accreditation, staffing, administration and governance." With the exception of the matter of accreditation it would be difficult to find a black college president who is not committed to this goal though all of them face a struggle in trying to convince boards of trustees and regents that this is not only right, but also that students and younger alumni now will settle for nothing less. The securing of control is for a purpose. As Harding phrases it, "the Black University and its students are guided essentially by the central purpose of service to the black community on every technical and personal level possible." This is not yet the central purpose of either staff or students at Negro institutions of higher learning. Career training for individual advancement and grooming for becoming a member of the black bourgeoisie is still probably the central purpose rationalized in terms of the comfortable delusion that by just getting ahead each individual is advancing the race. Those who control black institutions will, of course, have to decide whether they want to shift that purpose toward committing black institutions to a mission as they always claimed to do until the 1930's.

If such a purpose were to be accepted, it is likely that those private institutions that survive the financing crises of the seventies are likely to realize it most fully, because they are free in a sense that publicly-supported institutions are not. Harding states the problem of black liberation in terms of the continuation of a centuries-old struggle against white racism and imperialism, with the black experience in the United States being only a special variant along with the experience in Africa and the West Indies. Black student pressures have already gone a long way toward securing the restructuring of curricula in the humanities and social sciences to include black studies explicitly or implicitly. Insofar as this is done the mere teaching of the truth documents this analysis of the black experience. Institutions with such an emphasis automatically heighten the level of self-respect and self-confidence of black students. They also develop, among students and staff, the resources for sharing the meaning of the black experience with white and black educational institutions at all levels in their immediate geographic area.

The transformation of intensified black awareness into constructive action takes on intellectual dimensions at the university as contrasted with what are sometimes called "street tasks." Harding reassures those who charge a plot to lower intellectual standards when he says the black university "cannot possibly be a place of escape from the demands of rigorous academic discipline." But the goal becomes the pursuit of academic excellence with a purpose—not for its own sake or for just "getting it made": "statisticians, physicists, chemists, systems analysts, linguists, biologists, engineers, botanists, agronomists—all are developed in the midst of a constant dialogue concerning the future toward which black people must move and the role of science and technology in that movement. For no subject matter is neutral in the Black University (just as no subject matter is really neutral in the White University)." This is a traditional Hampton-Tuskegee approach raised to a higher intellectual and political level.

Harding did not discuss the black university within the context of an emerging pluralistic social system, although there is nothing inconsistent between his ideas and such a model. Another model has been presented recently by a white scholar which suggests a more integrationist version of the black university concept. Arnold Schuchter in *Reparations: The Black Manifesto and Its Challenge to White America* envisions a key role for the predominantly black institutions in what he calls a "strategy of redress" for black Americans coupled with the mobilization of forces to oppose the "military-industrial complex" which, he feels, "more than any other factor in American politics . . . is denying blacks (and disadvantaged whites) the immense and growing bounty of well-being within the grasp of this nation." He presents an elaborate plan for channeling $100,000,000 in funds from the wealthy white churches of the country available in response to James Forman's dramatic reparations movement, into a Redress Mutual Fund that could finance projects such as a Second Income Trust Plan, a New Community Development Fund, and a Capital Ownership Insurance Corporation. Crucial to Schuchter's strategy of redress is the establishment of Centers of National Reform which "would have to develop a program for dealing with the problem of blacks simultaneously in rural and central city America." They would function as "a national advocate agency for blacks." More than one center is envisioned; they would operate on a decentralized basis, with one center providing over-all direction. It is proposed that initially about four Centers of National Reform housing a total of about one thousand persons structured and administered principally by blacks should be created in the South and linked to consortia of black colleges, which, except for half a dozen of the strongest ones, face financial crisis. He states further:

> There are several good reasons for choosing the South and its private church-supported black colleges as the principal location for Centers of National Reform. Black colleges in general enroll about 130,000 students, about two thirds in private schools, comprising about 60 percent of all black undergraduates. With a few exceptions, these institutions serve the most educationally disadvantaged college students in the nation. Lack of adequate government, philanthropic, corporate and church support has intensified the stigma of inferiority that attaches to these creations of racism and a Southern caste system. Only a major injection of new capital combined with a radical reformulation of the traditional role and curriculum offers hope of converting these colleges into viable educational institutions. This new mission, the antithesis of the missionary education which led to their founding, would emphasize the education and training of blacks *and* whites for roles as agents of change in American society. This mission requires that black colleges become magnets for the most promising black and white college-age students now attracted to Northern campuses for lack of a substantial alternative . . .
>
> Some steps toward the concept of NCRs already exist. In August 1969, a Five-Day Black University sponsored by the National Association for African-American Education was held in Atlanta, Georgia, where an estimated one thousand persons from all parts of the nation met to deal with the problems that black people face in white America. The principal focus was on radically changing traditional educational programs in the nation in order to make them more relevant to black people. The concept of Centers of National Reform in effect institutionalizes and broadens the Five-Day Black University.[42]

Schuchter, like Du Bois and Harding, sees black colleges as having a national mission. I have preferred to discuss a more restricted role—

their possible *regional* function in carrying out a second southern Reconstruction with Black Power playing a creative role as it did in the first one.

The campuses of the private black institutions might well become the locale for black "think-tanks" and talent-pools upon which all types of black community movements and institutions can draw for counsel and advice as well as instruction and technical assistance: the community considering incorporation and needing a study of its tax base; black organizations planning to have Rev. Leon Sullivan's Opportunities Industrialization Centers (OIC) consider them for setting up a shopping plaza and needing a survey before they send a representative off to Philadelphia; a group of welfare mothers who are trying to prepare a petition and need a college student to help shape it up; the SCLC planning an attempt to help a group of black and white textile workers who are forming a union and need a background paper on the county; a cooperative that wants help in an educational program; a project for giving dental service to some rural kids (as Howard University recently did) and needs some student assistants; a high school trying to put on a program of African and Afro-American culture. Blacks would have to be in a majority and in control, even though whites whom they want to work with them would not be excluded.

It is possible to visualize a group of undergraduates studying diligently for their degrees but all devoting *some* of their time—not all of it—to community projects instead of to fraternity and sorority rituals, or graduate and professional students maintaining liaison with the black community as they develop their own skills. This would mean developing a type of faculty and student body somewhat different from that of the past, or a collective reorientation of the existing college community. As older professors flow out to the well-paid jobs in those northern universities that are raiding, growing numbers of young Ph.D.'s are now available who want to teach in the South if the institutions are dedicated to the tasks of black liberation. Now that black high school students have a wider range of options than in the past, and black private institutions do not have to carry the entire load of ambitious upward-mobile youth, they may be in a position to set up new unorthodox admission criteria—for instance, to make "leadership potential" and what used to be called "seriousness of purpose" a decisive trait when all other things are equal (and those other things need not be test scores on the conventional entrance examinations but, rather, intellectual potential that has been demonstrated in other ways or attested to by secondary school teachers). Acceptance on the basis of special aptitudes with provision for remedial work in weak areas might become the rule instead of the exception. The possibility of tapping the new talent pool in the southern two-year community colleges might be carefully examined. National recruitment, as in the past, not regional recruitment, should be the goal, but with a commitment on the part of students accepted on scholarship to work in the South after graduation for a specified period of time. Working with student bodies of this type would demand a much higher amount of student participation in decision-making and a willingness to risk expressions of militancy not usually welcomed. But southern institutions learned to live with such students during the Desegregation Decade.

The conventional private black institutions cannot radicalize themselves enough to be acceptable to the most militant youth and there is no reason why they should try. They should state frankly what their distinctive contribution to the black liberation movement is—*intellectual* tasks not "street" tasks—and then develop a modus vivendi with the new experimental institutions that the angry young para-intellectuals (as Martin Kilson of Harvard calls them) are setting up, such as Malcolm X Liberation University in North Carolina. There is no reason why staff and graduate students from conventional institutions should not lecture occasionally for the militant experimental institutions, make audio-visual aids available to them, or extend them library privileges, while inviting them and their students to symposia and conferences to enrich the experiences of their own institutions. Some institutions may already have experience of this type to share with others.

The role of publicly-supported institutions will, of necessity, have to be a quite different one from that of private colleges, but it is an equally important one in a functional division of labor for black liberation. Their basic task will probably turn out to be training for careers in the public white-collar sector—teachers, social workers, and, one hopes in the future, city and state civil servants, agriculturalists, home economists, and personnel for business and industry. Through their interchange arrangements with predominantly white institutions in a unitary system they will have the opportunity to continuously feed students into the state schools of law, medicine, dentistry, library science, and social work where they do not offer such work themselves. They might even set up manpower training targets, state-by-state, as colleges in developing nations do, and gear their work to meeting them. Some of these institutions will have black studies programs, and while they are likely to be less wide-ranging than those in private institutions, they can be related to one of the primary functions of the black segment of public unitary systems—education of white students in other segments so they can educate their predominantly white associates after graduation as to what the new pluralism should and can mean.

How a wide range of types of black colleges and universities can deliberately work out a functional division of labor in carrying forward the task of black liberation is no easy problem to solve. It may demand new types of institutional structures to keep open channels of communication between them in addition to the organizations now devoted to joint fund raising. What we already have is a very loose division of labor that has grown up without planning but is recognized as such. One barrier to closer coordination of programs for black liberation will be the struggle for sheer survival and the necessity to compete for resources increasingly scarce when measured against the challenges presented by the future. But black internal integration needs to proceed at an accelerated rate, knitting together churches, schools, businesses, and voluntary associations, in order to maximize the Black Power Potential for achieving structural integration into the interracial economic and political systems, local, state, regional, and national.

References

1. Some of the more readily accessible sources for detailed data on black higher education during the formative period are W. E. B. Du Bois, ed., *The College-Bred Negro* (Atlanta: Atlanta University Press, 1900); Edwin R. Embree and Julia Waxman, *Investment in People: The Story of the Julius Rosenwald Fund* (New York: Harper and Brothers, 1949); Horace Mann Bond, "The Negro Scholar and Professional in America," in John P. Davis, ed., *The American Negro Reference Book* (Englewood Cliffs, N. J.: Prentice-Hall, 1966), pp. 548-589; Virgil A. Clift, "Educating the American Negro," in Davis, ed., *American Negro Reference Book,* pp. 360-395; and St. Clair Drake, "Negro Americans and the Africa Interest," in Davis, ed., *American Negro Reference Book,* pp. 662-705. See also Horace Mann Bond, *The Education of the Negro in the American Social Order* (New York: Prentice-Hall, 1934).

2. Du Bois, ed., *College-Bred Negro,* p. 65.

3. *Ibid.*

4. Drake, "Negro Americans and the Africa Interest," pp. 679-688.

5. W. E. B. Du Bois, "Negro Education," *Crisis* (February 1918), reprinted in Meyer Weinberg, ed., *W. E. B. Du Bois: A Reader* (New York: Harper and Row, 1970), pp. 161-171.

6. The atmosphere created upon some black campuses by a combination of southern racist influences and New England missionary attitudes that led to student resentment can be inferred from John Sekora's article, "Murder Relentless and Impassive: The American Academic Community and the Negro College," in *Soundings: A Journal of Interdisciplinary Studies,* 51 (Fall 1968), 237-264. He extends his caustic criticisms to the contemporary situation. Two articles by Du Bois are relevant, "Negroes in College," *The Nation* (March 3, 1926), and "The Hampton Strike," *The Nation* (November 2, 1927).

7. W. E. B. Du Bois, "A Graduate School," *Crisis* (June 1929), reprinted in Weinberg, ed., *W. E. B. Du Bois,* pp. 175-176.

8. Embree and Waxman, *Investment in People,* pp. 105-106.

9. *Ibid.*

10. W. E. B. Du Bois, "Does the Negro Need Separate Schools?" *Journal of Negro Education* (July 1935), reprinted in Weinberg, ed., *W. E. B. Du Bois,* pp. 278-288. Weinberg also presents an article written seven years before when Du Bois was espousing the opposite position, "Pechstein and Pecksniff," pp. 270-273, but with a general statement on the need for getting the most out of separate institutions during the transition to a completely open society—originally published in *Crisis* (January 1934), pp. 276-277. The 1942 article on "The Cultural Missions of Atlanta University" appears on pp. 187-200.

11. Embree and Waxman, *Investment in People,* p. 106.

12. *Ibid.*

13. For a summary of these cases see Clift, "Educating the American Negro," pp. 360-395.

14. See James Forman, *Sammy Younge, Jr.* (New York: Grove Press, 1968).

15. This fact has been documented as part of a scholarly and perceptive study, "Negro Students and the Protest Movement," by Donald Matthews and James Prothro, in James McEvoy and Abraham Miller, eds., *Black Power and Student Rebellion* (Belmont, Calif.: Wadsworth Publishing Co., 1969).

16. A discussion of Gomillion's activities is given from a radical perspective in Forman, *Sammy Younge,* pp. 230-235.

17. Two articles relevant to these developments in Patricia W. Romero, ed., *In Black America, 1968: The Year of Awakening* (Washington: United Publishing Corporation, 1969) are Prince E. Wilson, "Some Aspects of

the Education of Black Americans, 1968," pp. 89-131, and St. Clair Drake, "The Patterns of Interracial Conflict in 1968," pp. 41-51. A clear concise statement on the relation of Black Power to conventional politics, including a discussion of coalitions, is presented in Stokely Carmichael and Charles V. Hamilton, *Black Power: The Politics of Liberation in America* (New York: Random House, 1967).

18. For a discussion of the conceptualization of Negro-white relations in terms of caste-class and ethnic-class see St. Clair Drake, "The Social and Economic Status of the Negro in the United States," *Dædalus* (Fall 1955), pp. 771-777. See also Milton Myron Gordon, *Assimilation in American Life* (New York: Oxford University Press, 1964) for a discussion of several conceptual models of ethnic relations.

19. *The Negro Worker* by Sterling Spero and Abram Harris (New York: Columbia University Press, 1931) presents a scholarly account of the interplay between northern industrial needs and Negro migration from the Civil War to 1921. For a comprehensive discussion of the migration-adjustment process, see August Meir and Elliott M. Rudwick, *From Plantation to Ghetto* (New York: Hill and Wang, 1966).

20. Table 1, "Per Cent Distribution of Negro Population by Region, 1960 and 1968," in Romero, ed., *In Black America,* p. 495. In the spring of 1969, one source reported that the Negro influx to cities had slowed to its lowest rate in twenty years. "The Demographic Profile and Where It Points," *Newsweek* (June 30, 1969), p. 18.

21. Philip M. Hauser, "Demographic Factors and the Integration of the Negro," *Dædalus* (Fall 1965), p. 852.

22. *The Social and Economic Status of Negroes in the United States, 1969,* BLS Report No. 375, p. 7. In Romero, ed., *In Black America,* p. 231, it is noted that "some 300,000 nonwhites moved into the suburbs in the early 1960's largely in segregated developments . . . the percentage of Blacks in suburbs between 1960 and 1966 dropped from 8.9 to 4.6 per cent."

23. See projections in *Report of the National Advisory Commission on Civil Disorders* (New York: Bantam Books, 1968), pp. 245-247, 391. The 1970 census returns indicated that Atlanta had moved over the 50 per cent line between 1960 and 1970. The black population, by 1970, was over 40 per cent though not yet one-half in Baltimore, Birmingham, New Orleans, and Detroit.

24. *Social and Economic Conditions of Negroes in the United States,* U. S. Department of Labor, BLS Report No. 332, 1967, "Non-white Families in Poverty Areas of Large Cities, 1960 and 1966," p. 93. See also *The Social and Economic Status of Negroes in the United States, 1969,* BLS Report No. 375, Section II, "Income and Poverty." Poverty areas are defined in terms of a high proportion of family incomes below $3,000, high proportion of children in broken homes, very low median education level, high volume of substandard housing, and high proportion of males in unskilled jobs.

25. *Ibid.*, "Employment Conditions in Nine Seriously Disadvantaged Slum Areas, November, 1966," p. 97, and "Families by Sex of Head, by Income Group, 1966," p. 71. See also, pp. 37 and 93.

26. *Ibid.*, "Fertility Rates, 1955-1965," p. 77.

27. *Ibid.*, p. 94.

28. See "The Black Mood: More Militant, More Hopeful, More Determined," *Time* (April 6, 1970), pp. 28-29. All polls since 1966 have indicated a high degree of sympathy among black respondents for "rioters." In the spring of 1970, 64 per cent in a Harris poll agreed with the statement, "Panthers give me a sense of pride." *Time* (April 6, 1970), p. 29.

29. See "Number and Per Cent of Persons Below the Poverty Level and of Persons Receiving Welfare, 1967 and 1968," in Romero, ed., *In Black America,* p. 497. In 1968, 35 per cent of the Negro population was reported below the poverty line as compared with 10 per cent of the whites. *The Social and Economic Status of Negroes in the United States, 1969*, BLS Report No. 375, p. 24.

30. A Time-Harris poll in the spring of 1970 reported 40-42 per cent of the black respondents in favor of supporting militant leadership and "taking to the streets" in order to "make real progress" and 68 per cent in favor of boycotts against whites who discriminate against blacks. *Time* (April 6, 1970).

31. *Social and Economic Conditions of Negroes in the United States,* BLS Report No. 332, 1967, pp. 39-40, and section X.

32. The data on changes between 1950 and 1960 have been summarized from Leonard Broom and Norval D. Glenn, *Transformation of the Negro American* (New York: Harper and Row, 1965). Statistics for the period 1960-1967 are from the BLS Report No. 332, cited above, and for 1968 and 1969 from *The Social and Economic Status of Negroes in the United States, 1969*, BLS Report No. 375, Section II, "Income and Poverty" and Section III, "Employment."

33. *The Social and Economic Status of Negroes in the United States, 1969,* BLS Report No. 375, Section III, "Employment."

34. *Ibid.*, pp. 46 and 47. Among the government agencies were Upward Bound and the Education Opportunity Act of 1968, and New York's College Bound Program. Among privately sponsored agencies were experiments such as Harlem Prep and Cleveland's Dropouts Anonymous.

35. See the methodological note in Andrew Billingsley, *Black Families in White America* (Englewood Cliffs, N. J.: Prentice-Hall, 1968).

36. The concept of institutional racism shifts the emphasis from a consideration of personal prejudices to the manner in which organizational procedures operate to the disadvantage of minority groups. See Louis L. Knowles and Kenneth Prewitt, *Institutional Racism in America* (Englewood Cliffs, N. J.: Prentice-Hall, 1969).

37. William Brink and Louis Harris, *Black and White: A Study of Racial Attitudes Today* (New York: A Clarion Book, 1966), pp. 258, 264.

38. Paul Sheatsley, "White Attitudes Toward the Negro," *Dædalus* (Winter 1966), pp. 217-238.

39. Brink and Harris, *Black and White,* p. 220.

40. The following table indicates the rapid increase in the number of registered voters in six states:

Increase in Number and Per Cent of Registered Black Voters in Six Southern States, 1962-1968

State	*1962*	*1966*	*Fall 1968*	*Per cent of Negroes of voting age registered, 1968*
Texas	242,000	400,000	540,000	83.1
Arkansas	68,970	115,000	130,000	67.5
Virginia	110,113	250,000	255,000	58.4
Alabama	68,317	250,000	273,000	56.7
Georgia	175,573	300,000	344,000	56.1
Mississippi	23,920	175,000	251,000	55.3

SOURCE: Edward F. Sweat, "State and Local Politics in 1968," in Romero, ed., *In Black America,* p. 110.

In 1968, Georgia was at the top of the list of southern states with black elected officials, having twelve members of the lower house and two senators as well as six city councilmen. Both Tennessee and Texas had black men in their upper houses, six and eight respectively, as well as two each in the lower house, and there were seven city councilmen in Tennessee and one in Texas. In Virginia, eighteen blacks had been elected to city councils and one person to the senate; Florida had a senator, too, and eight city councilmen. The following states had no black representatives in state legislatures, but each had city councilmen: Alabama (twenty-nine), South Carolina (sixteen), Louisiana (fourteen), Arkansas (eleven), North Carolina (nine), Mississippi (six). By 1969, throughout the South there were 218 black city councilmen, 90 school board members, 38 members of county governing boards, 30 state legislators, and 17 mayors. A black candidate for governor had been defeated in North Carolina, as had candidates for Congress in Georgia, Mississippi, and South Carolina. See Edward F. Sweat, "State and Local Politics in 1968," in Romero, ed., *In Black America,* pp. 133-146; and Arnold Schuchter, *Reparations: The Black Manifesto and Its Challenge to White America* (Philadelphia: Lippincott, 1970), pp. 152-153.

41. "Plural societies," according to one useful definition, are "those that are segmented into two or more groups that have distinct and duplicatory sets of institutions, except in the political and economic spheres where the institutions are shared . . . Many, if not most, plural societies are politically and economically dominated by one of the constituent groups." Pierre L. Van den Berghe, *Race and Ethnicity* (New York: Basic Books, 1970), p.

14. The new element in the southern situation is the movement away from caste relations toward a more equalitarian separateness in a variety of new situations.

42. Schuchter, *Reparations,* pp. 150, 152-154. The author underestimates the extent to which the concept of *interracial* Centers of National Reform, located on black campuses, differs from the spirit and objectives of the younger black people who were associated with the Five-Day Black University.

Notes on Contributors

ELIAS BLAKE, JR., born in 1929, is president of the Institute for Services to Education. The Institute is involved in major programs of curriculum development with a number of black colleges, including a graduate program emphasizing teaching in the freshman year of college. Mr. Blake is the author of a study of racial unrest in six city high schools for the Commission on Civil Rights.

ANDREW F. BRIMMER, born in 1926, is a member of the Board of Governors of the Federal Reserve System. He is the author of *The Framework of Industrial Organization in India* (Cambridge, Mass., 1954), *Life Insurance Companies in the Capital Market* (East Lansing, Mich., 1962), *Survey of Mutual Fund Investors* (Securities and Exchange Commission, 1963), and *Poverty in the United States* (Committee on Education and Labor, House of Representatives, 1964).

HENRY ALLEN BULLOCK, born in 1906, is professor of history and sociology and chairman of the Ethnic Studies Program at the University of Texas. Mr. Bullock is the author of *A History of Negro Education in the South* (Cambridge, Mass., 1967) and coauthor of *The School in the Social Order* (Scranton, Pa., 1970).

ST. CLAIR DRAKE, born in 1911, is professor of anthropology and sociology and chairman of the program in African and Afro-American Studies at Stanford University. He is the author of *Race Relations in a Time of Rapid Social Change* (New York, 1966) and *Black Metropolis,* rev. ed. (New York, 1970).

WINFRED L. GODWIN, born in 1926, is president of the Southern Regional Education Board. Mr. Godwin is the author of *Physicians for the South* (1960) and coeditor of *Community Colleges in the South* (1962). He is chairman of the board of *Change* magazine.

CONRAD K. HARPER, born in 1940, is a lawyer associated with Simpson Thacher & Bartlett, New York City. He was formerly employed by the NAACP Legal Defense and Educational Fund, Inc.

PATRICIA ROBERTS HARRIS is a partner in Strasser, Spiegelberg, Fried, Frank & Kampelman, Attorneys, Washington, D. C. She is a former dean and professor of law at Howard University School of Law and former United States ambassador to Luxembourg.

VIVIAN W. HENDERSON, born in 1923, is president of Clark College, Atlanta. He is the author of *The Economic Status of Negroes: In the*

Nation and in the South (Southern Regional Council, 1963) and *The Advancing South: Manpower Problems and Prospects* (Twentieth Century Fund, 1965).

TOBE JOHNSON, born in 1929, is coordinator of undergraduate Afro-American studies, Atlanta University Center, and professor of political science, Morehouse College. Mr. Johnson is consultant to the Southern Association of Colleges and Schools for institutional self-studies in black schools and a board member of the Southern Education Foundation.

MACK H. JONES, born in 1937, is associate professor of political science, Atlanta University. He is the author of *Black School Board Members in Southern Politics* (Southern Education Foundation, 1970) and president of the National Conference of Black Political Scientists, 1970-1971.

C. ERIC LINCOLN, born in 1924, is professor of sociology and religion at Union Theological Seminary and adjunct professor of religion at Columbia University. He is the author of *The Black Muslims in America* (Boston, 1961), *My Face Is Black* (Boston, 1964), *Sounds of the Struggle* (New York, 1967), *The Negro Pilgrimage in America* (New York, 1968), and *Profile of Martin Luther King, Jr.* (New York, 1969). Mr. Lincoln is founding president of the Black Academy of Arts and Letters and president of the American Forum for African Study.

S. M. NABRIT, born in 1905, is executive director of the Southern Fellowships Fund. He is the author of scientific papers on marine life. Mr. Nabrit is a member of the board of directors of Brown University, Benedict College, Maryville College, and Washington Technical Institute, a member of the National Academy of Sciences' Institute on Medicine, and a member of the Management Committee of the United States/South Africa Leader Exchange Program.

THOMAS F. PETTIGREW, born in 1931, is professor of social psychology at Harvard University. He is the author of *A Profile of the Negro American* (Princeton, 1964) and *Racially Separate or Together* (New York, 1971). Mr. Pettigrew is currently doing social psychological survey research on white voters for black mayoralty candidates in Gary, Cleveland, Los Angeles, and Newark.

WILLIAM J. TRENT, JR., born in 1910, is assistant personnel director of Time Inc. and former executive director of the United Negro College Fund, 1944-1964. He is a member of the Boards of the National Council on Philanthropy, the State Communities Aid Association, and the National Urban League.

MICHAEL R. WINSTON, born in 1941, is instructor in history at Howard University. He is coauthor of *Ordeal of Democracy: The Negro in the United States, 1945-1970* (New York, 1971). Mr. Winston was formerly associate director of the Institute for Services to Education, Washington, D. C., and assistant dean of the College of Liberal Arts, Howard University.

Issues of *Dædalus* in Print

These may be ordered from the *Dædalus* Subscription Office, the American Academy of Arts and Sciences, 280 Newton Street, Brookline, Massachusetts 02146.

The Historian and the World of the Twentieth Century *(Spring 1971)*

Historical Studies Today *(Winter 1971)*

The Making of Modern Science: Biographical Studies *(Fall 1970)*

Rights and Responsibilities:
The University's Dilemma *(Summer 1970)*

Theory in Humanistics Studies *(Spring 1970)*

The Embattled University *(Winter 1970)*

Dædalus Dialogues *(Fall 1969)*

The Future of the Humanities *(Summer 1969)*

Ethical Aspects of Experimentation with Human Subjects *(Spring 1969)*

Perspectives on Business *(Winter 1969)*

Philosophers and Kings: Studies in Leadership *(Summer 1968)*

Historical Population Studies *(Spring 1968)*

Students and Politics *(Winter 1968)*

America's Changing Environment *(Fall 1967)*

Toward the Year 2000: Work in Progress *(Summer 1967)*

Color and Race *(Spring 1967)*

Religion in America *(Winter 1967)*

Fiction in Several Languages *(Fall 1966)*

Tradition and Change *(Summer 1966)*

Conditions of World Order *(Spring 1966)*

The Negro American—2 (special issue, *Winter 1966)*

The Negro American—1 (special issue, *Fall 1965)*

The Contemporary University: U.S.A. *(Fall 1964)*

Continued

Population, Prediction, Conflict, Existentialism *(Summer 1964)*

The Professions *(Fall 1963)*

Themes in Transition *(Summer 1963)*

Perspectives on the Novel *(Spring 1963)*

The American Reading Public *(Winter 1963)*

Current Work and Controversies—2 *(Summer 1962)*

Science and Technology in Contemporary Society *(Spring 1962)*

Excellence and Leadership in a Democracy *(Fall 1961)*

Symbolism in Religion and Literature *(Summer 1958)*

Tenth Anniversary Index: 1958-1968

Issues of *DÆDALUS* out of Print

See hard-cover books based on these issues, listed on following pages.

The Conscience of the City *(Fall 1968)*

Creativity and Learning *(Summer 1965)*

Utopia *(Spring 1965)*

Science and Culture *(Winter 1965)*

The Woman in America *(Spring 1964)*

A New Europe? (special issue, *Winter 1964)*

American Foreign Policy—Freedoms and Restraints *(Fall 1962)*

Youth: Change and Challenge *(Winter 1962)*

Evolution and Man's Progress *(Summer 1961)*

Ethnic Groups in American Life *(Spring 1961)*

The Future Metropolis *(Winter 1961)*

Arms Control (special issue, *Fall 1960)*

The Russian Intelligentsia *(Summer 1960)*

Mass Cultures and Mass Media *(Spring 1960)*

The Visual Arts Today (special issue, *Winter 1960)*

Quantity and Quality *(Fall 1959)*

Current Work and Controversies—1 *(Summer 1959)*

Myth and Mythmaking *(Spring 1959)*

Education in the Age of Science *(Winter 1959)*

On Evidence and Inference *(Fall 1958)*

The American National Style *(Spring 1958)*

Science and the Modern World View *(Winter 1958)*

Books Published from Issues of *DÆDALUS*

Virtually all the issues of *Dædalus*, in expanded form, appear also as books in hard covers and in subsequent paperback editions. Inquiries should be directed to the respective publishers.

Hard-cover Editions

The Embattled University, edited by Stephen R. Graubard and Geno A. Ballotti. George Braziller, Inc., 1970. $6.95.

Philosophers and Kings: Studies in Leadership, edited by Dankwart A. Rustow. George Braziller, Inc., 1970. $7.50.

Experimentation with Human Subjects, edited by Paul A. Freund. George Braziller, Inc., 1970. $6.95.

The Conscience of the City, edited by Martin Meyerson. George Braziller, Inc., 1970. $6.00.

America's Changing Environment, edited by Roger Revelle and Hans H. Landsberg. Houghton Mifflin Company, 1970. $6.95.

Students in Revolt, edited by Seymour Martin Lipset and Philip G. Altbach. Houghton Mifflin Company, 1969. $8.95.

Color and Race, edited by John Hope Franklin. Houghton Mifflin Company, 1968. $6.95.

Toward the Year 2000: Work in Progress, edited by Daniel Bell. Houghton Mifflin Company, 1968. $6.50.

Conditions of World Order, edited by Stanley Hoffmann. Houghton Mifflin Company, 1968. $6.50.

Fiction in Several Languages, edited by Henri Peyre. Houghton Mifflin Company, 1968. $6.00.

Creativity and Learning, edited by Jerome Kagan. Houghton Mifflin Company, 1967. $6.95.

The Negro American, edited by Talcott Parsons and Kenneth B. Clark. Houghton Mifflin Company, 1966. $10.00.

Utopias and Utopian Thought, edited by Frank E. Manuel. Houghton Mifflin Company, 1966. $6.50.

Continued

The Contemporary University: U.S.A., edited by Robert S. Morison. Houghton Mifflin Company, 1966. $8.00.

Science and Culture, edited by Gerald Holton. Houghton Mifflin Company, 1965. $6.00.

The Professions in America, edited by Kenneth S. Lynn. Houghton Mifflin Company, 1965. $5.00.

The Woman in America, edited by Robert Jay Lifton. Houghton Mifflin Company, 1965. $6.95.

A New Europe?, edited by Stephen R. Graubard. Houghton Mifflin Company, 1964. $10.00.

The American Reading Public, edited by Roger H. Smith. R. R. Bowker Company, 1964. $7.95.

Youth: Change and Challenge, edited by Erik H. Erikson. Basic Books, 1963. $7.50.

Excellence and Leadership in a Democracy, edited by Stephen R. Graubard and Gerald Holton. Columbia University Press, 1962. $6.50.

Evolution and Man's Progress, edited by Hudson Hoagland and Ralph W. Burhoe. Columbia University Press, 1962. $5.50.

The Future Metropolis, edited by Lloyd Rodwin. George Braziller, Inc., 1961. $6.00.

Arms Control, Disarmament, and National Security, edited by Donald G. Brennan. George Braziller, Inc., 1961. $6.00.

The Russian Intelligentsia, edited by Richard Pipes. Columbia University Press, 1961. $6.75.

The Visual Arts Today, edited by Gyorgy Kepes. Wesleyan University Press, 1960. $8.50.

Quantity and Quality, edited by Daniel Lerner. The Free Press of Glencoe, Inc., 1961. $5.95.

Evidence and Inference, edited by Daniel Lerner. The Free Press of Glencoe, Inc., 1959. $5.95.

Symbolism in Religion and Literature, edited by Rollo May. George Braziller, Inc., 1960. $5.00.

Continued

PAPERBACK EDITIONS

THE EMBATTLED UNIVERSITY, edited by Stephen R. Graubard and Geno A. Ballotti. George Braziller, Inc., 1970. $3.95.

PHILOSOPHERS AND KINGS: STUDIES IN LEADERSHIP, edited by Dankwart A. Rustow. George Braziller, Inc., 1970. $3.75.

EXPERIMENTATION WITH HUMAN SUBJECTS, edited by Paul A. Freund. George Braziller, Inc., 1970. $3.50.

THE CONSCIENCE OF THE CITY, edited by Martin Meyerson. George Braziller, Inc., 1970. $3.00.

AMERICA'S CHANGING ENVIRONMENT, edited by Roger Revelle and Hans H. Landsberg. Beacon Press, 1970. $3.95.

STUDENTS IN REVOLT, edited by Seymour Martin Lipset and Philip G. Altbach. Beacon Press, 1970. $3.95.

COLOR AND RACE, edited by John Hope Franklin. Beacon Press, 1969. $2.95.

TOWARD THE YEAR 2000: WORK IN PROGRESS, edited by Daniel Bell. Beacon Press, 1969. $2.95.

FICTION IN SEVERAL LANGUAGES, edited by Henri Peyre. Beacon Press, 1969. $2.95.

THE FUTURE METROPOLIS, edited by Lloyd Rodwin. George Braziller, Inc., 1969. $2.95.

RELIGION IN AMERICA, edited by Robert N. Bellah and William G. McLoughlin. Beacon Press, 1968. $3.45.

MYTH AND MYTHMAKING, edited by Henry A. Murray. Beacon Press, 1968. $2.95.

THE NEGRO AMERICAN, edited by Talcott Parsons and Kenneth B. Clark. Beacon Press, 1967. $3.95.

CREATIVITY AND LEARNING, edited by Jerome Kagan. Beacon Press, 1967. $2.45.

UTOPIAS AND UTOPIAN THOUGHT, edited by Frank E. Manuel. Beacon Press, 1967. $2.45.

Continued

SCIENCE & CULTURE, edited by Gerald Holton. Beacon Press, 1967. $2.45.

THE CONTEMPORARY UNIVERSITY: U.S.A., edited by Robert S. Morison. Beacon Press, 1967. $2.45.

THE WOMAN IN AMERICA, edited by Robert Jay Lifton. Beacon Press, 1967. $2.45.

A NEW EUROPE?, edited by Stephen R. Graubard. Beacon Press, 1967. $3.45.

THE PROFESSIONS IN AMERICA, edited by Kenneth S. Lynn. Beacon Press, 1967. $1.95.

SYMBOLISM IN RELIGION AND LITERATURE, edited by Rollo May. George Braziller, Inc., 1966. $1.95.

THE CHALLENGE OF YOUTH, edited by Erik H. Erikson. Anchor Books, 1965. $1.45.

CULTURE FOR THE MILLIONS?, edited by Norman Jacobs. Beacon Press, 1965. $1.95.